GAY ADU STAR DIRECTORY

OVER 2,000 PORN STAR VIDEOGRAPHIES
PAST TO PRESENT

Edited By
Bruce Wayne

companion press

laguna hills, california
http://www.companionpress.com

COMPANION PRESS, PO Box 2575, Laguna Hills, California 92654

Printed in the United States of America
First Printing 2000

ISBN: 1-889138-22-3

Cover photo of the late Christian Fox photographed by and courtesy of Per Lui © 2000.

Contents

Top-10 Porn Stars of All Time

In 1999 we, at Companion Press, asked our website visitors, our mail-order customers—and anyone else we could think of, to send us a list of their Top-10 gay porn stars of all time. Any gay porn star could be nominated.

Each entry became part of a free drawing and the randomly selected winner won a free copy of this book as the prize. The contest ran for nearly a year and we received hundreds of responses.

It certainly wasn't scientific, but the results are still interesting. There were a few surprises, but for the most part the list contains the names you'd probably expect to see.

Whether you agree or disagree with the list, we invite you to send us *your* list of Top-10 gay porn stars of all time, before the next edition of this directory is published, and you'll automatically be entered in our next free drawing. One lucky winner will receive a free copy of the next edition. Will these 10 stars continue to reign? It's up to you, the readers and the fans.

So here they are, the Top-10 gay porn stars of all time, in order of votes—out of the more than 2,000 stars listed in this book—according to *our* survey.

Top-10 Porn Stars
1. Ken Ryker
2. Jeff Stryker
3. Lukas Ridgeston
4. Joey Stefano
5. Aiden Shaw
6. Jeff Palmer
7. Johan Paulik
8. Kevin Williams
9. Mike Branson
10. Derek Cameron

10 Runners Up (Alphabetical)
11. Rod Barry
12. Rex Chandler
13. Tom Chase
14. Matt Gunther
15. Ryan Idol
16. Mason Jarr
17. Lance
18. Matt Ramsey
19. Hal Rockland
20. Vince Rockland

10 Second Runners Up (Alphabetical)
21. Talvin DeMachio
22. Casey Donovan
23. Rick Donovan
24. Chad Douglas
25. Anthony Gallo
26. Al Parker
27. Jeremy Penn
28. Marco Rossi
29. Zak Spears
30. Jack Wrangler

Acknowledgements

Compiling a directory covering three decades and thousands of stars is, to say the least, an enormous—never ending—project that would not be possible without the generous help of hundreds of individuals.

First and foremost, I want to thank Mario Solano for typing in most of the information in this directory. And for calling, e-mailing and writing letters to all of the studios to request information and photos. And then for following up and following up again.

Second, I'd like to thank Mickey Skee for his helpful books and for introducing us, at Companion Press, to the directors, the porn stars and the many behind-the-scenes people who make it possible for this industry to continue pumping out the product.

Many thanks to the studios and the stars who provided or varified information: Barry Gallop at Kristen Bjorn, Bruno at Oh Man! Studios, Craig Latker at Hot House, Brian Mills at Titan Media, Freddie Berkowitz at Video 10, Mike Donner and Danny Cross at All Worlds Video, Michael Yoens at Falcon, Tom at Catalina, Robert Prion at Galaxy, Debbie Rubio at HIS Video Gold, John Owens at Man 2 Man, Michael LaBarbera at Hollywood Sales, John Travis and Scott Masters at Studio 2000, Mike Lamb and Sean Zullo at Watershed, Jo-Ann Manzo at Pacific Media, Laura Hardin at Bel Ami, Bob East at Odyssey, Phil St. John at Tribal Pulse, Thor Stephens at Thor Productions, Marci Hirsch at Vivid, Nick DiMartino at U.S. Male, Jennie Joyce at Totally Tight, Mikhal Bales at Zeus Studios and everyone else at the studios who helped in large and small ways.

Thanks also to Butch Harris for offering to give us his feedback on this directory and share his expertise prior to publication. Porn fans will want to check out his amazing gay search engine at http:// www. ManNet.com.

To Cyrus at Discount Video in San Diego for his helpful list of videos and his suggestions.

To Conan the Vulgarian at *X Factor* magazine in Phoenix, Arizona for his feedback and suggestions.

To Leo Buck for his knowledge of the history of this business and for sharing it with us.

To porn stud Will Clark for his helpful, fact-filled newsletter

"Porn Star Confidential." Check out his website: at www.willclark usa.com. porn star

To Editor William Spencer for his many helpful comments about the stars.

To all of you who directed us to the "Dead Porn Star List" at http://www.rame.net/faq/deadporn and to Tim Evanson who supplied most of the gay information for this memorial site.

To Per Lui for his wonderful cover photo of the late Christian Fox, who he photographed on a number of occassions and who "borrowed" his camera after the cover shoot for this book—and never returned it. And for sharing other behind-the-scenes information about many of the stars in this book.

Most of our information in this directory came directly from the studios or the stars, but each of the following sources also proved to be useful in researching this directory and especially when double checking facts. We thank them all and recommend them highly.

Adam Gay Video Directory 1991 - 1999 Editions (Knight Publishing)

Autopornography: A Memoir of Life in the Lust Lane, by Scott O'Hara (Harrington Park Press)

Bad Boys of Video #1: Interviews with Gay Adult Stars, by Mickey Skee (Companion)

Bad Boys of Video #2: Interviews with Gay Adult Stars, by Mickey Skee (Companion).

The Bijou Video CD-Rom Catalog, by Bijou Video of Chicago, www.bijouworld.com.

Boy In The Sand: Casey Donovan All-American Sex Star, by Roger Edmonson (Alyson).

Making It Big: Sex Stars, Porn Films and Me, by Chi Chi LaRue, with John Erich (Alyson).

PORN KING: The Autobiography of John C. Holmes, by John C. Holmes with Laurie Holmes and Fred E. Basten.

Sorry I Asked: Intimate Interviews With Gay Porn's Rand and File, by Dave Kinnick (Bad Boy).

Sticky Remote: Pocket Gay Video Guide 1998, by Butch and Lance and *J.C. Adams* (OLS Publishing).

Superstars #1: Gay Adult Star Guide, by Jamoo (Companion).

Superstars #2: Gay Adult Star Guide, by Jamoo (Companion).

Unzipped magazine, the gay adult entertainment publication, edited by John Erich.

Wonder Bread And Ecstasy: The Life And Death of Joey Stefano, by Charles Isherwood (Alyson).

The X-Rated Gay Video Guide, by Sabin (Companion).

About This Directory

Who Is This Book For?

Over the years Companion Press has received hundreds of calls and letters from video stores and from fans asking us for a directory of gay porn stars and a complete list of each of their videos.

It took a while, and a half dozen people working on it off and on, but here it is, the only complete gay porn star videography—in a handy, easy to use, book format.

This is not an encyclopedia and it's not a photo book. It's a porn star videography book designed for video stores, fans and industry professionals.

How Complete Is This Directory?

Every porn star that we know of who made a movie since the early 1970s, when full-length gay porn videos became legal and began being widely distributed, is listed here.

How Is The Directory Organized?

In an easy, A to Z format. Each porn star videography includes the name of the actor, brief information about the actor (whenever available) and a complete list of his videos. If you want to know which studio produced the video, or when

it was released, simply turn to the "Video Title Index" at the back of the book.

We placed the studio and date at the back of the book in an index to keep the book small and handy. To list the studio and date next to each video would have doubled the size of the book.

How Many Stars Are Included?

This directory lists over 2,000 stars. So, we're pretty confident that we have just about everyone. Of these, only a couple hundred have become legends and only a handful have become icons.

How Did We Gather The Information?

As you can imagine, this has been an ongoing project for a number of years. We started by contacting all of the studios. We asked them to send us their complete list of videos and stars so we could ensure an accurate directory. Some did, some didn't.

We also contacted every porn star we could reach, past and present, and asked them for their list of videos.

After going directly to the source, we went to the videos themselves. We discovered that often an actor is listed on the box cover but is not actually in the video. Whenever possible we tried to verify that the actors listed on the box actually appeared in the videos.

How Can You Purchase The Videos Listed In This Directory?

At the back of the book you'll find a "Studio Directory & Video Buyers' Guide." Many of the videos listed here are no longer available for purchase but this guide should make it easy to find out from your local video store if they are available for rent.

Porn Star Name Variations

Many of the porn stars listed in this directory have used more than one name. Whenever possible we've included all names and listed the actor by the most popular name we are aware of. Usually the most popular name first then in parenthesis, also know as (aka so and so).

Video Title Variations

Video titles often appear one way on the box, and another way on the promotional material. Every effort has been made to verify titles.

Video Studio Variations

A number of studios have gone out of the business over the years. Often their videos are purchased by new studios and re-released under a new studio name. We have made every effort to indicate all studio names that we are aware of.

Video Date Variations

We have tried to include dates for every video, but this has proven to be one of the most difficult piece of information to obtain. Every effort has been made to let you know if a video is new or an old.

Feel Free To Contact Us

Have we left off one of your favorite stars? Have you discovered a mistake or incorrect information that needs to be corrected? Do you have information about any of the stars that would help us update their bios?

If so, please let us know and we'll make the correction or addition before the next edition and add you to the acknowledgements for your contributions. We'd especially like to hear from the stars and studios themselves.

You can send e-mail to the publisher Steve Stewart at sstewart@ companionpress.com or mail to PO Box 2575, Laguna Hills, CA 92654.

Thank you in advance for helping to make this the best directory available for fans of the porn stars—past and present.

Bruce Wayne, Editor

Gay Porn Stars From A to Z
(1970s, 1980s, 1990s)

A

SCOTT AARON
A blond, surfer-boy next
door model from the
1980s.
Desert Paradise
Mountain Fever

ROD ABBOTT
1990s model.
Bad Boys
Boys in the Office
Brown Paper Wrapper
Carnival
Deliver Ring
Destination: West
Hollywood
Fetish
For My Eyes Only
Freshman Fever
Hard Pressed
Hard Talk
Heat
How Big is Big?
Interior Motives
Knight Out with the Boys
Las Vegas Love Gods
Making of "Knight Out with
   the Boys"
Man Scent
Mansplash
Method & Madness
No Fluff, Just Stuff
O Is For Orgy
San Francisco Bed &

Breakfast
Secret Boys Club
Sex Gallery
Superstud Fever
Take It Like a Man
Through the Looking Glass
Training Session
Trick Time

MILTON ABDALLA
1990s model.
Brazilian Bath Boys Part 2
The Men From Ipanema

SAM ABDUL
Dark-haired model and
1990s actor-turned-
director.
Bed Tales
Big Merger, The
Boys Will Be Boys
Brotherly Love 2
Cockeyed Eagle, The
Conflict Of Interest
Dish
Hard Ass
Hole Different Ball Game, A
Male Instinct
Male Seduction

JOEY ACCIOLY
1990s model.
Leather Obsession
   3 & 4
Forever Orgies 1

ELIO ACOSTAS
Give It To Me Straight
Threesome

TONY ACOSTA
The Big Shot

TAZ ACTION
A youthful blond, 1990s
bottom. Actor and writer,
originally from Wisconsin.
Bottoms Up
A Cut Above
Freshman Fever
Hardball
Hard Labor
Hell Knight
Men With Tools
Obsessive Desires
Portholes
Scent of Leather
Thrust Fault
Toys Bi Us

BRIAN ADAMS
Light brown haired model
from late '80s. Former
boyfriend of Joe Cade.
Better Than Ever
The Big One
G.I. Mac
Handtools
Main Attraction, The
Main Event, The
Neighborhood Watch
Rites of Fall, The

Rites of Summer, The
Surge Men are Very
   Receptive
Surge Men at Their Best

CHETT ADAMS
1990s model.
Relentless
Shameless

CORKY ADAMS
(aka Shawn Young, Sean
Young) Dark-haired, youth-
ful 1990s model.
Club 18-23
College Jocks' Foot Fetish
Corky's Vacation
Freshman Years
Hung Man Meat
Its Raining Men
Jeff Stryker's Underground
The Other Side of
   Big Bear
Pleasure Principle
Pucker Up
Sex Fly
Top it Off
Young Men On The
Pleasure Trail

CORY ADAMS
1980s model.
Beyond Hawaii
Boot Camp Buddies
Catalina Down and Dirty
Catalina Orgies, Vol. 1
Class Reunion
Cousins
French Lt's Boys
Leo Ford: the Making of
   a Superstar
Military Men
Sailor in the Wild

San Francisco Orgy
Sex in the Great Outdoors
   1 &2
X-tra Large

DANNY ADAMS
Unexpected Persuasion

DEVON ADAMS
(See Grant Fagan)

DIRK ADAMS
(aka Lance Michaels)
1990s model.
Always Available
All That Jizz
As Big as it Gets
Below the Decks
Big Deposit
Cockland
Country Hustlers
Crossing Over
The Drifter
Flyin' Solo
Gay for the Weekend
Good Dick Hunting
Hustler Way
In the Shadows
Men of Magnum
My Big Brother
   U.S.M.C.
Other Side of Big Bear
Pounderosa, The
Raw Meat
Rent to Bone
Sex Invaders
Something About Larry
Special Forces
Spin the Bottle Orgy
Straight Talk
West Hollywood Stories
While the Cat's Away

JULIAN ADAMS
1990s model.
Ranger Nick 2
Sweat & Wet

MARC ADAMS
Powergrip

PAUL ADAMS
Born April 6. 1990s model.
Fit for a Man
Tall Tail

REN ADAMS
(aka Ren Lickitt & Devon
Michaels) Handsome,
dark-haired, 1990s model.
5'11," 8" cock, versatile.
Born in Abbeville, South
Carolina. Resides in
Los Angeles, California.
Anal Attraction
Blue Collar-White Heat
Brief Exchanges
Clothes Make the Man
Cut Above, A
Danny's Anal Addiction
Dream Team
Drill Me Good
Fantasy Fight
Faultline Sextimes
Gay Video Guide All-Star
   Softball Game #1
Hair Plug
Hard Act
Hard Drive
Hole In The Wall
Honolulu HardBodies
It's a Gang #1
License To Thrill
Man Construction
No Secrets
Protector, The

Raw Discipline
Rear End Window
Rearin' to Go
Ren's Den #1-6
Rip and Strip
Rodeo Wrestling #1
Rude Awakening
Rush, The
Sexposure
Single For The Weekend
Slave Workshop Boston
Smell of a Man 2
Spring Fever
Taxi Tales
Through The Looking
Glass
Upfront
Wet and Wild
Young Memories

RICK ADAMS
California Blue
Flashbacks
San Francisco Orgy

SHANE ADAMS
Star Maker

SHAWN ADAMS
Handsome blond, late
1990s model.
The Bartender
How To Get A Man In Bed
Intrusion
Just One Favor
Men

TOM ADAMS
1990s model.
Choke 'Em 3
God Was I Drunk
Spiked

TROY ADAMS
All Men Do It
It Happened One Day

CHETT ADDAMS
Can't Say No
One Way or the Other
Shameless

RUSH ADDAMS
A cute, dark-haired, 1990s
model, hung thick.
Back to Front
Behind The Barn Door
Blue Collar, White Heat
Good Vibrations
Handjobs 2
Roommate, The

ADRIAN
Desert Paradise II:
Revenge!
Schlong Blade

KIRK ALAN
Born September 5, 1965,
Woodland, California. 6'2,"
9" cock. Top. A 1990s
model.
Fallen Angel 2
Focal Length
Get It On Line

STEVE ALAN
1990s model.
O is for Orgy

CLIFF ALEXANDER
Even Steven

ETHAN ALEXANDER
1990s black model.
A.W.O.L.

Black American
Black Renegades
Ho Ho Ho!!!
Hung Man Meat
Pumping Black

JEREMY ALEXANDER
Young Guys
Young Shooters (Solo)

KEVIN ALEXANDER
Black Renegades
Cruisin' for a Gang Bang
Driveshaft
Everything A Man Wants
Make it Count
Men Matter Most
Nothing Else Matters
One Way or the Other
Point Of Entry
Pushover
Relentless
Shameless
Stop At Nothing
Whatever It Takes

ZACK ALEXANDER
Born September 26, 1976
in Los Angeles. Smooth,
youthful-looking model.
5'11" with dark brown hair
and eyes. Late 1990s
model.
Beach Head
Brothers Behaving Badly
Das Butt 2
Fit for a Man
It's Raining Men
Young Guys
Young Shooters (Solo)

MARK ALLAN
Any Excuse For Sex

Earning His Keep
Leather Weekend
More Than Friends

SPENCE ALLAN
Hard Labor
The Night We Met
The Visit

CHASE ALLEN
Born May 27. Mature,
hairy-chested, late 1990s
model.
Leather Intrusion Case 1:
Flaming Dragon
Leather Obsession 5—
    Mission Possible
Look Of Leather
Our Trespasses
Thick of It
Tools of the Trade

CHRIS ALLEN
One of the more memo-
rable versativel bottoms of
the '80s. 8" uncut cock.
Auto Erotica: Best of Sex
    in Cars
Bad Boys, Vol. 24 & 26
Bi-Coastal
Bi For Now
Blown Away
California Wet
Chip Off the Old Block
Cousins
Coverboy
Down to His Knee
Drawing Tricks
Fade In
Fade Out
Firsts
Flesh
Fun Size

Getting It
Getting Off Campus
Hot Shots, Vol. 1, 2, 4 & 9
Hot Splash
Hunk
King Size
Male-O-Gram
Man Size
Manholes #2
Men in Motion #1
Midnight Special #4:
    Surf's Up
Modern Men, Modern Toys
More Than a Mouthful
New Wave Hustlers
Nine-and-a-Half Inches
Nothing But the Best
Old Reliable #42:
    Big Time Excitement
Old Reliable #48:
    Totally Uncut
One Size Fits All
P.S. Connection #2
Picklin' the Cucumbers
Rangers
Sex in the Great Outdoors
    Part 2
Shooting Stars #6:
    Chris Allen
Solo Guys
Squirts 1-3
Stud Struck
Studbusters
Studio X
Totally Uncut
Tub Stubs
U.N.C.U.T. Club of L.A.
Winners

MORGAN ALLEN
(aka Alex Brown, Morgan
Sommer, Morgan Alan)
Born May 17, 1968 in

Hollywood, California into
a Mormon family. Grew
up in San Diego. 6', blue
eyes, black curly hair. Was
a Mormon missionary in
Québec, Canada for 2
years. Speaks French flu-
ently. Went to Hampshire
College in Amherst, MA.
Resides in Silverlake,
California. Co-founder/
owner of the Cybersocket
directory, web-magazine,
and www.cybersocket.com
web site.
Daytime Voyeur
Desert Paradise 1 & 2
Four Men
Good Fellas, Bad Fellas
    (Alex Brown)
Hot Laguna Knights
    (Morgan Sommer)
Hot Spot
In The Shadows
Palm Springs Cruisin'
Sexcuses
Tempted
Threesome

PAT ALLEN
Getting Off Campus
Inevitable Love
Men In The Sand 2
When A Stranger Comes

RICK ALLEN
Mature, dark-haired, 1990s
leather daddy.
Shameless

BRAD ALLMAN
(see Chris McKenzie)

TONY ALVARANZO
Leather Men 2
Sexual Thoughts

JOEY AMORE
(aka Joey Morelli & Joey
Violence) 1990s model.
Back in the Saddle
Naked Highway
Workin' it Out

ANDEL
Youthful, cute, Czech
Republic model from the
1990s with light brown
hair.
Andel's Story
Andel's Story 2: The
Running of the Bulls
Czech Bi Demand
Czech Is In The Male
Impromtus
Inn Bi The Road
Puda

MATTHEW ANDERS
(aka Matt Anders)
Born January 30, 1973
Poland. Cute, young,
blond, 5'8," 6 1/2" uncut,
versatile 1990s model.
Bad Ass Lieutenant
Body Heat
California Kings
CatalinaVille
Cream Team, The
Gay for the Weekend
Getaway Weekend
High Tide
Lusty Leathermen:
Mechanic on Booty
Men of Magnum
Soaked

Summer, The First Time
Uncut Weekend
Uninvited, The
Uninvited Images

TODD ANDERS
(see Chris McKenzie)

ZAK ANDERS
Batter Up!

CRAIG ANDERSON
1989 model. Only made
four films.
Beach Dreamer
Health Club Gigolo
International Guide to
Fellatio
Pin Me

SCOTT ANDERSON
Boys of San Francisco
Face to Face
Pacific Coast Highway

T. J. ANDERSON
(see T. J. Scott)

VAL ANDERSON
A 1970s model.
Seven in a Barn

PETRE ANDRAAS
Raging River

ALEX ANDRADE
Hard On Demand
Earning His Keep

B.J. ANDREWS
Any Way I Can

DREW ANDREWS
Born April 18. Handsome,
hunky, brown-haired, 1990s
model.
Anonymous Sex
As Big as it Gets
At First Glance
Barracks Glory Hole 3
Big Boyz Club 4
Birthday Blowout
Boot Camp Buddies
Chasing Andy
Corporate Ladder, The
Cruising Game, The
Dial "S" for Sex
Dive!
Dreams of Discipline
Eroto Wrestling
Full Body Contact
Gang Bang Ranch Hand
Getting Personal
Goodfellas/Badfellas
Good Samaritan, The
Hairsteria
Hand of Fate
Hartley's Crew
Hills Have Bis, The
Jamie Hendrix's
 Interviews 1
Johnny Hormone
L.A. Daze
Like Father Like Son
Liplock
Locker Room Sex Brawl
Logan's Journey
Lovers Lane
Lusty Leathermen
Mall Crusin' X-L
Man Hunt, The
Marine Obsessions
Mechanic on Booty
Mount The Big One
My Big Brother U.S.M.C.

New Meat
Night Feast
Our Trespasses
Outdoor Ecstacy
Play With Fire
Policemen's Balls
Poolman Cometh, The
Pounderosa, The
Pressure
Pumping Up
Red, Hot & Safe
Runway Studs
Sex Session
Straight Exposure
Straight Men
Switchcraft
Technical Ecstasy
That Old Whorehouse
Top it Off
Trixxx of the Trade
Undress for Success
VamBires
Warehouse Heat
Webmaster
West Hollywood Sex Party

IAN ANDREWS
Caught In The Military #1

JAKE ANDREWS
One of the top stars of the 1990s. This dark-haired hunk, reportedly moved to Australia.
Abduction 2: Conflict
Billy's Tale
Blow Me Down
Boot Black 1 & 2
Breakaway
Built Tough
Chasers
Code of Conduct 1 & 2
Deep End

Desert Hart
Dickted
Dirty White Guys
Fame and Flesh
Fit for a Man
Friction
Greased Up
Hard As Marble
Hardbody 2000 (non-sex)
Hidden Instinct
Highway Hunks
High Tide
Hot Blades
Hot House Files
Hotwired: Viewers' Choice
Hung Riders
Idol Country
In Man's Country
Iron Will
Jawbreaker
Link
Link 2 Link
Matinee Idol
On the Mark
On the Rise
The Other Side of Aspen 4
Our Trespasses
Peep-O-Rama
Receiving End
Rock Solid
Secret Sex 3
Splash Tops
Stud Valley
Summoner, The
Swallowers, The
Taking of Jake, The
That Old Whorehouse
Toolkit
True Stories
Try Again
Workin' Stiff

JASON ANDREWS
1990s model.
All About Steve
Behind the Barn Door
Bigger They Come
Brawn's Rod
Damien, One Night of Sin
Exposed
Hold Me Again
Honorable Discharge
Hot Pursuit
Jockaholics
Juice Bomb
Just In Time
Long Distance Lovers
Motor Crotch
Palm Springs Paradise
Piece of Cake
Sex, Guys & Videotape
Shadows in the Night
Star Gazing, Vol. 3
Take Down
Taken to the Max
Tough Terrain
Stiff Cocktail
Wet and Wild

JIM ANDREWS
Sex Toy Story #2
Sucker

KYLE ANDREWS
Can't Say No
Every Man's Desire

MARK ANDREWS
Late '80s blond model with a swimmer's body.
As Time Goes Bi
Below The Rim
The Bi-Analyst
Bi Golly
Bi Inferno

The Bi-Spy
Bi Valley, The
Big Merger, The
Big Switch 2:
    The Bachelor Party
Boner
Brotherly Love 2
Busted
Camp Pokahine
Cellblock Sinner
Chain Male
Club House #5
Cockeyed Eagle, The
Cool Moon
Cruisin' 2: More Men On
    The Make
Dirty Pictures
Double Exposure
Dream Team
4 Alarm Studs
Group Therapy
Horny Rent Collector
Horsemeat
Idol Worship
Ivy League, The
Knight Out With The Boys
Lava Flow
Liquid Love
Macho Money
Made To Get Laid
Madness & Method
Majestic Knight
Making Of "Knight Out With
    The Boys"
Male Seduction
Man Alone
Mandriven
Manplay
Mean Streak
Memories Of Summer
Men On The Loose
Method & Madness
Military Issue

Muscle Club, The
Neighborhood Games
A Night With Strangers
Open House
Over The Edge
Payne In The Ass
Personal Service
Power Play
Preferred Stock #1
Raw Recruits
Rex: Take One
Rimshot
Rump Ranger
Sailing To Paradise
Sexcess
Sexologist
Smokin' Butts'
Spring Fever
Strip Search
Strip Tease
Studmania
Studz
Switch Hitters 6 & 7
Ten Plus (Vol. 2)
Trick Time
Truth, Dare Or Damian
White On White
Wild Country
Young And Notorious

MILES ANDREWS
1990s model.
Happiness is a Big Cock

RYAN ANDREWS
Bi-Cepts
Class Reunion
Saturday Night Special

DIRK ANGELES
Too Big to Handle

ANGELO
(aka Angelo Moore,
Steven Moore and Steven
Angelo Moore) 1980s
model.
Angelo Loves It
Big Packages
Blow Bi Blow
Buckets of Love
Climactic Scenes #101
Cody Exposed
Fantasies of Brazil
Frat Brats
Hard Choices 2
Hawaiian Heat
Heaven Too Soon
Hot Shots, Vol. 22:
    Raw Bears
Hot Shots, Vol. 28:
    Hot Pickups
In Deep
Larger Than Life
Malibu Poolboys
Mustang Ranch
My Best Friend
Neptune
Orgy at the Funhouse
Show it Off
Surf's Up
Unchained Men

MAC ANGELO
1980s model.
One Track Mind
Pleasure Ridge
Single For The Weekend

NICK ANGELO
1990s model.
Positively Yours
A Tale of Two Brothers

TONY ANGELO
(aka Tony De Angelo, Joey D' Angelo) dark-haired, 1990s model.
Backdrop
Coming Out, Coming Hard
Fan Male
Malibu Pool Boys
Pleasure Theater
Raising Hell
Rigid Video 1
Rings
Sterling Ranch
Trail Tails
Ultimate Desires

BRIAN ANGER
A late 1990s model.
Jockstrap

KEITH ANTHONI
New York model from the late '80s.
All Tied Up
Catching Up
El Paso Wrecking Corp.
Flesh & Fantasy
In Heat
In the Name of Leather
Leather Rituals
Night Before, The
Pier Groups
Sex Toilets
So Many Men,
   So Little Time
Swallow It

ANTHONY
(aka Antonio) 1990s model.
Blatino Party L.A.
Crammin' for the Big One
Cummin' Of Age

Hawaiian Vacation 2
Huddle Up
Kept: A Way of Life
Latin Sex Thing
My Big Brother U.S.M.C.
Rent to Bone
Star Maker
Supersize II
ThunderBalls
WhiteWalls

CHASE ANTHONY
Can't Say No
Every Man's Desire
First Time Tryers #11

CHRIS ANTHONY
Hot Firemen
Top It Off

DAVID ANTHONY
Sizzle

JAY ANTHONY
Born April 4. Brunet, late 1990s model.
Four Men
Winged

JOSE ANTHONY
Man Trade Solos

MARC ANTHONY
Not the same actor as Marc Anthony below. Born April 7. Originally from New Jersey, this 5'10" bisexual top man now resides in Florida. 1990s model.
South Beach Summer

MARK ANTHONY
1990s model. Not the same actor as Marc Anthony above.
Butt Bruisers
Mo' Bigga Butt
Sure Thing

MICHAEL ANTHONY
Born February 4.
Best Of All II
Free Delivery
Motel California
Rear Delivery
Royal Flesh
Size of the Matter
Two By Ten
When a Stranger Comes

TEX ANTHONY
A bisexual porn legend of the '80s.
Best Bi Far #2
The Best of Times
Bi-Bi Love
The Big Switch
Bisexuals a Go-Go
Bisexual Fantasies
Foreplay
Hard
Hard to Believe
Hot Shots, Vol. 8: Orgies
Hot Shots, Vol. 9:
   Hot Blonds
Hot Shots, Vol. 15:
   Bottoms
Hot Shots, Vol. 17:
   Meat Market
Make Me Hard
Naked Lunch
Neverending Studs
Palm Springs
   Connection 2

Play Safely
Private Collection
  Screen Test
Quickies #6: The Revenge
Rushes
Social Studies
Spring Semester
Tough Iron
Young and the Hung, The

ANTONIO (see Anthony)

JUAN ANTONIO
Das Butt 2
Schlong Blade
Tomorrow Will Come

MARCO ANTONIO
Born April 24. Resides in
Argentina. Native
Argentinians Marco
Antonio and Jean Rivera
are lovers who came to
the U.S. in 1997 and
entered the porn video
business. They returned to
their native country where
they continue to make
porn videos for American
studios.
Apprentice, The
Club 18-23
Current Affairs
First Time Tryers 6
Games We Play, The
Indulge 2
A Jock's Dream
Latins
A Love Story
Positively Yours
Sharp Shooters
Tale End of Summer
Winged

SAL ANTONIO
A dark-haired, South
American model from the
1990s.
Coming Together
Hold Me Again
Hologram
Hot Ticket
Jackpot
Liquid Love
Lords of Leather

MAREK ANTONOV
1990s Czech Republic
model.
Lucky Lukas

ADAM ARCHER
Bigger They Come
Boner
Break In
Delirium
Down Home
Easy Riders
Hard at Work
Inner Circle
Jumper
Keeping Time
Male Instinct
Night We Met, The
Overnight Service
Powertool 2: Breaking Out
Prince Charming
Ripped
Sex Shooters
Take Down
True
Visitor, The
Water Sports

SCOTT ARDEN
Black Lust, White Passion
Interview 1 & 2

Spanking Master, The

KEITH ARDENT
Died September 9, 1992
from AIDS-related causes.
dark-haired, hairy chested
model with a mustache.
Bad Ass
Bi And Large
Black Book
Crosswire
Forty Plus
Goodjac
Master Hyde
Raw Footage
Sex Junkies
Sex Toys
The Shaft

ROBERTO ARIAS
A late 1980s Latino actor.
Bears and Cubs
Best of Joe Simmons, The
Black Alley: South of
  the Border
Blow Bi Blow
The Boxer 1
Boys on Fire
Buckets of Love
Butt Darts
By Day/Bi Night
Cat Burgler
Climactic Scenes #101
Cowboys & Indians
Danny Does Dallas
Dueling Dicks
Engine #69
Fantasies of Brazil
Guys With Tight Asses
Hard Ball
The Harder the Better
Headin' West
In the End Zone

Los Hombres
Men of Size
Pool Boy
Ram Man 1 & 3
Raw Footage
River, The
Rock Hard
Rumble
Secret Action Man
Seduction II: The Heat
    is On
She-Males Undercover
Smokin' Butts
Soldiers
Soul & Salsa
Switch Hitter IV: The
Grand Slam
Thumbs Up
Tips
Tongue Dancing
Wide Load
Winged

GREGG ARLEN
1990s Studio 2000
exclusive.
Rosebud
West Hollywood Hope

JOSE ARMANDO
(aka Jesus Armando)
A Latino model from 1990.
Adrenaline
Advocate Men Live 5
Boxer 2, The
Built Like A Brick House
Cabana Boys
For Sale by Owners
Gentlemen Only
Hombres
Latin Power
Latinos Working Hard
Men: Skin and Steel

Overseas Trade
Real Men of the New West
Traffic School Was Never
Like This!
Uncut Fever, Part 2
Uncut Gems: Diamonds
    in the Raw
Up and Over

JULIAN ARMANIS
Young Czech Republic
model.
English Student, The

ROCKY ARMANO
Big Guns
Bulge: Mass Appeal
Hard Men
Hot Rods

HODGE ARMSTRONG
Born May 25. Hunky 6'3"
jock-next-door 1990s
model with light-brown hair
and blue eyes. Resides in
Wisconsin.
First Time Tryers
Fox Tales
Matador
Said & Done
Show Me the Money
White Hot
Why Marines Don't Kiss

JAKE ARMSTRONG
Cute, boy-next-door late
1990s model with light-
brown hair.
Daredevils
Don't Dick with the Devil
It's Raining Men
My Brother's Best Friend
Tall Tail

ROBERT ARTHURS
Skinny Dipping

DAVID ASHFIELD
(aka Billy Evans, Bob
Holloway) A blond, 1980s
legendary top. 5'11."
AC/DC Hookup
Bad Boys Dormitory
Below the Belt
Best Friends II
The Best of Blacks
The Best of Surge, Vol. 1
Bi-Coastal
Bi-Mistake
Bigger They Come, The
Blown Away
Boys Can't Help It
Campus Jocks
Classmates
Climactic Scenes #101
Coverboy
Cum Shots 102
Delivery Boys
Fade In
Fantasize
Firsts
Flesh
Foreplay
Freshmen
Full Load
Fun Size
Getting It
Getting Off Campus
Gidget Goes Bi
Golden Boys, The
Hard at It, Volume 2
Heart Throbs
H.E.A.T.
Hot Numbers, Vol 1 & 2
Hot Off the Press
Hot Shots, Vol. 1, 2 4 8,
    14, 20, 30

Hot Splash
Hotel Hell
Hunk
In Hot Pursuit
Jobsite
Lifeguard
Locker Room Fever
Magnum Griffin, Vol II
Men in Motion
Manheat
Manholes #2
Mansplash
Mantalk
Maximum Oversize
Men in Motion #3
Men of Size
Men on Site
Men on the Loose
Midnight Special #4:
    Surf's Up
Mind Games
Mix n' Match
More Mind Games
Move Over, Johnny
Neverending Studs
Nightcrawler
Nine-and-a-Half Inches
Nuts and Butts
Old Reliable #73:
    The Size of the Matter
One Size Fits All
The Pizza Boy
    (He Delivers)
Play Safely
Probe Vol. 2: Three's
    Company
Rites of Spring, The
Santa Monica Boulevard
Secret Action Man
Sex Hunt
S.F. Packing Company
Size of His Toys, The
Spring Break

Star Shots 1 & 3
Stiff Sentence
Strange Places, Strange
Things
Strokers
Stud Fuckers
Therapy
Think Big
Tongue Dancing
Trash, Vol. 4: Huge Meat
Unchained Men
Wide Load

MICHAEL ASHLEY
1990s model.
Good Vibrations
Home Wrecker
Jackpot—On The Road To
    Vegas
Juice Bomb
Latin Bandit
Latin Encounters
Legend Of Joey Stefano
Moment Of Truth
Point Of Return
Power Driver
Rump Ranger
Sexcess
Stickpussy
Sunsex Boulevard
Tales Of The Backlot

PETER ASHLEY
Hard Men 2
Main Attraction, The
Top Man

GEOFF ASHTON
1990s model.
Billy Herrington's Body
Shop

ROSS ATKINS
A 1990s, blond, boy next
door model.
Amateur 2
Gang Bang Alley
Hollywood Kid, The
Love Muscle
Sex Party
Sex Test, The
Thunder Blue
Tony's Big Brother

AUSTIN
(aka Austin Ashley)
Born October 11. Tall,
blond, boy-next-door-look-
ing late 1990s model. Lives
in Los Angeles.
A Day In The Life of Austin
Handsome Drifters
Hard Focus
In Love
Interview 1
Naked Highway
Nude Science

AARON AUSTIN
Straight identified 1990s
model.
Aaron Austin: A Day In
    The Life
Cody Exposed
Hidden Agenda
Hot Properties
Hung Up
Inside Karl Thomas
Insiders, The
Into The Night
Jockaholics
Journey, The
Look Of A Man, The
Masquerade
Memories Of Summer

Men Of Forum
Mentor
Obsessively Compulsive
On The Rise
One Track Mind
Original Sin
Risky Sex
Safe Sex: A Gay Man's
 Guide
San Francisco Bed &
Breakfast
Sex Wrestling
Single White Male
Skin Tight
Solid Flesh
Splash Tops
Spring Fever
Steel Away
Sunsex Boulevard
Switch Hitters 7
Take It Like A Man
Twin Exposure
Tyler Scott- A Day Of
 Decadence

ALEX AUSTIN
1990s model.
Boys From Bel Air
45 Minutes Of Bondage
Friendly Desire
Hard Ball
House Of Tricks
Magnified
Obsessive Desires
Officer And His Gentleman
One Track Mind
Pleasure Ridge
Power Driver
Reveille
Ruthless
To The Hilt
Trophies: Class Of '94

BRAD AUSTIN
Low Riders

CORY AUSTIN
Phi Kappa Sucka'

JEFF AUSTIN
Blond bottom from the
 '90s.
The Backroom
Built Tough
Boot Black 2
Clothes Make the Man
Drummond's Auditions
Guy Next Door
Hard Lessons: Sex Ed 2
Hot Cops 2
Hot Copy
Leather Obsession 4 -
 Forever
Muscledaddy's Boy
Toys/Jake
Orgies Pt 1

JOE AUSTIN
Saving Ryan's Privates

JORDAN AUSTIN
Bound & Shaved
Club 18-23
Getting Ahead
Kept: A Way of Life
Men 4 Men On The Net

KEITH AUSTIN
I Saw What You Did
Kept: A Way of Life

KENT AUSTIN
(see Jack Ryan)

SCOTT AUSTIN
1990s model.

Big Thrill, The
Hotel California

WARD AUSTIN
Minute Man 5
Rawhide Roundup!

JACQUES AUVRAY
1980s model.
Carnival In Venice
Getting Even
Street Smart

SCOTT AVERY
One of the more memo-
rable stars of the past.
All-American Boy, The
Best of All Matt Sterling
Best of Surge, Vol. 1, The
Big Shooters 4 & 5
Blown Away
Boys Just Wanna Have
 Sex
Coverboy
Dirty Load
Hard Disk Drive
Hot Male Mechanics
International Skin
Job Site
King Size
L.A. Boiling Point
Manholes #1
A Matter of Size
Men in Motion #6
Size Talks
Something Wild
Spring Training
Studbusters
Totally Awesome
Tyger Tales
What the Big Boys Eat

ETHAN-MICHAEL AYERS

Dark-haired, blue-eyed boy-next-door model and San Diego resident. Will always be known as one of the pornstars who was befriended by Andrew Cunanan, the serial killer who murdered Gianni Versace in 1997.
Backseat BJ
Barracks Glory Hole 4
Dirty Leather Dive!
Forced Service
Four Men
Our Trespasses
Playing With Fire
Plugged
Try Again
White Fire

B

NINO BACCI
Road Home, The

JACK BAILEY
God Was I Drunk

PAUL BAIN
1990s model.
Big Delivery
Command Performance
Double Crossed
Down Home
Manticipation
Midnight Run
Pitch A Tent

BEN BAKER
(aka Benjamin) 1980s model.
Boys of San Francisco
Class of '84, Part 2
Games
Hot Trash
Kip Noll and the
    Westside Boys
A Night at the Adonis
Pacific Coast Highway
Rear Deliveries
Revenge of the Nighthawk
Skin Deep

CORY BAKER
All the Right Boys
All the Way In
California Homegrown
Desert Heat
Dirty Jocks
Eighteen Candles
    (18 Candles)
Growing Years
Mikey Likes It
A Physical Education

DERRECK BALDWIN
Men 4 Men On The Net
Millitary Issue 3:
    Ask & I'll Tell
Orgies Pt 1

GARRETT BALDWIN
Off Duty

LEE BALDWIN
Popular, dark-haired, 1980s model. Went on to produce his own videos.
Assplay 1 & 2
Better Than Bi
Bi-Heat, Vol 5, 9, 10
Bone Alone
Butt Crazy Boys
    (Custom Tape #2)
Clippers
Crazy Horny Nutz
Dares
Days Gone Bi
Dickey-Lickey
Guyz-N-the Burbs
Jac Attack
Jerk-Off (dir.)
Leather Me Down,
    Do Me Toys
Man Eaters
Master Hyde
Men Behind Bars
My Sister, My Brother
Piss Party 5
Posed to Expose
Prison
The Rod Squad
Sex Behind bars
Slaves
The Spanking Master 2
Straight to Bed
Suck (dir.)
Three Little Pigs
Tongue in Cheek
Tough Choices
Underground Sex Club
Weekend at Large

LEX BALDWIN
Early '90s, gay-for-pay actor and brother of straight porn star T.T. Boy.
King Of The Mountain
Man Of The Year
Powertool 2
Sex Bi-Lex
Straight To Bed

REX BALDWIN
(aka Billy Slater)
Best of Leather: Part 1
Chance Encounter
Driven Home
Hot Blades
Hot Cops 2
Hung Up
Knight Gallery 2
Leather Obsession
Limited Entry
Long Play
Naughty Little Brother
No Reservations
Original Sin
Pet Boys
Quick Study
Wear It Out
Workin' Hard

SCOTT BALDWIN
Born July 30, 1971 in
Crystal City, Virginia. 5'5-
1/2," 7" cock. Resides in
West Hollywood, Calif-
ornia. A popular bottom
from the '90s.
Officer and His
    Gentleman, An
Backstage Pass
Big River
Boys and Their Toys 2
Center Spread 2
Cream of the Crop
Cruise Control
Double Vision
A Few Fresh Men
Flashpoint
Getting in Tight
Hold Me Again
House Rules
Knight Gallery
Man to Men

Man's Touch (CD)
Manhattan Skyline
Men of Forum 1 & 2
Mentor
Nice & Hard (CD)
Our Trespasses
Prisoner of Love
Rags to Riches
Santa Monica Place
A Taste of Leather 2
Technical Ecstasy
Total Corruption
Trickmaster, Zack
True Stories
Uncut Club 5
Virtual Viewer
    Photodisk (CD)

DANIEL BALL
976-Stud

BAM
Born March 21. Popular
black star of the 1990s.
A.W.O.L.
Bam
Bam 2: Thug
Black Leather Gang Bang
Black Men Cruisin'
    Crenshaw
Black Muscle Machine 2
Black Warriors
Hard to Swallow
Marine Chronicles, The
Straight Cocksuckers

TONY BANDANZA
Danger Zone
Blade's Real World
Outdoor Ecstacy

VIC BANDERA
Hot to Trot

Splashdown!

VINCE BANDERO
(aka Vince Bandera)
Born June 2. Resides in
San Francisco. 5'5," 7"
uncut, top. A Latin model
from the '90s.
The Bite 2
Full Up!
Glory Holes of San
Francisco
Humidity
Live Feed
Stock
Stuffed
Suck Daddy
Working It Out

ROB BANKS
(see Ryan Fox)

DEX BANNING
Late 1990s model.
Nude Science

SEAN BANNING
Just Blondes
Mr. Footlong's Made In
America, Wildside

PAUL BARESSI
Former *Playgirl* centerfold
and 1980s and '90s,
mature, hairy-chested
model turned director.
China and Silk
Cops, Jocks and Military
    Feet
Driving Hard
Falconhead 2
Foot Loose
G.I. Mac

Goodfellas/Badfellas
Hot Male Mechanics
Hot Shots, Vol. 13:
   Bisexual
L.A. Plays Itself
L.A. Tool & Die
Men of the Midway
Razor Closet
Sulka's Wedding
Water Sports
What the Big Boys Eat

CHRIS BARLOW
1990s model.
Sit Tight

TIM BARNETT
Blond, all-American '90s
model.
Abduction 2: The Conflict
An Officer and His
   Gentleman
Captain Stud and His
   Seamen
Center Spread 2
Driven Home
Driven To It
Dynastud
Hard Bodyguard
Hole, The
Initiation, The
Intensive
Limited Entry
Man to Men
Mirage
On the Rise
Original Sin
Prisoner of Love
Thriller
Ty Me Up
Valley of the Bi Dolls
Wanted

ROD BARRETT
It's Raining Men

CHUCK BARRON
(aka Andrew Michaels)
A handsome, dark-haired,
gay-for-pay, 1980s model
from Orange county,
California.
The Best of Jon Vincent 1
Bi and Beyond 3
Bi and Sell
Bigger The Better 2, The
Billboard
Buddy System
Buddy System II:
   Camouflage
Cowboys & Indians
Cream of the Crop
Crossroads
Cruisers: A Reunion of
   Friends
Down, Down, Down
   (wrestling)
Eight Men In
Favors
Filth
Foreign Affairs
French Kiss
A Friendly Obsession
Hard Knocks
Heads or Tails
Hidden Man
Honorable Discharge
Horney Rent Collector
Hot Summer Knights
Imagination
In the Stretch
It's A Gang: Video Series 1
Jock City
Karen's Bi-Line
Lights! Camera! Action!
Long Hard Ride

Lovers Coming Home
Macho Money
Man Scent
Moment Of Truth
My Own Private Mexico
The Nasty Boys
Nasty Rays
Paul Norman's World of
Sexual Oddities
Painted
Private Files
Privilege
Psychedelic Dreamers
Pumping Up: Flex II
Ranger Nick II
The Rites of Manhood
Roommate, The
Screwing Screw-Ups
6969 Melrose Lane
Slam Dunk
Slick Willies
Special Reouest
Studmania
Summer Knights
Three's on Their Knees
Through The Looking Glass
Thumbs Up!
To the Bone
Tool Of The Trade
Total Corruption
Trick Stop
Tricked
Tube Steak
Valley Heat
Voltage
Where The Night Takes You

JEFF BARRON
A Hot House leather daddy
of the 1990s.
Bottoms Up
Dr. Good Glove
Doctor's Orders 1 & 2

Gut Reaction
Layin' Pipe

THOM BARRON

Blond, blue-eyed, hunky
1990s model from
Germany.
Berlin Army Nights
Best of Titan: Collector
   Series 2
Betrayed
Billy 2000
Breaking Point
Dildo Sex Slaves
Dr.'s Orders Part 1:
   Manipulation
Fever
Fluid
French Connection 1-2
Guarding the Jewels
Hard On Site
Hard Use
A Love Story
Orgies Pt 2
Sting: A Taste For Leather
Stock
Tourist Trade
The Verdict
Wet Warehouse #3:
   The Party

ROD BARRY

Born December 5. An ex-
Marine and one of the
most popular and cutest,
blond, gay-for-pay porn
stars of the '90s.
Barracks Glory Hole 5
Beach Buns
Beach Head
Breaking & Entering
Burning
Club 18-23

Complexxx, The
Cowboy Jacks
Current Affairs
Dare Devils
Dirty White Guys
Fox Tale
Full Body Contact
Gold Diggers
Hand of Fate
High Tide
Hot to Trot
Humidity
Just You and I
Lesson Learned, A
Link
Mantasy Island
Maximum Cruise
Mercury Rising
Mountain Patrol
New Coach, The
Oh Brother
On the Prowl Again
Red, Hot & Safe
Show Me the Money
Tall Tail
Uncut Weekend
Uniforms Only
White Hot
X-Press Male

KURT BATEMAN

Boys Camp Memories
Cover Models
Deep Inside
Desert Paradise
Oasis
Obsession: The Ultimate
   Experience
On Top
Pleasure Peak
Summer Heat
Surf's Up

JIM BATTAGLIA

Bad Boys Dormitory
The Best of Stud
The Best Stallions
Big and Hard
Big Men on Campus
Campus Jocks
Dirty Picture Show
Flesh and Fantasy
Hard
Hot Shots, Vol. 8, 13, 15
Idol, The
Men in Motion #1
Men on the Loose
Neverending Studs
Play Safely
Spirit is Willing, The
Stud Show
Three Day Pass

KURT BAUER

Dark-haired, hairy-chested,
1980s model.
Advocate Men Live!
Beef
The Best of Kurt Bauer
Bi and Beyond
The Big One
Bulge: Mass Appeal
Catalina Blonds
Discharged
Down for the Count
Exchange, The
Locker Room Sex
My Best Buddy
Paul Norman's World of
   Sexual Oddity
Size of His Toys, The
Top Man
Video Games #11

CODY BAWDUNIAK

Body of Art

Leather After Midnight
Leather Confessions
Leather Pit

DENNIS BAXTER
Black Mischief

MARK BAXTER
Born July 25. A versatile top or bottom from the early '90s.
Big Bang
Bottoms Up
Doctor's Orders 1 & 2
Hot Pursuit
Jumpin' Jacks
Mission Accomplished
Private Workout
Raw Material
Special Handling
True Stories

BEAU BEAUMONT
(aka Ryan Edwards)
Popular 1980s blond, jock-next-door model.
All That Counts
Bat Dude & Throbbin'
Best of Adam Grant, The
Best of All Matt Sterling
Cocktales
From Maui With Love
Hard Labor
Head of the Class, Part 2
Heat In The Night
Hot Shots, Vol. 44: Golden Boys
Island Heat
New Love
Pledge Masters
Point of No Return
Powerful II
Say Goodbye

Stryker's Best Powerful Sex
Ten is Enough
Trip to Paradise Beach

KYLE BECKER
Born July 28. Latin-looking '90s model.
Betrayed
Current Affairs
Fit for a Man
High Tide
In Deep: Miles To Go
Summer Reunion: The Best Parts of Summer

PAULO BELEZ
Porno Tonight Show, The

TORY BELL
1980s black actor.
Basic Black #7
Black Lust, White Passion
Black Sex Party
Black Sweat
Black Workout 3

TONY BELMONTE
1980s model.
Alley Action
Arms Of Forgiveness
Badlands
Behind His Back
Big Shots
Brats
Breaking And Entering
Caged Heat
Calendar Man, The
California Dream Inn
Cramming For The Big One
Cruisin'
Danger Alley

Day Dreams
Decent Proposal, A
Desert Maneuvers
Desert Paradise
Destination: West Hollywood
Down & Out
Dreams Come True
Frat House: Memories Of Pledge Week
Filth
Friendly Desire
Great Lengths
Guest, The
Happy House
Hard Times
Hell Weekend
Hole Different Ball Game, A
Hollywood Tails
Hot And Nasty
Hot Pursuit
Imagination: Action Gone Wild
It's A Gang #2
Jock City
Leather Temptation
Male Order Sex
Man Construction
Men In Love
Men Of The Moment
Midnight Sun
Moon Also Rises, The
Movin'
976 - Hot
No Cruisin' Zone
Outcall Lover
Party Animals
Party Favors
Payne In The Ass
Personal Service
Playing With Power
Playtime

Private Files
Pure Attraction
Raw Stock
Rear End Window
Rear Ended
Ripped
Secret Report
Sexcuses
Silverlake Inn
Songs In The Key Of Sex
Special Deliveries
Strong Man Scent
Strokes
Strong Man Scent
Sweat Motel
Tennis Court Daze
Tight Leather
Wall, The 1-3
Wild And Loose
X-Tasy

LUKE BENDER
(see Steve Kennedy)

CLINT BENEDICT
A dark-haired, mature, mid-
'90s model. West Holly-
wood resident and
masseur.
Abduction 2: The Conflict
Below the Rim
Bike Bang
Dynastud
House Rules
Hush
Lovers, Tricks & One Nigh
Stands
Magnified
Slave Auction
Wild Ones, The

JAY BENJAMIN
Ft. Lauderdale Hustlers

BRAD BENNETT
Can't Say No
Every Man's Desire

JIM BENSON
(see Jim Bentley)

RAY BENSTON
Do Me Evil

JEFF BENTLEY
A blond, 1980's model.
Bait
The Best of Times
Boys Just Wanna Have
  Sex
Cruisin' for Lust
Desert Heat
Dirty Jocks
Dynastud
Good Men Go Bad
Ivy Blues
Men on the Loose
P.S. Connection 1 & 2
Social Studies
The Spirit is Willing
2x10
Video Games #6

JIM BENTLEY
(aka Jim Benson)
Born May 24. One of the
big names of the 1980s.
This blond boy-next-door
type still makes personal
appearances today, per-
forming in clubs across the
country. When we spoke to
him in 1998 he was writing
his autobiography. He
made two comeback videos
in 1999.
Advocate Men Live 4

All-American Boy, The
All the Way
Behind Closed Doors
Best Wishes
Bi-Day Bi-Night
Big Show Off
Bi the Way
Bi-Surprise
Black Brother-White
  Brother
Boys on Call
Breakthrough
Buster: The Best Years
Butch and Masculine:
  Eagle 1
Cabin Fever
Castro Commando
Climactic Scenes #101
Daddy's Revenge
Danny Does Dallas
Danny Does 'Em All
Dirty Tricks
Dogs in Heat
Do Me Dirty
Easy Prey
Entertainment Bi-Night
Fire in the Hole
Foolin' Around
Fucking Around
Getting It
Gym Tales
Haulin' & Ballin'
Health Club Gigolo
Heroes
Historic Affairs
Hot High and Horny
Hot Shots, Vol. 2, 3, 4, 5
  & 10
Interracial Affairs
J.S. Big Time
Just Men
Made for You
Magnum Griffin, Vol. 6

Major Meat
Making it Huge
Manholes #2
Marine Obsession
Matinee Idol
Men Together
Moonlusting
New Zealand Undercover
A Night at Alfies
Nuts and Butts
Officer Dick
Portrait of a Gay Man
Ripe for the Harvest
San Francisco Sex
Secret Action Club
Sex Alley
Shooting Porn
Shooting Stars #4:
   Jeremy Scott
South of Market Leather
Splash Shots 1 & 2
Spokes II
Strokers
Swing Shift
Switch Hitters 1, 2 & 9
A Taste of Leather
They Work Hard for the
   Money
Thinking Big
Ticket to Ride
Tough Competition

ROLF ERIC BERGMAN
A mature 1980s model.
Absolutely Uncut
Beater's Digest
Men: Skin and Steel
Skinner Jacks
Trash, Vol. 8: Uncut Cocks
Uncut Gems: Diamonds in
   the Raw

PETER BERLIN
Though he only made a
few films, he became one
of the porn legends of the
1970s. A San Francisco
resident with long blond
hair and a huge dick, he
posed for numerous skin
magazines of the day.
Blueboys 1 & 2
Nights In Black Leather
Search (solo)
Solo Videos 1-3
That Boy
Waldeslust

STEPHAN BERTOLI
Dark-haired, mid '90s
model.
Another Man's Pleasure
One Man's Poison

SHAYNE BEST
A South African who now
resides in London. 1990s
model.
The Caller

BRUNO BIANCHI
Anchor Hotel, The
Tomorrow Will Come

BOB BIRDSONG
Connoisseur Collector
Classics
Hayride
Lodestar
Ram Charger

ANDREW BISHOP
Late 1980s model.
Between the Sheets
Challenge, The

Exiled
Hot for His Bod
Hot Shots, Vol. 50:
   Men at Work
Jackhammer
Joker's Wild
Rear Window
Trading Up
Truth, Dare or Damian

DERECK BISHOP
Born November 9th,
Missouri. 6'1," 8 1/2" cut,
versatile. 6'1," dark-haired,
late 1990s model.
Back Seat BJ
Chained Desires
Gates of Hell
Gay For The Weekend
Hand to Mouth
Hot Tub Fever
The Hotel
Inter-Racial Interrogation
Love Inn Exile (softcore)
Military Issue Part #3
Mount of the Big One
My Secret Collection
Orgies Pt 1
Picture Perfect
Private Members
Saving Ryan's Privates
Sodom
West Hollywood Sex Party
When The Wife's Away

PETER BISHOP
Born in Foley, Alabama. Ex-
Navy man and popular mid-
'90s bottom.
All Night Long
Another Man's Pleasure
At Your Service
Below The Decks

The Big Score
Bottoms Up
Bulletin Board Buddies
Bullring
Camp Pokahiney
Chi Chi Larue's Hard Body
  Video Mag. 4
For Your Pleasure
Hungry Eyes
Leather Night
New Pledge Master
No Reservations
Oklahomo!
Slip It In
Squeeze Play
Sunshine Supermen
Thursday Morning Workout
When A Man Wants A Man

STEPHEN BISHOP
A dark-haired model from
the 1980s.
Anything, Anytime
Cousin Buck
Make It Hard
Manholes
My Masters
Navy Blue
Tramps

KRISTEN BJORN
One of the most popular,
handsome, and award-win-
ning director's of the '90s
and of all time. Began his
career as a porn actor for
Falcon in the 1980s and a
as photographer for skin
magazines.
Advocate Men Live 5 (Act)
Amazon Adventure (dir.)
The Anchor Hotel (dir.)
Big Summer Surprise (Act)

Biker's Liberty (actor)
Call of the Wild (dir.)
Caracas Adventure (dir.)
Caribbean Beat (dir.)
Carnival in Rio (dir.)
Champs (dir.)
Comrades in Arms (dir.)
Gansters at Large (dir.)
Hot Times in Little
  Havana (dir.)
Hungarians (dir.)
Hungary for Men (dir.)
Island Fever (dir.)
Jackaroos (dir.)
Jungle Heat (dir.)
Manhattan Latin (dir.)
Manly Beach (dir.)
Manwatcher (dir.)
Montreal Men (dir.)
Mystery Men (dir.)
New Breed, The (actor)
Paradise Plantation (dir.)
A Sailor in Sydney (dir.)
Thick as Thieves (dir.)
Tropical Heatwave (dir.)
The Vampire of
  Budapest (dir.)
A World of Men (dir.)

VICTOR BJORN
Danger Zone
Phi Kappa Sucka'

AUSTIN BLACK
Born September 19th,
Austin, Texas. 6'0", 9"
cock, top. Mature, African-
American, late 1990s
model.
At Skinner Jack's
Bachelor Party, The
Balls To the Wall Vol 5-9
Batter Up

Best of Blacks, The
Big Guns 2
Big Salami, The
Black Balled 2
Black Gang Bang 1 & 2
Black Heat
Black Leather Gang Bang
Black Magic, White Heat
Black Man on Top
Black Moves
Black Raven Gang Bang
Boy's on Call
Brickbat #2
Castro Commandos
Challenge, The
Chicago Meat Packers
Chocolate Desert
Cumplete and Uncut
Danny's Anal Ordeal
Das Butt
Demolition Man
Dogs in Heat
Down and Dangerous
Duo Series, Vol. 6:
  Escape into Black
Easy Prey
Escape into Black
Foreskin Quarterly
F-Train to Castro
Gang Bang-Rich Boy
GBM (Gamma-Beta-Mu)
Grip of Passion, The:
  Love or Lust
Hard at It, Vol. 2
House of Games
Hustler Blue
In the Grip of Passion
In the Mix
Larger Than Life
Latin Jack Off
Latino Power
Leather Boy Rebellion
Low Riders

Male Box
Manly Persuasion
Mix it Up
Nubian Horses
Other Man, The
Paint the Town Black
Palm Desires
Party Hard
Pledges of Gamma Beta
  Mu, The
Popular Mechanics Gang
Bang Power Sex 4 Part 1
Punishment Contest 3
Real Men of the New West
Running With the Bulls
Said & Done
Sex Acts
Sgt. Marc Mann's Manly
Persuasion
Soul and Salsa 1 & 2
Stiff Summer Cocktails
Stud Search
Ticket To Ride
Truth or Fantasy
Uncut Glory
Viva Latino
Wet Daddy

CORY BLACK
1980s model.
Men Matter Most
Powergrip

KENDALL BLACK
Blue Collar Fantasies
Sizzlin' Studs

ROBERT BLACK
dark-haired, late 1990s
model heavy into leather.
Fetish Sex Fights 3
Hell Razer 3

SETH BLACK
Born March 31, Arcadia,
California. 5'8," 7" cock.
Known for his tan and for
his bottoming. 1990s
model.
Babes Ballin' Boys #3
Battling Briefs
Behind His Back
The Bite 2
Bound to Fool Around
Busted
Club Butt II: The
  Private Party
Cop Sins
Cruise Park
Desert Maneuvers
Dude Watch
Equestrian Club, The
Eroto Wrestling 1 & 2
Fine Daze
Full Body Contact
Hard Focus
Historic Affairs
Latin Balls 2: Huevos
Hustler Way
Hustler's Alley—Men In
Demand Insertion
Kick Boxer, The
Mat Muscle Mayhem 5
Maximum Cruise
My Own Private Mexico
Naked Underneath
976-Jock
Nude Getaway
On the Move
Penetration on
Pennsylvania Ave.
Photo Op
Plugged
Razor Close
Room Mated
Runway Studs

S.S. Gigantic
Saving Ryan's Privates
Sea 'n Men
Sex Story 2
Show Me The Money
Size Does Matter
Spin the Bottle Orgy
Steel Blades
Tailspin
Tormentors's Conquest
Trade Off
Wild Sex In America
WeHo Alley
XXX
XXX.Man.Com

TRENT BLACK
(aka Cliff Trent)
Born February 22.
Handsome, 1990s model
with light brown hair from
Texas.
Don't Dick with the Devil
Four Card Stud
Manhungry

JIM BLACKBURN
(aka James Blackburn)
Last seen living and work-
ing in West Hollywood,
California.
Action On Melrose
Big Box Office
Built To Last
Caged Heat
Clippers
Delusion
Experiment, The
Going Down On The Farm
Guest, The
Guys N' The Burb
Leather Me Down Do
  Me Toys

Lords Of Leather
Moving
Prison
Secret Report

KEITH BLADE
Best Of Leather: Part 2
Bi-Conflict of Interest
Conflict Of Interest
Into Leather
Man About Town

CHRISTIAN BLAIR
Brothers Behaving Badly
Full Body Contact
You Sexy Thing!

JIM BLAIR
Rebel 1980s

BLUE BLAKE
(aka Bleau Blake)
Born August 5, 1963,
Nottingham, England.
Resides in Studio City,
California. This former mili-
tary man began as a Colt
model. 9 inches, uncut.
1990s model.
Badboys
Balls In Play
Black and Blue
Blake Twins Raw and
   Uncut
Blow the Man Down
Butt Buddies
Caged Desires
A Clockwork Blue
Cockfight
Dudes
Fantasy Play For Gays
Getting Even With David
Gino Colbert's Hunk

Hunt 8
Guys With Giant Dicks
Hair Fetish and Gay Men
Hardworkers
Hidden Instinct
Idol Dreams
Jeff Stryker's Underground
Johnny Hormone
Just Men
Kink
Lube Job
Man's Touch
Men in Blue
Men In Uniform
Military Muscle
Muscle Bound
Muscle Up
My Bitch
Night Walk
Nothin' Nice
Orgies 1
Orgy Boys 2
Our Trespasses
Peep-O-Rama
Perfect Ten's—Male
Porn Fiction
Posing Strap
Ram Jet
Red, White & Blue
Ryan Block's Black And
   Blue
Seeds of Love
Sergeant Blake and
Sergeant Stone
Shoot The Chute
Taste of Leather 2
Twincest
Uncut Dicks
Virtual Viewer (CD Rom)
Wild Ones, The

BOBBY BLAKE
Born August 11 in

Memphis, Tennessee. 6'0",
10 1/2" cut. Popular black
'90s top.
Adventures of A. Rocky
   and Bill Winkler, The
Alibi for a Gang Bang
Balls to the Wall 35
Bam
Bam 2: Thug
Beef Jerky
Big Guns II
Black American
Black & Lethal
Black & Proud 2
Black Bolts, White Nuts
Black Bone-A-Thon
   Volume 1, 2, 3, 4
Black Brigade
Black Cargo
Black Gang-Bang 5-6
Black Horses
Black in the Saddle
Black Justice
Black Leather Gang Bang
Black Lovers
Black Market
Black Mischief
Black Mouthfuls
Black Muscle Machine 2
Black Nubian Fantasies
Black Passion
Black Power
Black, Ripped & Stripped
Black Rose
Black Secret
Black, Sex and Leather
Black Warriors
Blatino Party L.A.
Chocolate Dessert
Ebony Kings
Fantasies of White and
   Black
Gang-Bang Belgium Boy

Gang Bang Movers
Goldilocks and the Three
Bi Bears Hard Body 2000
High Rollin a Black Thang
Hot Chocolate
Huge Black and Delicious
Hung Man Meat
In the Mix
Iron Cage
It's the Size That Counts
Junk Yard Dog
Mt. Fuckmore
Other Side of Big Bear
Popular Mechanics Gang
    Bang
Power Surge: Power
    Fist Trilogy 3
Pumping Black
Pumping Up
Puppy Up
Sleazy Gang Bang
Straight Cocksuckers
Soul Patrol
Underboss, The
Wet Daddy
White Nuts & Black Bolts
Zebra Love

CESAR BLANCO
1980s model.
Best of the Blacks, The
Breaker Blue
BulletPac 10: Hot Latinos
Raw Footage
Soul & Salsa 1 & 2

DAKOTA BLAZE
Cruisin' for a Gang Bang
Handsome Ransom
Love In Dakota

BOB BLEEKER
Hotter Than Hell

New York Men

JAMIE BLEU
Dock 9
Growing Years
Ivy Blues
Lifeguard
Magnum Griffin, Vol. 13
Mansplash
Midnight Special #5:
    Boys of Beverly Hills
Move Over, Johnny
On Fire
Private Pool Party
Seven Card Stud
Stick Shift
Totally Awesome

MICHAEL BLEU
Never Ending Studs
Pure Fantasies

DANNY BLISS
(aka Danny Bliss Elliott)
A very young looking,
dark-haired, boy next door
1990s model. Lives in Los
Angeles.
Alone At Last
Bat Dude & Throbbin'
Beach Blanket Boner
Best of Original Recipe
Home Video
Bi Golly
Big Dare, The
Blue Collar
Boot Camp I& 2
Danny's Anal Ordeal
Deception, Part 1: Happy
    Birthday to You
Deception, Part 2:
    Hard Justice
Dirty Pool

Dream Team
Extra Day, The
Guys In Jocks And Jockeys
Here Comes Peter
Horny Rent Collector
I Dream Of Weenie
Joker's Wild
Knights Of Thunder
Las Vegas Love Gods
Lights! Camera! Action!
Masquerade
Meaning Of Sex, The
Mentor
Mounted Police
Moving In
Muscle Club, The
Need You Tonight
Neighborhood Games
Original Recipe Home
    Video 3
Orgy At The Funhouse
Pay To Play 3
Pits, Tits And Feet
Private Dancer
Private Games
Rearended
Rex: Take One
Rump Ranger
Salsa Fever
Santa's Coming
Secret Report
Sex Mates
Sizzlin' Studs
Spank Me Paddle Me
Steel Pulse
Straight Up
Superstud Fever
Taxi
Tease Me!
Tickled Butch Guys
Tricked
2 Hard Up
Undercover

Waterworks
Wet Dreams
Wet Load
Wet Sex
X-Tasy
Young And Notorious
Young Warriors

RYAN BLOCK
(aka Juaquin)
Born September 8. Popular
Latin/black star of the mid
'90s. Also worked behind
the camera. Top, and
occassional bottom.
Absolute Sex
Alone At Last
At Your Service
Bed And Breakfast
Bi Laddin
Black All American
Black Jack Fever
Black Workout 5
Blow Me Down
A Brother's Desire
Color Me Bad
Cruisin' The Balcony
Eight Men In
Fluffer, The
Guess What?
GV Guide All-Star Softball 1
Hard As Marble
Hard Ass
Hard Body Video Mag. 3-4
Hidden Man
Hot House Lodge
Hurricane Hard-On
In The Mix
Latin Instinct
Long Shots
Morning Ritual
Never Say Never
Night Walk

Ninety Dirty Minutes
Oral Fixation
Portrait Of Sex
Raw Stock
Rear View
Seeds Of Love
Stripper Service
Stroke It
Strong Man Scent
Supermodels Of Advocate
    Men
Switch Hitters 8
Temptation
10 Plus Vol. 2
These Bases Are Loaded 2
Toilet Tramps
Twin Exposure

DAVE BLOOM
Bi, Bi Love
Bisexual Fantasies
Heat Goes On
International Skin
P.S. Connection #1
Social Studies
Spirit Is Willing
Tough Iron

GAVIN BLUE
1990s model.
976-Stud
1-800-Hunk
www.Orgy

MICHAEL BLUE
Motor Punks
Weekend At Large

SANDY BLUE
Big Packages
Boys, Boys, Boys
Boys On The Block
Lust Boys

Painting Party
Show It Off
Suckulents

BLAINE BOGART
1990s model.
Object of My Erection, The

ANDRE BOLLA
Born May 4, 1957 in
Seattle, Washington.
Resides in Los Angeles,
California. 5'8 1/2", 9"
cock. Primarily Top. Has
appeared in straight videos
as well. 1990s model.
Advanced Gay Sexual
    Fantasies
Alibi for a Gang Bang
All Black, All Gay
Back in Town
Black and Huge 2
Black and Lethal
Black Assets: The Movie
Black Attack II
Black Bone Parties
Black Brigade
Black for More
Black Gang Bang
    2,3,4,5,6,8
Black Gold
Black Handfulls IV
Black Heat
Black, Large and in
Charge
Black Lovers
Black Men Do
Black Men on Top
Black Mouthfulls 1 & 2
Black On Black
Black Raven Gang Bang
Black Sex and Leather 1-2
Black Workout 6, 9

Black, Large and in Charge
Bone Yard
Breakers
Brick Bat 3
Brothas Gettin' Down 1-10
Butt Breakers
Cockland: Hair Trigger 2
Colossal Combo, Vol. 43
Dark Secrets
Dreamin': A Black And Latin Fantasy Duo XV
Gang Bang Belgium
Gang Bang Mover
Gang Bang Revenge
Gang Bang Towel Boy
Geared Up
Going Greek
Guys Who Crave Hard Dicks
Hairy Hunks
Hard and Kinky 14
Hard as Stone
Inter-Racial Interrogation
Interview with a Black Man
Iron Men of Porn, Vol. 3
Jack City
Juice in the Hood
Kinky Leather Lads
Lords of Leather
Meet Your Man: Andre Bolla
Men Of Magnum
Mixin' It Up
No Secrets
On To Something Big
Penetration
Pinball Wiz
Reflections in Black
Run With The Bulls
Sexx Pitt
Sudden Urge
Tailgate Party 2

Wet Daddies
Working Hard
XXX Volume 10
Zebra Love

RICK BOLTON
Handsome, hunky, brunet star of the early '90s. Went on to direct for Bob Jones.

Behind The Barn Door
Big City Men
Bi-Ology
Body Search
Bound, Shaved And Enslaved
Butch Hardon's Private Home Movie
Car Wash Out
Caught In The Act 3
Dirk's Dirty Sex Garage
Doctor's Sex Dungeon
Down Bi Law
Electro Anal Kink 2
Forced Fuck Fantasies
From Feet To Meat
Hell Weekend
Hey Tony, What's The Story?
Hung, Paddled And Plugged
Key West Bellhop
Master's Sex Toys
Military Kin
Military Sex Initiation
Motor Shop Skinheads
Motor Shop Enema Slaves
1230 West Melrose
Paddle Me Please
Peep Show Booth
Punishment
Pits, Tits And Feet
Private Games
Rearended

Rimming Slaves
Rough Sex
San Francisco Boot Masters
Sex Clubs Of San Francisco
Shadow Dancer
Shooters
Shower Room Slaves
Slave Trainer
Sleepless In San Francisco
Stiff Cocktail
Straight Bound For Pleasure
Straight Boy Shave Down
Straight Construction Site
Stripped, Whipped And Washed
Take Down
Thief's Punishment
Tickled Butch Guys
Toe The Line
Torture Alley
Trucker's Pig Stop
Trucker's Sex Dog
Uncut Fuck Buddy
Video Store Sex Studs
Washed Out Anal Buddies
Waterworks

J.J. BOND
1990s model.
Mantasy Island
Read Bi All
Spiked
SWM

SCOTT BOND
Born in Canada, this handsome, boy-next-door model from the late 1980s died from AIDS-related complications.

Discovered by Chi Chi
LaRue.
Backdrop
Best of Ryan Yeager, The
Best of Scott Bond, The
Big Delivery
Classified Action
Object of Desire
Rise, The
Sex in the Great
   Outdoors 3

THOMAS BOND

Born July 22nd in the
Midwest. 6'0," 8" cock, top.
1990s model.
Adventures of Straight
Man's Pass
All That Jizz
First Time Tryers 12
Lick It Up
MVP: Most Valuable Player
My Best Friends Woody
Pounderosa, The
Weho Confidential
You've Got Male

SEBASTIAN BONNET

1990s Czech Republic
model.
English Student, The

SASHA BOROV

1990s model.
Anchor Hotel
Manwatcher
Thick as Thieves

ANDRAS BORSOS

Hungarian Rhapsody

LEE BOWMAN

French Erections

ROB BOXXER

Layin' Pipe

CHARLIE BOY

Dark-hared, youthful
model, discovered in 1994
by Catalina during a model
search.
Beat Off Frenzy 2
Call Boy
Hung Riders
Secret Sex 3: The
Takeover
Sex House

TONY BOY

(aka Tony Lorenzo)
1990s model.
Biker Pigs From Hell

STEVE BOYD

A 1970s model.
Eureka Bound
Kansas City Trucking Co.
Magnum Griffin #2
Raw Country
Self Service

TIM BOYD

Behind His Back
Bullring
Court Martial
Cummin' Of Age
Desert Paradise
Drop 'Em
Lust Shack
The Playboys
Pleasure Ridge
Raw Recruits
Virgin Territory
Wall 3, The
Wear It Out

ROC BOYER

1990s model.
Northern Exposures
Woody's

KYLE BRADFORD

Give & Submit
Leather Meets The Mat

TOM BRADFORD

Bijou

DAVID BRADLEY

Handsome, mature, late
1990s brunet model with
blue eyes.
Ass Lick Alley
Full Up!
In Deep: Miles To Go
Sit Tight
Spiked
Stock
Stuffed

PHIL BRADLEY

Very handsome, hairy
chested, mature, early '90s
model. Resides in Los
Angeles.
Barn Storm
Big Drill, The
Bondage Memories
Hand Jobs 3
Hart Throb
Jockaholics
Montreal Men
Sex Crimes
Some Body Is Watching
Thriller
Total Corruption
Wet Load
Wild Horses

MATT BRADSHAW
Won Best Top and Best Group Scene in 1996 for Falcon's *The Renegade.* Handsome, dark-haired, 1990s model.
Backstreet BJ
Breathless
Bustin' Loose
Butt Bruisers
Chained Desires
Chi Chi La Rue's Hardbody 2000.2
Code of Conduct 2
Dark Side of the Moon
Dildo Sex Slaves
Dirty White Guys
Down on Me
Dynastud 3
Extreme Measures
Glory Holes of L.A.
Guys Like Us
Harley's Crew
Hot Cops 3
In the Deep End
Last Taboo, The
Leather Party, The
A Love Story
Man Trade Solos
Masters of Discipline
Matador
Maximum Maxon
Morning, Noon & Night
My Secret Collection
964 Dicks St.
Perfect Gift, The
Renegade, The
Ripe for Harvest
Road Home, The
Said & Done
Scenes in Leather
Schlong Blade
Sex Club Initiation

Spank me Man!
Take One: Guys Like Us
Thunderballs
Turn of Events
Worked Over

JASON BRANCH
Born December 5. Resides in San Francisco. 6' 1," 8 inch cock. Mature, hairy-chested late 1990s model with light brown hair.
Ass Lick Alley
Bondage Hangover
Chapters
Final Link, The
Glory Holes of San Francisco
Iron Will
Phoenix Rising
Serviced
Skuff
Sting: A Taste For Leather
Up For Grabs

ERIC BRANDON
Brian's Boys

KYLE BRANDON
Born June 30. Handsome and very popular leather daddy. Reportedly retired from the business in 1999.
Ace in Your Face
Chip Daniels' Video Studbook
Code of Conduct
Dirty Stories
Fallen Angel 1-2
Gamemaster
Hot Cops 1 & 2
Jockstrapped
Masters of Discipline

Photoplay
Playing to Win
Raw Material
Swallow
Tools of the Trade
Tradewinds
Uniform Code

MICHAEL BRANDON
(aka Mike Phillips)
Air Male
All Hands on Dick
All the Way
Best of Street Times Video, The
Blow Your Own Horn
Boy, Oh Boy
Boys, Boys, Boys
Butt Boys in Space
Come Blow Your Own Horn
Idle Pleasures
Lovers Coming Home
Oral Orgy
Pegasus 2
Ranger Nick
Sexy Billy Blue
Shacking Up
Sweet in the Bootie
Tender Trick
Token, The

TONY BRANDON
1990s model.
Hot Cops 3
The Last Taboo
South Beach Heat

AARON BRANDT
(aka Adam West)
Born June 3. 1990s model.
First Timer
Gaywatch

Hot Male Mechanics
Jump On It
No Faking It
Top Men
Our Trespasses
Splashdown!
Take One: Guys Like Us

BILLY BRANDT
Cute, young, blond, late
1990s Australian discovery.
Absolute Arid
Taken Down Under

MIKE BRANSON
Born May 28. dark-haired,
hunky, horse-hung, 1990s
Falcon exclusive.
Basic Plumbing 2
California Kings
Chosen, The
Current Affairs
Freshmen, The
Hardline
High Tide
Hotwired: Viewers' Choice
Manhandlers

TONY BRAVO
Real name Michael Pietri.
Popular '80s pornstar died
July 25, 1990 from AIDS-
related illness.
Advocate Men Live
Best of Jeff Stryker, The
Best of Stud, The
Best of the Biggest, The
Boystown: Going West
    Hollywood
Discharged
The Other Side of Aspen II
Powertool
Santa Monica Blvd

Video Games #1

MICHAEL BRAWN
A Chicago native. Won the
Gay Video Guide performer
of the year in 1993.
Brawn's Rod
Cowboys And Indians
Friendly Obsession
Full Length
Going Down In Style
Good Vibrations
GV Guide Gay Erotic Video
    Awards
Hard Body Video Mag. #2
Hart Throb
Heat In The Night
He-Devils
International Guide To The
    Fine Art Of Fellatio
Island Heat
Juice Bomb
Kiss Off
Laid To Order
Rites Of Manhood, The
Somebody Is Watching
Waterworks
Wet Load
The Wild Ones

GEORGE BRAZIL
Late 1990s model.
Nude Science

PEPE BRAZIL
Dune Buddies
Fire Island Fever

MARK BRENNAN
1980s model.
Kip Noll & The Westside
    Boys

RICK BRENNAN
1980s model.
Kip Noll & The Westside
    Boys

YURI BRESHNEV
A 1990s model.
Thick as Thieves

DAN BREWER
Road Home, The
Webmaster

MARK BREWER
Object of My Erection, The

MICHAEL BRITTEN
Full Service
Undercover
Young Gladiators

TONY BROCCO
Erotikus
Major Meat
Men Of Lake Michigan
Naked Truth
Sexual Suspect
Swallow
Thick Of It
Total Corruption 2

DARYL BROCK
Born August 14. A
Canadian model from the
mid '90s.
Backseat BJ
Big As They Come 2
Boot Black
Butt Munch
Captain Stud and His
    Seamen
CD Ram: Sex Star
    Interactive

Desert Oasis
Forever Hold Your Piece 2
Greaseguns
Hung Riders
Idol Inn Exile
Jawbreaker
Link 2 Link
Mirage
Nightheat
Nutcrackers
The Other Side of Aspen 3
Other Side of Aspen 4, The
   Redwood Ranger
Saddle Tramps
Secret Sex 2 & 3
Sex House
Sex Posse
Skuff
Slave Auction
Summer of Scott
Randsome
Tony's Thing
Wet Daddy

GLENN BROCK
Youthful 1970s model.
A Ghost of a Chance

TOM BROCK
A very handsome and
hunky, porn legend of the
'80s with a smooth body,
light-brown hair and blue
eyes.
Best of All Matt Sterling
Bigger Than Life
Bulge: Mass Appeal
Catalina Classics
Catalina Down and Dirty
Catalina Men
Director's Best:
   John Travis, Vol.1
In Your Wildest Dreams

Inch by Inch
Probe Vol. 3: Tom Brock
They Grow 'em Big

JASON BRODERICK
(aka Shadoe Thomas)
1990s model.
Born To Please
Chi Chi Larue's Hardbody
   Video Mag 4
Coming True
Cowboys Get The Blues
Dick Diving
Friendly Desire
Hole In The Wall
Low Rent
Naughty Little Brother
Night Watch
Overcharged
Party Favors
Raw Stock
Romeo And Julian
Stripper Service
Summer Daze

MARK BRODY
Hairy-chested, masculine
model from the mid '90s.
Bad Moon Rising
Barracks Glory Hole 3
Breakthrough
Courting Libido
Leather Intrusion
Leather Lust
Men 4 Men On The Net
Millitary Issue 3:
   Ask & I'll Tell
Prisoners of Lust
River Patrol

JEREMY BROOKS
Palm Springs resident.
1990s model.

Fast Action
Getting Straight
Object of My Erection, The
Return to Camp YMAC

KRISTIAN BROOKS
Cute, blond, youthful
1990s model.
Das Butt 2
Dream Team
Chasers
Family Values 2
Fever
Fine Daze
Forest Rump
Getting Straight
Hardcore
High Tide
The Hitchiker
Hotel California
Hotter Than Life
Lesson Learned, A
Love Inn Exile (softcore)
Manhungry
Maximum Cruise
Mountain Patrol
Reform School
Confidential
Summer Reunion: The
   Best Parts of Summer
Tales From the Backlot #2
Tank Tops
Time Cops
West Hollywood Hope

MARVIN BROOKS
976-Stud
1-800-Hunk

RUSTY BROOKS
Cute, young, blond boy-
next-door from early
1990s.

Bad Boys
Coming Out, Coming Hard
Corporate Head
Driving Hard
Foreign Competition
Graduation
Hotel L.A.
Huge Double Impact
Jet Set Sex
L.A. Sex Stories
Latin Encounters
Lover, Cheaters and
Maneaters
Men on A Budget
Mind Blower
Never Enough
976
Rex: Take One
Savage Blue
Take Me Home
Tough Choices
Uncut Fantasies

DANNY BROWN
(aka Dany Brown, Richard
French aka Robert French)
Very popular 1980s and
'90s French-Canadian
model.
Attraction
Bad Boys
Bear Hugs
Bears and Cubs
Best of Back Alley Video
Bi-Dacious
Big Deposit
Big Packages
Blow Bi Blow
Boot Camp 1&2
Boy Toy, The
Boys Night Out
Breaker Blue
BulletPac 12: Black Bullet

Butt Darts
Carnival Tails
Castro Motel
Climactic Scenes #101
Cream of the Crop
Crossing Over
Deep in Hot Water
Excess
Flexx
Fucking Around
Hand in the Fire
Headin' West
Heads Up
Heavenly
Hot Cocks (non-sex)
Hot Shots, Vol 20, 22, 23,
    27, 29, 33
In the End Zone
Innocent Bi-Standers
Inside Vladimir Correa
Interview, Volume 2
Made for You
Magnum Griffin, Vol. 12
Mall Cruisin' X-L
Meet Me At The Orgy
My Fantasy
Night Maneuvers
Nuts and Butts
O is for Orgy
Perils of Danny
Powerful II
Ram Man
Rites of Fall, The
Rooms
Seduction
Seduction II:
    The Heat is On
Seduction IV: Sex Storm
Sexologist
Soldiers
Soul & Salsa 1 & 2
Spanking New:
    Drive it Home

Stiff Competition
Straight Boys Do
Stud Fuckers
Stud Search
Surfer Guys
Tasting Mr. Goodbar
Tell Me Something Dirty
3-Way Cum, Vol. 1
Tips
Top Man
Two Handsful 2
Unchained Men
Untamed
Weekend Wildcats
Working Pleasure

JIM BROWN
Black Orient Express
Black Sex Therapy
Never Ending Studs

KEN BROWN
El Paso Wrecking Corp.

MALEEK BROWN
(aka Maleek Jones)
Born January 26th, 1979,
Arizona.San Francisco resident. 5'11", 8" cock. Top.
1990s African-American
model.
Titan Men 2 & 3
Youthful Offenders 18-25

JEFF BROWNING
A youthful-looking bottom
from the mid 1990s.
Cybersex
Double Exposure
Face Down
Fountains Of Youth
A Jock's Tale
Junior Varsity 2

Oh! So Tender
Outcall Lover
Prison Fever
Rumpster, The
6969 Melrose
Sleepless In L.A.
Stiff
Straight Shooters
Summer Seduction
Tiger Cub Club

LEE BRUBAKER
Hot Stuff
Turned On

BRUNO
(aka Bruno Will)
Best of Brentwood
Best of Colt, Vols.3, 8, 12
Bruno and Shane: Hayride
Good Neighbors
In and Out
Laid Back
Master Lesson
Pleasures in the Sun
Rip Colt's Sex-Rated
Home Movies

JOE BRUNO
Ft. Lauderdale Hustlers

KARL BRUNO
(aka Kurt Lundgren)
Greased Up
Hot Guys #3
In Man's Country
A Letter To Three Men
Riptide!
Sexx Pitt
Total Corruption 2

DION BRUTON
(see Ty Fox)

JIM BUCK
Born August 19th, 1968 in
Louisiana. Resides in New
Orleans. Very popular, late
'90s, award-winning porn
star top. Dark hair, 5'11",
8" cock, with a Prince
Albert pierced penis.
At Twilight Come The
Flesh-Eaters Dr. Jerkoff
and Mr. Hard
Fallen Angel
First Time Tryers
Goldiggers
Hardcore
Mardi Gras Cowboy
Naked Highway
Our Trespasses
Tale of Two Brothers
Toolbox

TONY BULLIT
1990s model.
Stuffed

ADAM BURKE
Pocket Rockets

JACK BURKE
Big Brother Is Watching
   You
Break Down
Brothers Should Do It
Eureka Bound
Golden Boys
Gunslingers
Pacific Coast Hwy.
These Bases Are Loaded

KENT BURKE
Born July 2. 1990s model.
Burgle Booty
Magic Bed, The

Plumbers Liquid
Weho Confidential

NED BURKE
Chained
Games Without Rules
Sons of Satan

CHRIS BURNS
Died February 26, 1995
from AIDS-related causes.
Real name was Danny. A
blond, porn legend of the
'80s known for his bottom-
ing. Made a return in the
early '90s.
Alleycats
Bad Habits
Bait
Below the Belt
Big Time
Catalina Orgies, Vol. 1
Dangerous
Dynastud
Family Values
For Sale or Rent
Getting It
Gunslingers
Hard and Throbbing
Hidden Cameras
Hot Shots, Vol. 9, 14, 23,
   24, 25, 35 & 40
Hot Trash
King Size
Larger than Life
Lewd Conduct
Locker Room Sex
Magnum Griffin, Vol. 7
Man's Hand #14
Master Hyde
Men of the Midway
Midnight Special #6: Boys
   of the Hollywood Spa

Mr. Drummer Finals 1986
My Masters
Nightcrawler
Nighthawk in Leather
Old Reliable #103:
  Blonds On Top
Pleasure Beach
Private Pleasures of
  John C. Holmes
Rawhide (1981)
Revenge of the Nighthawk
Room for Rent
Room Service Plus
Shacking Up
Size of His Toys, The
Skin Deep
Skin Flix
Social Studies
Spank
Spring Break
Star Shots 1 & 3
Stiff Sentence
These Bases are Loaded
Three Little Pigs
Toilets
Tony's Iniation
Windows
Wrestling Meat 1 & 2

TOM BURNS
Boys Will Be Boys
Dynastud
Eagle Pack #4
Hard As They Come
Outpost
Prostitute, The

TREVOR BURNS
1990s model.
You've Got Male

DAVID BURRILL
(aka Rick Long)

Popular 1980s, all-
American, boyish-looking,
dark-haired porn star and
song writer.
Advocate Men Live 3
Backstrokes
Big & Thick
Danny's Anal Ordeal
  (as Rick Long)
Inside David
Interviews, Vol 1
Latin Men
976-CUMM
One Night Stands
  (non-sex)
Rolls, The
Private Cover Boy
Say Goodbye
Wide Load

SCOTT BURTON
Cop Sins
Straight Men

BUSTER
(aka Jeff Cole)
Died February 10, 1991
from AIDS-related causes.
A cute, blond, surfer-boy-
type porn legend of the
1980s.
Best of Blonds 3, The
Big & Thick
Big Surprise, The
Bigger the Better, The
Briefs: The Best of John
  Summers
Buster And Billy (short)
Buster Goes to Laguna
Buster: The Best Years
Hot Numbers, Vol. 1, 2 & 4
Night Fever
Night Flight

Sailor in the Wind
Sex in the Great Outdoors
Smokin' Butts

BUTCH
Very busy, late '80s early
'90s star.
Beach Dreamer
Big Memories
Black Book
Black Pac 88
Boys will be Boys
Busted
Catalina Blonds
Crosswire
Cum Shots 102
Dirty Tricks
Excess
Fantasy Bytes
Fast Idle
Fratrimony
Friendly Obsession
Full Service
G.I. Mac
Hard-On Hard Bodies
He-Devils
Hot, Hung & Hard
In the Grasp
Juice
Made for You
Main Attraction
Manimal
More of a Man
Next Valentino, The
Offering, The
Paradise Found
Rough Riders
Seduction
Size Talks
Straight Boys Do
Tall Timber
Think Big
Touch Me

Under Cover

ERIC BUTLER
Black Balled 2
Fantasies of White & Black
White Movers, Black
Shakers
White Tails, Black Tails

KEN BUTLER
Chapters

RAY BUTLER
Special Handling

C

LOUIS CABRERRA
1990s model.
Saving Ryan's Privates
My Best Friends Woody

VINCE CABRETTI
Hard Rock High
House Boys
Lust Boys
Matters In Hand
Mirrors, Mirrors
Swim Meat #2
Touch of Class

JOE CADE
A legendary butch bottom
from the '80s. The dark-
haired, well built model is
now a weight trainer who
lives in West Hollywood.
His lover is one of the
biggest porn stars of the
'90s, Falcon exclusive,
Tom Chase.

Behind Closed Doors
Better Than Ever
Bi and Beyond 3
Cruisin'
Fantasy Suite
Hard to Believe
Hot Shots, Vol. 39: Uncut
Hunks, 2
Low Blows
Made for You
Powerful II
Rites of Fall, The
Splash Shots
Surge Men at Their Best
"10" Plus

JUSTIN CADE
Better Than Ever
Golden Guys
In Your Wildest Dreams
A Night Alone With Al
Parker
Personals
Splash Shots
Turbo Charge
Very Receptive
Working Hard For the
Money

JOEY CAFFERIO
Outdoor Ecstacy

ALLAN CAGE
Homo Erectus
Taking The Plunge

CHANCE
Cute, blond, boy-next-door
1990s model.
An American In Prague
Johan's Big Chance

CHANCE CALDWELL
Born June 30. Blond,
mature star of the early
'90s.
The Abduction 1, 2&3
Big Merger
The Big Switch 3:
Bachelor Party
Bi Inferno
Bi-Madness
Cellblock Sinner
Chance Of A Lifetime
Corporate Head
Crotch Rockets
Cuming Attractions
Dallas Does Hawaii
Down And Out
Drop 'Em
Everybody Does It
Full Body Contact
Handsome Ransom
Heaven Too Soon
Holding Their Own:
Self-Sucking Soldiers
Hot Day In L.A.
It's A Gang Video Series 1
Kickboxing
Love Muscle
Male Seduction
Mr. Blue
Muscle Force
Night Walk
A Night With Strangers
Nymphomania
O Is For Orgy
The Other Side Of
Hollywood
Physical Exam
Poolman Cometh, The
Powertool 2
Preferred Stock 1
Provacative
Raising Hell

Roommate, The
Rump Ranger
Scent Of Man
Secret Dreams
Sex Bi-Lex
Skinny Dipping
Slippery When Wet
Songs In The Key Of Sex
Swimming Pool Orgy
Tease, The
10 Plus 1 & 2
Tight Leather
Virgin Territory

DIRK CALDWELL
(aka Eric Dahl & Keith
Panther) Young-looking,
5'8," blond star of the
1980s.
Big Favors
Big Packages
Big Shooters 2
Blonds, Blonds, Blonds
Boys on Film
Cross Over
Fantasy Boys
Head of the Class 2
Hot Shots, Vol. 28: Hot
    Pickups
I Like to Watch: Stroke #45
Interview 2
Main Attraction, The
Mustang Ranch
One Hot Day
Powerline
Private Collection
Private Dick
Recruiter
Screen Test 2
Seduction V: Taking Full
    Charge
Streaks
Taxi

Transitory States
Wet Dreams
Young Lovers

MARCO CALLES
Men Together
Pocket Rockets
Principal of Lust

SERGIO CALUCCI
Hairy chested, dark-haired
model from the late 1980s,
early '90s.
Cool Hand Dick
Dirty Laundry
First Mate
G-Squad
Headstruck
Hombres
Iron Man Pumping Up:
    Flex 2
Lunch Hour
Ranger Nick 2
To The Bone

CURT CAMDEN
Men With Tools

DEREK CAMERON
Born June 27, 1971 in Bay
City, Texas. West Holly-
wood resident. 5'7," 7-1/2"
cock. Mainstream-model-
handsome and very popular
star of the late 1990s.
The Big Thrill
Centerfold Men
Chosen, The
Fever
Heatwave
Jeff Stryker's Underground
Journey to Italy
Just Guys

Love Inn Exile (softcore)
Manhandlers
Man Watch
Morning Music
Nude Science
On Your Knees
Red, White and Blue
Three Brothers
Tradewinds

STEVE CAMERON
House Boys
Weekend Adventure

TONY CAMERON
10 Plus 1 & 2
Bullring
In Man's Country
Leather Pit

ALEC CAMPBELL
(aka Hogan Maloney)
1990s Australian model,
discovered by Kristen
Bjorn.
Command Performance
Drifter, The
Grand Prize
Jackaroos
Manly Beach
Summer Memories: My
    Buddies
Wet Load
Wild Country

GIORGIO CANALI
(aka Rocco Rizzoli)
A 1980s uncut legendary
top.
Best Little Warehouse in
    L.A., The
Best of Colt, Vol. 1
Best of Colt, Vol. 2

Best of Colt, Vol 12
Best of Jon King
Brothers Should Do It
Catalina Down and Dirty
Catalina Orgies, Vol. 1
Class Reunion
Director's Best: William
Higgins, 1
Every Which Way
Games
Lifeguard
Lockerroom Fever
Main Attraction, The
Malibu Days, Big Bear
Nights
Members Only
One In A Billion
Other Side of Aspen
Skin Deep
Splash Shots
These Bases Are Loaded

SERGIO CANALI
1980s model.
California Summer
Desert Heat
Dirty Jocks
Foreplay
French Lt's Boys
Hot Shots, Vol. 12:
Uniforms
Hot Shots, Vol. 17: Meat
Market
Manholes 1 & 2
Man Talk
Men on the Loose
Mikey Likes It
Play Safely
Spirit is Willing, The
2X10
Whiteload

MARCUS CAINE
Cadet
Flesh and Fantasy 2
Switchcraft

TYSON CANE
Born May 17. Handsome
black actor and 1998
Unzipped cover model.
Another ex-military man.
Anchor Hotel, The
Chocolate Dessert
Freshmen, The
Hard Workout
Home Bodies
In the Mix
Inter-Racial Interrogation
Link 2 Link
Men 4 Men
On the Net
Perfect Gift, The
Selection 2, The

SEAN CANNON
Bi Dream of Genie
Boys, Boys, Boys
Cousins Should Do It
Cream of the Crop
Hot Shots, Vol. 44:
Golden Boys
Knockout
Paramedic Alert
Pay to Play 2
Pool Boy
Rites of Manhood, The
Tips

STEVE CANNON
Born August 18, 1966 in
Upland, CA. Now resides
in Chicago. 5'11", 8" cock
with a Prince Albert.
Bottom. 1990s model.

Aching for Punishment
Biker Pigs From Hell
Driven
Equestrian Club, The
Expose
Fallen Angel 1 & 2
Family Secrets
Family Values
Fetish Sex Fights
Hardcore
Hard Hats
Hot Spot
Link
Masters of Discipline
Outlaw Bikers
Raw Discipline
Sodom
Spankfest 6
Total Corruption 2

CRIS CAPELLI
Home Bodies
Staten Island Sex Cult

ANDRE CARDINAL
Sure Shot

MITCHELL CAREY
A 1970s model.
Tuesday Morning Workout

NICHOLAS CARLISE
A Lesson Learned
Lovers Lane

GIAN CARLO
A 1980s model.
Fire Island Fever
Greenhorn
Oh Brother
Private Collection
Strokers
Turned On

JUAN CARLOS
Swell

BRAD CARLTON
Air Male
Big Business
Bubble Butt
By Attractions
Dream Doll
Every Which Way
Full Service
Guys Who Take It
House Boys
Make a Wish & Blow
One Hot Day
Painting Party
Private Dick
Ram Man
Rites of Summer
Rites of Winter
Rooms
Taxi
X-Poseur

CHAZ CARLTON
Born October 22, 1967, in
the South. 6'0," 7 1/2" cut.
1980s model.
All Men Do It
Alley Katt
Anonymous Sex
Big Pick Up, The
Blow Me Down
Body of Art
Butt Bruisers
Call Boy
Caught In The Military #2
Cop Stories 1 & 2
Court Martial
Cruise Park
Desert Sands
Dream Lover
Fast Moves

Flavor of Leather, The
Four Men
Getting Ahead
Going West
Good Samaritan, The
Guest Services
Hard Cock Jock
Hard on Site
He Gotta Have It
Hose 'em Down
Hot Properties
Hot Springs Orgy
Hustler Way
I Am Curious Leather
Intrusion
A Jock's Dream
A Jocks Tale
Leather Lover
Leather Party
My Secret Lust
Night In Leather, A
O is for Orgy
Oh What A Site
On The Move
One Track Mind
Phi Kappa Sucka'
Pillow Talk
Prize Fight
Quick Relief
Right Hand Man
Romping Roommates
Room Services
Runway Studs
Sex is in the Air
Show Me The Money
Studio Tricks
Summer Money
13th Step, The
Total Deception
Touch Me There
Trade Off
Travelin' Wild
Uniforms Only

Virgin Territory
Weekend Sex Camp
Wet Dreams
White Walls

COLE CARPENTER
A porn legend of the '80s.
Blond, versatile and hung.
Advanced Disrobics
Best Bi Far #2
Best of Both Worlds, The
Bi-Ceps
Bigger They Come, The
Double Exposure
Every Inch a Winner
Naked Lunch
Passion by Fire:
   The Big Switch, 2
Rushes
Spring Break
Strokers
Tyger Tales
Young And The Hung, The

JOEY CARR
Cute, youthful, 1980s
model.
Born To Please
Fully Serviced
Jump On It
Militia Men

MIKE CARR
Dangerous
Fake Out
Huge H.E.A.T.
One in a Billion
San Francisco Orgy
Screen Play
Wilde House

CARLOS CARRERA
Shooting Stars

SEAN CARRERA
A 1990s Latin model.
All About Last Night
Bi-Conflict of Interest
Bite, The
Cruising Park
Danny's Back
Deception, Part 1:
    Happy Birthday to You
Deception, Part 2:
    Hard Justice
Foot Fetish
4 Alarm Stud
Frat House: Memories of
    Pledge Week
Getting In Tight
Great Lengths
Heat
Hollywood and Vine
Hollywood Tail
In the Men's Room
Kick Boxing
Les Hommes
Lights! Camera! Action!
Manhandler
Midnight Hard-On
Mounted Police
One Track Mind
Orgy Club, The
Picture Perfect
Private Games
Raising Hell
Ready to Serve
Rimshot
Santa's Coming
Sex Depot
Sex Bazaar, Part I & 2
Sex Shooters II
Smokin' Butts
Studz
Tool of the Trade
X-treme Close-Up
You Bet Your Ass

PAUL CARRIGAN
Born August 18 in
California. 6'0," 8" cock.
Versatile. Mature, dark-
haired 1990s model.
After Hours
Arrested Voyeur
Bad Ass Lieutenant
Balls in Play
Balls to the Wall 35 & 36
Bare Bodies
Bathroom Cruisers
Biagra
Big Boys Club 1-2
Birthday Blowout
Body of Art
Body Shop
Bondage Buddies
Both Ways
California Creamin'
Camp Pokahiney
Captive Men 6
Caught In The Military #2
Cheap Motel Sex
Cockfight
Company We Keep, The
Cop Corruption
Cop Stories #2: The
Cover Up
Cruisin'
Cum Bustible
Dick Undercover
Driven By Lust
Drop 'Em
Dynastud 3
Freshman Recruits
Gianfranco Delivers
Glory Holes of LA
Goodfellas/Badfellas
Hair Trigger
Hell Bent For Leather
He's Worth It
Hill's Have Bi's

Hot Firemen
Hot Sex Pick-Up
Hot Sheets
Hung Jury
I Saw What You Did
Indulge
Internal Affairs
Jockstrap
Le Sex Salon
Leather After Midnight
Leather Connection
Leather Intrusion Case 1:
    Flaming Dragon
Leather Dream
Leather Night
Leather Training Center
Leather World
Love In Dakota
Love Money
Lure, The
Lusty Leathermen:
Mechanic on Booty
Making The Team
Measure For Measure
Men's Room
MVP: Most Valuable Player
Nefarious
Night of the Living Bi-Dolls
Nude Getaway
Olympians, The
Orgies Pt 3
Palm Desires
Picture Perfect
Plugged In
Priority Male
Pushed to the Limit
Red, White and Blue
Rescue 69-11
Ring, The
Rocket Ryder
Scenes in Leather
Selection Part 1, The
    (Solo)

Sex and Sensuality
Sex In Leather
Sex On The Beach
Sexologist
Sexpionage
Showboys
Star Maker
Studio Tricks
Supersize It
Spanking Master 4, The
Things You Can Do in
   Leather
Three Brothers
Time in the Hole
Ultimate Reality
Weekend Sex Cramp
West Hollywood Stories
You Sexy Thing!

TROY CARRIGAN
Stuffed

ALEX CARRINGTON
Born in Los Angeles July
3, 1968. Resides in
Hollywood, California.
Dark-haired, olive-skinned,
and very prolific late '80s
and '90s porn star. 6'1,"
10-1/2" uncut, top.
Alone and Private 2
Apprentice, The
Ass Tag
Bad Ass Lieutenant
Balls to the Wall 5 - 8
Bathroom Buddies &
   Plumbers Helpers
Best of Sam Abdul, The
Bi Spy, Stallion (Bi)
Big Dare, The
Bi-Sexual & Built (Bi)
Big Drill, Video 10
Blue Moves

Boom Ball Black
Boomerang
Brats
Break In
Brothers Behaving Badly
Buffalo Meat
Buns of Steel
Buttboys of Barcelona
Cat Burglar
Cock Hog
Cock Lock
Coming Together
Cum Shots 102
Cut Club, The
Cut vs Uncut: A
   Competition
Damien, One Night of Sin
Dick Smoke
Dickted Dirty Dreaming
Dirty Dreaming
Dirty Pool
Doggie Style
Down & Out
Eight Men In
Eroto Wrestling
Expose
Extra Service
Fantasy Bytes
Few, Proud And Naked 2
Foreskin Madness Four
   for More
French Kiss
Fresh
Funboy Three
G.I. Jocks-Out Of The
   Ranks
Hard Balls
Health Club
Hole In One
Hollywood Hunks
Hot Chili Peppers
Hot Tamales
Huge Double Impact

I Love Foreskin
Imagination: Action
   Gone Wild
In Your Face
Inside Of Me (Bi)
Jammed Packed
Loaded
Lost in Vegas
Mack Pack 2: Dicked
Male Instinct
Man Hole
Manwich
Measure of a Man
Mindscape 2
Model Behavior
Mouth Organ
Mr. Footlong's Made In
   America
Mr. Meatman
My Cousin Danny
Need You Tonight
976-Cumm
Over The Top
Palm Springs Paradise
Peter Pepper, Vol. 7-8
The Playboys
Private Dancer Private
   Games
Rodz, The
Room for Rent
Roommated
Rugged
Runway Studs
Sand Blasters
Sea N Men
Seanmen
Screwed, Blued and
   Tattoed
Secret Action Man
Sex in Public Places
Sex Story 2
Shadows In The Night
Size Matters

Sleazy Motel Gang Bang
Smoking in the Boys
Room
Snafu
Solitaire
Some Men Are Bigger
Than Others
Summer of Derek Thomas
Supershots 6 Take Me
Home
Take Me Home
10 Plus, Volume 2
Three's on Their Knees
Tree Swallow
Triple Play
True Confessions Uncut
Club #1,2,5,
Uncut Club
Uncut Weekend
Visitor, The
Weekend Liberty
Weekend with Howie
When the Wife's Away
Whole Nine Yards, The
Wild Country

KYLE CARRINGTON
All American Boy
Hot Male Mechanics
Tough Competition

**ERIC CARSON
(see Chris Ramsey)**

SAM CARSON
Born November 13, 1961,
New Mexico. 5'9", 8" cock.
Versatile, hunky, blond,
late '90s star.
Ass Lick Alley
Aussie Pool Party
Bewitching
Camp Pokahiney

Customer Service
Das Butt
Expose
Fox's Lair
Friction
Guy Next Door
Hair Trigger
Hot Guys #3
Hot Springs Orgy
INNdulge Palm Springs
Just One Favor
Leather Tricks
Lube Job
Morning, Noon & Night
Nude Science
Online Connection
Palm Springs Orgy
Portrait of Lust
Said and Done
Sex and Sensuality
Shoot 'N' Porn
Tales From the Backlot 2
Try Again
Weekend Sex Camp

ERIC CARTER
Driveshaft
Every Man's Desire
Make it Count
Point Of Entry
Powergrip
Unexpected Persuasion
Whatever It Takes

J.C. CARTER
Born July 27, 1962,
Chicago, Illinois. 5'6", 8'
1/2" cock. Versatile.
Popular black actor from
the late '90s.
Bad as I Wanna Be
Bam
Black Attack 2

Black Balled 2
Black Cargo
Black Entry
Black Market
Black Passion
Black Patriot
Blatino Party L.A.
Dark Journeys 2
First Time Tryers 6
Gettin' my Freak On
Iron Cage
It's the Size That Counts
Jeff Stryker's Underground
Pledges of Gamma Beta
Mu, The
Street Fair Meat
White Movers, Black
Shakers
White Tails, Black Tails

ROB CARTER
Break Down
El Paso Wrecking Co.

ADAM CARTIER
Czech Republic model.
Lucky Lukas

JUSTIN CASE
Getting Personal
Give It To Me Straight
I Am Curious Leather
In The Shadows
O is for Orgy
Sexcuses
Sex Toy Story
Summer Obsession
13th Step
Working It Out

KIP CASEY
1980s model.
Runway Studs

COUGAR CASH
Asphalt Jungle
Asphalt River
Best of Black Knights, The
Best of Latin Man Video
Best of Rick Savage, The
Big Delivery
Black Betrayal
Black Hammer
Bound Body Worship
Castro Commando
Chicago Meat Packers
Club Pleasure
Color Me Bad
Cruisin' the Balcony
Dogs in Heat
Do Me Dirty
Dream Maker
Electro Anal Kink 2
Everybody Does It
Fast Idle
House of Bondage
Hard Focus
Hot House Lodge
Hot Pursuit
In a Jock's Locker
Interior Motives
Keeping Time
Men Together
Moon Over Bangkok
Obedience Lesson
Pantera's Pleasure Party
Parade Week Lockdown 2
Penetration
Playground, The
Powerdriver
Rigid Video, Vol.1
Roped and Delivered
San Francisco Sex
Servicemen
Shoot
Slippery When Wet
Stiff Coctail

Take It Like a Man
Top This
Truths and Dares
Webmaster
Weekend at Large
What Men Do

CARLOS CASINO
Born in 1976. Uncut, 8"
cock, 5"7". Late 1990s,
youthful-looking Latino
model. Resides in
Southern California.
Hispanic Mechanics
Latin Men Do
Mi Pinga Loca
Virtual Sexuality

BLAKE CASS
Bigger They Come, The
California Wet
Century Mining
Exchange, The
Faces
Firsts
Hot Shots, Vol. 14:
   Tight Buns
Hot Shots, Vol. 20:
   More Tight Buns
L.A. Boiling Point
Making it Huge
Manholes #2
More Than a Mouthful
Move Over, Johnny
Stiff Sentence
Therapy
Uncut Club of L.A., The

LOU CASS
A tall, dark-haired porn leg-
end of the 1980s.
Advocate Men Live 2
All the Way

Best of Joey Stefano, The
Bi-Heat, Vol. 8
Concrete Lover
Double Solitaire
Full Service
Gang Bangers
Kevin Goes Wild
Man of the Year
Oral Orgy
Pleasure Theater
Powerline
Private Dick
Private Lives of Lou Cass
Sex Waves
Sexy Billie Blue
Solo Flight
Squirts, Vol. 8: The Pickup
Stroke 'N Men
Weekend Workout

JIM CASSIDY
All American Boys in Heat
Anything, Anytime
Chapter Three
Connoisseur Collector
Classics
Deep Compassion
Desires of the Devil
Hard as They Come
Inside Bill Eld
Lodestar

KEITH CASSIDY
Thriller

RICK CASSIDY
Four Card Stud

STEFANO CASTELLO
1990s model.
Summoner, The

EDMUNDO CASTRO
1990s model.
Men From Ipanema, The

ROBERTO CASTRO
Le Voyeur
Sleaze

BENJAMIN CATES
Advocate Men Live #6

PIETRO CATTANI
Summoner, The

PAOLO CENTORI
Handsome, dark-haired,
1990s Italian model.
As Big as It Gets
Back to K-Waikiki
Big Deposit
Burning Desire
Crossing Over
Desert Paradise 2
Going West
Hard Times
Hard Working Men
In the Shadows
K-Waikiki
Latin Sex Thing
Meet Me At The Orgy
Meet Ray Harley
Pumping Up
Sex Session
Touch Me There
Uniform Ball 1
Uniforms Only
While the Cat's Away

MIKE CESAR
1990s model.
Alex's Leather Dream
Big Boyz Club 3
Boot Camp Buddies

Dildo Sex Slaves
Greased Lightening
Latin Sex Thing
Leather Intrusion Case 4:
    Down To The Wire
Mall Cruisin' X-L
Mi Pinga Loca
Mouth Organ
Poolman Cometh, The
Rent to Bone
Sex Club Initiation
Sliders
Straight Talk
Swimming Pool Orgy
Tank Tops
Things to Cum
Viva Latino!

MICHAEL CHADS
Mature, dark-haired, 1990s
model.
A Hidden Man
Hologram
Hot Ticket
Model Behavior
Sex Crimes
South Beach Heat
Tony's Big Brother
X-treme Close Up

CHUCK CHAMBERS
Black Men Do!
Pumping Black

GLENN CHAMBERS
Even Steven
Top This

CHRIS CHAMPION
All American
Beat Off Frenzy
Full Package
Jawbreaker

Jump On It
Too Damn Big
Measuring Up

DAVE CHANDLER
Real name David Kemple.
A Utah native, he reportedly committed suicide by
drug overdose March 5,
1999 in his Las Vegas
home. When we met him
at the CES show in
January 1999 he was so
excited about getting into
porn that this handsome,
6'2" newcomer could hard-
ly wait for his next video.
This would be his only
video performance.
Night Riders

KYLE CHANDLER
Apply Within

REX CHANDLER
Born August 14, 1966 in
Mount Clemens, Michigan.
Resides in West
Hollywood. 6'5," 10" cock.
One of the biggest gay-
for-pay superstars of the
1980s.
Best of All Matt Sterling II
Chi Chi LaRue's Screwing
    Screw Ups
Cocktails
Deep in Hot Water
Dish
Gay Video Guide All Star
    Softball Game #1
Heat in the Night
Idle Pleasures
John Summers' Screentest

Mag. 1
Just Between Us, You
    Promise
Made for You
Man-Rammer, A Battle of
    Size
Men With Big Toys
Morning Ritual
Rage & Honor
Rex Chandler: One on One
    (solo)
Rex Take One
Screwing Screw Ups
Sleepless
Videolog 2: Director's Cut
View to a Thrill 2: Man With
    the Golden Rod

TOMMY CHANDLER
(aka Richard Granger)
A tall, bisexual top from the
late 1980s.
Bedtime Stories
Bigger The Better 2, The
Gridiron
Pacific Coast Highway 2
Return Of Grant Fagin, The
Spellbound For Action
Slam Dunk
Stroke, The

JOHN CHARLES
Flesh & Fantasy
Private Collection

MICHAEL CHARLES
Head Trips
Strange Places, Strange
Things

BRAD CHASE
A Chicago native.
Bed Tales

Cut Club, The
Knight Moves
On the Lookout
Sex Bazaar 1 & 2
Summertime Blues
Willing to Take It

RICK CHASE
Dark-haired, blue-eyed,
mature-looking mid 1990s
model.
Body to Die For , A 1 & 2
Dream Team
Last Taboo, The
One Hot Summer
Uncle Jack
Whatever You Say, Sir!
Workin' It Out

TOM CHASE
Born March 6, 1965,
Columbus, Ohio. Resides
in West Hollywood, Calif-
ornia. 5'10," 10' 1/2", top.
Backwoods
Big Thrill , The
California Kings
Chasers
Chosen, The
Code of Conduct 1 & 2
Cruisin #3
Driven
Fever
Freshmen, The
Heatwave
High Tide
Hotwired: Viewers' Choice

DEAN CHASSON
(aka Champion)
1970s model.
Ace In The Hole
Best of Eric Manchester,

The
The Big Deal
Brothers
Catalina Down and Dirty
Catalina Men
Look, The
Magnum Griffin, Vol. 13
Male Stampede
Muscle, Sweat & Brawn
Out of Control
Pool Party
Seven in a Barn
They Grow 'em Big
Tuesday Morning Workout

MIKE CHAVEZ
(see Mike Lamas)

YURI CHEKOV
Bend Over Buddies
Hungarian Rhapsody

NICK CHEVALIER
Born April 26, 1973 in
Provence, France. Resides
in Versailles, France.
Discovered by Chi Chi
LaRue in Paris. 6", 8 1/2."
Aching For Punishment
Americans in Paris
An American Man in Paris
Chip Daniels' Video
Studbook
Desert Hart
French Connections Part
    One: Temptation
French Connections Part
    Two: Conquest
Galaxy Boys
Gang Bang Frenchman
Gang Bang
Guys With A Rise
S.S. Gigantic

Size Does Matter
Spankfest 6
Suck Daddy
Time Cops
West Hollywood Stories

BEAU CHILDS
A popular 1980s porn star,
his name was chosen no
doubt because he always
looked so young.
Birthday Boy
Cover Models
Hard Rock High
In the Raw
Memories of 18
Orgy at the Fun House
Swim Meat
Wide Load

MICK CHRISTIFER
Big Favors
Boys Just Wanna Have
Sex
Fast Friends
Good Sex!
Heat Goes On
International Skin
Strokers

JAYDEN CHRISTOPHER
Fantasies of Black & White

**JONATHON
CHRISTOPHER**
Boot Camp Buddies
Insertion
Leather World
Orgies Pt 1

MARK CHRISTOPHER
Big Shooters #2
Flesh Tones

MICHAEL CHRISTOPHER
A well hung, brown-haired,
bisexual porn legend of the
'80s.
Arousers, The
Best Little Warehouse in
L.A., The
Best of Blonds, The, 1 & 2
Bore 'N' Stroke
Catalina Down and Dirty
Catalina Orgies, Vol. 1
Class Reunion
Coverboy
Director's Best: William
Higgins, 1
Doing It
Easy Entry
Every Inch a Winner
Fade In
Fade Out
A Few Good Men
Gayracula
Hard and Throbbing
Hard Fantasies
Hard to Come By
Hot Numbers, Vol. 1, 2, 4
Hot off the Press
Hot Shots, Vol. 2: J/O
Hot Shots, Vol. 3, 4, 7, 9
How I Got the Story
Juice
The Last Surfer
Lifeguard
Making it Huge
Manholes #2
Men and Steel
Men in Motion #5
Mind Games
Muscle Studs
Obsession: The Ultimate
Experience
Pleasure Beach
Printer's Devils

Rodeo
Shooting Stars #2:
    Michael Christopher
Shore Leave
Skin Deep
Strictly for Ladies Only
Tony's Initiation
Trick Time
What the Big Boys Eat

TIM CHRISTY
Busy Boys
Catching Up
Erotica Video-30 #1
Everything Goes
Heavy Equipment
Incest-Brother Love
Palace of Pleasures
Round Up
School's Out
Six Card Stud
Station to Station

AARON CLARK
Mountain Cruisin'
Tutor Me

JAROD CLARK
Mid 1990s blond bottom.
Full Length
Just Can't Stop
Lords of Leather
The Naked Man
Workin' Stiff
Handball Marathon Part II
Smoky
Tijuana Toilet Tramps

WILL CLARK
Born March 9, 1968 in
Wausaw, Wisconsin. Will is
a red-headed, 5'8", 7 1/2'
versatile bottom. One of

the most likeable guys in the biz, this popular and charismatic star of the late '90s is also a writer (read his columns in *Skinflicks, Dude* and other gay magazines) and a tireless fundraiser for AIDS charities. He resides in West Hollywood. Visit his website at www.willclarkusa.com

Boss Man
Bound for Leather
Bound to Fool Around
Country Hustlers
Dildo Sex Slaves
Dr. Good Glove
Doctor's Orders 2
Fantasies of White and
    Black
Fetish Sex Fights 3
Freshman Recruits
Hardcore
Hellbent for Leather
HOMOgenized
Hot Firemen
Hotel, The
Immersion
In and Out Express
Indulge Part 2
Invaders From Uranus
Island Guardian
Kink
Leather Obsession 5:
    Mission
Liquid Latex
Making the Team
Man Watch
Night Walk
Porno Tonight Show, The
Possible
Private Parts

Redwood
Sex Ed 5: Street Smart
Snafu
Sodom
Tail End of Summer
Take It Deep
Take One: Guys Like Us
Things to Come
Uninvited

ROY CLARK
Youthful 1970s model.
A Ghost of a Chance

SCOTT CLARK
A 1990s model.
Fade In
Fade Out

VINCE CLARK
More Dick Fisk

DEAN CLARKE
A 1990s model.
Black Attack 2
Black Entry
Swell

GREG CLARKE
Cramming For The Big
    One
In Touch Auditions 2 (solo)
Lusty Leathermen:
Mechanic on Booty
Straight Talk
West Hollywood Sex Party

NICHOLAS CLAY
Born February 2. With green eyes and dark hair, this 6'2" late '90s model with a 9-1/2" cock resides in San Francisco.

Ass Lick Alley
Full Up!
In Deep: Miles To Go
Serviced
Spiked
Up For Grabs

ERIC CLEMENTS
Big Men on Campus 1979
Choice Cuts
Deep Fantasies
Hot Lunch
Hot Stuff
King Size: The Best of
J.W. King
Rear Admiral
Trouble Shooters
Wet Shorts

ADAM CLINE
Leather Intrusion Case 1:
    The Flaming Dragon
Leather Men
Leather Pit
Sex On The Beach

DAVID CLINE
Blow Out
Happily Ever After
Leather Playhouse
Leather Triangle
Night In Leather
Personals
Pick Up
Rescue 69-11
Steel Away
Working Day & Night

PAUL CLINTON
Hard Choices
House Boys
Imperfect Strangers
Like Father, Like Son

More
Mountain Fever

KEVIN COBAIN
Born January 30. A San Diego resident. Blond, 5'8", 7" cock.
A Body to Die For 2
Grease Guns 2
Uncle Jack
Whatever You Say, Sir!
Workin' It Out

VINCE COBRETTI
(aka Vinnie Cobretti) A young, dark-haired model from the early '90s.
Bad Boys
Beat Street Boys
The California Stud Pups
Commercial Sex
Cool Hand Dick
Good Samaritan, The
Hard Moves
Hard Rock High
Hot Tub Fever
House Boys
In the Stretch
Lust Boys, The
Matters in Hand
Mirror, Mirror
Oral Reports
Phi Kappa Sucka'
Spring Clean Up
Swim Meat 2
Touch of Class

RANDY COCHRAN
A versatile, black porn legend from the '80s, with a 9" cock. Lives in Los Angeles.
All American Boys in Heat
Bad Boys, Vol. 24 & 26

Bears and Cubs
Best of Blacks, The
Best Stallions, The
Bi the Way
Bigger and Better
Black All-American 2
Black Attack
Black Balled
Black Bullet
Black for More
Black Force
Black Jacks
Black Lust, White Passion
Black Magic, White Heat
Black Male
Black Sweat
Boys Night Out
BulletPac 12: Black Bullet
Cabana Boys
Catalina's Black Gold
Collage 1 & 2
Coming From Above
Crazed
Deep Chocolate
Dildo Kings
Eagle Pack 5
Gidget Goes Bi
Great Balls of Fire
Guys Who Crave Black Cock
GV Guide All-Star Softball Game 1
Hard at It, Vol. 2
Hard Line
Haulin'-n-'Ballin'
Head of the Class
Headin' West
Heatwaves
Hotshots, Vol. 19: Black and White Buns
In the Black
In Thrust We Trust
Innocent Bi-Standers

Interracial Affairs
Making it Big
Male Order Sex
Manstroke
Men in Motion #1
Men of Size
Men on Site
Mocha Madness
Night Maneuvers
Picklin' the Cucumber
Pretty Boy
Private Pool Party
Probe Vol. 4: Black and Blond
Pump
Pumping Black
Rod's Raiders
Rumble
S.F. Packing Company
A Scent of Man
Soul and Salsa 1 & 2
Stud Fuckers
Tasting Mr. Goodbar
Three-Way Cum, Vol. 1
Thunderbolt
Trash, Vol. 4: Huge Meat
Trash, Vol. 8: Uncut Cocks
Try Anything Once

CLAUDE COCTEAU
Very cute and boyish dark-haired Czech Republic model.
English Student, The

PAUL CODER
Advocate Men Live 2
Behind Closed Doors
The Best of Back Alley Video
Big Packages
Boys Night Out
Cousins Should Do It

Cum Shots 102
Take (non-sex)
Hard to Resist
Hot Shots, Vol. 18, 20,
    21, 27
House Boys
Raw Footage
Revenge: More Than I
    Can Take
The Rites of Fall
Size of His Toys, The
Streaks
Stud Search
Think Big
Transitory States
Undercover

CHRISTOPHER CODY
Cocky Cruisin'

MICHAEL CODY
Sex & Sensuality
Tools of the Trade

GINO COLBERT
(aka Sam Schad) Born
April 25. Very handsome
model turned award-win-
ning director from the
1980s and '90s.
Anywhere, Anytime
Best Wishes
Better Than Bi
Bi Analist (dir.)
Bi & Busty (dir.)
Bi Dream of Jeannie
Bi Inferno
Bi Madness (dir.)
Bi Medicine (dir.)
Bi Spy, The (dir.)
Black Balled (dir. & actor)
Black Jacks (prod. & actor)
Black Male (prod. & dir.)

Boner (dir.)
Boys on Fire (dir. & non-
    sex. cameo)
Boys Will Be Boys (dir.)
Boxer, The (prod & actor)
Boxer 2, The (dir.)
Brotherly Love (prod. &
    actor)
Brotherly Love II (dir.)
Buddy System 2:
    Camouflage
Busted
By Day, Bi Night
Cabana Boys (dir.)
Cat Burglar
Cherry, The (dir. & actor)
Climactic Scenes #101
Club Taboo
Cockeyed Eagle, The (dir.)
Cruisin' the Balcony
Danny Does Dallas (dir. &
    actor)
Danny Does 'em All (dir.)
Dickey-Lickey
Dirt Busters
Dirty Trick (dir.)
Dracula Sucks (dir./actor)
Dream Doll
Dreaming About Dick
    (dir. & actor)
Dueling Dicks
Eyes of A Stranger
First Timers: Amateur
    Trilogy #1 (dir.)
Gidget Goes Bi (dir./actor)
Great Balls of Fire
Guys Who Eat Cum
Guys with Tight Asses
Hard Balls
Hard To Hold
Harder the Better, The
Hawaiian Eyes
Headin' West (dir.)

Honorable Discharge
Hooked on Hispanics
Horsemeat (dir.)
Hot Cocks (non-sex)
Hung and Dangerous (dir.)
In His Corner
In the End Zone (dir.)
Imagination
Innocent Bi-Standers
    (dir. & actor)
Inside Vladimir Correa
    (dir.)
Interracial Affairs
J.S. Big Time
Just You and Me 2 (dir.)
Kevin Goes Wild
Les Hommes
Loving Butch
Make a Wish and Blow
Male Instinct
Male Taboo (dir. & prod.)
Manhandler (dir.)
Manstroke (dir.)
Matters in Hand (dir.)
Men Behind Bars
Mix-N-Match (dir.)
Muscleman (dir.)
My Sister, My Brother
Night Boys, The
    (dir. & actor)
Night Maneuvers (dir.)
A Night with Strangers
    (non-sex)
Oral Orgy
One Hot Day
Pretty Boy (dir.)
Pumping Black
Queens Behind Bars
Ram Man #3 (dir.)
Rod Squad, The
Rump Ranger
A Scent of a Man (dir.)
Secret Action Man

(co-dir. & actor)
Sex Behind Bars
Sexy Billy Blue
She-Males Undercover
She's a Boy
She's a He
Smokin' Butts
Split Decision
Stryker's Best Powerful
   Sex
Stud Fuckers
Stud Vision
Student Bodies Too
Switch Hitters VI: (dir.)
Tasting Mr. Goodbar
Teammates
Thirteenth, The: It Was a
   Friday
Tongue Dancing
Tough Guys Do Dance
Transitory States (dir.)
Unchained Men (dir.)
William Higgins Preview
   Tape#2

BRYCE COLBY
Dr. Good Glove
Flashpoint
Guest Services
Workin' Stiff

NED COLBY
In His Corner
Men Behind Bars
My Sister, My Brother
Sex Behind Bars

JEFF COLE (See Buster)

RICK COLEMAN
Airmale
Buddy System
Dreammen

Dude Beach
Fantasy Bytes
Foxhole
Hot Shots, Vol. 50:
   Men at Work
Manrammer
Raising Hell
Stud Ranch
Sunday Brunch
Teammates

DAMIEN COLETTA
A 1990s model.
Make it Count
You've Got The Touch

CHRIS COLLINS
Don't Hold Back
Men Matter Most
Natural Response
Powergrip
Pushing The Limit
Unexpected Persuasion
You've Got The Touch

KEVIN COLLINS
Big Shooters #4
Body Scorcher
California Wet
Eighteen Candles
F-Stop
Firsts
Manholes #1
Never Big Enough
Shooting Stars #1: Chris
   Thompson
Studio X
Young Hot Studs

NIC COLLINS
Born in Arizona. 5'10", 8"
cock. Versatile.
After Hours

Balls in Play
Behind His Back
Big Rigs
Blow Hard
Camp Pokahiney
Cat Men Do!
Four Men
Jamie Hendrix's
   Interviews 1
Leather Temptation
Like Father, Like Son
Lust Shack
Married Men
Men With Tools 2
Missionary Position
MVP: Most Valuable Player
My Dick Is Bigger 2
Oklahomo
Quick Relief
Romping Roommates
Roughing It
Sexual Thoughts
Slurp!
Smell of a Man 2
Sucker
Summer Obsession
Tell Me About Sex
Tempted
Rush, The
Trying It On For Size
Ultimate Reality
Wall 3, The

STEVE COLLINS
(aka Joe Andrews) Early
1980s, hairy-chested,
uncut model.
Big Shooters #6
Biggest One I Ever Saw
California's Golden Boys
Company We Keep, The
Falconhead 2
Gayracula

Hard Men at Work
Hard Money
Hustlers, The 1-3
I Do
Non-Stop
Private Pleasures of John
  Holmes
Valley Boys

ALEX COLT
The Bartender
Hot Guys #4
It Happened One Day
Just One Favor

ANDREW COLT
(aka Andrew Cole)
Escort, The
Made To Get Laid
Obsessively Compulsive
Receiving End
Summer Daze
Working Stiff

ANTHONY COLT
Getting In Tight

BRETT COLT
The Night We Met

CHRIS COLT
The Selection Part 1
  (Solo)

SHANE COLT
Best Of Leather: Part 3
He's Worth It
Leather Obsession 3 & 5
Letter To Three Men
Night In Leather
Orgies Pt 3
We've Got Them All
Wet Warehouse

THOMAS COLT
Cat's Tale

TRAVIS COLT
Come With Me
Thrust Fault

DILLON COLTER
Leather Obsession 5
Orgies Pt 3
The Selection Part 1
  (Solo)
The Sex Files

DANNY COMBS
Falconhead 2: The
  Maneaters
Giants 1 & 2
Hard Money
Hot Stuff
Knockout
Marco's Friends
Screen Play
Soap Studs
Trick Time
Uncut
Valley Boys
X-Tra Large

TRENT COMEAUX
Captive Men 6
Forced Pleasures
Immersion
Island Guardian
Link to Link
Liquid Latex
Russo's Sex Pig
Sex Acts
Slave Camp 2
Spank Me, Man!
Uncut Glory
Walked Over

JEREMY CONDON
Board Meeting
Bronco Bunch
Power Force
Seducers Sizzle
Suckulents
Sweet Meat, Lost
  Innocence
Swim Meat 2
Young Squirts

CHAD CONNERS
Born June 23. Handsome
boy-next-door blond bottom
from the '90s.
After Hours
All The Way Inn
Black & Blue
Blow Out
Boys Next Door
Bullseye
Cop Stories #2:
  The Cover Up
Download
Erotikus
Face Down
Getting Ahead
Hard Ass
The Hole
Hung Up
Initiation, The
Journey
A Letter To Three Men
Limited Entry
Muscleforce #4 - Chad
Masculine Men
Matinee Idol
Mavericks
Never Too Big
Nightwalk
Night Watch 2
Nude Men Can Jump
Orgies Pt 4

Overcharged
The Pornographer
Possession
Power Trip
Quick Study
Riptide!
Rope Tricks
Ruthless
Squeezeplay
Steel Away
Summer's Tall Tales
Tall Tales
Tommy Boy
Wet Warehouse

DANNY CONNERS
A 1980s model.
Anything, Anytime
Chain Reaction
Heroes
Hot Shots 6
I Need It Bad
Ivy League
Rough Idea
Street Kids
Young Ones
Young Yankees

DAVE CONNORS
A porn legend of the '80s.
Died from AIDS-related ill-
ness.
The Biggest One I Ever
   Saw
Boys In The Sand 2
Dirt Bikes
One In A Billion
One, Two, Three

JOSH CONNORS
(Real name Erik
Greenman) Best known as
the roommate of Andrew

Cunanan, the serial killer
who murdered Gianni
Versace in 1997.
Hotter Than Life
A Tale of Two Brothers

MARK CONNORS
A 1970s model.
Adam & Yves

GEORGE CONOVER
The Biggest One I Ever
   Saw
Boys In The Sand 2
Dirt Bikes
One, Two, Three
One In A Billion

JON CONRAD
Palace Of Pleasures

JEFF CONVERSE
One of the more memo-
rable stars from the late
1980s.
Giants
Other Side of Aspen 2, The
Powertool 1 & 2
Saddle Tramps 2
Spring Break
Spring Training
Winners

MITCH COOKE
Bat Dude
Dreamen
Hard To Be Good
Teammates

CLINT COOPER
Discoverd by Chi Chi
LaRue in Paris in 1998.
Another Man's Hand

Final Link, The

STEWART COPELAND
An early 1990s model.
Dickey Lickey
Dirty Tricks
Dreaming About Dick
In His Corner
My Sister, My Brother
Night Boys

JAKE CORBIN
A cute, boyish looking,
brown-haired, 1980s
model. Died September
27, 1992 from AIDS-relat-
ed causes.
Boys on Fire
Cruisin'
Dreaming About Dick
Frank Vickers, Vol. 3
Full Service
In His Corner
The Men of 550
Night Boys
Pacific Fever
Runaways
Screen Test 2
Scum
Secret Asian Man
Three Little Pigs
Undercover

TOM CORD
All Tied Up
Dynamite
Eight Inches Or More
Grey Hanky Left
Leather Lover

DONOVAN COREY
Balls to the Wall 36
Home Work

JAY COREY
Arms Of Forgiveness
Badlands
Big Date, The
Black And Blue
Body Search
Caged Heat
California Dream Inn
Chain Male
Come And Get It
Craze!
Danny's Back
Delirium
Dirty Dreaming
Dirty Laundry
Down & Out
Dreams Come True
Experiment, The
Fast Company
Frat House: Memories
  Of Pledge Week
Great Lengths
GV Guide Gay Erotic
  Video Awards 1
Hell Weekend
Hollywood And Vine
Horny Rent Collector
In The Men's Room
Juice Bomb
Keeping Time
Latin X
Lights! Camera! Action!
Mad Masseur, The
Meaning Of Sex, The
Men In Love
976 - Hot
Party Animals
Pure Attraction
Rearended
Risky Sex
Secret Report
Selling It
Skin Tight

Someone To Watch
Special Deliveries
Straight To The Zone
Stud Ranch
Stud Wanted
Sweat Motel
Thunder Blue
Tool Of The Trade
  Trade
1230 West Melrose
Twin Exposure
Wild And Loose

ROB CORONE
Gay Weekend Away

VLADIMIR CORREA
A popular, late 1980s
Brazilian model.
Best Wishes
Bi & Busty
Bi Dream of Genie
Bi Inferno
Bi-Medicine
Bi 'N' Large
Big Time
Black & Latino Working
  Hard
Black Salsa
Boxer, The 1 & 2
Cherry, The
Club Tattoo
Cruising Park
Days Gone Bi
Dirt Busters
Dirty Tricks
Double Standards
Fantasies of Brazil
Full Grown Full Blown
Gays, Bis, She-Males and
Haulin'-n-Ballin'
Hawaiian Desire
Hermaphrodites

Hot Cocks
Hung and Dangerous
Incessant
Inside Vladimir Correa
Interracial Affairs
Latin Jackoff
Latin Power
Latinos Working Hard
Male Seduction
More
Muscle Studs
New Recruits
Out of Bounds
Rock-Hard
Sexy Billy Blue
Smokin' Butts
Student Bodies Too
"10" Plus
They Grow 'em Big
Tommy Boy
Twice the Fun

GILBERTO CORREIA
A 1990s Latin model.
Brazilian Bath Boys
Breakin'Em In 1 & 2
Brazilian Bath Boys 2

DAN CORTEZ
Asian Persuasion 2
Flesh and Fantasy 2

PHIL CORTEZ
Buddy System
Buddy System 2

TONY CORTEZ
Mountain Cruisin'
Trade

DONOVAN CORY
Desert Paradise
I Am Curious Leather

Sex Toy Story
Summer Obsession

DOUG CORY
Best Of All 1 & 2
Celebrity Sex
Sizing Up
Stryker Force

JOHN CORY
Casting Cocks (solo)

NICK COUGAR
Blond, hairy-chested,
youthful-looking model
from the early 1990s.
Bare Bottoms
Best of Eric Manchester
Big One, The
Crosswire
G.I. Mac
Low Blows
Mannequin Man
Powerline
Pumping Up: Flexx II
Ranch Hand
Rites of Fall, The
Superhunks
Switch Hitters V:
    The Night Games
Tim Lowe's Weekend
Adventure
True Confessions
Untamed

DEAN COULTER
Born April 24th in Seattle.
5'8", 7' cock. Versatile bottom. Cute, husky, late
1990s star with light brown
hair.
Best of Titan: Collector
    Series 2

Chapters
Fallen Angel 2
Immersion
Swell

ANTHONY COX
All Night Long
BulletPac II: Battle of the
Bulge
Climactic Scenes #101
Crazed
Dude Ranch
4-hour 4-skin
Gimme It All
Goosed (bi)
Harder the Better, The
Imperfect Strangers
In the End Zone
Las Vegas Orgy
New Meat
Night Maneuvers
Sex Drive 2020
Soldiers
Stud Fuckers
Surge Men are Very
Receptive
3-Way Cum, Vol. 1
The Voyeur

COREY COX
Black Attack 2
Black Brigade
Black Men Do!
Black Patrol
Black Renegades
Ho Ho Ho!!!
Iron Cage
Men at Magnum
Pledges of Gamma Beta
    Mu, The
Special Forces
White Movers, Black
Shakers

LOGAN COX
Basic Plumbing 2
Four Card Stud

MIKE COX
Campus Jocks
Dick Day Afternoon
Motel California
Never Ending Studs

TED COX
A very popular 1980s
bisexual model.
Best of Adam Grant, The
Best of Matt Powers, The
Best of Street Times
    Video, The
Black and Beyond: The
Darker Side
Boys on the Block
Cherry, The
Courting Libido
Cum Shots 102
Do Me Dirty
Don't Leave Me/Locker
Room Billy
Guys Who Eat Cum
Guys With Tight Asses
Hard Balls
Hard Labor
He-Devils
Honesty
Hot Cocks
Hot Shots, Vol. 42:
    Face Shots
Hot Shots, Vol. 49:
    Torrid Trios
In the Stretch
International Guide to
    Fellatio
Iron Man
Kevin Goes Wild
Knockout

Lewd Conduct
Lifeguard on Duty
Pay to Play 1 & 2
Personals
Rise, The
Rodz, The
Sailor in the Wild 2, Sex,
   Lies and Videocassettes
Sex Is In The Air
Sex Shooters
Shacking Up
Some Men are Bigger
   than Others
Smokin' Butts
Sparky O'Toole's Excellent
   Adventure
Sparky's Wild Adventure
Straight Boys Do
Stiff Competition
Stroke, The
Sweet Meat, Lost
Innocence
Switch Hitter V: The Night
   Games
Tender Trick
Tight Jeans
True Confessions
Weekend Wildcats
Young Hustlers

JOE CRAIG
Auto Erotica: the Best of
   Sex in Cars
The Best of All Matt
Sterling
Big & Thick
Bigger the Better, The
Buster: The Best years
FratHouse Memories
Getting It
Like A Horse
Master of Discipline
Preppy Summer

Sizing Up

STEVEN CRAIG
(aka Steven Kreig)
1980s Falcon model. Died
in 1990.
Gridiron
Iron Man
Lifeguard
Plunge
Revenge
Slam Dunk

BILL CRANE
A brown-haired, youthful-
looking model from the
early 1990s.
Best of Back Alley Videos
Best of Jonathan Strong
Bull Pen
Callguys, U.S.A.
Cream of the Crop
Cousins Should Do It
Davy and the Cruisers
Heat in the Night
Man in Motion
Neptune
Painting Party
Paramedic Alert
Point of No Return
Rites of Manhood, The
Rites of Spring, The
Shacking Up
Sizzle
Spanking New: Drive it
   Home
Straight Boys Do
Superhunks II
Taken by Storm
Tips
Tough Guys Do Dance
Two Handfuls 2
Weekend Wildcats

DENTON CRANE
A late 1980s model.
Bring Your Own Man
Cousin Buck
Hot Roomers
Long Johns
Manholes
My Masters
Navy Blue Hanky Left
Raunch 2
They All Came
Toilets
Tramps

EDDIE CRANE
Bare Bottoms
Bronco Bunch
International Guide to
Fellatio
Like Father, Like Son
Lust Boys
Power Force
Sweet Meat, Lost
Innocense
Ten Is Enough
Tongue Dancing

**CHRISTOPHER
CRAWFORD**
The Come Back
You Sexy Thing!

DOLPH CRAWFORD
Four By Four
Three The Hard Way
Too Hard To Hold

ERIC CRAWFORD
A 1970s model.
Adam & Yves

MICHAEL CRAWFORD
Born in Virginia. 6'0", 6"

cock. Bottom.
Big Shot, The
Das Butt 1 & 2
Hotel, The
Hotel California
Kickboxer
Men in Blue
Mountain Patrol
Soaked
Uncle Jack
Uninvited, The
Uninvited Images

JONATHAN CRISTIPHER
Face Riders
Hell Bent for Leather
Insertion
LeatherWorld
On the Move
South of the Border
Ranger in the Wild
Uniform Ball 1-2

SAM CROCKETT
Born in Charlotte, North
Carolina. Mature model
with brown hair. 6'1", 8"
cock, top.
Alley Boys
Asian Persuasion
Below the Decks
Big Black Bed, The
Boot Camp Buddies
CatalinaVille
Cat Men Do!
Chip Daniels' Video
Studbook
Choice, The
Company We Keep, The
Corporate Ladder, The
Crossing the Line
Detour
Dial "S" For Sex

Dirty Stories
Extreme Measures
Family Secrets
Fast Action
Fine Daze
Flavor of Men, The
Flesh and Fantasy 2
Forced Pleasures
Full Body Contact
Happily Ever After
Hot Firemen
Hot to Trot
Hung Riders 2
In and Out Express
In the Deep End
Last Taboo, The
Leather Bound
Locker Room Sex Brawl
Malibu Beach Hunks
Men's Room
My Brother's Best Friend
Naked Highway
Night of the Living Bi-Dolls
Party of One
Perfect Gift, The
Played Pressure
Positively Yours
Pressure
Priority Male
Ryker Files, The
Schlong Blade
Showboys
Staff, The
Stag Party
Studio Tricks
Summer Reunion: The
    Best Parts of Summer
Sure Thing
Tank Tops
Technical Ecstasy
Things to Cum
Throat Spankers
Thunderballs

Toolbox
Why Marines Don't Kiss

BRENT CROSS
Born May 24. Hunky,
brown-haired, boy-next-
door, gay-for-pay, late '90s
star with an enormous
dick.
Before and After
Big Deposit
Butt Munch Chasers
Choke 'Em
Crossing Over
Dark Side of the Moon
Dirty White Guys
Family Values
Hawaiian Illustrated
HOMOgenized
Hot Guys
Hot Spot
Huddle Up
I Saw What You Did
In Love
In the Shadows
Jeff Stryker's Underground
Johnny Hormone
Just Guys
Man Hunt, The
Men in Blue
Orgies Pt 2
Pure
Reform School
Confidential
Rope Tricks
Sex Invaders
Sharp Shooters
Tailspin
Wet Warehouse Part 2:
Drenched

DEREK CRUISE
A handsome, smooth-bod-

ied brunet and very popular
1990s model.
All About Steve
Chi Chi Larue's Hardbody
Video Mag 4
Cruise Control
Dish
Few Fresh Men, A
Forum Video Magazine
Getaway, The
GV Guide Gay Erotic Video
Awards 2
Lovers, Tricks & One Night
Stands
Network Q #28: Inside The
Gay Porn Film Industry
Outlaw Bikers
Secret Sex 1 & 2
Thrust Fault
Toilet Tramps
Valley Of The Bi Dolls

JASON CRUISE
An early '90s, youthful-
looking, brown-haired
model from Florida.
Best of Back Alley Video
Best of Jonathan Strong
Best of Rick Savage, The
Cool Hand Dick
Deep Inside Jon Vincent
Free to Be Wild
Hard Moves
Hard to Resist
Hawaiian Desire
Hot for His Bod
Hot Shots, Vol. 46 & 47
Hot Summer Knights
In the Briefs
In the Stretch
Knockout
Lustful Paradise
Man in Motion

My Soul Desire
Pay 2 Play
Summer Knights
Taken by Storm

TOMMY CRUISE
Born in Los Angeles. 5'11",
6" cut, bottom. Very popu-
lar, late '90s gay-for-pay
star.
Asian Persuasion 2
Before and After
Billy 2000
Cop Stories #1: The
Scandal
Cruisin' for a Gang Bang
Dare Devils
Foot Patrol
Gamemaster
Goosed (bi)
Hard To Keep Down
Joe's Big Adventure
Love Inn Exile (softcore)
Private Passions
Rosebud
Seduction, The Part 4
Underboss, The
West Hollywood Hope
Wet Daddy

ANTHONY CRUZ
(aka Tony Cruz)
Hotter Than Life
Latin Balls 2: Huevos
Virtual Sexuality

KENNY CRUZ
Attack of the Amazing
Colossal Latino

SEBASTIAN CRUZ
Games We Play, The

ROB CRYSTON
Back to Front, The
Big Drill, The
Bigger the Better 2, The
Bite, The
Black Mischief
Bodymasters, The
Brawnzmen, The
Brief Encounters
Centerspread 3
Chi Chi Larue's Hardbody
Video Mag. 1
Cocksure
Damien, One Night Of Sin
Deception, Part 1: Happy
Birthday to You
Deception, Part 2, Hard
Justice
Desert Drifters
Dirty Pool
Disconnected
Down Bi Law
Dream-Seeker
Fast Company
The Fluffer
G.I. Jocks: Out Of The
Ranks
Going Down In Style
Gv Guide Gay Erotic Video
Awards #1
Highway Hunks
Hole Patrol
Hot Ticket
House For Sale—Sex
Idol Thoughts
Juice Bomb
Just Men
Long Play
Lords Of Leather
Lovers, Tricks & One Night
Stands
Manticipation
Mavericks

Men On Call
Mine's Bigger Than Yours
Motor Crotch
Muscle Bound
Neighborhood Games
Night Walk
Nuts, Butts And Glory
Personals
Privilege
Picture Perfect
The Pornographer
Privilege
Proud
Rassle
Reflections
Roll In The Hay
The Roommate
Secret Sex 1 & 2
Sex Between The Lines
Sex Posse
Shoot
Single White Male
Skin Tight
Slave Trainer
Smoky
Snowbumz
Steel Away
Studz
Summer Buddies
Sunsex Boulevard
Switch Hitters 7
Taken 2 The Max
Tales Of The Backlot
Thick Of It, The
Toilet Tramps
Tommy Boy
Tool Of The Trade
Totally Exposed
Tricked
Twin Exposure
2 Hard Up
Voice Male
Wanted Man, A

Waterworks
Weekend Liberty
Wet And Wild

MILOS CSABA
Buffed, blond haired 1999
Hungarian model.
Hungarian Heat

MICHAEL CUMMINGS
All the Right Boys
All the Way In
Angelo Loves It
Ball Blasters
Below the Belt
Big Time
Boys Camp Memories
California Wet
Campus Jocks
Cashload
Chip off the Old Block
Chris Noll's Fantasies
Deep Inside
Down to His Knee
Extreme Urge
Firsts
Getting Off Campus
Good Sex
Hard Disk Drive
Hawaiian Heat
Hot off the Press
Hot on His Trail
Hot Shots, Vol 8: Orgies
Imperfect Strangers
It's the Size That Counts
L.A. Boiling Point
Man Size
Manholes #1
More Than a Mouthful
Naked Lunch
Never Big Enough
New Wave Hustlers
Nightcrawler

Out of Bounds
P.S. Connection 1
Pleasure Peak
Sex Drive 2020
Sex Waves
Shooting Stars #2:
    Michael Christopher
Shooting Stars #3:
    Michael Cummings
Show it Hard
Star Shoots #6
Stiff Sentence
Summer Heat
Teddy's Bare
Totally Awesome
2X10
Uncle Mike Meets Howard
Video Games #6

TONY CUMMINGS
Born December 13, 1973,
North Carolina. Resides in
Washington, DC. Cute,
young, dark-haired late
1990s model. 5'10", 7"
cock, bottom.
Alley Boys
Apprentice, The
Beverly Hills Hustlers
Club 18 to 23
A Day in the Life of Austin
Driven
Hard For The Money
He's Worth It
Hot Guys 1 & 2
Indulge 1 & 2
Pleasure Principle
Ranger In The Wild
Road Home, The
Sex and Sensuality
Sharpshooters
Something Very Big This
    Way Comes

South Beach Heat
Striptease

ALEX CUMMINS
My Dick Is Bigger 2

BILL CURRY
Best Of Colt #2
Main Attraction, The
Members Only

JOEL CURRY
A pornstar bottom from the
'80s. Committed suicide
October 2, 1995.
Bi-Sexual Fantasies
Dynastud
Fleshtones
Lusty Lovers
Mansplash
Naked Lunch
Sighs
Swing Set
2X10

QUINN CURTIS
How I Got The Story
Made To Order

D

DAVID DABELLO
(aka David Silva)
Bears and Cubs
The Best of Eric
Manchester
Better Than Ever
Beyond Briefs
Down for the Count
Gotta Have It
Hard at It, Vol. 2
Heart Throbs

New Meat
Northwest Passage
Picklin' the Cucumber
Surge Men are Very
Receptive
Try Anything Once
Video Games 5 & 8

ERIC DAHL
(see Dirk Caldwell)

DAKOTA
(aka Dcota)
A New Mexico native.
The Best of All Matt
Sterling II
Buttbusters
Compulsion
Cruisin' II: More Men on
    the Make
Mission Accomplished
Score 10
Stroke 'N' Men
Sun Devils
View to a Thrill 2: The Man
    With the Golden Rod

DEAN DAKOTA
San Diego Summer

JEFF DAKOTA
(See Jeff D. Kota)

GREG DALE
Best of Times
Class of '84 Vol. 1 & 2
The Cruiser
Freshman Fantasies
His Little Brother
Hot Trash
The Idol
L.A. Tool & Die
Manhandler

A Night At Halstead's
Rear Deliveries
Rushes
Skin Flix
Tough Iron
Turned On
Wet Shorts

JACK DALLAS
(See Chris Lopez)

NICK DALLAS
California Blue
Handyman
Hitchhiker
Paradise Park

DAMIEN
(aka Damian, Steve Lyons)
Tall, very handsome, dark-
haired, Italian-looking
model from the late '80s.
For a time his boyfriend
was pornstar Tony
Erickson.
Bad Break
Best of Danny Sommers
    (non-sex)
Best of Ryan Yeager, The
Boy Next Door, The
Butt Busters
Chi Chi Larue's Hardbody
    Video Mag1
The Coach's Boys
Convertible Blues
Damien, One Night Of Sin
Head Struck
Hot Pursuit
In Your Fac pe
Inner Circle, The
King of the Mountain
Leo & Lance
Majestic Knights

Man of the Year
Mannequin Man
Master Piece
Mating Game
Overnight Service
Primitive Impulse
Privilege
Read My Lips
Return of Grant Fagin, The
Rimshot
Scoring
Sex in Tight Places
Steel Garters
Sterling Ranch
Strictly For Ladies Only
Summertime Blues
Total Corruption
Toweling Off
Truth, Dare or Damian
Valley of the Bi Dolls

BEN DAMON
Born March 26. Resides in
San Francisco. 5' 11", 8-
inch cock.
Billy Herrington's Body
   Shop
Coal Miner's Son
Gang Bang Ranch Hand
Stuffed
Youthful Offenders

BOB DAMON
Dirty Picture Show
L.A. Tool & Die
Trouble Shooters

DREW DAMON
Born October 2, 1975.
Resides in Canada. 10"
cock.
Fever
French Connection 2

Stock

JUSTIN DAMON
(aka Justin Dee)
Born September 15. Blond
haired, boyish-looking late
1990s model. Resides in
Los Angeles.
Fresh Trade
Late Night Porn
Penal Pen Pals
Too Many Tops
Youthful Offenders

MICHEL D'AMOURS
Born August 6 in Ottawa,
Ontario, Canada. A hand-
some, dark-haired, French-
Canadian, jock-next-door
and 1990s model. 5'5," 7"
cock.
Abduction 2 & 3
Call of the Wild
Desert Train
Dirty Pool
Home Grown
Imagination: Action
   Gone Wild
Is Your Big Brother Home
Laid To Order
Lost In Vegas
Montreal Men
River Patrol
Slave Camp
Thriller

TONY DANCER
Basic Plumbing 2

DANE
Chip Off The Old Block
Uncut Club of L.A.

BRETT DANIELS
Every Man's Desire
Men Matter Most
Pushing The Limit

BRIAN DANIELS
Born October 23. Cute,
dark-haired, cute, youthful
model from the late 1990s.
Billy 2000
Blade
California Kings
CatalinaVille
Caught In The Military #2
Cowboy Jacks
Current Affairs
Deep in the Brig
A Love Story
Mercury Rising
Mountain Patrol
Ready to Serve
Reform School Confidential

CHIP DANIELS
Handsome, hunky, dark-
haired 1990s model turned
director.
Backdrop
Best Of All II
Big as They Come
California Dream Inn
Chip Daniels' Video
   Studbook (non-sex)
Deception, Part 1 & 2
Fast Idle
Full Length
Going Down In Style
Grease Guns
GV Guide All-Star Softball
   Game #1
Hard Talk
Into the Night
Jawbreaker

Lowe Down
Mack Pack #4: The Other
   Side of Hollywood
Mack Pack #5: Toolkit
The Male Triangle
Man Country
On the Lookout
Overload
Please Don't Tell
Rawhide
Room Service
Scorcher
Special Handling
Tool Kit

JEREMY DANIELS
Relentless
Shameless

JOE DANIELS
Any Boy Can

MIKE DANIELS
Do Me Evil

PIERCE DANIELS
Died July 8, 1995 from
AIDS-related illness.
Anonymous Sex
Bait
The Best of Surge II
Better Than Ever
Big Shooter #3
Built to Last
Century Mining
Chip off the Old Block
Double Exposure
Elements of Passion
Faces
Firsts
Foreskin Fantasy
Glory Hole of Fame
Gotta Have It

GV Guide Gay Erotic Video
   Awards 1
Hard Talk
Hollywood Gigolo
Hot Roomers
Hot Shots, Vol. 5, 7, 8, 12
Hung and Dangerous
Lovers and Friends
Lusty Lovers
Manholes 1 & 2
Men and Steel
Men in Motion #3
Military Secrets
Muscle Fever
Nightcrawlers
No Cruising Zone
Paradise Beach
Perfect Ten
Quickies #2
Rodeo
Roughed Up At the Spike
Sex Drive 2020
Sex Hunt
Sex Waves
Sighs
Star Shots #6
Studbusters
Surge Men at Their Best
Therapy
Thinking Big
To Protect and to Serve
Tough Stuff
A Trip to Paradise Beach
Tyger Tales
Windows

WES DANIELS
Late '80s, dark-haired
model, reportedly left the
business and now lives in
North Carolina.
Alley Action
Bedtime Stories: Tales to

Keep You Up
The Best of Chad Knight
Beyond It All: The Real
   Thing
The Big Dare
The Body Masters
Body Search
The Brawzmen
Brief Encounters
Caged Heat
Chi Chi LaRue's Hardbody
   VideoMag 1
Choose me
Clippers
The Coach's Boys
Daddy, Daddy
Danger Alley
Deception, Part 1 & 2
Delirium
Disconnected
The Drifters
Easy Riders
The Extra Day
Fan Male
Hard at Work
Hidden Man
Immoral Thoughts
Inner Circle
Into the Night
It's A Gang, Video Series 1
Juice Bomb
Jumper
Keeping Time
Leather Teddy
Long Distance Lover
Majestic Knights
Memories of Summer
Midnight Sun
Mindscape 1 & 2
Model Behavior
Morning Ritual #2
Moving In
The Muscle Club

Need You Tonight
Palm Springs 92264
Picture Perfect
Ripped
Sex in Wet Places
Sexpress
Snowbumz
Songs in the Key of Sex
Special Deliveries
Star Gazing #1
Steel Garters
Sterling Ranch
Straight to the Zone
Total Corruption
To Thine Own Self Be True
  True
Truth, Dare or Damian
The Visitor

GREG DALE
(aka Dale Arnold)
The Best of Times
Class of '84, Part 2
Freshman Fantasies
Hot Trash
The Idol
L.A. Tool & Die
Manhandler Collection
A Night at Halsted's
Rear Deliveries
Rushes
Skin Flix (aka Deep Thrust)
Tough Iron
Turned On
Wet Shorts

CHRIS DANO
(aka Eddie Van Ness)
Born October 12. Late '80s
and '90s, Mature, Hawaiian
model.
Alley Katt
The Best of Adam Grant

Biagra
Bi Sex Club
The Big Switch III: Bachelor
  Party
Black Gang-Bang 8
Black Passion
Blatino Party L.A.
Brother Trouble
Clothes Make the Man
Demolition Man
The Drifter
Face Riders
Foxhole
Full Service
Gang Bang Ranch Hand
Handtools 2
Handsome Randsom
Head of the Class II
Hombres Latinos
Hot Copy
Hot Spot
I Like to Watch
Inches Away
Jeff Stryker's Underground
A Jock's Dream
Leather Intrusion Case 4:
  Down To The Wire
A Letter To Three Men
Matador
Naked Underneath
Night of the Living Bi-Dolls
Over the Rainbow
Photo-Op
Private Dick
Reunion
Rock Off
Sex Bi Lex
Throat Spankers
Total Corruption 2
Toys for Big Boys
Uncut Glory

JOHN DANTE
(aka John Mercato)
Any Way I Can
Campus Men
Don't Hold Back
Hungry for Hole (as
Mercato)
Latin Knockout
Make it Count
Quintet in Ass (as Mercato)

BILLY DARE
Youthful, dark-haired, late
1990s model.
Deep in the Brig
Forced Service
F-Train to Castro
Link 2 Link

MARCO DASILVA
Woody And His Peckers

CARL DAVENPORT
Bull Pen
Hidden Instinct
Orgies Pt 1
Peep-O-Rama
Together Again

DEVIN DAVENPORT
Early '90s, blond, jock next
door model.
Afternoon Delight
Backdrop
Bone Alone
Hand Jobs
Mine's Bigger Than Yours
My First Love
Reunion
Weekend Liberty

JOHNNY DAVENPORT
(aka John Davenport and

John "10-Inches"
Davenport in hetero videos)
A blond hair, blue eyed
pornstar legend from the
'80s. Resides in New
Mexico.
As Big As They Come
Bad Boys Club
Best Bi Far
The Best of John
Davenport
The Best of Kevin Williams
The Best of Kurt Bauer
Big Bad Boys
Big Guns
The Bigger They Come
Catalina Classics
Director's Best:
    John Travis, Vol. 1
Dreaming of You
Full Grown/Full Blown
Glory Hole of Fame
Handtools
Heartbeat
Hot Rods: The Young and
    the Hung II
Hot Shots, Vol 15: Bottoms
Hot Shots, Vol. 36: Student
    Affairs
In Hot Pursuit
Innocence Lost
Magnum Griffin, Vol. 8 & 10
My Best Buddy
Oasis (as Mike Pager)
Perfect Summer
Powerline
Powertool
Sunstroke
Switch Video #2
Trading Up
The Young and The Hung

TY DAVENPORT
Alley Katt
Behind His Back
Cruise Park
Desert Maneuvers
From Hair to Eternity
Leather Dream
Leather Men
Leather Night
Leather Party
Leather Triangle
Leather World
Love In Dakota
Night In Leather
Sex Toy Story #2
Virgin Territory

ION DAVIDOV
A 1990s Lukas Ridgeston
co-star from the Czech
Republic.
Johan's Big Chance
Lucky Lukas

JOHNNY DAVIDSON
Cop Corruption
Cop Daddies Playtime
Free Delivery
Laguna Beach Lifeguards

BOBBY DAVIS
A blond, uncut model from
the late 1980s.
As Big As They Come
Bulging Jockstraps
Collage
Deep Chocolate
Foreplay
Foreskin Dreams
Full Grown/Full Blown
Gotta Have It
Heavy Crusin'
Hot Shots, Vol. 39:

Uncut Hunks 2
Hot Shots, Vol. 47:
    Newcomers
Looking Good
Major Meat
Mantalk
Memories of Eighteen
Motel California
New Love
Old Reliable #62: Uncut #4
Pleasure Peak
Quickies #6
Red Hot Redheads
Straight Boys Do
Surfer Guys
Sunstroke

BRAD DAVIS
Asian Persuasion
Aussie Pool Party
Butt Bruisers
Flavor of Leather, The
Full Up!
Glory Holes of L.A.
Hard Workout
A Jock's Dream
Meet Ray Harley
964 Dicks St.
Razor Close
Spiked
Wacky Wack-Offs 1
X-Press Male

CONNOR DAVIS
Butt Bruisers
Straight Talk

DARREN DAVIS
Anonymous Sex
Cream Team, The
From Hair to Eternity
Internal Affairs

JOHN DAVIS
A 1970s model.
Adam & Yves

JON DAVIS
A 1990s model.
West Hollywood Hope

MARK DAVIS
Brian's Boys

RICK DAVIS
Just Blonds

SCOTT DAVIS
Handsome, blond, 1990s model.
Coach's Boys, The
Coal Miner's Son
Cramming For The Big One
Cut Vs. Uncut
Dynastud 2: Powerhouse
  Foot Patrol
Forum Video Magazine
Hold Me Again
Hot Cargo
Hotel California
Humidity
Jockstrap
Journal, The
Mind Blower
My Best Friends Woody
9-1/2"
Read Bi All
Saving Ryan's Privates
Something About Larry
Switchcraft
Weho Alley
Young Men On The
Pleasure Trail

SEAN DAVIS
(aka Foot Long Sean)

Australian model discovered by Kristen Bjorn.
Jackaroos
Manly Beach
Basic Plumbing
Forum Video Magazine
Full Length
Grease Guns
Men With Tools
Summer Fever
True Stories
Saddle Tramps
Escort, The
Grease Guns
House Rules
Men With Tools
Saddle Tramps
Summer Fever
True Storles: Tales From
  The Hot House Flies
Woody's

THARON DAVIS
Born June 25, 1958 in
Bayonne, New Jersey.
5'10", 8," cut, top or bottom. According to Leo
Buck "Tharon 's "Big
Break" came when a
reviewer referred him to
Joe Gage. His first experience on camera was
opposite "Porn Legend"
Jack Wrangler. Davis also
founded the "L.A.
Footmen" fetish group.
Babe
Bi-Bi American Style
Getting Ahead
Girls U.S.A.
In the Name of Leather
  Orgy
Street Kids

Subway
Tough Guys

TONY DAVIS
Youthful, blond and uncut.
One of the most memorable and most prolific porn
actors in the late '80s.
All Hands on Dick (bi)
All Night Long
Beach Dreamers
The Best of Jon Vincent 1
Bi & Sell
Bi Mistake
Blow Bi Blow
Bootcamp 1 & 2
Bound and Tickled in New
  York
Boy, Oh Boy
Boys Night Out
The Boy Toy
Brotherly Love
Buddy System 2:
Camouflage
BulletPac II: Battle of the
  Bulges
Carnival Tails
Castro Motel
Climatic Scenes #101
Cowboys & Indians
Cum Shots 102
Dreaming About Dick
Dueling Dicks
Fantasies
Fantasies of Brazil
Fond Focus
Frat Brats
A Friendly Obsession
G.I. Mac
Guys with Tight Asses
Hard Knocks
Hard to be Good
The Harder the Better

Headin' West
Heartbeat
Heavenly
Highway Patrol
Hot Pages
Hot Shots, Vol. 19: Black and White Buns
Hot Shots, Vol. 20, 21, 23, 24, 28, 42
Hung and Dangerous
Hung Guns
Illusions
In the End Zone
Island Heat
Knockout
Long Hard Ride
Magnum Griffin, Vol II
Manimal
Massive Meat
Matters in Hand
The Men of 550
My Soul Desire
Mystic Museum
Night Maneuvers
One Hot Day
Party Favors
Pay to Play
Pretty Boy
Raw Footage
The Rites of Spring
The River
The Rodz
Rumble
Screwing Screw-Ups
Seduction
Seduction 4 & 5
Size 12: Confessions of a Foot
Smokin' Butts
Tasting Mr. Goodbar
Thumbs Up!
Tips
3-Way Cum, Vol. 1

Unchained Men
Uncut Fever 1 & 2
Who's Dat Boy?
Wolf Boy
X-Poseur

JOHNNY DAWES
Real name Brian Lee. Handsome and popular model from the 1980s. Died July 25, 1989 from AIDS-related causes at age 34.
Bad, Bad Boys
Big Boys of Summer
A Big Business
Boys Night Out
Butt Darts
Climactic Scenes #101
Daddy Dearest
A Dance with Death (dir.,non-sex)
Doing It
Dude Ranch
Games
Hard & Throbbing
Hardline
Hot Numbers, Vol. 2
Hot Pages: Bound for Lust
Hot Shots, Vol.. 41: Rim Shots
In the End Zone
Knockout
Pleasure Beach
The Private Pleasures of John C. Holmes
Revenge of the Nighthawk
Skin Deep
Soap Studs
3-Way Cum, Vol. 1
Toilet Training
Trick Time
Who's Dat Boy?
The Wilde House

DON DAWSON
(see Duncan Mills)

PAUL DAWSON
Ass Lick Alley

SKY DAWSON
A pornstar legend from the '80s.
Big Summer Surprise
Bikers Liberty
Champs
Johnny Harden & the Champs
Hot shots, Vol. 30, Hot Jocks
Rawhide (1981)
Sex Session
Steve Scott's Turned On

MARCUS DAY
Lap It Up

DCOTA (see Dakota)

BRIAN DEAN
Desert Maneuvers
Leather Intrusion Case 3: Flesh Puppets
Leather World
Sex Toy Story #2

DAVID DEAN
Early 1990s blond haired model.
The Best of Black Alley Video
The Best of Black Knights
The Best of Rick Savage
Black All-American
First Mate
Free to be Wild
Hole in One

Iron Man
It's Good to be Bad
Man in Motion
The Rockmore Files
Snowbound
Spanking New; Drive it
  Home
The Stroke
Tell Me Something Dirty

GARY DEAN
A very handsome, 1990s
brown-haired, gay-for-pay
jock next door model from
Albuquerque, New Mexico.
Bone Alone
Breaking & Entering
Cheap Tricks
Delivery Ring
Dorm Fever
The Experiment
The Guest
Happy House
Hard Talk
Head or Tails
Joey
L.A. Underground
My Cousin Danny
Newcomers
1230 West Melrose
Payne In The Ass
Pool Man
Secret Dreams
Sex Posse
Star Gazing 2
Training Sessions
Underground
Upwardly Mobile

JOHNNY DEAN
Born June 19, Milwaukee.
5'10", 7" cock. Versatile.
Corporate Ladder

Drill Me Good
Rosebud
Show Your Pride
Wrestling Video

KELLY DEAN
A dark-haired, 1980s gay-
for-pay model.
Bound To Please #2
Show It Hard
Size of The Matter
Some Old Friends 3
Spanking Master

KEVIN DEAN
Born June 1 in Canada. A
mid '90s, boyish-looking
model who had one of the
biggest dicks in the history
of porn.
Download
Forced Entry
Measuring Up
Night Walk
On the Prowl
The Other Side of Aspen
  3 & 4
Rawhide

MIKE DEAN
Best Little Warehouse
  in L.A.
Better Than Ever
Catalina Down and Dirty
Catalina Orgies, Vol 1.
Class Reunion
Dude Ranch
Shore Leave
Surge Men are Very
Receptive
Surge Men at Their Best
Young Olympians

**TONY DE ANGELO
(see Tony Angelo)**

CAL DECKER
Immersion

DIRK DECKER
Free Delivery

JIM DECKER
Batter Up!

**ERIC DEGIORGIO
(see Eric Di Giorgio)**

MIKE DEITZ
Supersize It

COY DEKKER
Born August 15th,
Baltimore, Maryland. 5'6",
8" cock, versatile.
Cumbustible
Getting in Tight
Hard As Marble
Hidden Instinct
The Male Triangle
Men of Forum
Please Don't Tell
Rawshock
Relentless
Rocket Ryder
Teacher Sucks
Thick Flesh

MICHAEL DELFINO
Bronc Rider
Super Jock

GINO DEL MAR
Ball Blasters
Beach Ballers
Deep Inside

Fade In
Fade Out
Hot on His Tail
Hot Trash
It's the Size That Counts
Mind Games
Obsessed
Star Shots #2
Tall Tales
Uncut Dreams

JOSE DEL NORTE
(see Jose Garcia)

TALVIN DEMACHIO
(aka Tal Demarco)
Born August 2, 1971,
Mannassas, North Virginia,
Price William County.
Resides in Washington,
D.C. 5'5", 7 1/2" cock. Top.
Arousal: 45 Degree
Boomerang
Fluid
Hard Focus
Hard Part 1
Live Feed- Watching You,
    Watching Me
Matador
The New Coach
The Selection #6
Size Matters, Titan Men 2
Striptease
Suck Daddy
Take One: Guys Like Us

ANTHONY DEMARCO
Free Delivery
Latin Cops
Off Duty
Rear Delivery

BRUNO DEMARCO
Throttled

J.D. DEMARCO
Blue Line
Burning Desire
Camp Pokahiney
Cat Men Do!
Happily Ever After
In the Shadows
Mt. Olympus Pool Party
Pheromones
A Tale of Two Brothers

MIKE DEMARCO
A 1980s mature looking,
dark-haired, former *Playgirl*
model.
The Arousers
Bait
Biagra
Hard Men At Work
How I Got The Story
In The Heat Of The Knight
Tony's Initiation

VINCENT DEMARCO
Can't Say No
Don't Hold Back
Driveshaft
Every Man's Desire
Everything A Man Wants
Make it Count
Natural Response
Nothing Else Matters
One Way or the Other
Point of Entry
Powergrip
Relentless
Shameless
Stop at Nothing
Unexpected Persuasions
Whatever it Takes

You've Got the Touch

PETER DEMETRI
Handyman
Hitchhiker
Man O Man
Stud Struck

STEVEN DENNIS
Delicious
Obsessed
On Fire
Founder

J.T. DENVER
Bare Tales
Best Bi Far #2
The Best of Kevin Williams
Bulge: Mass Appeal
Delivery Boys
Giants
Hot Rods: The Young and
    the Hung II
Men in Motion 4 & 5
Out of Bounds
Passion By Fire: the Big
Switch 2
Probe Vol. 2: Three's
Company
Switch Video #2
They Work Hard for Their
    Money
The Young and the Hung

JACQUES DERIVES
Carnival In Venice
Coming Soon
Sex Drive
Tough & Tender

RICHARD DERRECK
Confessions
Motorsexual

LEO DESILVER
All Heated Up
Biagra
Bi Sex Club
First Time Tryers 12
Getting Personal
Goosed (bi)
Jamie Hendrix's
    Interviews 1
Working It Out
Hard Working Men

LUKE DEVALLE
Straight Talk

JACK DEVEAU
A 1970s model.
Adam & Yves

JEFF DEVINS
I Live For Sex
Principal of Lust

BRAD DEVLYN
Summer Reunion

DE'VOUR
Any Boy Can

JOHNNY DIAMOND
(see Gianfranco)

SEAN DIAMOND
(aka Chris Phifer)
Blond, boy-next-door bot-
tom star from the mid '90s.
The Backroom
Big Kahuna, The
Black Balled
Centerspread
Fantasy Fights 5 & 6
Forced Entry
Idol Worship

In The Penthouse
In Your Ear
Jawbreaker
Lava Flows
Matinee Idol
Nasty Rays
Officer And His Gentleman
Personals
Pleasures Of The Flesh
Possession
Riptide!
Sailing To Paradise
Steel Away
Travelin' Wild
Urge, The
Urgent Matters

DANIEL DIAMANI
Best Wishes
Club Taboo
Ful Load
Haulin' 'n' Ballin'
Hot to Trot
(Let Me Be Your) Loverboy
Superhunks
Switch Hitters 2
Weekend Workout

TONY DIANGELO
Hold Me Again

BRIAN DIAZ
An early '90s Latin model.
Hola!
Salt & Pepper Boys
Solo Collection 9
Tony's Initiation
Wilde House
Wrestling 10

BRUNO DIAZ
Thick as Thieves

MELCHOR DIAZ
(aka Melchor Agular)
Died in 1995 from AIDS-
related causes. One of the
first Latino porn star leg-
ends from the '80s.
Beef
The Best Stallions
Down to His Knee
Dynastud
Foreskin
Hard
Hard to Believe
Hollywood Gigolo
Hot Shots, Vol. 15: Bottoms
Hunk (as Melchor Agular)
International Skin
Lifeguard
Los Hombres
Mantalk
More Uncut Men
Mustang
The Night Boys
Nightcrawlers
Nighthawk in Leather
Nightflight
Oral Orgy
Performance
Pieces of Eight
Room for Rent
Rushes
Sexy Billy Blue
Social Studies
Solitary Sin: Eagle 8
Star Shots #4
Stiff Sentence
Strange Places, Strange
    Things
Traffic School Was Never
    Like This
Windows
Wrestling Meat

RICKY DIAZ
Boys Behind Bars 2

SONNY DIAZ
Driveshaft
Every Man's Desire
Make it Count
Nothing Else Matters
You've Got The Touch

NICK DIBONA
Off Duty

ACE DICKSON
Glory Holes of San
Francisco

MICHAEL DICKSON
Coming Soon
Sex Bazaar

SEAN DICKSON
All Night Long
Analized
Bustin' Loose
CatalinaVille
The Company We Keep
Man Watch
Mouth Organ
MVP: Most Valuable Player
Over the Rainbow
Palm Desires
Raw Material
Ripe for Harvest
Rope Tricks
The Selection Part 4 (Solo)
Self-Suckin' Dildo-Ridin'
   Rampage
Straight Men Caught on
Tape
Tormentor's Conquest
Uninvited, The
Wet Warehouse 2

Whatever You Say, Sir!

DANIEL DICICCICIO
Boys in the Sand

ERIC DI GIORGIO
(aka Eric De Giorgio)
Batdude & Throbbin'
Blow Bi Blow
Boner
The Calendar Man
Carnival
The Challenge
Cut vs. Uncut
Filth
First Timers: Amateur
   Trilogy 1
A Hole Different Ballgame
Huge Double Impact
Jet Set Sex
Laid Off
L.A. Underground
Las Vegas Orgy
Love of Lust
The Nasty Boys
Nasty Rays
A Night with Strangers
Original Recipe Home
   Video 8: Fully Loaded
Original Recipe Home
   Video 9: Hard Meat
A Scent of Man
Silverlake Inn
Steamed
Sweat Motel
Teammates
Tease Me
Texas Size 12
Tongue and Cheek
The Whole 9 Yards

DAVID DIAMANI
Best Wishes

Club Taboo
Full Load: Maximum
Overdrive
Haulin'-n-Ballin'
Let Me Be Your Lover Boy
Pegasus 2: Hot to Trot
Squirts, Vol. 8: The Pickup
Superhunks
Switch Hitters II
Twice the Fun
Weekend Workout

JOEY D'FALCO
Sex Acts

**GAVIN GEOFFREY
DILLARD**
Born in North Carolina.
Appeared in a few porn
videos in late '70s early
'80s.
Wrote a biography *In The
Flesh: Undressing for
Success* in 1998.

CAMERON DILLON
Boot Camp Buddies

JACK DILLON
Born in Kansas City,
Missouri. Brown hair, well
built, early '90s model and
6" top.
Abduction, The 2 & 3
Big Ones, The
Body Search
Butt Busters
Coming Together
Compulsion-He's Gotta
   Have It
Cruisin' 2
Powertool 2
Predators, The

JEFF DILLON
Blond, jock-next-door star
from the early '90s.
Bigger The Better 2, The
Day Dreams
Highway Hunks
Limited Entry
Magnified
Manhattan Skyline
Men At Work
Physical Education
Rassle
Thrust Fault
Voice Male

KEITH DILLON
Camp YMAC
Mountain Fever
Southbay Boys
We're Off

TROY DILLON
In Love

DAVID DILORENZO
Hot On The Trail
Sex Drive
Thick 'N Creamy

DINO DIMARCO
Hairy, mature, dark-haired
1990s model.
All American
Bad Ass Lieutenant
The Big Shot
Blade's Real World
Daddy's Revenge
Dream Lover
The Equestrian Club
Freshman Recruits
Full Body Contact
Gamemaster
Hard as Marble

The Hotel
Hungry Eyes
Journal, The
Leather Obsession 6 The
   Search
Lost In Las Vegas
Lube Job
Lust Shack
Lusty Leathermen:
Mechanic on Booty
Men of Magnum
Naked Highway
Night Walk
Pleasure Principle
Provacative
Red, Hot & Safe
Right Hand Man
Rock Off
Sex Pit #2
Sodom
South Beach Heat
The Stalker
Tailspin
Tomorrow Will Come
Uncut
Underboss, The
Wet Warehouse #3:
   The Party

ED DINAKOS
A 1980s bodybuilder and
model.
Minute Man 6 & 9
Muscle Ranch

**GEOFFREY "KAREN
"DIOR**
(aka Rick Van, Geoffrey
Karen Dior) Actor-turned-
director, songwriter and
performer. Known primarily
as a drag diva, Dior made
headline news in the '90s

as part of an Eddie Murphy
scandal. Has appreared in
many television sitcoms
and commercials.
Arms Of Forgiveness
Bedroom Eyes
Bi And Busty
Bi Golly
Black Leather, White Studs
Brats
Brown Paper Wrapper
Cut Above, A
Decent Proposal, A
Delirium
Express Male
Fag Hags
Fan Male
Foot Fetish
Frat Pack
Give It To Me Straight
Hard On Demand
Hole Different Ball Game, A
Hose Man
Immoral Thoughts
Karen's Bi-Line
Leather Weekend
Mad Masseur, The
More Than Friends
Muscle & Thickness
Night Walk
976
Painted
Personal Service
Pumping Up: Flexx 2
Pure Sex
Ripped
Rodz: Boys in the Band
Sand Blasters
Secret Sex 3: The Takeover
Solid Flesh
Steel Garters
Stickpussy
Summer School

Tennis Court Daze
To The Bone
Tough Choices
White On White

DAN DIXON
Penetration on
Pennsylvania Avenue

"Big" PETER DIXON
Born May 5, 1963 in
Chicago, Illinois. 6'3," 10-
1/4" cock. A Chicago resi-
dent, the tall, blond Dixon
also writes a column for
Gay Chicago magazine.
Born to Be Wild
Bustin' Loose
Down in the Dunes
Gypsy for Dicks
In the Bushes
The Men of Lake Michigan
Private Parts
Red, Hot & Safe
Room Service
Sleeping Booty
Toilet Room Trilogies

MIKE DIXON
California Surfsiders
Freshman Fever
Oh, So Tender

SAM DIXON
Born March 5, 1968 in
Maine. Resides in Santa
Monica, California. Former
cop-turned-pornstar-turned
director. Masculine, dark
hair, 6'0," 8" cock, top.
All You Can Eat
Bar None
Beach Head

Boomerang
Chained Desires
Exxxit From Exxxodus
Four Men
Fox Tale
Gold Diggers
Hard-core
Hawaiian Illustrated
Hollywood Knights
Homosexual Tendencies
Hot Sheets
Hustler Blue
Journal, The
Lost in Vegas
Missionary Position
Player, The
Pleasing the Master
Reform School
Confidential
Said and Done
Sex Fly
Sex Invaders
Steel Trap
Tales From The Backlot 2
The Player
Time in The Hole
Turning Tricks
Twins
Uninvited, The
XXX.Man.com
Young Men On The
Pleasure Trail

BRAD DODGER
Batter Up!

MICHAEL DODSON
All Hands On Dick
Big Boys of Summer
California Dreamin'
Ride The Swell
Streaks

DOMINO
Darkly handsome early
'90s star.
Deep End
Hard Knocks
His Big Brother
Idol Worship
Magnified
Manrammer
Manhattan Latin
One Track Mind
Other Side of Hollywood
Revenge
Rex-Take One
Toolkit

LORENZO DONADO
Stock

REX DONAHUE
Preppy Summer
They Work Hard For The
Money

TODD DONAHUE
Bad Boys Club
Buddy System
Freshman
Good Men Get Bad
Motel California
Pleasure Peak
Power Force
Spring Break

CHRIS DONNEL
Jamie Hendrix's
Interviews 1

CASEY DONOVAN
(Real name Cal Culver)
Born November 2, 1943 in
East Bloomfield, New York.
Died August 10, 1987 in

Florida from AIDS-related illness. A star of the 1970s, considered by most to be the first gay porn superstar. Roger Edmonson's biography: "Boy In The Sand, Casey Donovan: All-American Sex Star" was published in 1998 and is a must-read for porn fans.
The Back Row 1972
The Best of Superstars
Boys in the Sand
Boys in the Sand, Part 2
Casey
Chance of a Lifetime
Dracula
Erotikus: A History of the Gay Movie
Forty Plus
Fun and Games
Fucked Up 1986
Hand in Hand Preview Tape #1
Heatstroke
Hotshots
Inevitable Love
L.A. Tool and Die
Men & Film (as Cal Culver)
Men In The Sand
Moving
Non-Stop
The Other Side of Aspen
P.M. Preview Tape #4
Sleaze
Split Image
Superstars
Non-adult film roles:
Ginger
Misty Beethoven
Score

CHAD DONOVAN
Dark-haired, handsome and hung star from the '90s. Last seen living in Los Angeles.
Auto Fellatio
Beat Off Frenzy
Big As They Come 2
Biker Pigs From Hell
Blow Me Down
By Invitation Only
Chained Desire
Chip Daniels' Video Studbook
Come and Get It
Deep End
Hot Cops 3
Jockstrapped
J.S. Big Time
Just Guys
Man Country
Mavericks
Nights in Eden
Party Line
Pitch a Tent
Rawhide
Ryker's Revenge
Secret Sex 2
Trophies
Workin' Stiff

RICK DONOVAN
A 1980s legendary top with one of the biggest dick's in porn history. 5'11," 10" cock. Resides in San Diego.
The Arousers
Bi and Beyond
Big and Thick
The Big Ones
The Bigger the Better
The Biggest One I

Ever Saw
The Boys of Company F
Captain Stud and his Seamen Dish
Cum Shots 102
Dynastud 1 & 2
The Few, The Proud, The Naked 1&2
Getting It
Giants, Part 1
Hard to Come By
Hard to Swallow
Heroes
Hot Shots, Vol. 1, 3, 4, 20, 26, 30
Ivy League
King Size
Latin Tongues
Leo Ford: The Making of a Superstar
Lifeguard
Men and Steel
More of a Man
On Top
Paul Norman's World of Sexual Oddities
Pleasure Mountain
Private Collection
Private Collection
Screentest
Screentest
Sailor in the Wild
She's a Boy
Sgt. Swann's Private Files
Star Shots #1
Stick Shift
Think Big
Video Games, Vol. 1 & 2
William Higgins Preview Tape #2

ROD DONOVAN
Think Big

TONY DONOVAN
(aka Mike Donovan)
Born March 29, 1979 in
Los Banos, California.
Resides in Los Angeles,
California. Boyishly good
looking, 5' 9," 13" cock.
Entered the biz at 18,
straight out of high school.
The Dream Team
Freaks
Getting Straight
Guarding the Jewels
Hardbody 2000
Meet Jake/Solo
Ryker's Revenge
Something Very Big
Technical Ecstasy

DREW DORNAN
Hot to Trot

CHAD DOUGLAS
A masculine, porn star
daddy from the 1980s.
Below the Belt
Big Guns
Giant Splash Shots 2
Hot Shots, Vol. 25: Brief
Encounters
In Your Wildest Dreams
Larger Than Life
Manrammer
Man Size
Seduction
Someone's Watching
Spokes 2: The Graduation
Spring Break
Tyger Tales

CHIP DOUGLAS
Mikey Likes It
Physical Education

MATT DOUGLAS
Wild Sex In America

**ETHAN ALEXANDER
DRAKAR**
The Other Side of Big
  Bear

MATT DRAKE
Fast Action

RICK DRAKE
Another Man's Pleasure
Best Of Leather: Part 2
Dream Lover
Friction
Guy Next Door, The
Hole, The
Hose 'Em Down
Hot Guys #3
Hot Springs Orgy
Hot Stuff
Into Leather
It Happened One Day
Just One Favor
Leather Playhouse
Measuring Up
Obsessive Desires
The Pornographer
Prisoners Of Lust
Sexx Pitt
Visit, The
While I Was Sleeping

LEE DRIVER
Sit Tight

PAVEL DUBCEK
(aka Max Pellion)
One of the new breed of
'young 90s stars from the
Czech Republic.
Americans in Paris

Andel's Story
Andel's Story 2: The
  Running of the Bulls
Czech Is In The Male
Frisky Summer 2
Inn Bi The Road
Mantasy Island
Puda

ASHLEY DUBOIS
Broadway Boys
Subway
Trisexual

JAVIER DURAN
A cute, young, Latin model
and native of Argentina dis-
covered in the late '90s.
Argentine Tangle
Bye Bi Buenos Aires
God Was I Drunk
Hot Times in Little Havana
How The West Was Hung
Mantasy Island
Read Bi All
Spiked

NOUR DUSTIN
Anonymous Sex
Hairsteria

DWAN
Anything, Anytime
Chain Reaction
Christopher Rage's Orgy
Fade In
Fantasy Man
Hot Shots, Vols. 35 and 40
Inevitable Love
Jailmates
Man O' Man
Rodeo
Squirts #2: Two Meets One

Squirts #3: Hot Encounters
Stud Struck
Windows

LOU DYE
Eyes of a Stranger
High Riders

KENNY DYNELL
Manholes
My Masters
Raunch 2
Toilet Tramps

KEITH DYSON
The Intruders
Skin Torpedoes
Superhunks

E

JON EAGLE
9-1/2"

MATTHEW EASTON
Born April 11. A 1990s
model.
Alley Boys
Journey, The
Mr. Footlong's Made In
America
On The Prowl
Pick Up
Positively Yours
Ryker Files, The
A Tale Of Two Brothers

SHAWN EASTON
Big Shooters 4
Body Scorcher
Fade In
L.A. Boiling Point

Rangers
Rodeo

JOHN EDDY
Too Big to Handle

EDUARDO
Born February 15, 1968,
Cuba. 5'10", 8" uncut.
Versatile. A hairy, Latin
hunk and late '90s model.
Alex's Leather Dream
All About Sex
Alley Boys
Analized
Australian For Leather
Bewitching
Biker Pigs From Hell
Boomerang
Born To Please
Brief Tales
Chasing Andy
Cheap Motel Sex
Chicago Erection Company
Clubhouse
Customer Service
Dallas Does Hawaii
Desert Train
Expose
Fault Line Sex Time
Fully Serviced
Gang of 13
Hairsteria
Hair Trigger
Hairway To Heaven
Hairy Chested Hunks
Happily Ever After
Hard On Demand
INNdulge Palm Springs
Jeff Stryker Underground
Knight Men #3:
    Thick & Throbbing
Latin Obsession

Latin Showboyz
Leather Bound
Leather Men 1 & 2
Leather Obsession 6
Leather Triangle
Leather Virgin
Leather Weekend
Long Play
Lost Loves
Love Money
Male Order Sex
Marine Fever
Matador
Men Together
Men With Tools 2: Nailed
Morning, Noon & Night
Mountain Jock
Naked Truth
Natural Born Driller
No Faking It
Nude Science
Online Connections
Physical Exam
Portrait of Lust
Priority Male
Pure Sex
Raw Discipline
Raw Street Meat
Rip 'n' Strip Wrestling
Said & Done
San Francisco Sex
The Selection 3
Sex and Sensuality
Sex in Leather
Sexual Suspect
Shoot 'N' Porn
Special Forces
Straight Men:
    Caught on Tape
Studio Tricks
Sudden Urge
Things You Can Do
    in Leather

Threesome
Tomorrow Will Come
Tools Of The Trade
Try Again
Weekend Sex Camp
Wet Warehouse 2

BURT EDWARDS
Handsome, blond, boyish-looking jock-next-door 1980s model.
Blue Summer Breeze
Brothers
Hurts So Good
I Want More
Out Of Control
Riverman

DEAN EDWARDS
A 1990s model.
Home Bodies

JOE EDWARDS
A 1990s model.
Black Men Do!

LUKE EDWARDS
Boot Camp Buddies

MARK EDWARDS
Body Scorcher
Fade Out
Making It Huge
The Spirit Is Willing

EL GRECO
Born October 29 in Czech Republic. Light brown hair, 6'2," 6" uncut.
Andel's Story 2: The
    Running of the Bulls
Impromptu
Inn By the Road

Mantasy Island

ALEX EINGANG
Casting Couch
Master Hyde
A Young Man From
Nantucket

BILL ELD
1970s model.
Adam & Yves
Best of Colt
Connoisseur Collector
Classics
Destroying Angel
Good Hot Stuff
Inside Bill Eld
Pool Party
Reflections of Youth
Rip Colt's Sex-Rated
Home Movies
Sex Magic
Strictly Forbidden
Try To Take It
Workmen's Compensation

FRANK EMMANUEL
Coming Soon
Street Smart

BRUCE EMORY
Minute Men 4

JON ERIC
Mature, late 1990s model with light brown hair.
Bootie Nights
Mass Appeal
Technical Ecstasy

CARL ERIK
Born June 6. A mid '90s daddy.

Les Hommes Au Natural
The Other Side of Aspen 3
The Other Side of Aspen 4
Possession
Sure Shot
Woody's

BRAD ERICKSEN
Hairy daddy star from the mid '90s.
Best Of Leather: Part 1
A Brother's Desire
Cool Moon
Don't Hold Back
Hair Klub For Men Only
Hardball
Honorable Discharge
In The Jeans
J.S. Big Time
Leather Obsession
Leather Obsession 4 -
    Forever
Leather Party
Made To Get Laid
Men Of Forum
Model Behavior
Naughty Little Brother
Ninety Dirty Minutes
Orgies Pt 1
Porno Tonight Show, The
Protector, The
Raw Recruits
The Road To Hopeful
Single White Male
Slip It In
Summer's Tall Tales
This End Up
Tough Terrain
X-Treme Closeup

LEIGH ERICKSON
(aka Marc Bennett)
A porn star legend from the

'80s.
Big & Thick
Giant Men
Giants
Hot Men
In Your Wildest Dreams
Men in Motion 1 & 6
Nightflight
Rockhard
Size Talks
Sizing Up
Splash Shots II
Too Big For His Britches
The Troy Saxon Gallery 1

PETER ERICKSON
Any Way I Can
Shooting Stars

SHANE ERICKSON
Boyish, blond-haired, blue-
eyed, 1980s model.
Cover Models
Surf's Up

TONY ERICKSON
(see Tony Sinatra)

ALVIN EROS
Fire In The Hole
Leather Lust
Principal of Lust
Sex Is In The Air

RICK ESTEPHAN
Born January 3, 1968, San
Juan, Puerto Rico. 5'8", 9
1/2" uncut. Top.
Ace in Your Face
Alley Katts
Bare Bodies
Black Boot Diaries
Black Mischief

Breathless
Brother to Brother
California Creamin'
Chicago Erection Co.
Das Butt
Dynastud #3
Flasher
Full Release
Hot Sex Pick-Up
Le Sex Salon
Leather Connection
Leather Dreams
Leather Intrusion #3
Leather Party
Look Of Leather
Lusty Leathermen:
Mechanic on Booty
Married Men
Men Under Siege
Naked Underneath
Mr. Blue
Oklahomo
Weho Confidential
Runway Studs
Sex Hostage
Straight Cocksuckers

BRIAN ESTEVEZ
(aka Mike Raymond &
Michael Wayne) dark-
haired, late '80s model.
Bisexual a Go-Go
Bi-Sexual Fantasies
California Dreamin'
Catalina Blonds
Cross Over (bi)
Engine 69
Frat Brats
Glory Hole of Fame
Guys Who Eat Cum
Hard Fucking Buddies
Heavenly
Hung Guns

Incessant
In Deep
In the Raw
Inside Expose
Manstroke
Men At Work
Men in Motion 3 & 5
Powertool
Seduction III: Passion
Obsession
Seduction V: Taking Full
   Charge
Show It Hard
Throb
The Young and the Hung

BILLY EVANS
(see David Ashfield)

CORY EVANS
After Hours
All Night Long
Behind The Barn Door
Come As You Are
Fighting Dirty
For Your Pleasure
Handjobs 2
Hardhats
Johnny Hormone
Pinned
The Pornographer
Ripe For Harvest
Sperminator, The
Thursday Morning Workout
1230 West Melrose
Visit, The
We've Got Them All
While I Was Sleeping

ERIC EVANS
Born December 28, 1966,
in Woodland Hills,
California. Resides in

Burbank, California. 5'10,"
7 1/2" cock. Hairy, mature
star from the '90s.
All American Man 2
At Your Service
Australian For Leather
Balls To The Wall
    Vol. 8-10 & 20
The Bartender
Below the Decks
Best of Leather 3
California Blonds #2
Chicago Bound
Cockland
Come With Me
Coming Together
Conflict of Interest
Cruising Grounds
The Cut Club
Desert Hart
The Equestrian Club
Fetish Sex Fights 2, 3
Gates of Hell
Gay for the Weekend
The Getaway
Getting it Firm
Good Vibrations
Greased Lightening
Grizzly
Hard Bodyguard
Hawaiian Dreams
He's Worth It
Hole Patrol
The Hotel
Hotel L.A.
In Your Face
Inside Men 2
Iron Stallions
Juice Bomb
Knight Moves
Laid for Work
Las Vegas Love Gods
Leather Men

Love of Lust
The Making Of A Gay
    Video
Male Box
Maximum Maxon Video
Measuring Up
Melrose Manor
Mesmerized
Motel Cowboys
On-line Connections
The Protector
Prowl, 1 & 2
The Rainman
Rough Road Ahead
Sex Between The Lines
Sex Bi-Lex
Sex Hostage
Sodom
Stiff
Switch Hitters #10
Taxi Tales
Tight Rope Series 29 & 30
Tough Terrain
Troy Likes It
Unique Gay Positions
Wear It Out
Wet Dreams
When The Wife's Away

ROB EVANS
Doctor's Orders 2

MARK EVERETT
Get it On Line
Gut Reaction
Handball Marathon 3
Leather Bound
Leather Obsession 4
Mo' Betta Butt
Sexx Pitt
Working Stiff

JOSH EVERS
Born June 17, 1977, Los
Angeles. 5'10," 6" cock.
Versatile.
Bootie Nights
Getting Ahead
Lap It Up
976-Stud
1-800-Hunk
The Pounderosa
Sexpionage
Trail Blazers
Wanna Be In Pictures?
Weekend at my Brothers
www.Orgy

F

NICK FABRINI
A dark-haired, hairy chest-
ed, well hung late 1980s
model.
Better Than Ever
Big Memories
Cum Shots 102
The Exchange
Flexx
Hot Shjots, Vol. 21:
    Big Ones!
Manimal
More
The Size Counts
Some Men are Bigger
Than Others
Sun-Kissed
Surge Men at Their Best
Think Big
Try Anything Once
Video Games #8

FABRITZIO
Hotel Montreal

Party In My Pants

GRANT FAGAN
(aka Grant Fagin, Devon
Adams) Brown-haired,
youthful boy-next-door
model from the late 1980s.
Auto Erotica: The Best of
   Sex in Cars
Boys in the Office
The Boys of Summer
First Experiences
Growing Years
I Lick It 'Cuz I Like It
Interview, Vol. 4
Jackhammer
Knight Moves
Make Me Hard
The Moon Also Rises
Motel California
The Pizza Boy—He
   Delivers
Private Moments
Rebel (as Devon Adams)
The Return of Grant Fagin
Southern Comfort
Spring Semester
Too Big for His Britches
The Young and the Hung

JOE FALCO
Leather Report
Minute Man 2

GIORGIO FALCONI
Actor turned agent.
Black & Blue
Exile
For His Own Good
GV Guide All-Star Softball
   Game 1
Leather Temptation
O Is For Orgy

One Track Mind
Over The Edge
Sex And The Single Man
Tell Me About Sex
Tight Leather
Top Man Security
Top Men

JOHN FARLEY
Powertool
Styker Force

TOM FARRELL
Died September 2, 1993
after being struck by a hit
and run driver.
Cops, Jocks & Military
   Feet
Corporate Head
Easy Riders
Foot Loose
Grapplin'
Huge Double Impact
Jumper
Muscleforce
My Own Private Kentucky
   Studs
On The Lookout
Rearended
Scorcher
Sexpress
Shake That Thing
Shooters
Straight Studs 2
The Visitor
Wild Obsession
Wild Streak

**CODY FEELGOODE
(see Randy Mixer)**

JANOS FEKETE
An American In Prague

Johan's Big Chance

JEFF FELICIANO
 All Heated Up
Big Deposit
Crossing Over
Driven By Lust
Latin Sex Thing
Touch me There
While the Cat's Away

JOHN FELL
Forbidden Portraits
Sex, Lives & Video
Cassettes
Ten Is Enough

JOHN FERAGE
Call to Arms

KORATH FERENG
Dark and slightly hairy
young 1999 Hungarian
model.
Hungarian Heat
Raging River

DON FERNANDO
Dreams Bi Night
Switch Hitters 2 & 4

SASCHA FETISOV
Johan's Big Chance

CODY FIELDS
(aka Kody Fields,
Christopher Zale)
A 1990s models.
Always Available
Apply Within
As Big as it Gets
Back to K-Waikiki
The Crusin' Game

Danger Zone
The Equestrian Club
Hard to Keep Down
Hard Working Men
Hot Spot
Insertion
Jeff Stryker's Underground
L.A. Daze
Link
Locker Room Lust
Lovers Lane
Orgies Pt 1
Phi Kappa Sucka
Playboys, The
Quick Relief
Raw Meat 1
Reform School
Confidential
Rent to Bone
Romping Roommates
Saving Ryan's Privates
Something's Up
Spankfest 6
S.S. Gigantic
Steel Trap
Straight Exposure
Uniform Ball 1-2
Warehouse Heat
While the Cat's Away

DOMINICK FILLA
An American In Prague
Johan's Big Chance

RICHIE FINE
Popular boyish-looking
'90s model.
Club 18-23
Fine Daze
Forest Rump
Hand of Fate
Hot Guys #2
Hustler Blue

It's Raining Men
Pleasure Principle
Skateboard Sliders
Sliders
So Fine
Things to Come

DICK FISK
1970s star killed in an auto
accident.
The Axe Master
Cruisin' the Castro
Help Wanted
More Dick Fisk
The New Breed
The Other Side of Aspen
Spokes
Steam Heat
Try to Take It

PETER FISK
Bijou
Boys in the Sand

TYLER FLANNERY
San Diego resident. Will
always be known as one
of the pornstars who was
befriended by Andrew
Cunanan.
A Tale of Two Brothers

DIRK FLETCHER
Discovered by Chi Chi
LaRue.
Boot Black
Courting Libido

LON FLEXXE
(aka Lon Flexx)
Born January 7, 1965.
Died September 15, 1995
from AIDS-related causes.

Was a resident of West
Hollywood and a New
Mexico native.
Bad Boys
The Best of All Matt
Sterling 1 & 2
The Best of Joey Stefano
Big Bang
Billboard
Blow Your Own Horn
Boys on the Block
California Stud Puppy
Commercial Sex
Cousins Should Do It
Cowboys & Indians
Cum Shots 102
Davey & the Cruisers
Dish
Fidelity
For Sale by Owners
GV Guide Gay Erotic
    Video Awards 2
Hard Balls
Hard Moves
Hard Labor
Heat in the Night
He-Devils
Hot Shots, Vol. 41:
    Rim Shots
Hot Shots, Vol. 44:
    Golden Boys
Inside Expose
The International Guide to
Fellatio
John Summers' Screentest
    Mag. 1
Just Between Us, You
    Promise
Knights of Thunder
Lunch Hour
Lustful Paradise
Male Taboo
Manstroke

Men At Work
The Men of Tough Guys
More of a Man
Personals
The Plunge
Ranger Nick II
The Rockmore Files
Sailor in the Wild 2
Sex in the Great
Outdoors 3
Sex, Lies and
Videocassettes
Sex Shooters
Sexmates
Some Men are Bigger
Than Others
Steel Pulse
Straight Boys Do
Straight Up
Stud Squad
Ten is Enough
Tough Guys Do Dance
Trade-Off
Untamed

BILLY FLYNN

A very cute, brown-haired,
barely legal, boy next door
model from the early '90s,
with a huge dick. Unfort-
unately, he didn't stick
around long.
Fresh
Home Movies

MASON FLYNT

Born June 20, 1969,
Lexington, Massachusetts.
6'2," 9 cock, top. A 1990s,
dark-haired, mature, porn
star daddy. Lives in Los
Angeles.
Fetish Sex Fights #2

Hellrazer
Lap It Up
Prowl 1 & 2

DEAN FORBES

Locker Jocks

DOUG FORBES

Dark-haired, mature, mid
'90s model.
Another Man's Pleasure
Big Showoff
Leather Story
A Letter To Three Men
One Man's Poison
The Road to Hopeful

AL FORD

(aka Malcolm Ford)
All American Boys In Heat
Boys of Baja
Cashload
Fast Friends
Hard at It, Vol. 2
Hot Shots, Vol. 20: Ticket
Home
Hot Shots, Vol. 30: Hot
Jocks
On Top
Picklin' the Cucumber
Private Pool Party
Quickies #7
Sunstroke
Thumbs Up

BRETT FORD

All Man
Badlands
Bedroom Eyes
Beginnings
Blowout
Boot Black
Butt Munch

Choose me
Dicked
Dirty Pillow Talk
Dominator
Dreams Come True
Elements of Passion
Fighting Dirty
Flesh and Fantasy 2
The Fluffer
Hot Pursuit
Idol Dreams
The Initiation
Knight Gallery 2
Long Play
The Lure
Man to Man
Mack Pack, Vol. 1-4
The Midnight Sun
My Cousin Danny
One and Only Dominator
Original Sin
Play With Size
Playing With Power
Ryker's Revenge
Sex Invaders
Sex In Wet Places
Sex Posse
Sexpress
Soaked
Songs in the Key of Sex
Stockade
Stud Ranch
The Swallowers
Technical Ecstasy
These Bases Are Loaded 2
Time Cops
To Protect and Serve
Uncle Jack
X-tasy

BUCK FORD

Confessions
Motor Sexual

CARL FORD
Chained
Sons of Satan
Station to Station

DAMIEN FORD
Born July 17.
Goodfellas/Badfellas
Red Blooded Americans
Take One: Guys Like Us

DANE FORD
All the White Boys
The Best of Times
Big Shooters #5
Blown Away
Body Scorcher
Boyfriends
Boys Camp Memories
California Dreamin'
Cruisin' West Hollywood
Deep Inside
Delicious
Down to His Knee
Firsts
Full House
Getting It
Hollywood Gigolo
Hot Shots, Vol. 8: Orgies
Hot Shots, Vol. 10, Sweat
Hot Shots, Vol. 37: Penal
  Code
Hot Splash
J. Brian's Flashbacks
Male-O-Gram
Mansplash
Midnight Special #2
Nine-and-a-Half Inches
Plug Me Up
Preppy Summer
The Prostitute
Splash Shots 2
Summer Heat

Tall Tales
Teddy's Bare
Totally Awesome
An Uncontrollable
  Obsession
Video Games #6
Video Games #10

KENNY FORD
Call to Arms

LEO FORD
Born in Dayton, Ohio. Died
July 15, 1991 in a motor-
cycle accident while living
in Hawaii. A blond super-
star of the '80s, Ford was
a versatile top or bottom
and will always be consid-
ered one of the biggest
names in the biz.
Best Bi Far
The Best of Blonds
The Best of Blonds 2
Blonds Do It Best
Carnal College
Catalina Blonds
Catalina Down and Dirty
Catalina Orgies, Vol. 1
Class Reunion
Director's Best: William
  Higgins 1
Games
Hot Shots, Vol. 3: Cum
  Contest
Hot Shots, Vol. 4: Contest
  Continues
Hot Shots, Vol. 9: Hot
  Blonds
J. Brian's Flashbacks
Leo & Lance
Leo Ford: The Making of a
  Superstar

(dir. & actor)
Lifeguard
New York City Pro
New Zealand Undercover
Passion by Fire: The Big
  Switch, 2
Rock 'n' Roll Peep Show
Sailor in the Wind
Santa Monica Blvd.
Spokes
Star Shots #4
Stiff Sentence
Style
The Summer of Scott Noll
William Higgins Preview
  Tape #2

NICK FORD
Manhungry
Mercury Rising
Red Alert

RAFE FORD
You've Got Male

RANDY FOREMAN
Basic Plumbing 2
Manwatcher

MATT FOREST
Late '80s, early '90s, dark-
haired model.
Angelo Loves It
Battle of the Bulges
Big Time
Bi-Cepts
Boystown
Down for the Count
Eighteen Candles
Full Grown
Full Blown
Full House
Gotta Have It

Hot on His Tail
Motel California
Perfect 10
Pleasure Peak
Pounder
Sunstroke
Switch Hitters
Tall Tales
Throb

ALEX FORREST
Angelo Love It
Battle of the Bulges
Big Time
Bi-Cepts
Boystown
Down for the Count
Eighteen Candles
Full Grown, Full Blown
Full House
Gotta Have It
Hot on His Tail
In Heat
Motel California
Perfect 10

BRENNAN FOSTER
Cute, blond 1990s Falcon
exclusive. Looks like he
could be Kevin Williams'
younger brother.
Basic Plumbing 2
Current Affairs
French Connections 1-2
Hotwired: Viewers' Choice
Red Alert
Summer Reunion: The
    Best Parts of Summer

CODY FOSTER
A Denver native with light
brown hair and all-
American good looks.

1990s model.
Basic Plumbing
Bi-Ology
Bigger The Better 2, The
Cody Exposed
Grease Guns
Malibu Pool Boys
Reunion
Star Gazing
Whitefire
Workin' Stiff

DEVYN FOSTER
(aka Monte Fiero)
A darkly handsome, Latin-
looking star from the mid
'90s.
Bedroom Lies
Boot Black 2
Captain Stud And His
    Seamen
Centerspread 1-3
Fire In The Hole
Foulplay
GV Guide All-Star Softball
    Game: #1
Hand To Hand
The Hole
Hole Patrol
Illicit Love
The Initiation
Intensive
Limited Entry
Meanstreak
Mentor
New Pledgemaster
Oral Fixation
Original Sin
Personals
Prisoner Of Love
Rival, The
Santa Monica Place
Smooth Operator

Trickmaster
True Stories
Urge, The
Voyeur

RAINY FOSTER
Happily Ever After

ALLAN FOX
(aka Allen Fox)
Hard Men 2
Hot Rods
Rock Hard
Uncontrollable Obsession

CAMERON FOX
Very cute, jock-next-door
brunet. Late 1990s model.
In Deep: Miles To Go
Serviced
Sting: A Taste For Leather

CHRISTIAN FOX
Born in Canada in 1974.
Died from a reported drug
overdose October 1996 in
New Orleans, where he
lived. A cute, blond, gay-
for-pay bottom, Fox is pic-
tured on the cover of this
book.
Big River
Blowout
Chance Encounter
Chi Chi Larue's Hardbody
    Video Mag. #4
Courting Libido
Dirty Pillow Talk
Driven Home
The Guy Next Door
House Rules
Hung Up
In Man's Country

Knight Gallery 2
Long Play
Look Of A Man
Manhattan Skyline
Matinee Idol
Power Trip
Quick Study
Roll In The Hay
Summer Fever
Wet Dreamers
Whitefire

DYLAN FOX

Six foot-one, Fox hailed
from the South.
Arms of Forgiveness
Bi Inferno
Big Box Office
Big Delivery
Brats
California Dream Inn
Cops, Jocks & Military
   Feet
Corporate Head
A Cut Avoce
Delusion
Dirty Dreaming
Down Home
Drifters, The
Flesh Den
For His Eyes Only
Hell Weekend
Hologram
Hot Ticket
Immoral Thoughts
L.A. Boot Bottom
Male Seduction
More Than Just Strangers
Neighborhood Games
Prison
Private Invitation of Billy
   Houston
The Producer

Savage Blue
Secret Shore Leave
Selling It
Sex Depot
Sex Shooters
Shake That Thing
Slave Trainer
Songs in the Key of Sex
Steel Garters
Stiff Piece
Stud Ranch
Tennis Court Daze
The Thick of It
Toe The Line
Two Fistfuls
Waterworks

GUY FOX

Handsome, young 1980s
model. Brother of Scott
Fox.
Bound Boys In Slave
   Hollow
Going Down On The Farm
More Guys In Bondge
Shaving Studs
Slave Boy Toy
Slave's Submissions
Tickling 101

KASPER FOX

Balls of the Wild

MICHAEL FOX ('80s)

Black Hombres
Black Shafts
Blond And Blond
Getting Down

MICHAEL FOX

9-1/2"

NED FOX

Chained
Sons of Satan

RYAN FOX

(aka Rob Banks)
Blond, buffed, mid '90s
model.
Centerspread 3
Fox's Lair
Powertrip

SCOTT FOX

Young, 1980s model and
brother of Guy Fox.
Bound Boys In Slave
   Hollow
Foot Frenzy
Going Down On The Farm
Shaving Studs
Slave Boy Toy

SEAN FOX

(aka Dusty and Dusty
Sands) Discovered by
William Higgins in 1982.
Best Little Warehouse in
L.A.
Bi Dream of Genie
Concrete Lover
Dream Doll
Fond Focus
He-Devils
Hollywood Hunks
Interview, Volume 2
Just Between Us, You
   Promise
Lewd Conduct
A Little Nookie (hetero)
Low Blows
Private Cover Boy
The Rodz
Secret Action Man

Stud Vision
Switch Hitters V: The Night
  Games
Tongue Dancing

STEVE FOX
(Rommel E. Hunt)
Born July 4, 1965. Committed suicide, using a handgun, October 23, 1997, in a Georgia hotel room. 6'2," blond bottom. Discovered by John Summers.
All American
Buttbusters
Compulsion
Flashpoint
Foul Play
Fox's Lair
Johnny Hormone
Secret Shore Leave

TOM FOX
(aka Tom Foxx)
A 1980s model.
After Hours
When Straight Men Stray

TY FOX
(Jeffrey Dion Bruton)
Top man Ty reportedly lost his his wife and his job as a high school PE teacher when he was outed as a pornstar in 1997 by *The Washington Post.*
Come and Get It
Cream of the Crop
Down on It
Fox Tales
Fox's Lair
Hawaiian Illustrated
Hot Day In L.A.

Manhattan Skyline
Man Construction
Playing With Fire
Revenge of the Bi Dolls
Ty Me Up
Ty's Back
White Fire

TONY FRANCO
Full Grown, Full Blown

DANTE FRANKLIN
Black Rose, The
Hung Man Meat
Pumping Black

JOHN FRANKLIN
Crossing Over

ROSS FRANKLIN
Oh, Brother!

SCOTT FREE
Hold Me Again

**RICHARD FRENCH & ROBERT FRENCH
(see Danny Brown)**

JOE FULLER
A late 1970s model.
Down for the Count
Someone's Sons
Wrestling 34

LANE FULLER
A California native and former marine. Resides in San Diego. Boyfriend of Kevin Williams.
Absolute Aqua
Tales From The Foxhole

MIKE FULLER
Doctor's Orders 1 & 2

TODD FULLER
An early '90s model.
All the Way In
Bedroom Eyes
The Boy Next Door
Coming Home
The Cut Club
Glory Hole of Fame 2
Heat
Knight Moves
Loaded
Marine Muscle
Off Duty Maneuvers
One Night Stand
Rimshot
The Rolls
Straight Studs
Two Fistful
Warhead

PAT FULTON
Four In Hand
Gunslingers
Little Brother's Coming Out
Made to Order
Winners Circle

G

AARON GAGE
A porn star legend from the early '80s.
Bi Heat, Vol. 6, 8, 10
Brian's Boys
Catalinas Down & Dirty
Catalina Orgies, Vol. 1
Class Reunion
Dirty Tricks
Dreaming About Dick

Leo and Lance
Sailor In The Wild
Sex in the Great Outdoors
	1 & 2
Student Bodies
Winner Takes All

NICHOLAS GAGE
Hawaiian Vacation 1 & 2

JOHN GAINES
(see John King)

ANTHONY GALLO
(Antonio Morias)
Analized
Black Passion
Blatino Party L.A.
Butt Bruisers
Chicago Bearfest
Cop Sins
Court Martial
Doctor's Orders 2
Fantasies of White and
Black
Forced Service
From Hair to Eternity
Gang Of 13
Getting In Tight
Hell Razer 3: The Sacrifice
Homeboy Gets It...All
Huddle Up
Hung Riders, The
Inside Karl Thomas
Internal Affairs
Invaders From URanus
Jawbreaker
Johnny Hormone
Latin Cops
Latin Obsession
Latins
Leather Obsession 6: The
	Search

Locker Room Sex Brawl
A Love Story
Lusty Leathermen:
	Mechanic On Booty
Man Country
Man Watch
Meet Ray Harley
Men With Tools
Measure For Measure
Millitary Issue 3:
	Ask & I'll Tell
Moving Target
Night Feast
Orgies Pt 4
Party Line
Peep-O-Rama!
Receiving End
Runway Studs
Secret Sex 3: The
Takeover
Sexpionage
Sleeping Booty
Smell Of A Man 2
Special Forces
Straight Cocksuckers
Stud Valley
Together Again
Top It Off
Uncut Glory
Undress for Success
Viva Latino!
Wanted

ALEX GAMBLE
Black Muscle Machine 2

FLEX GAMBLE
Mature-looking, shaved-
headed, African American
model from the late 1990s.
Black Power
Black Rose, The
Black Warriors

Penal Pen Pals
Stroke My Digits

JOSE GARCIA
(aka Jose Del Norte)
Dick Day Afternoon
Room Service Plus
Valley Boys
Wilde House
Wrestling 7, 13, 14, 22

DENNY GARDNER
Battle of the Bulges
Hot Latinos

ROD GARETTO
Born August 7.
Angels By Day, Devils Bi
Night
Back in the Saddle Again
Balls to the Wall 35
Basket Fever
Bed Tales
The Best of Jonathan
	Strong
Best of Sam Abdul
Bi & Busty
Bi Inferno
Bi Intruder
Bi Madness
Bi Medicine
Bi Mistake
Bi Spy
Big Memories
Black & Latino Working
	Hard
Black Salsa
Boot Camp 1 & 2
Bound to Please, Vol. 1
The Boxer 1 & 2
Casting Couch
Cat Burgler
The Cherry

Come Clean
Convertible Blues
Cybersex
Delicious
Dorm Fever
Dream Doll
Dueling Dicks
Fag Hags
Fantasy Boys
Fantasy Bytes
Filth
Gays, Bis, She-Males &
    Hermaprhodites
Getting It On
Great Balls of Fire
Guys with Tight Asses
Hardcorps
Hard-On Hard Bodies
Hard Labor
Health Club Gigolo
Highway Hunks
Hoghounds 2
Hombres
Horsemeat
Hot Cocks
Hot Shots, Vol. 42: Face
    Shots
Hot Shots, Vol. 49: Torrid
    Trios
Hot Shots, Vol. 50: Men at
    Work
How Big is Danny?
Hung and Dangerous
Inside Vladimir Correa
In The Jeans
Interview, Vol. 1
Just Men
Latin Instinct
Latin Magic
Latin Power
Latinos Working Hard
Lee Hunter's Laguna
    Adventure

Los Hombres
Low Blows
Made To Get Laid
Male Instinct
Male Taboo
Manhandler
Manstroke
Men of Steel
My Fantasy
Naval Focus
Need You Tonight
Obsession: Hot Rods of
    Steel
Old Reliable #114: The
    Size of the Matter
Old Reliable #156
Old Reliable #158: Hola!
One Hot Day
Pool Man
Queens Behind Bars
Rock-hard
The Rod Squad
Romeo and Julian
Rump Ranger
Salsa Fever
Screwing Screw-Ups
Secrets and Fantasies
Sex Change
Show it Hard
Show it Off
Sunday Brunch
Swap Meat
Sweat Motel
Switch Hitters VI: Back in
    the Bullpen
Taken by Storm
Tattoo Parlor
Temptation
Tight Jeans
Tommy Boy
Top to Bottom
Tough Guys Do Dance
Vice Cop

The Voyeur
Whistle While You Work

EDDIE GARFIELD
Naked City Nights
Wild Side
Young Yankees

AXEL GARRETT
Born in 1969. Cute, young,
boyish and blond, this ex-
military man, discovered by
Dirk Yates, became popular
in 1989. He made a come-
back in 1999.
Dirk Yates' Private
    Collection
Family Affair, A
Few, The Proud, The
Naked, The 1&2
How The West Was Hung
Kiss Off
Men For All Seasons
Miss Kitty's Litter (bi)
Reflections 2
Trade-Off

BO GARRETT
Born December 25, 1968,
Mobile, Alabama. Resides
in Nevada. 6'2," 10" cock,
Top. This daddy is known
for his full-body tattoos.
Biker Pigs From Hell
Just Men
Mavericks
Nightwatch 2
Rebel Biker
Saddle Tramps 2
Slick

ROY GARRETT
Died April 3, 1992 from

AIDS-related causes.
Anything, Anytime
Boots and Saddles
Cell Block #9
Centurians of Rome
Forbidden Portraits
Handsome
Heatstroke
Hot Shots, Vol. 13:
Bisexual
Men Come First
Red Ball Express
Tough Guys
Young Ones

TAD GARRETT
Arms Of Forgiveness
Blue Collar- White Heat
Fast Company
Horny Rent Collector
Knight Heat
Mindscape
Naked Prey
Neighborhood Games
Night With Strangers, A
Producer, The
Selling It
Smoky

ALLAN GASSMAN
Big Deposit
Crossing Over
Desert Paradise 1 & 2
Red, Hot & Safe

MICHAEL GAYLORD
Action at Melrose
Back to Front
The Big Lift
Black & Blue
Bone Alone
Built to Last
Cheap Trick

Cut Loose
Deliver Ring
Dirty Laundry
Fast Company
Fever
Friend to Friend
Jet Set Sex
Joey
Leather Angel
The Mad Masseur
Movin'
Newcomers
976
No Fluff, Just Stuff
Return to Badlands
Secret Dreams
Snowbumz
Stockade Studs
Studmania (dir. & actor)
Studz
Training Sessions
Trick Stop
X-Treme Closeup

SHANE GEAR
(aka Shane Gere)
Dirty Works
Disconnected
For My Eyes Only
Hotel Hombre
Latin Bandit
The Mad Masseur
Max Hardware
Reckless
Savage Blue
Sexposure 2
State Of Mind
Sunsex Boulevard
Tubesteak

LANCE GEAR
Born October 13. A hairy,
mature, shaved-headed

late 1990s model. 5'11" with
an 8" cock, he resides on
the East coast.
Easy Inn

GAVIN GEOFFREY
Advocate Men Live #5
Stryker Force
Track Meat

JOE GERE
Buster: The Best Years
Getting It
Night Flight
Salt & Pepper Boys
Trilogy

MIKE GERE
A 1980s model from
Texas.
Pizza Boy
Powertool
Spring Semester
Sticky Business
Two Handfuls
Young & Hung

WOLF GEYSER
Just Blondes

IAN GHORGY
Raging River

GIANFRANCO
(aka Johnny Diamond)
Born March 20. Dark and
handsome mid '90s star.
Boys Will Be Boys #1
Down on It
Erotikus
Family Secrets
Forever Hold Your Piece 2
Guest Services

Hot Properties
In Good Hands
Sex Hunt
Riptide
The Roommate

JOE GIBBONS
And early 1990s model.
Bigger Than Life
Celebrity Sex
Heatwaves
The Look
Rock Hard

TODD GIBBS
Raw Material
Road Home, The

MIKE GIBSON
A 1990s model.
Beyond Hawaii
Delivery Boy
Frat House Memories
Oasis
Preppy Summer
Route 69
Sticky Business

STEVE GIBSON
A youthful, blond, buffed
Australian model from the
1990s.
Adrenaline
The Best of Jonathan
   Strong
The Best of Matt Powers
California Blonds
Club Men
Desert Drifters
Foreign Affairs
Foreign Competition
Hard Steal
Hot for His Bod

Hot Pursuit
Hot Shots, Vol. 29: More
   Raw Rears
Hot Shots, Vol. 46: Street
   Meat
Idol Eyes
Jockathon
Joker's Wild
Kiss-Off
Lunch Hour
Palm Springs 92264
Point of No Return
Rassle
Razor Closet
Redwood
Rooms
Shoot
Sperminator
Taken by Storm
The Wild Ones
White Steel

MARCUS GIOVANNI
A 1970s model.
Adam & Yves

GREG GIRARD
Eighteen Candles
Head Trips
Rangers
Something Wild

KEVIN GLADSTONE
Black Brother/White
   Brother
Black Forbidden Fantasies
Black Orient Express
A Family Affair
Golden Years
Haulin'-n-Ballin'
Hung and Horny
Interracial Affairs
Man's Hand #115

The Massage Boys
Mr. Wonderful
My Straight Friend
New Recruits
Oral Orgy
Student Bodies Too
Twice the Fun
Weekend Workout
Who Killed Cock Robin?

KEVIN GLOVER
Actor-turned softcore video
producer. Was a nude
Playgirl model in 1986.
Advanced Disrobics
Anywhere, Anytime
Boot Camp 1&2
The Boy Toy
Hot Pages
Hot Shots, Vol. 27:
   Super Studs
Hot Shots, Vol. 28:
   Hot Pickups
Inside Expose
Jerker (prod.)
Knight Out with the Boys
Love Bites (star & dir.)
   (non-sex)
Man's Hand #13
Method & Madness
The Making of "Knight Out
with the Boys"
Midnight Riders
The Next Valentino
On Common Ground
Pool Boy
Power Trip
Ride the Swell
Secret Fantasies (co-dir.)
Seduction III: Passion
Obsession
Seduction V: Taking Full
   Charge

Split Decision
Thumbs Up!
Tips
Top Man
Warhead
Who Killed Cock Robin?
Working Hard for the
Money

BOBBY GOLDEN
Born April 28. 1990s
model.
Skateboard Sliders
Man Watch

JEFF GOLDEN
Youthful, brown-haired
1980s model.
Bound to Please
Hollywood Hunks
Interview 3
Spank 'Em Hard

JIM GORGA
A 1970s model.
Seven in a Barn

MIKE GRACE
Hung and the Restless
New Cummers

MAX GRAND
(aka Lash, Maxx)
Born July 5. 6' Latin from
El Salvador.
Resides in West
Hollywood.
At First Glance
Bad Ass Lieutenant
Big Showoff
Bondage Buddies
Boot Camp Buddies
Bound to Rise

Breakaway
CatalinaVille
Chicago Meat Packers
Cockland
Cop Sins
Cruisin' the Balcony
Cut vs. Uncut
Daddy Trains
Das Butt 2
Domestic Servitude
Down in the Dunes
Everybody Does It
Face Down
The Games We Play
Goodfellas/Badfellas
Guest Services
Hairsteria
Hard at Work
Historic Affairs
Hot Springs Orgy
Hotter Than Life
House of Games
Iron Cage
Just in Time
Latin Obsession
Latin Tongues
Leather Confessions
Low Riders
Midnight Run
Morning, Noon & Night
9-1/2 Inches
On the Move
The Other Side of Aspen
    3 & 4
Palm Springs Weekend
Penetrating Moves
Photoplay
Pocket Rockets
Razor Close
Room-Mated
Roped and Drilled
Sand Storms
Schlong Blade

Sex Acts
Sex Invaders
Strait Jacketed
Summer Fever
Taken to the Max
Tools of the Trade
True Stories
Try Again
Uniforms Only
Viva Latino!
Wet Warehouse

**RICHARD GRANGER
(see Tommy Chandler)**

TY GRANGER
Locker Jocks 1982

ADAM GRANT
The Best of Adam Grant
The Best of Jeff Stryker
The Best of Joey Stefano
Billboard
Handtools 2
Head of the Class, Part 2
Idle Pleasures
In Hot Pursuit
John Summers Screentest
    Mag.1
Lust
Paradise Beach
Sailor in the Wild 2
A Trip to Paradise Beach
View to a Thrill

DAVID GRANT
A pornstar legend from the
1980s.
California Blonds
Desert Fox
Don't Kiss Me, I'm Straight
Eaten Alive
The First Time

Hidden Instincts
The Long Hot Summer 2
Once in a Blue Moon
The Producer
Rear Window
Someone is Watching
Total Impact

GORDON GRANT
A mature, dark-haired porn
star legend from the
1970s.
The Best of Colt, Vol 3, 4,
    6, 12, 13
Crotch Watcher
The Day the Marines
    Came
Hammerhead & House
Boat
The Lifeguard
Hot Truckin'
Pleasures in the Sun
Working Late

JIMMY GRAY
Beater's Digest
Cult Manhood
Max Makes it Big
Skinner Jacks

MICHAEL GRAY
Big Guns
Bigger Than Life
The Bigger They Come
In Hot Pursuit
Man Size
Passion By Fire

TYLER GRAY
Born April 16.
Beach Heat
Gangsters at Large
Handsome Drifters

The Last Taboo
Men with Tools 2

BART GREEN
All The Way
Butthole Banquet 2
For Sale or Rent

CHRIS GREEN
Member of the band the
"Johnny Depp Clones" and
has done music for porn
videos. Resides in West
Hollywood.
All Night Long
Chi Chi Larue's Hardbody
Video Mag. 4
Courting Libido
Fluffer, The
Hands On
Hung Riders, The
Posing Strap
Secret Sex 2: The Sex
    Radicals
Secret Sex 3: The
    Takeover
Songs In The Key Of Sex
Valley Of The Bi Dolls

MICHAEL GREEN
Bijou

MITCH GREEN
Early 1990s black actor.
Asphalt Jungle
Asphalt River
The Best of Back Alley
    Video
The Best of Joe Simmons
Black Alley: South of the
    Border
Black Workout 3
Borderblack Workout 3

Dogs in Heat
Hard at Work
Hard to Resist
In a Jock's Locker
Luck of the Draw
Lust
A Night With Strangers
Pumping Black
Rap 'N Vette
Spare Room
The Token

WES GREEN
Blue Summer Breeze

BILLY GREENWAY
Make It Hard
Young Yankees

TIMMY GREER
Paradise Park
Stud Force

MIKE GREGORY
Early 1990s, dark-haired,
Italian actor.
Behind Closed Doors
The Best of Kurt Bauer
Bi & Beyond 1 & 2
The Big One
Catalina Blonds
Every Which Way
Les Hommes
Locker Room Sex
Made for You
My Best Buddy
Paul Norman's World of
Sexual Oddities
The Pledge Masters
Powerline
Top Man
The Young Cadets

SEAN GREGORY
All Tied Up
Death Scorpio
In Search Of The Perfect Man
Light Blue Hanky Left
Long Johns
Rough Ideas

TODD GREY
San Diego Summer
Think Big
Try Anything Once

DAVID GRIFFIN
Actor turned producer. Founded Griffin Intl. video studio in 1998.
Ass Rustler
Big City Men
The Bigger They Come
Black and Blue
Brown Paper Wrapper
Chain Male
Craze!
Daddy Stories
Drill Me Good
Dude Beach
Favors
Filth
Fucking Good!
Happy House
Hidden Man
Honolulu Hard Bodies
I Dream of Weenie
In the Men's Room
In the Mix
Leather Angel
Lights! Camera! Action!
Macho Money
The Meaning of Sex
Mounted Police
Moving In

Muscle Talk
My Own Private Mexico
The Orgy Club
Ouch
The Producer
Psychedelic Dreamers
Sex Between the Lines
Sex Shooters
Tattoo Parlor
Through the Looking Glass
Tool of the Trade
Waterworks

JEFF GRIFFIN
Black Workout 2
Boys of the Hollywood Spa

AARON GRIFFITH
Home Work

SERGEI GRIGORIEV
An American In Prague
Johan's Big Chance

SEBASTIAN GRONOFF
Born in Russia. Hairy-chested, mature, late 1990s model.
Betrayed
Hard to Hold

ALEXI GROMOFF
(aka Ivan, Gabor)
Handsome, dark-haired young 1990s Russian model.
Comrades In Arms
Gangsters at Large
Manwatcher
World of Men

GINO GULTIER
Balls to the Wall 35

Bare Bodies
Big Boys Club
Big Boyz Club 3
Blatino Party L.A.
Cruisin'
Cruisin' the Men of L.A.
Dickin' Around
Dr. Discipline
Employee of the Month
Four Rooms
Gay Pride Parade
Latino Posse
Latin Sex Thing
Latin Stories
Pacific Rim
Virgin Territory
Working Pleasure

MATT GUNTHER
Born 1963. Died May 27, 1997 from a heart attack. Also had AIDS. 5' 11." Considered by most to be one of the top performers of the '90s.
The Abduction
Big Bang
Boot Black
Buttbusters
By Invitation Only
Cool Hard Dick
Coming Out: The Challenge
Cruisin' II: More Men on the Make
Deep Inside Jon Vincent
Dreaming In Blue
First Mate
Full Length
Gentlemen Only
Grand Prize
Hole in One
Hot Shots, Vol. 44:

Golden Boys
Idol Eyes
Inside Expose
Into the Night
Les Hommes
The Long Hot Summer 2
Long Play
Man Driven
Man in Motion
Mean Streak
Men in Love
Men With Tools
Model Behavior
My Cousin Danny
On the Rocks
One More Time
Raising Hell
Screwing Screw-Ups
Slave Auction
Steamy Bondage Hard-On
Stranded: Enemies and
   Lovers
Straight To The Zone
Stryker's Best Powerful
   Sex
To the Bone

H

VIC HALL
A 1980s model.
Big Lift, The
Chicken Hawks
Dirty Pillow Talk
Forced Entry
Great Lengths
Hard Lessons: Sex Ed 2
Hole, The
Idol Universe
Interview #2
Just One Favor
Keeping Time

Mindscape
Mindscape 2: The Final
   Chapter
Mr. Footlong's Made In
   America
Muscle Bound
Naked Prey
Pick Up
Safe Sex: A Gay Man's
   Guide
Steel Away
Tease, The
Total Corruption 2
Toweling Off
Travelin' Wild
VamBires

JEFF HALSEY
A 1990s model. 5'1,1" 160
lbs., 7 1/2" cock, top. Born
in Redlands, California.
Chapters
Stuffed

FRED HALSTED
(aka Fred Halstead)
Died in 1988 from an over-
dose of sleeping pills. One
of the 1970s superstar
tops, Halsted directed him-
self in his videos.
Breaker Blue
El Paso Wrecking Corp.
Erotikus: A History of the
   Gay Movie
Fast Friends
Hot Shots, Vol. 7: Daddies
Hot Shots, Vol. 13: Both
   Ways
L.A. Plays Itself
Mustang
A Night at Halsted's
Nighthawk in Leather

Pieces of Eight
Revenge of the Nighthawk
Sex Garage
Sex Tool
Three Day Pass

TROY HALSTON
A 1990s model.
Beached
The Cruising Game
Family Secrets
Fly By Night
Fox Tale
Gang-Bang Movers
Hardline
His Big Brother
Hollywood Knights
Hotwheels
Hot Laguna Knights
Insertion
In Training
Naked Highway
Selection 2, The
Sexologist
Sexpress
The Sex Rangers
Spellbound for Action
Steel Trap
Take A Peak
The Taking of Jake
Thunder Balls
Timeless Encounters
Whatever You Say, Sir!
White Hot

MARK HAMILL
Stuffed

ERIC HAMILTON
Man Watch

MARC HAMILTON
Born January 5, 1959,

Upstate N.Y. Resides in
Minneapolis, Minnesota.
5'11," 7" cock. Versatile.
Bareback
Bob Jones Dog Training
 Video
CatalinaVille
Deep in the Brig
Fallen Angel
Firewater
First Time Tryers Vol. 3
Glory Hole Pigs
Hand to Mouth
In House $ervice
L.A.P.D.
Piss Boy Marc:
 The Solo Video
Power Pissing
Raw Meat Vol. 3
Rim City
Slave Brothel
Stud Fee
Technical Ecstasy
Uninvited
Water Sports Videos:

NATHAN HAMILTON
Anonymous Sex
Cream Team, The
Gay Weekend Away

BUCK HAMMER
Mo' Betta Butt
Mo' Bigga Butt

JACK HAMMER
Bi, Bi American Style
Stud Force

JAKE HAMMER
My Secret Lust

JENS HAMMER
Stock

JEFF HAMMOND
Handsome and hung, dark-
haired 1980s model.
All Night Long
Bad Boys' Ball
Best Of All 2
Down Home
Driving Hard
My Own Private Kentucky
 Studs
Never Too Big
On The Lookout
Piece Of Cake
Slip It In
Take Me Home
To The Hilt

STEVE HAMMOND
A legendary top from the
late '80s. Blond, well built
and very handsome.
Advocate Men Live 5
Backstrokes (solo)
The Best of All Matt
Sterling II
Big & Thick
Briefs: The Best of John
 Summers
Mission Accomplished
The Next Valentino
The Pledge Masters
Ryan Idol: A Very Personal
 View (solo)
Stryker Force
The Troy Saxon Gallery 1
 (narrator)
Touch Me
Young Gladiators

TONY HAMPTON
All About Steve
Beat Off Frenzy: 2
Beat Patrol
Built Tough
Dirty Pillow Talk
Forced Entry
Layin' Pipe
Man Country
Manticipation
Night Watch
One Man's Poison
Power Trip
Secret Sex 3: The Takeover
Summer Of Scott
Randsome
Urgent Matters

ALEX HANAK
Czech Republic, 1990s
model.
Lucky Lukas

BRIAN HANCOCK
God Was I Drunk

CURT HANSEN
Brian's Boys

RYDER HANSEN
(aka Ryder Hanson)
Born in Germany in 1962.
Died from AIDS-related ill-
ness in 1989. Real name
Wolfgang Praegert. A porn
star legend from the '80s.
The Best of Surge
Buster: The Best Years
By Initiation Only
Chain Reactions
Faces
Getting Off Campus
Head Trips

Heroes
Hot Shots, Vol. 6: Kinky
Hot Shots, Vol 37: Penal
   Code
Magnum Griffin,
   Vol. 6, 8 & 9
Making it Huge
More Than a Mouthful
Mr. Drummer Finals 1985
One, Two, Three
Room for Rent
Seven Card Stud
Strange Places, Strange
   Things
Stroke: Foreskin
Thinking Big
Tough Competition
Uncut
Wild Oats
Windows

TRACE HANSEN
A 1990s model.
Iron Will

TREVOR HANSEN
Blond, well built early 1990s
model.
Buttbusters
Compulsion-He's Gotta
   Have It
First Time, The
Heaven Too Soon
Men With Big Toys
Muscle Force
Raising Hell
Someone's Watching

BRIAN HANSON
A 1990s model.
South Beach Vibrations

BRAD HANSON
Born July 14th, Montana.
5'11", 8" cock, versatile.
Late 1990s model.
Resides in Los Angeles.
At First Glance
Black Hot Rods
Boy Was I Drunk Last
   Night
1st time Tryers
God Was I Drunk
In Touch Vol. 2
Men of Magnum
Object of My Erection, The
Opposites Attract
Raw Meat 1-4
Young Guys

BRIAN HANSON
A 1990s model.
Cop Bound
Cops at Play
Cop Training 1-2
The Corporate Ladder
Desert Train
Don't Dick With the Devil
Dreams of Discipline
Forced Pleasures
Gonna Blow
Leather Punks
Military Sex Pass
Police Daddy
Rookie Patrol
Shades of Black
South Beach Buns
Surf, Sand and Sex
Trucker Daddies

DREW HANSON
A 1990s model.
Big Salami, The

ERIC HANSON
A dark-haired, 1990s
model.
California Kings
French Connections 1-2
The Freshmen
Hot Wheels
Mercury Rising
Rock Solid
Summer Reunion: The
   Best Parts of Summer

JOHNNY HANSON
Tall, dark and handsome
1990s model with dark hair
and a huge cock.
Chip Daniels' Video
Studbook
Download
The Other Side of Aspen
   3 & 4

PAUL HANSON
An early 1990s black
model.
Alibi for a Gangbang
Blackballed
Black & Bound, Vol. 1-2
Black & Hung, Part 2
Black in Demand
Black Leather
Black Men Cruisin'
   Crenshaw
Black Mouthfuls
Black Nubian Fantasies
Black, Ripped & Stripped
Black Street Fever
Black Workout, Part 6
Brothas Gettin' Down
Duo Series 3: Episodes
   VI & VII
GV Guide All-Star Softball
   Game #1

Heavenly Acres
In Thrust We Trust
Paul Hanson's Star Search
Salt & Pepper Boys

ROMEO HANZ
A 1980s model.
Big Boys of Summer
Bigger and Better
The Boy Toy
Boys Night Out
California Dreamin'
Frat Brats
Hot Shots, Vol. 23:
   Massive Meat
Hot Shots, Vol. 24: Hot
   Hunks
Hot Shots, Vol. 27: Super
   Studs
In Deep
In the Raw
Men of Size
My Brother, My Lover
Who's Dat Boy?
Wide Load
Working Hard for Their
Money
Young Squirts (solo)

ACE HARDEN
Boys Town: Going West
   Hollywood
Century Mining
The Golden Boys
Hard to Swallow
Seven Card Stud
Stokers
Studbusters
Windows

JOHNNY HARDEN
Model and straight actor
with a legendary cock.

Mostly did solo videos and
auto-fellatio.
The Best of Colt, Vol. 2:
   Overload
The Best of Colt, Vol. 5
   California Fox
Cruisin' the Castro
Johnny Harden & The
   Champs
Pieces of Eight

SCOTT HARDESTEY
All The Way Inn
Hot Stuff
Measuring Up
Never Too Big
Open Windows

BUTCH HARDON
Butch Hardon's Private
   Home Movie
Folsom Street Sex
More Steamy Bondage
   Hardons
Straight Bound for
   Pleasure
Video Store Sex Studs

ROCK HARDON
Cute, young and hung,
dark-haired, 1990s model.
Action On Melrose
The Big Lift
Bonus Pay
Broadway Studs
Chain Male
Come As You Are
Convertible Blues
Derek Powers' Blueboys
Dirty Works
Freshman Fever
The Hollywood Kid
It's A Gang: Video Series 1

Mix It Up
Morning Rituals 2
Newcomers
Playing With Power
6969 Melrose Lane
Sticky Gloves
Trophies
Tubesteak
Young And Notorious

SCOTT HARDMAN
A 1990s model.
Back To Front
Bi-Conflict Of Interest
Coach's Boys, The
Conflict Of Interest
Cream Of The Crop
Cruise Control
Cut Vs. Uncut
Deep In The Brig
Need You Tonight
Into Leather Part 2
Making Of A Gay Video
Sex In Leather
Ty Me Up!
Wild Country

MICHAEL HARDWICK
A 1970s model.
Adam & Yves

BEN HARDY
Sure Shot

CHIP HARDY
A 1990s model.
A Lesson Learned
Turn of Events

DIXON HARDY
(see Frank Sterling)

DARREN HARKER
Caller, The

RYAN HARKER
Cell Block 9
Oil Rig 99
Tough Guys

RAY ED HARLEY
Hairy-chested, dark-haired,
mature, late 1990s model.
Backstage Pass
Big Guns 2
CatalinaVille
Harley's Crew
Meet Ray Harley

NICK HARMON
A 1980s model.
All Hands on Dick (bi)
The Bi-Analyst
Boy, Oh Boy!
Climactic Scenes #101
Fantasies
From Maui with Love
Hung Guns
Idle Pleasures
In the End Zone
Mannequin Man
Never Say Good Bi
Nuts and Butts
Ranger Nick 1 & 2
Seduction IV: Sex Storm
Unchained Men

REX HARMON
Backstrokes

TERRY HARMON
His Little Brother

BLAKE HARPER
Born October 19th, 1968,

outside the U.S. 6'0", 7
1/2" cock, versatile. Cute,
hairy-chested, dark-haired
'90s model.
Ass Lick Alley
Chapters
Descendant
Focal Length
Full Up!
Glory Holes of San
Francisco
In Deep: Miles To Go
Serviced
Sting: A Taste For Leather
Up For Grabs

MATT HARPER
(see Will Seagers)

STEVE HARPER
Batter Up
A Body to Die For
Hot to Trot
House of Games
Ryker's Revenge

VINCE HARRINGTON
(aka Lana Luster)
A West Hollywood resident,
Harrington has become
best know for his roles in
drag in the late '90s.
As Time Goes Bi
Bi Valley, The
Driven Home
In Deep
Sexx Pitt
Tennis Court Daze
Young Hustlers

BOBBY HARRIS
Manly Persuasion

BRETT HARRIS
The Arousers
Getting It

DAMIEN HARRIS
(Bill Marlowe)

DARRYL HARRIS
Early 1990s black model.
The Best of Blacks
Black and Bound, Vol 1&2
Black and Hung, Part 2
Black in Demand
Black Leather, White Studs
Black Workout 3
Duo Series, Vol. 1
Duo Series, Vol. 2:
Episodes IV & V
Duo Series, Vol. 5:
Episodes X & XI
Heavenly Acts
Soul & Salsa 1 & 2
Working it up with
    Bobby Joe

ROB HARRIS
Call to Arms
Gut Reaction

ROBERT HARRIS
A young looking, brown-
haired, 1980s model.
Bi Heat, Vol. 3:
    Last Call for Alcohol
Bi Heat, Vol. 4:
    Quick Study
The Best of John
Davenport
The Bigger They Come
Cruisin'
Days Gone Bi
Every Inch a Winner
Haulin' n Ballin'

Hot Shots, Vol. 14:
   Tight Buns
Measuring Up
On Top
Perfect Summer
Stick Shift
Sticky Business
Stryker Force
Vice Cop

STONE HARRIS
A 1990s model.
Phi Kappa Sucka'
Quick Relief
Romping Roommates

BILL HARRISON
(aka Ronnie Shark)
Died October 18, 1991
from AIDS-related causes.
Actor turned director.
Bare Tales (dir.)
The Biggest One I
   Ever Saw (dir.)
Bijou
Black Velvet
Hideaway Bed
Sex Machine
Size Talks (dir. as Shark)
Too Big For His
   Britches (dir.)
Tyker Tales (dir.)

ADAM HART
Born August 7, 1969 in
Tampa, Florida. 6,' 8-1/4"
cock. Florida resident. Very
handsome, blond, gay-for-
pay model and director in
the mid 1990s.
Deep Desire
Desert Hart
Fame & Flesh

Hard Core
Hart Attack
Hart Throb
How to Get a Man Into Bed
Just One Favor
Nights in Eden
Sexologist
Tainted Love
Take Down
Voyeur

BRIAN HART
Aaron Austin: A Day In
   The Life
Head Of The Class Part 2
Long Distance Lovers
Memories Of Summer
Single White Male
Superhunks

JOEY HART
Born October 11, 1974 in
Fort Bragg, North Carolina.
5'6", 7 1/2" cock. Bottom.
A Body To Die For 2
Body Worship
Don't Dick With The Devil
Hard Core
Hard Focus
Hummer
The New Coach
Night Riders
Nude Oil Wrestling 23
Nude Science
Read Bi All
Rosebud
Ryker's Revenge
Spiked
Summer Reunion: The
   Best Parts of Summer
West Hollywood Hope

K.C. HART
(aka Wesley Parker)
Born September 16, 1974,
Orange County, California.
Resides in Santa Monica,
California. 5'7", 8 1'2"
cock. Blond, 1990s top.
All You Can Eat
Analized
Back Seat BJ
Bad Ass Lieutenant
Beverly Hills Hustlers
Boomerang
Cat Men Do!
Chip Daniels' Video
   Studbook
The Choice
Country Hustlers
Crossing the Line
Dark Side of the Moon
A Day In The Life Of
   Austin
Daytime Voyeur
Dude Watch
Extra Service
Extreme Measures
Flyin' Solo
Forced Service
49 F-Train To Castro
Give It To Me Straight
Hand to Mouth
Hardline
Heat Of The City
Hot Cops #3—The Final
   Assault
Hot Laguna Knights
Hunk Hustlers
Invaders From Uranus
Jeff Stryker's Underground
Just Blondes
Just Guys
Killer Looks
Latin Obsession

Leather Obsession 5—
Mission Possible
Lucky Stiff
Lust in the Hay
Malibu Beach Hunks
Mirage—from the XXX
   Files
Nine Holes
Palm Springs Crusin'
The Player
Plugged In
Punk
Pure
Reunion
Rope Tricks
Sea Men
Sea n men
Sex After Hours
Sharp Shooters
Show Boys
Snafu
Snowbound In Manhattan
Special Forces
Street Boyz
Summer of '44
Summer Love
Tail End Of Summer
Tailspin
Touch Me There
Uncut Weekend
Underground
Working Fantasies
XXX, Blue Men You
   Sexy Thing

T.J. HART
Goosed (bi)
SWM

KIP HARTING
Mature, blond, 1990s
model.
Piece Of Cake

Shades Of Grey
Tough Terrain
Wild Country

CHRIS HARTS
Asphalt River
The Best of Scott Bond
Classified Action
Dream maker
   (pro. & actor)
Extra Sex
Fast Idle (pro. & actor)
Handjobs
J.D. Slater's Confessions
Once in a Blue Moon
Say Union Yes
Secret Meeting
Sex in the Great Outdoors,
   Part 3
Sex Is (docu)
Star Gazers
The Token
Top Brass
Underground Homo
   Hard-Core

ROY HARWOOD
L.A. Tool & Die

TOMMY HAWK
Leather Men 2
Look Of Leather

BRIAN HAWKS
(aka Brian Hawkes, Shawn
McIvan)
The Arousers
Big & Thick
The Bigger the Better
Brian's Boys
Fantasize
Hard Money
Hot Numbers, Vol.1-4

Jocks
Like A Horse
Locker Room Fever
One Size Fits All
Printers Devils

TERRENCE HAWKE
Model and director of his
own very popular amateur
video series. Resides in
San Francisco.
New Meat 1-7

MATT HAWKES
As Big as They Come
The Best of Back Alley
   Video
Cashload
Down to His Knee
Full Grown/Full Blown
Full House
Hard Balls
Hard to Resist
Hot on His Tail
Hot Shots, Vol. 10: Sweat
It's the Size That Counts
Las vegas Orgy
Obsession: The Ultimate
   Experience
Plug Me Up
Ram Man
Shacking Up
Sun-Kissed
3-Way Cum, Vol. 1
Tight Friendship

VADIM HAUSMAN
Czech Republic model.
Lucky Lukas

TANNER HAYES
Born November 16. 5'8,"
9" cock. Resides in San

Diego. Originally from Idaho.
Ass Lick Alley
First Time Tryers #9
Jarhead
A Lesson Learned
White Tails, Black Tails

KYLE HAZARD
Bullet Pack 1, 3, 4 & 9
Dirt Bike
501

JAMIE HENDRIX
Handsome, blond boy-next-door actor-turned-director from the '90s.
Anal Mania 3
Arms of Forgiveness
Bathroom Buddies
California Blonds
Call Boys
Cellblock Sinner
Crusin' 2: More Men on the Make
Desert Fox
Hustlemania
Laguna Summer
The Long Hot Summer 2
The Mad Masseur
Mechanics on Duty (dir.)
The Moon also Rises
Movin'
Object of Desire
On Cue (dir.)
Preferred Stock #1
Rockhard 2
Rump Ranger
Secret Fantasies (actor and co-dir.)
Shaft Sliding
Strictly Forbidden
Stud Ranch

Takin' Care of Mike
White Steel

BILL HENSON
A legendary bottom from the '80s.
The Best of All Matt Sterling
A Matter of Size
Military Men
The New breed
Private Collection
Screentest
Sailor in the Wild
Sex in the Great Outdoors 1-2
Winner Take All

MIKE HENSON
Cute, dark-haired, young looking 1980s model. Lives in Los Angeles.
Bad Boys Club
The Best of Jeff Stryker
The Best of John Davenport
The Best of Kevin Williams
The Best of Mike Henson
Big & Thick
Big Bad Boys
Big Guns
Bugle: Mass Appeal
Full Load: Maximum Overdrive
Glory Hole of Fame
Hot Rods: The Young and the Hung 2
In Hot Pursuit
Military Men
More of a Man
My Best Buddy
Powertool 1 & 2
Score 10

Two Handsful

STEVE HENSON
A popular 1980s model.
The Bigger the Better
Giants
Inch by Inch
Like A Horse
Other Side of Aspen
Pizza Boy
View to a Thrill

BILLY HERRINGTON
Former Colt model-turned pornstar in the late 1990s. Buffed, hairy-chested with brown hair.
Body Shop
Tales From The Foxhole

GRANT HICKSON
Any Boy Can

HANK HIGHTOWER
Born October 12 in Long Beach. Hunky, hairy, Cuban daddy, Hank is one of the few pornstars to use his real name. He now lives in San Francisco.
All About Steve
Australian For Leather
Basketballs
Bear Hugs
Buttsluts Of The Castro
Chi Chi Larue's Hardbody Video Magazine 4
Conflict Of Interest
Cop Corruption
Courting Libido
Easy Prey
Faultline
Force Of Nature

Free Delivery
Getting In Tight
Grizzly
Hoghounds
Into Leather
Johnny Hormone
Kink
Lap It Up
Like Father, Like Son
Long Play
Lost In Las Vegas
Matinee Idol
Men With Tools
Military Issue 2
Nightwalk
Nymphomania
Obessively Compulsive
Pornocopia
Rags to Riches
Romeo and Julian
Roughed Up at the Spike
Sex Trigger
Stripper Service
A Taste of Leather
Total Corruption 1&2
Trade
Ty Me Up
Watering Game
Webmaster
Wharfmen

BRUCE HILL
1990s model.
Ass Lick Alley
Bi-Sexual Nation
Cruisin' for a Gang Bang
Getting Ahead
Goosed (bi)
Measure For Measure
My Secret Lust
Nefarious
Sexpionage

DAVID HILL
House of Tricks
Physical Education

TYLER HILL
Desert Hart
In Deep: Miles To Go
Stock

SCOTT HOGAN
An early 1990s model.
The Abduction 2&3
The Big Ones
Blond Obsession
The Challenge
Club Men
Compulsion
Craze!
A Day in the Life
Dorm Fever
Dude Beach
Hollywood Tails
Honolulu Hard Bodies
Hot Summer Knights
Hustlemania
Joker's Wild
Knight Moves
Las Vegas Love Gods
The Long Hot Summer 2
Mein Kock
Men of Steel
Piece Work
Play to Pay 3
Private Dancer
Rear Window
Someone's Watching
Summer Knights
Superstud Fever
The Tattoo Love Boy
Tricked
Valley Heat

MAX HOLDEN
Chi Chi Larue's Hardbody
   Video Mag. 1
Hologram
Hot Ticket
Idol Thoughts
Night Watch 2
One Man's Poison
Pocket Rockets
River Patrol
Sex Between The Lines
Tony's Big Brother

CHAZ HOLDERMAN
(aka Chaz Holdaman,
Hans Reger) A youthful-
looking, dark-haired, porn-
star legend from the '80s.
Beach Ballers
The Best Men
The Best of Blonds
The Best of Times
Boys Camp Memories
Boys Town: Going West
Hollywood Club Taboo
Deep Fantasies
Deep Inside
Foreplay
Freshman Fantasies
Full House
Good Times Coming
Hard to Believe
Heavy Cruisin'
Hot Wired
I Was a She-Male for
   the FBI
It's the Size that Counts
Lifeguard
Like a Horse
Male-O-Gram
Manheat
Man Size
Men of Action

Military Men
Motel California
Muscle Fever
Oasis
Obsessed
On Fire
On Top
Perfect 10
Plug Me Up
Pounder
Quickies #4
Raw Rimmers
Rushes
Santa Monica Blvd.
Sex Drive 2020
Sex Hunt
Slumming
Social Studies
Summer Heat
Tall Tales
Too Big For His Britches
Tough Iron
  (as Hans Reger)
Try Anything Once
Uncut Dreams
Uploading It
Video Games 6 & 8
When a Stranger Comes
The Young Cadets

MARK HOLLAND
I Live For Sex

NICK HOLLIDAY
Batter Up!

DOMINIC HOLMES
Too Big to Handle

JOHN HOLMES
Died March 13, 1988 from
AIDS-related causes.
Famous straight "King of

Porn" who appeared in
over 200 straight videos
and the handful of gay
videos listed here.
Biggest of Them All
Black Velvet
Pool Party
Private Pleasures of John
  C. Holmes
Problem of Size
Sex Machine
Single Handed
Super Studs
Too Hard To Handle

DANIEL HOLT
dark-haired 1980s daddy,
died November 20, 1993
from a reported drug over-
dose.
Alleycats
Anything, Anytime
The Best Stallions
Big Shooters #5
Body Scorcher
Captive Men
Chain Reactions
Christopher Rage's Orgy
Closed Set 2
Daddy Dearest
501
Foreskin Fantasy
Giants, Part 2
Hard at It, Vol. 2
H.E.A.T.
Hot Shots, Vol. 8: Orgies
Hot Shots, Vol. 15:
  Bottoms
In the Name of Leather
Job Site
The Last Surfer
Le Voyeur
Looking Good

Making it Huge
Men & Films
Men Will Play
Midnight Special #1
Modern Men, Modern Toys
Navy Blue Hanky Left
New Wave Hustlers
A Night Alone with Al
  Parker
Nighcrawler
Non-Stop
One Night Stand
Rangers
Rawhide
Red Ball Express
Rock Creek Gang
  (actor and co-dir.)
Room Service Plus
Safe Sex
Sleaze
Subway
Therapy
Trisexual
TurboCharge
Video Encounters of the
  Sexual Kind
The Wilde House
X-tra Large

BOB HOLLOWAY
(see David Ashfield)

STEVE HOOD
Mo' Betta Butt
Mo' Bigga Butt

PETER HORNE
Winged
Slave Toy

ERIK HOUSTON
Best Of All 2
Hot Guys 2

In The Jeans
Jockaholics
Scorcher
Wet Load
Wild Horses

KURT HOUSTON
Born February 25, 1964.
Died August 22, 1997 in
Hamilton Canada at age
33. His death was reported
as kidney failure.
Alley Boys
Night Walk
Possession
Raw Material
Seamen First Class
Sex & Sensuality

VICTOR HOUSTON
Boys in the Sand II
Cocktails
Head Waiter
Hunk
The Hustlers
The Hustlers, Parts 1, 2, 3
Latin Lovers
Men In The Sand 2
Pier Groups
Top Man

TOM HOWARD
Bear Hugs

PAUL HOWELL
Big Brother Is Watching
You
Hard Man at Work
Room Service Plus
Wilde House

BRETT HUGHES
Behind His Back

Cruise Park
Cruisin'
Desert Maneuvers
Leather Lover
Smell of a Man 2

DAVID HUGHES
Arkansas Luggage
Best Solos
Body Scorcher
Boys of the Hollywood Spa
Century Mining Co.
L.A. Boiling Point
Seven Card Stud
Show it Hard
Squirts #2
Trisexual Encounters 2
Tub Studs

JIMMY HUGHES
Youthful 1970s model.
A Ghost of a Chance

ADAM HUNT
Eighteen Candles

BRAD HUNT
Handsome, boyish, dark-
haired model from the mid
1990s.
Baby It's You
The Big Score
By Invitation Only
Flashpoint
I.M.L. Uncut
Men of Lake Michigan
One Man's Poison
Rear Ended
The Road to Hopeful
This End Up

DOUG HUNT
Gay Weekend Away

BILL HUNTER
(aka William Hunter)
Died in 1998. Actor turned
director.
A Big Business
Boy, Oh Boy!
Heartbeat
Hot, Hung and hard
Hot Shots, vol. 25:
    Brief Encounters
In the Raw
More
The Size Counts
Spare room
Tough Choices (dir.)
Underground: Homo
Hardcore

BRAD HUNTER
Bear Hugs
Club 18-23
Tall Tail
Tomorrow Will Come
Whatever You Say, Sir

BROCK HUNTER
Young, hairy chested,
brown-haired, 1990s model.
Coming Together
Hologram
Keeping Time
Midnight Sun
Military Issue
Model Behavior

CHASE HUNTER
Born May 16. Originally
from the mid west. Sandy
haired, mustached, mid
'90s model.
Basic Plumbing 1 & 2
Breakaway
The Chase Is On

Download
Hold Me Again
House Rules
Riptide

CHUCK HUNTER
(aka Esteban) brown-
haired, 1990s model dis-
covered by Kristen Bjorn.
Caribbean Beat
Command Performance
Drifter, The
Falcon's Grand Prize
Grand Prize
Hot Pursuit
Idol Thoughts
Piece Of Cake
Stood Up
Wild Country

CORY HUNTER
Can't Say No
Don't Hold Back
Make it Count
Nothing Else Matters
Pushover
Stop At Nothing

GLEN HUNTER
Doctor's Orders
A Love Story
Orgies Pt 4
Worked Over

K.C. HUNTER
Leather Meets The Mat

KYLE HUNTER
Alley Boys
Cram Course: Sex Ed 3
Night Walk
Street Smarts: Sex Ed 5
Take One: Guys Like Us

Vacation Spot

JEFF HUNTER
Big Brother is Watching
  You
Down on the Farm
Gunslingers
Hunk
Kept After School
Little Brother's Coming Out

MORGAN HUNTER
Early 1990s dark-haired
model.
Bait
High Tech
Hollywood Gigolo
Perfect Ten
Private Pool Party
Rushes
S.F. Packing Co.
Social Studies
Tall Tales
Uncut Dreams

SCOTT HUNTER
Born December 8th, 1967,
Pennsylvania. 5'10", 7"
cock, versatile.
Focal Length

SEAN HUNTER
Cute, dark-haired, boyish
looking, jock-next-door
1980s legend.
All The Way In
Best Of Sam Abdul
Come Clean
Fetish
Grip Of Passion, The
How Big Is Big?
Interview Vol. #3
Jackhammer

Knight Heat
Made To Get Laid
Mind Blower
Off Duty Maneuvers
Oh, So Tender
Picture Perfect 2
Private Moments
Secret Boys Club
Special Reouest
Stud Valley
Stud Wanted
Thrust Fault
Warhead

I

RYAN IDOL
Born August 10. One of
the most popular gay-for-
pay tops from the late '80s
and early '90s. In 1998 he
fell from a four story NYC
apartment and survived.
Has spent much of the late
'90s on stage.
The Best of All Matt
Sterling 2
GV Guide Erotic Video
  Awards 1 & 2
Idol Country
Idol Eyes
Idol in the Sky
Idol Thoughts
Idol Worship
Jockathon
Just You and Me 2
Letters From the Heart
  (hetero)
The Road Home
Ryan Idol: A Very
  Personal View
Score 10

Trade-Off

TONY IDOL
A 1990s model.
All Night Long
Down On It
Idol Dreams
Idol Inn Exile
Idol Universe
Jawbreaker
Lovers, Tricks And One
   Night Stands
Revenge Of The Bi Dolls
Roommate, The
Seeds Of Love
Stargazing 5

PAUL IRISH
Men In The Sand 2

MARCUS IRON
Born October 18. Mature,
dark-haired, late 1990s
model. Resides in San
Francisco. 8" cock.
Descent
Dr.'s Orders Part 1:
   Manipulation
Glory Holes of San
   Francisco
Iron Will
Man Eater
Serviced
Skuff
Splashdown

SHAWN ISLANDER
A buffed, brown-haired,
1990s model. Resides in
Los Angeles. This is the
correct spelling of his first
name, according to Shawn,
himself.

Bi Sex Club
976-Stud
1-800-Hunk
www.Orgy

SERGE ISTAVAN
Dark and handsome 1990s
Hungarian model.
Hungarian Heat
Raging River

PATRICK IVES
A 1990s model.
Always Available
Bootie Nights
Cop Corruption
Daddy Stories
Daytime Voyeur
Dick Diving
Drill Me Good
Erotikus
Exiled
Fever
Fire In The Hole
Gang Bang Ranch Hand
Hard Working Men
Hell Knight
Here Comes Peter
Hot Springs Orgy
Hungry Eyes
Hurricane Hard-On
It's A Gang: Video Series 1
Keep The Tip
Latin Balls 2: Huevos
Leather Intrusion Case 2:
   Spider's Kiss
Leather Teddy
Lovers Lane
Measure For Measure
Mess Hall Maneuvers
Mr. Footlong's Made In
   America
MVP: Most Valuable Player

My Secret Lust
Nutt Crackers
Nymphomania
Open Windows
Overcharged
Penetration On
Pennsylvania Avenue
Point Of Return
Poolman Cometh, The
Portholes
Red Blooded Americans
Right Hand Man
Schlong Blade
Sex House
Sexual Suspect
Sexual Thoughts
Skinny Dipping
Stiff
Swimming Pool Orgy
Trixxx of the Trade
Virgin Territory
Wall 3, The

J

CORY JACOBSON
Black Brothers
Black Forbidden Fantasies
Black Force
Black Sex Therapy
New Recruits
Student Bodies

JEFF JAGGER
Chip Daniels' Video
Studbook
Fire In The Hole
Hot Cops
Overcharged
Sex Is In The Air

JIMMY JAGGER
Boys Can't Help It
Boys of Beverly Hills
Brothers Should Do It
Eighteen Candles
Flesh
Hunk
Thinking Big

TAYLOR JAKKS
A Canadian who now
resides in London.
Caller , The

CHAD JAMES
Hairy-chested, 1980s
model.
Bears & Cubs
The Best of Blacks
Big Time
Black Magic/White Heat
The Boy Toy
Cult of Manhood
The Day the Marines
Came
Hard at It, Vol.2
Head of the Class
Hot Shots, Vol. 20, 27, 28
In the Raw
Larger Than Life
Magnum Griffin, Vol. 11
Men on Site
Mocha Madness
New Meat
Old Reliable #76:
The Orgy!
Private Pool Party
Rod's Raiders
S.F. Packing Co.
The Size Counts
Stick Shift
Tease me!
What the Big Boys Eat

CHRISTOPHER JAMES
Blonds Do It Best
Hot Male Mechanics

CODY JAMES
A 1980s model.
Big as They Come
Blond Obsession
Breaking and Entering
The Carnival
Danger Alley
Dirty Pictures
Friends & Lovers
Gang Bang Alley
Hollywood Tails
Hotel L.A.
The Moon Also Rises
The Naked Prey
Never Enough
Personal Service
The Predators, Vol 1
Preferred Stock #1
Rear End Window
Safe Sex: A Gay Man's
Guide
Savage Blue
Smoky
Squirts, Vol 6:
Toothache Cure
Straight Studs 2
Stud Ranch
Take Me Home
Two Fistsful
Where the Night Takes
You

DANIEL JAMES
B.J.
Bound for Leather
Chicago Erection Co.
Dirty White Guys
Leather Intrusion 3
Slurp

Warehouse Heat

JOEY JAMES
Asian Persuasion 2

KEITH JAMES
After the Shot
Bait
Battle of the Bulges
Brothers Should Do It
A Few Good Men
Good Sex!
Hot Latinos
Longhorn Cowboys
Main Attraction
Man O' Man
Rangers
Single Handed
Skin Flix
These Bases Arer Loaded
Uncle Mike Meets Howard

LUCAS JAMES
dark-haired, darkly hand-
some young, late 1990s
model.
All That Jizz
Apply Within
Before & After
Brothers Behaving Badly
Club 18-23
The Complexxx
Cruise Park
Dream Team
Gang Bang Ranch Hand
Good Dick Hunting
I Know Who You Blew Last
Summer
Locker Room Lust
Nude Getaway
Reunion
Sex Fly
Spiked

Tomorrow Will Come
Young Guys
Young Shooters (Solo)

STEVEN JAMES
Brother Hustlers
Down To His Knee
That Boy

TIMOTHY JAMES
Brother Hustlers
Young 'N Eager

JAMOO
Born April 26th in Texas.
5'11, 8" uncut, top. Jamoo
is also a writer. His work
has appeared in *Freshmen*,
Unzipped and other maga-
zines. He is also the author
of two books, *Superstars#1*
and *The Films of Kristen
Bjorn* for Companion Press.
A-B-C's of Sex
Afternoons in Hollywood
Anal Attraction
Bacchus
Butt Service
Day of Decadence
Diary of a Gay Producer
Dicks and Robbers
Dominique's Bi Adventure
Firmest
Gilligan's Bi-land
Hair Plug
Hard Drive
Hoghounds 1 & 2
Hunk Hunt #1
A Latin Adventure
Latin Gallery
Latin Submission
Latin X
Naked Ghosts

The Naked Man
Off Beat and Path
Officer Dick
Party Partners
Personally Yours
Please Don't Tell (dir)
Ready For It
Refried Dreams
Sex f/x
Spring Meal
Summer Licks
Sunsex Blvd.
Toilet Tramps
Tyler Scott—
   A Day of Decadence

ADAM JANNIN
An American In Prague
Johan's Big Chance

CLIFF JARNO
In His Corner
Sex Behind Bars

MASON JARR
(aka Ron Payton)
Born March 31, 1976 in
Dayton, Ohio. Resides in
San Diego, California. Very
popular '90s straight-identi-
fied Latino model 5', 10."
Cock size 7".
Barracks Glory Hole 6
Choke 'Em 3
The Complexxx
Dirk Yates Private
   Amateur #100
The Few, the Proud, the
Naked 7
HOMOgenized
Jarhead
Link 2 Link
Montage

On the Prowl Again
Pucker Up
Sex After Hours
Straight White Male
SWM
XXX.Man.Com

LUC JARRETT
Betrayed
Sit Tight

NICK JARRETT
Blond porn star legend
from the '80s with an
enormous cock.
Fantasize
Gold Rush Boys
Hot Numbers, Vol. 1-2-3-4
The Summer of Scott Noll

BUD JASPER
Kansas City Trucking Co.

COREY JAY
Acres of Ass 1-2
Dr. Good Glove
Layin' Pipe
Link 2 Link
Mo' Betta Butt
Mo' Bigga Butt

MARSHALL JEFFERSON
Hot To Trot
Scores

DOUG JEFFRIES
Born January 11, 1966,
New York. Mature, dark-
haired, late 1990s model.
5'7", 8" cock, top.
All You Can Eat
Best of Titan: Collector
   Series 2

Beef Jerky
The Big Black Bed
The Bite
A Body To Die For
CatalinaVille
The Complexxx
Crossing the Line
Daytime Voyeur
Demolition Man
Desert Hart
Fluid
Happily Ever After
Hung Jury
Leather Obsession 6
Link
Measure For Measure
964 Dicks St.
Positively Yours
The Pounderosa
Private Parts
Red, Hot & Safe
Skuff
Sodom
Striptease
Things To Cum
Thrill Me!
Turn of Events
Unleashed Action
Up For Grabs
Weho Confidential
Why Marines Don't Kiss

DON JENKINS
Big Boyz Club 3

TOM JENKINS
Back in the Saddle

COLIN JENNINGS
As Good as it Gets
Brothers Behaving Badly
Caught In The Military #1
Chasing Andy

Cop Stories 1 & 2
Cream Team, The
Gang Bang Ranch Hand
Good Dick Hunting
I Saw What You Did
Kept: A Way of Life
LeatherWorld
Measure For Measure
My Big Brother U.S.M.C.
Naked Underneath
Playing with Fire
Policemen's Balls
Prize Fight
The Selection 3
Star Maker
Straight Talk
Supersize It
Undress for Success
X-Press Male
You Sexy Thing!

LEE JENNINGS
A late '80s, early '90s
brown-haired model and
New Mexico native.
Bedtime Stories:
    Tales to Keep You Up
Behind the Eight Ball
The Bi Analyst
Bi & Busty
Bi Cycling
Bi Mistake
Boot Camp 1&2
Boys on Fire
Brotherly Love
Commercial Sex
Dreamen
Dueling Dicks
Fantasy Boys
Foxhole
A Friendly Obsession
Gidget Goes Bi
Great Balls of Fire

Guys with Tight Asses
Hard Moves!
Heat
Hot Pages
Hot Shots, Vol. 42:
    Face Shots
Knight Moves
Make a Wish and Blow
Matters in Hand
Men At Work
Mission Accomplished
Much More Than I Can
    Take
One Hot Day
Private Workout
Rumble
Secret Action Man
Smokin' Butts
Stud Fuckers
Summertime Blues
Surge Men are Very
    Receptive
Switch Hitters IV: The
    Grand Slam
White Steel

MARK JENNINGS
Best Friends
Driven Home

ROCK JENNINGS
Winged

CAL JENSEN
(aka Al Jensen) A blond,
late 1980s model.
The Best of Michael parks
Boys, Boys, Boys
Cruisers: A Reunion of
    Friends
Deep in Hot Water
Foxhole
Glory Hole of Fame

Heat in the Night
The Jensen Sensation
Just Between Us, You
Promise
Plunge
Two Handsful 2
   (as Al Jensen)

CORT JENSEN
Blond-haired, early 1990s
model.
Foul Play

DEREK JENSEN
Well built, brown-haired
'80s model.
Bare Bottoms
The Big One
Bound to Please, Vol. 4
Brother Trouble 1-2
Frat Brat
Hard Choices II:
   Getting Even
Hollywood Hunks
In Deep
Interviews, Vol. 3
Lewd Conduct
Point of No Return
Powerline
Top Man

RACE JENSEN
A pornstar legend from the
'80s and a Falcon exclu-
sive.
Crusin'
Pledge Masters
Spokes 2,
Touch Me—It's Hot, It's
   Tender

RICK JENSEN
Huge

TYLER JENSEN
Down For The Count
Obsession

ED JEROME
Sgt. Swann's Private Files

BEN JOHNSON
Eighteen Candles

CHAD JOHNSON
A porn star legend from
the '80s. 6'2," exotically
handsome, dark-haired
and hairy chested model.
All the White Boys
Beach Ballers
Bulge: Mass Appeal
California Dreamin'
Cashload
Catalina Down and Dirty
Catalina Men
Cruisin' West Hollywood
Cult of Manhood
Delicious
Director's Best: William
   Higgins 1
Down for the Count
Down to His Knee
Flogging the Sausage
Full House
Man Size
Perfect Ten
A Physical Education
Pipeline
The Pizza Boy: He
   Delivers
Plug Me Up
Pounder
Tall Tales
Tall Timber
Too Big for His Britches
An Uncontrollable

Obsession
Uncut Dreams

CHRIS JOHNSON
As Big as it Gets
Black Attack 2
Black Entry
Black Men Do!
Black Patrol
Hot Spot
White Movers, Black
   Shakers
White Tails, Black Tails

DEAN JOHNSON
Big Score, The
Bullring
Cruisin' The Balcony
Daddy Dearest
Do Me Dirty
Easy Rider
First Time, The
Hot House Lodge
Hot Pursuit
In A Jock's Locker
Intrusion
J.S. Big Time
Jump On It
Leather Pit
Manhattan Skyline
Men Together
Pocket Rockets
Sex, Guys And Videotape
Stud Valley
Summer Buddies
Take It Deep
Thrust Fault
Together Again
Visit, The
When A Man Wants A Man

DENNIS JOHNSON
Basic Black 4
Black Attack
Black Lust/White Passion
Black Sex Party
Black Stallions
Black Sweat
Black Thunder
Black Workout 2
Coming From Above
Deep Chocolate 2
Old Reliable #50: Basic
   Black, Vol. 4
Old Reliable #75: Basic
   Black, Vol. 6
The Spanking Master

DUKE JOHNSON
Black Mischief

GREG JOHNSON
A Few Good Men

JEFF JOHNSON
Bi And Large
Black Pack

JOHNNY JOHNSON
Daddy Stories

MATT JOHNSON
The Best of Black Nights
Black & Forbidden
Black Bomber
Black Hammer
Cum Shots 102
Dark Men
Fever Pitch
I Love Foreskin
Make Mine Black
Manimal
Mo' Better Dudes
Moving Black

One Night Alone
Paramedic Alert
Stroke 'N' Men

O.G. JOHNSON
Night Flight
Other Side Of Aspen 2

PAT JOHNSON
Anything, Anytime
Le Voyeur
Oriental Dick
Safe Sex
Screen Test
Young Ones

BOB JONES
A 1970s model.
Adam & Yves

BUDDY JONES
Thick as Thieves

CATFISH JONES
Bad Ass
The Shaft

JESSE JONES
Forbidden Portraits
Oil Rig #99

LUCKY JONES
Mt. Fuckmore

MALEETK JONES
(see Maleek Brown)

ROB JONES
Cop Corruption
Off Duty
Rear Delivery

RYDER JONES
Centurians of Rome
Head Waiter
Hunk
New York Construction Co.

TONY LEE JONES
Internal Affairs
Inter-Racial Interrogation

TY JONES
A late 1980s black model.
Beef
The Best of Joe Simmons
Black and Bound,
   Vol. 1 & 2
Black Attack
Black Balled
Black Brother/White
   Brother
Black Champions
Black Fantasies
Black in Demand
Blackforce
Black Jacks
Black Magic
Black Male
Black Sweat
Black Workout 3
Boys on Fire
BulletPac 12: Black Bullet
Casting Couch
Castro Motel
Catalina's Black Gold
Club Taboo
Duo Series, Vol. 2:
   Episodes IV & V
Ebony Eagles
Gimme it All
Glory Hole of Fame
The Good Old Days
Hot Shots, Vol. 19:
   Black and White Buns

Hot Shots, Vol. 24:
Hot Hunks
Hot Shots, Vol. 27
Super Studs
Imperfect Strangers
Interracial Affairs
The Lovers
Men in Motion #1
On Fire
Pound Your Pud: Eagle 7
Probe, Vol. 4: Black &
Blond
Pump
Pumping Black
Solo Flight
Tour de Trans
Who's Dat Boy?

CASEY JORDAN
(As a hit mainstream song-
writer he uses his real
name Kyle Neven).
Born February 10, 1968 in
Salt Lake City, Utah.
Resides in Melbourne,
Australia. Late '80s, early
'90s porn star turned
songwriter. 5', 11," cock
size: 9 1/2".
The Backroom
Boot Black 2
Boyz in the Band
Buttboyz Blackjack (CD)
Down In The Dirt
Getting Even With David
Hair Trigger
Hard Lessons, Sex Ed 2
High Stakes Wrestling
1 & 2
Hoghounds 2
Hot Blades
Hunk Hunt 1
Inner Circle 2

Leather Sensations
New Pledgemaster
Perfect Summer
Pheromones The Smell Of
Sex
A Real Man
Ruthless
A Score Of Sex
Slam Bam Thank You Man
Spokes II
Tease, The
Touch Me, It's Hot, It's
Tender
Uniform Code —Sex Ed 4
XXX

CHRISTIAN JORDAN
A 1990s model.
West Hollywood Stories

CLAUDE JORDAN
(aka Claude Jourdan)
Canadian, discovered by
Kristian Bjorn in the early
1990s.
All American
Backstage Pass
Hart Throb
Laid To Order
Montreal Men
Northern Exposures
Score of Sex
Skin Tight
Somebody Is Watching
Sterling Ranch
Sure Shot
True Stories
Woody's

CRAIG JORDAN
Blue Streak
Hungry Hole
Log Jammin'

SERGEI JORDONOV
(Stefan Yanos)
East of Berlin
Gangsters at Large
Man Watcher
Thick as Thieves
Tomorrow Always Comes

BILL JOSEPH
Inch By Inch

TOTH JOSEPH
Raging River

SHADOW JOYCE
Big Favors
Big Shooters 1
Heat Goes On
Jail Mates
The Spirit is Willing

SHAWN JUSTIN
(aka Sean Justin)
Early '90s porn star daddy.
Abduction 2: The Conflict
Backstage Pass
Black Mischief
Chip Daniels' Video
Studbook
Club Sex-a-holics
Coming Together
Faultline Sextime
For His Own Good
Give It To Me Straight
Hologram
Hot Cops 2
Idol Thoughts
Juice Bomb
Just in Time
I Am Curious Leather
Like Father, Like Son
Looking for Mr. Big
Lost Loves

More You Get, More You Need
Picture Perfect
Privilege
Proud
Skintight
Slave Camp
Snowbumz
Stargazing 3
Summer Obsession
Tony's Big Brother

K

ERIC KAHNLER
Blue Summer Breeze

JIRKA KALVODA
Handsome and hunky Czech model with light-brown hair. Resides in the Czech Republic.
Andel's Story 2: The Running With the Bulls
Czech Is In The Male Rapture

DJAI KAMARA
Getting Even
Sex Bazaar
Sex Oasis

JOHNNY KANUUK
Head Waiter
New York Construction Co.

MICAL KASE
SWM

KIP KASEY
Burgle Booty
Drop 'em

First Timer
Goodfellas/Badfellas
Hard Up
Leather Confessions
Mr. Blue
Photo-Op
Plumbers Liquid
Sex On The Beach
Skinny Dippers
Virgin Tales #1: The Show

JAVIER KASKO
Bat Dude
Bigger & Better

JOHN KASS
California Blues
Daddy Does A Video
Slaves For Sale

**THOM KATT
(From the '80s)**
Died in 1992 from AIDS-related complications. A popular 1980s model.
Battle of the Bulges
Black Force
Black Heat
Cult of Manhood
Dorm Fever
Eagle Pack 8
Frat Brats
In Deep
Let Me Be Your Lover Boy
Old Reliable 377:
Someone's Son
Show it Hard
Solitary Sin
Someone's Sons
Wrestling 34

TOM KATT
(aka Thom Payne)

Hunky, muscle stud from the '90s.
Abduction 2 & 3
Alley Katt
Bad Boys' Ball
Behind The Barn Door
Best Of Leather: Part 2
Blackforce
Body Search
Cellblock Sinner
Chi Chi Larue's Hardbody Video Magazine #1
Come And Get It!
Cop Corruption
Cumming Attractions
Dorm Fever
Fantasy Fights 5 & 6
Full Length
Good Vibrations
Heaven Too Soon
Hot Guys
How To Get A Man In Bed
Idol Thoughts
Leather Obsession
Link 2 Link
Men Of Magnum
Orgies Pt 2
Palm Springs Paradise
Payne In The Ass
Raising Hell
Red, White & Blue
Secret Sex 2
Splash Tops
Tom Katt
Toolkit
Total Corruption 2
Visit, The
Wet N Wild
Wet Warehouse 2
We've Got Them All

STEVE KAYE
Hustlers

One, Two, Three
Split Image

MICHAEL KEARNS
L.A. Tool & Die

BRENDAN KEITH
Cadet

CAMERON KELLY
A popular and youthful-
looking, brown-haired,
uncut, gay for pay model
from the 1980s.
A Big Business
Big Boys of Summer
Bronco Bunch
Bubble Butt
By Day, Bi Night
Climactic Scenes #101
Dude Ranch
Hot Shots, Vol. 24:
  Hot Hunks
Mix N' Match
My Brother, My Lover
Old Reliable #153: Uncut 9
Orgy at the Funhouse
Private Cover Boy
The Rites of Fall
The Rites of Summer
Runaways
She-Males #19: Toga Party
Stud Squad
Taxi
Unchained Men
Uncut Dreams
Wet Dreams
Wild Trail

DAX KELLY
Born July 25. A 1990s bottom who changes his look
often, from blond to

redhead.
All You Can Eat
Beach Head
The Big Black Bed
The Corporate Ladder
Crossing the Line
A Day in the Life of Austin
Dreams of Discipline
Dr. Jerkoff & Mr. Hyde
Erotikus
Eroto Wrestling
Family Secrets
Hard Hats
Hot Guys
Hotter Than Hell
Men Only
Morning, Noon and Night
My Brother's Best Friend
On Your Knees
One Hot Summer
Orgies Pt 2
Photoplay
Rock Off
Sex Fly
Sleeping Booty
South Beach Heat
Spank Me. Man!
Sure Thing
Turn of Events
Wet Warehouse 2
Winged

DREW KELLY
Backdrop
Bad Boys
The Big Splash
Cops, Jocks & Military Feet
Dirty Pictures
Driving Hard
Grapplin'
Heat
Heaven Too Soon
Male Seduction

On the Lookout
Palm Springs 92264
Raising Hell
(Secret) Shore Leave
Shake That Thing
Straight Studs
Summertime Blues
Take Me Home
Truth, Dare or Damian
Two Fistfuls

MIKE KELLY
(see Eric Stryker)

KEVIN KEMP
(O'Neill, Troy Maxwell)
Adventures of A. Rocky
  and Bill Winkler, The
Black Entry
Black Muscle Machine 2
Black Patrol
Black Renegades
Black Rose, The
Black Secret
Black Warriors
Cat's Tale, A
Chocolate Dessert
Gang-Bang Movers
Hot Mix
Hung Man Meat
In the Mix
Mt. Fuckmore
The Other Side of Big
  Bear
The Perfect Gift
Private Parts
White Movers, Black
  Shakers
White Tails, Black Tails

NOEL KEMP
(see Eric Stryker)

CHAD KENNEDY
Serviced
Something About Larry
Sting: A Taste For Leather
Technical Ecstasy

MIKE KENNEDY
Hairy-chested and hunky
youthful-looking late 1990s
model.
Convictions
Stalled
Tranny World

REECE KENNEDY
Resideds in England.
Another Man's Pleasure
Easy Prey

RICK KENNEDY
Best Little Warehouse
   in L.A.
Frat House One
Hang 10

STEVE KENNEDY
(aka Luke Bender, John
Fell) Died in 1996 from
AIDS-related causes. A leg-
endary, dark-haired top.
The Abduction
The Best of Danny
Sommers
Black & Beyond: The
Darker Side
Carnival Tails
Deep in Hot Water
Fidelity
Fond Focus
Honesty
Hot Shots, Vol. 45:
   Latin Fever
Island Heat

Las Vegas Love Gods
Lunch Hour
Object of Desire
Once in a Blue Moon
Point of No Return
Powerful II
Private Workout
Read My Lips
Revenge: Much More Than
   I Can Take
The River
Sex in Tight Places
Slave Worship L.A.
Stryker's Best Powerful
Sex
Superstud Fever
Ten Is Enough
"10" Plus
To the Bone

TONY KENNEDY
Boys Can't Help It
Eighteen Candles
Flesh
Hunk
Jail Mates
Men and Steel
Platoon
Strange Places, Strange
   Things

JAY KENT
Choice Cuts
Kid Brother

JOE KENT
Hot Guys
Orgies Pt 2
Wet Warehouse Part 2:
   Drenched

MARK KENT
Gut Reaction

KEN KERNS
California Summer
Preppy Summer
The Young & the Hung

BRYAN KIDD
Lives in San Diego with
boyfriend Ryan Wagner.
Will always be known as
one of the pornstars who
was befriended by Andrew
Cunanan, the serial killer
who murdered Gianni
Versace in 1997.
Backseat BJ
The Big Black Bed
Birthday Blowout
Cat Man Do!
Cockfight
The Company We Keep
The Diary
Dr. Jerkoff and Mr. Hard
Family Values
The Flavor of Men
Flesh and Blood
Fox Tail
Hawaiian Illustrated
Just Guys
Law of Desire
Like Father, Like Son
Lip Lock
Log Jammer
Michael's Leather Dream
My Sister's Husband
Ram Jet
The Rush
Slurp!
Surf, Sand and Sex
Tales From the Backlot 2
Under Covers
Weekend Sex Camp
Wet Fantasies
White Hot

TONY KIDD
Cousins
Hard Money

RYAN KILGORE
Best of Colt 2
The Brig

GERARD KILIAN
An American In Prague
Johan's Big Chance

ALEX KINCAID
Born July 13. Mature,
brown hair, 1990s model.
All Night Long
Breakthrough
Chip Daniels' Video
Studbook
Crossing The Line
For Your Pleasure
He's Worth It
Hot Copy
Hot Firemen
Hot Guys 1 & 4
It Happened One Day
Leather Dream
Leather Obsession 3:
    Illusion
Man About Town
Men 4 Men On The Net
Night Heat
Nights In Eden
Officer And His Gentleman
Oklahomo!
On The Rise
Prisoners Of Lust
The Sex Files
Summer Fever
Try Again
Working Stiff

BILLY KINCAID
Iron Will

JOSH KINCAID
Against the Rules
Bullet 5, 8, 9

ANTHONY KING
Low Riders

BO KING
Physical Education

BRAD KING
Born July 27th, Hollywood,
California. 5'9," 6 1/2"
cock. Bottom.
Australian For Leather
A Body To Die For 1 & 2
CatalinaVille
Dial "5" For Sex
Don't Dick With The Devil
Escape To Fern Falls
Grease Guns 2
Hard To Keep Down
Hot To trot
Intimate Relations
The Kickboxer
Logan's Journey
Malibu Beach hunks
Maximum Maxon
Military Issue 3
Private Members
Redwood
Slave Toy
Slick
Things To Come
Uninvited, The

DAVID KING
Head Trip Hunk
Killing Me Softly

GRANT KING
(aka Grant Williams)
A blond, uncut British
model from the 1980s.
The Best of Street Times
    Video
Body Waves
Cabana Boys
Castro Motel
Cowboys & Indians
Davey and the Cruisers
Dirty Pool
Dungeon Slave Boys
Extra Sex
Fantasy Bites
Fatigue Relief
Grand Prize
Grapplin'
Highway Patrol
Hollywood Hunks
Illusions
Inside Expose
Junior Crew
Leather Me Down, Do Me
    Toys
Low Blows
Lust
Manstroke
Men in Love
More Than Just Strangers
Obsesively Compulsive
Olympic Proportions
Overseas Trade
Pool Boy
Private Games
Ram & Jam
The Rod Squad
Seduction III: Passion
    Obsession
Seduction IV: Sex Storm
Shadows in the Night
Shake that Thing
Slam Dunk

Sweet in the Bootie
Tips
Warloads
Wolf Boy
You Bet Your Ass

JACKSON KING
Manhungry

J.W. KING
Died December 5, 1986
from AIDS-related causes.
The Best of Colt, Vol. 2
The Best of Colt, Vol. 10:
Sunstrokes
The Best of Jon King
Big Men on Campus 1979
Brothers Should Do It
California Boys
Catalina Orgies, Vol. 1
Class of '84, Part 2
Deep Fantasies
Every Which Way
Face to Face
Gold Rush Boys
Hot Numbers, Vol. 2
Hot Shots, Vol. 3: Cum
  Contest
Hot Shots, Vol. 4: Contest
  Continues
Hot Shots, Vol. 6: Kinky
Hot Shots, Vol. 8: Orgies
Hot Shots, Vol. 9: Hot
Blonds
Hot Shots, Vol. 35:
  Cowpokes
King Size: The Best of
  J.W. King
Malibu Days/Big Bear
Nights
A Night at Halsted's
Nighthawk in Leather
Pacific Coast Highway

Palace of Pleasures
Performance
Rawhide
Skin Flix
Star Shots, Vol. 3
Strokers
Studhunter, Part 1 & 2
These Bases are Loaded
Three Days Past
Turned On
Wet Shorts
William Higgins Preview
  Tape #1

JON KING
(aka John Gaines.)
Died March 8, 1995 from
AIDS-related causes. One
of the biggest superstar
bottoms of the 1980s.
Assholes & Tongues
The Best of Jon King
The Biggest One I Ever
  Saw
Bikers Liberty
Bore 'N' Stroke
Boys on Call
Brothers Should Do It
Catalina Orgies, Vol. 1
Fade In
Fade Out
Getting It
Giants, Part 1 & 2
Gotta Have It
Hot Off the Press
Hot Shots, Vol. 1: All Star
  Review
Hot Shots, Vol. 3: Cum
  Contest
Hot Shots, Vol. 4: Contest
  Continues
Hot Shots, Vol. 7: Daddies
Hotel Hell

Inevitable Love
Kip Noll: Superstar
Latin Tongues
Locker Room Sex
Magnum Griffin, Vol. 12
The Main Attraction
Members Only
Perfect Summer
Printer's Devils
Screen Play
Star Shots #2
Studhunters, Part 1
These Bases are Loaded
  1 & 2
Trick Time
Tyger Tales
Wide Load
Wild Country
Wild Oats
William Higgins Preview
  Tape #1

NEIMAN KING
Obsessions
Platoon Sun Kissed

PETER KING
Best Men
Bulging Jockstraps
Down To His Knee
Full House
Hard to Believe
Motel California

STEVE KING
El Paso Wrecking Corp.
Twelve at Noon

TERRY KING
Gemini

RON KINNEY
Brian's Boys

JAY KIRK
Eyes of a Stranger
Their Tender Moments

ROB KIRK
A 1990s model.
Lap It Up
976-Stud
1-800-Hunk
Penal Pen Pals
Something About Larry
Technical Ecstasy
www.Orgy

DAVID KLAUS
Knockout
Nighthawk in Leather

AARON KLEIN
God Was I Drunk

DAMIAN KLEIN
Back in the Saddle

MARK KLINE
Preppy Summer
They Work Hard for the
Money

SHAWN KLINE
Tiger's Brooklyn Tails

TOM KLINE
Big Deal
Winner's Circle
Winner's Way

MIKE KLOUBEC
Beef
Best Wishes

BRENDAN KNIGHT
Born December 5, 1972 in

Portland, Oregon. 5'11," 8
1/2" cock. Bottom.
Body To Die For, A
Cat's Tale, A
Chained Desires
Four Men '97
Malibu Beach Hunks
Man Watch
Pressure
Private Members
Take A Peek

CHAD KNIGHT
Resides in Northern
California. dark-haired, boy
next door early 1990s
model.
Bad Moon Rising
Beach Blanket Bedtime
  Stories
Beach Blanket Boner
Bedtime Stories: Tales to
  Keep You Up
The Best of All Matt
  Sterling II
The Best of Chad Knight
Big River
The Big Switch III: Bachelor
  Party
Bullseye
Buttbusters
Chip Daniels' Video
Studbook
Coming Out
Compulsion: He's Gotta
  Have It
Cram Course: Sex Ed 3
Don't Kiss Me, I'm Straight
Driving Hard
Eyes of a Stranger
A Family Affair
Fetish
Fox's Lair

Glory Hole of Fame 2
Handjobs
Hard Bargains
Hardball
Hard Lessons
Heat of Passion
Heaven Too Soon
Hell Knight
He's Gotta Have It
Key West Voyeur
Kiss-Off
Knight Moves
Knight Out With the Boys
Live From Key West
Loaded
Lust Horizons
Lust Letters
Malibu Pool Boys
Mating Game
Marine Crucible
Mein Kock
Method & Madness
The Making of "Knight Out
  with the Boys"
The Other Side of Aspen
  3 & 4
Pacific Coast Highway
Pleasure Principle
Plugged In
Preferred Stock #1
Quick Study
Reflections
Remembering Times
  Gone By
Ruthless
Score 10
Scoring
Sexmates
Sexpress
Shooters
Someone in Mind
Someone is Watching
Spellbound for Action

Steel Garters
Straight Pick Up 3
Steel Garters
Summer Buddies
Striptease
Summer Buddies
Superstud Fever
Tales From the Backlot
Tales to Keep You Up
Traffic School Was Never
   Like This!
Trick Time
True
1230 Melrose
Ultimate Reality
Urgent Matters
Willing to Take It

CHRISTIAN KNIGHT
A 1990s model.
Hard Ball
Link 2 Link

DAVID KNIGHT
Casting Cocks (solo)

DIRK KNIGHT
All Men Do It

DOLPH KNIGHT
A mature, blond early '90s
model.
The Abduction 2&3
Fetish
Innocence Found
Majestic Knights
Men Who work it Alone
Powertool 2: Breaking Out
Score 10
Twic Pecs

ERIK KNIGHT
The Other Side of Big

Bear

MICHAEL KNIGHT
Mature-looking brunet and
late 1990s model. Resides
in W. Hollywood.
Bi-Agra
Bi For Pay
Jamie Hendrix's
   Interviews 1
Tapestry

RYAN KNIGHT
Bone Alone
Heat

TIM KNIGHT
California Golden Boys
Salt & Pepper Boys

ROB KNOX
A 1990s model.
Doctor's Orders 2

CRIS K.O.
Beeper Boys of El Barrio
Hispanic Monuments

JESSE KOEHLER
Mature, blond 1980s
model. Died in 1989 from
AIDS-related complica-
tions.
The Best of Blonds
Big Shooters #3
Boys Can't Help It
Boys Town: Going West
   Hollywood
Collage
Cult of Manhood
Dirty Load
The Exchange
Firsts

Getting It
Hard Disk Drive
Hot Shots, Vol. 1: Anal
Hot Splash
Hot Wired
Hunk
Imperfect Strangers
King Size
Lusty Lovers
Men Will Play
Midnight Special #1:
   Longhorn Cowboys
Move Over, Johnny
Outpost
Pleasure Peak
Poker Studs
The Prostitute
Rangers
Rock-Hard
Rod's Raiders
Sex Drive 2020
Squirts 1 & 3
Star Shots #1
Studbusters
Unloading It
The Voyeur
What the Big Boys Eat

GREG KOLB
Bronc Rider
Every Which Way

STEPHAN KOLLS
Heroes
Nothing But the Best
Tough Competition

ZOLTAN KORDA
A 1990s model.
HUNGarians

PETER KORMAN
A 1990s Czech Republic

model.
Lucky Lukas

JEFF D. KOTA
(aka Jeff Dakota)
We asked Jeff, himself, and
this is the correct spelling
of his name. A tall, blond,
youthful and uncut late
1990s model. Resides in
Los Angeles.
All Heated Up
Bi Sex Club
Both Ways (bi)
The Drifter
Driven By Lust
Ho Ho Ho!!!
Hot Mix
1-800-Hunk
976-Stud
Skateboard Sliders
Trade Off
www.Orgy

ERIK KOVAC
A 1990s model.
Summoner, The

JOHN KOVACS
Centurians of Rome
Head Waiter

KEVIN KRAMER
Born September 14.
Resides in West
Hollywood. A popular,
blond 1990s model.
Appeared in the non-porn
film "Hustler White" with
Tony Ward.
Below the Decks
Big Shooters
Biggest Piece I've Ever

Had
Centerspread
Chip Daniels' Video
Studbook
Coach's Boys
Deep In The Brig
GV Guide Gay Erotic
   Video Awards 2
Hard Bargains
Hell Knight
Hot Reunion
Imagination
J.S. Big Time
The Look Of A Man
Masquerade
A Matter Of Size
Mind Blower
Moving Target
Nights In Eden
Oh! So Tender
Olympic Proportions
Powerdriver
Proud 2
The Rival
The Rumpsters
Sexposure 2
Smokescreen
Stiff
Tales From The Backlot
Too Damn Big
Weekend With Howie

MARK KRAMER
Uninvited, The

TIM KRAMER
Died April 15, 1992 from
AIDS-related causes. A
cute, 6'2" blond, porn star
legend from the '80s and a
Florida native. Operated
his own nutritional prod-
ucts business in West

Hollywood.
Big Shooters #6
Biker's Liberty
Bullet Gold, Vol. 1-3
California Jackoff
Gayracula
Giants, Part 2
Heroes
Hot Numbers, Vol. 1
Hot Shots, Vol. 1: Anal
Hot Shots, Vol. 8: Orgies
Hot Shots, Vol. 9: Hot
Blonds
I Do
Magnum Griffin, Vol. II
Men of Action II
Men of the Midway
Mouth to Mouth
New Zealand Undercover
Solo Studs
Sunstroke
Tony's Iniation
Trick Time

MARK KRONER
Born in Salem, Ohio. 6'
1/2", 9" cock. Hairy, red-
headed, porn daddy top
from the late '90s.
Big Guns 2
Biker Pigs From Hell
Choke 'Em 2
Corporate Ladder
First time Tryers #6
From Hair to Eternity
Gang of 13
Gay For The Weekend
Hairsteria
Harley's Crew
Inter-Racial Interrogation
Lick It Up
Link
Saving Ryan's Privates

Sex Invaders
Show Your Pride
Swell
Things To Cum
Turn of Events
Uninvited, The
Winged

LOU KRUZE
From Maui with Love
Paradise Found
Rooms
Skin Torpedos
Warloads

LEX KYLER
Born August 13th, in
Virginia. Mature, shaved-
headed, late 1990s model.
5'11," 8 1/2 cock. Top.
Big Guns 2
Butt Munch
Cock Lock
Equestrian Club, The
Glory Holes of San
Francisco
Jumpin' Jacks
Lick It Up
Master Controls
Men Together
Pet Boy
Porno Tonight Show, The
Principal of Lust
Video Dreams

L

ROBERT LABATT
Northern Exposures
Woody's

JAME LA COSTA
Boys of San Francisco

CHRIS LADD
(aka Chris Starr)
Died November 14, 1990
from AIDS-related causes.
A Texas native. Very cute
and youthful-looking boy
next door 1980s model.
The Best of Adam Grant
Bi and Beyond III
The Bronco Bunch
Full Service
Gettin's it Good
Handtools
Hard Men II
Head of the Class Part 2
Love Bites (non-sex)
The Main Attraction
The Main Event
Memories of Eighteen
The Pledge Masters
The Rites of Manhood
The Rites of Summer
The Rites of Winter
Swim Meat
Superhunks II
View to a Thrill 2: Man With
    the Golden Rod
Young Jocks

ANTHONY LAFONT
Mature-looking brunet. Born
in France. Late 1990s
model.
Absolute Arid
Absolute Aqua

GENE LAMARR
A popular black 1990s
model with a huge, uncut
cock.
Balls to the Wall 35
The Best of Blacks
The Best of Joe Simmons

Black & Blue
Black & Bound, Vol. 1 & 2
Black & Hung, Part 2
Black Balled
Black Bullet #12
Black Fantasies
Black For More
Black Jacks
Black Leather
Black Magic
Black Male
Black Moves
Black Sex & Leather
BulletPac 12: Black Bullet
Butt Boys in Space
Casting Couch
Castro Motel
The Cherry
Duo Series, Vol. 1
Get It On
The Good Old Days
Guys Who Eat Cum
Guys with Tight Asses
Hard at It, Vol. 2
Hard Balls
Horsemeat
Hot Cocks (non-sex)
Hot Shots Vol. 48:
    International Males
Hung and Dangerous
In the Black
In the Raw
In Thrust We Trust
Inside Vladimir Correa
    (non-sex)
Kink
Love Thy Neighbor
M.A.G.I.C.
Pumping Black
The Rod Squad
Secret Action Man
Sexx Pitt
Soul & Salsa 1 & 2

Soul Dad
Whistle While You Work

MIKE LAMAS
(aka Miguel Lopez & Mike
Chavez) Hunky, Latin, mid
'90s model.
All American
Best of Leather: Part 1
Big River
Bullpen
Centerspread 1-3
Chi Chi Larue's Hardbody
   Video Mag. 3
Come Closer
Coming True
Cruisin' The Balcony
Cybersex
Do Me Dirty
Down On It
Face Down
Getting Even With David
Hole, The
Hot Guys #3
Idol Country
Illicit Love
The Initiation
Inside Karl Thomas
Into Leather Part 2
J.S. Big Time
Just One Favor
Knight Gallery 2
Leather Bound
Limited Entry
Lip Lock
Male Order Sex
The Male Triangle
Man To Men
Measuring Up
Knights In Eden
No Reservations
One Man's Poison
Orgies Pt 3 & 4

Outlaw Bikers
Pitch A Tent
Photoplay
Point Of View
Quickstudy
Rawhide
Sexabition
Slip It In
Stroking It—Uncut #1
Stud House
Tijuana Toilet Tramps
Top To Bottom
Total Deception
Wet Warehouse
What Men Do

TONY LAMAS
Bi & Beyond 2
In The Raw

ALAN LAMBERT
(aka Andrew Lambert)
Committed suicide with a
shotgun December 1992.
Brown hair, smooth-bodied,
jock-next-door model.
Bare Bottoms
Beach Dreamer
The Best of Jon Vincent
Boot Camp 1 & 2
Brother Trouble 1 & 2
Fatigue Relief
Grand Prize
Hard Ball
Hard to be Good
Highway Patrol
Hot Pages
Hot Shots, Vol. 25: Brief
   Encounters
Illusions
Locker Room Sex
Major Meat
Pool Boy

Rooms
Rumble
Seduction 3: Passion
   Obsession
Summer Buddies
Thumbs Up!
Warloads
Wolf Boy

DENNIS LAMBERT
French Erections

JASON LAMONT
Unexpected Persuasion

MARCUS LAMONT
Indulge Part 2

JEFF LANCASTER
Cute, blond, early 1990s
model.
Head of the Class
Screen Test

KEITH LANCASTER
Black Load

LANCE
(aka Lance Whitman)
A very popular blond,
uncut porn star legend
from the '80s from Arizona.
Backstrokes (Solo)
The Best of Blonds 2
Big & Thick
Blonds Do it Best
Carnal College
Catalina Blonds
Catalina Down & Dirty
Catalina Orgies, Vol. 1
Director's Best: William
   Higgins 1
Giant Splash Shots II

Good Hot Stuff
Good Times Coming
Hard Action
Hard to Believe
Leo and Lance
Leo Ford: The Making of a
  Superstar
Solo Studs
Student Bodies
Uncut Dreams
William Higgins Preview
  Tape #2

CHRIS LANCE
Dynastud
Inch by Inch
Other Side of Aspen 2
The Young and the Hung

ROD LANCE
A popular, blond, jock-next-
door-type 1980s model.
Anal Attraction
The Best of Blacks
Bigger and Better
Climactic Scenes #101
Come as You Are
Crazed
Cruisers: A Reunion of
Friends
Dude Ranch
Employee of the Month
Express Male
Fantasies
Gang Bangers
Happy House
Hard at It: Vol. 2
Hot Pages
In Deep
Looking Good
Men of the Moment
Northwest Package
O is for Orgy

Party Hard!
Plumbers Liquid
Pumping Up: Flexx II
Ram Man
Rooms
Spellbound For Action
Tasting Mr. Goodbar
The Thick of It
Throb
Trick Stop
Wild Streak

CHAZ LANCER
Below the Decks

SHANE LANCOURT
Desert Hart

DANNY LANDERS
For His Own Good
O is for Orgy
Sex Toy Story

JOE LANDON
Late '90s, all-American,
hunky and hung like a
horse, blond jock-next-
door model.
Apprentice, The
Joe's Big Adventure

RICK LANG
Cousins

TERRY LANG
Thick 'N Creamy

ERICH LANGE
A 1980s model from the
state of Washington.
Back to Front
Battle of the Bulge
Blond Obsession

Boys Night Out
Butt Darts
Climactic Scenes #101
Cocksure
Convertible Blues
Danny Does 'em All (bi)
Dirty Dreaming
Dude Ranch
Fantasy Boys
G.I. Mac
Hardline
Hard-on Hard Bodies
Hin Yin For Men
Horsemeat
Hot Shots, Vol. 19: Black
  and White Buns
House Boys
Hung and Dangerous
Ivy Blues
Love Bites (non-sex)
The Main Attraction
Male Taboo
Muscle Talk
The Next Valentino
Night Maneuvers
Obsession: The Ultimate
  Experience
Reunion
The Rites of Spring
The Rites of Winter
Sex Shooters II
Slick Willies
Smokin' Butts
Southbay Boys
Stiff Piece
Stud Ranch
Studz
"10" Plus
Tight Friendship
The Young Cadets

JAMES LANGE
Frat House One

RICK LANGE
Make It Hard

RENAUD LANVIN
Northern Exposures

TONY LANZA
The Main Attraction
Private Dick

ROBERT LARKIN
Attraction
The Best of Rick Savage
The Best of Street Times
Video
Cousins Should Do It
Cum Shots 102
Heartbeat
Hot Shots, Vol. 44:
Golden Boys
Hot Shots, vol. 49: Torrid
Trios
I Love Foreskin
Illusions
Lovers Coming Home
Midnight Riders
Neptune
Painting Party
Piece Work
Pool Boy
Power Force
Ram & Jam
Runaways
Sunday Brunch
Sweet Meat, Lost
Innocence
Touch of Class
White Foreskin

SVEN LARRIN
Black Stallions

DAVID LARSON
Cruisin' '57

GRANT LARSON
Originally from Illinois.
All About Last Night
Bi-Conflict of Interest
Blow Me Down
Boys From Bel Air
Center Spread 2
Chi Chi Larue's Hardbody
Video Mag. 3
Come With Me
Dish
Escort, The
Fulton Street
Getting Even With David
Going Down In Style
Hard Corps
Hidden Agenda
Hot Cargo
Idol Country
Initiation, The
Jock's Tale, A
Long Play
Made To Get Laid
Men With Tools
More Than Friends
Nymphomania
Original Sin
Power Driver
Prisoner Of Love
Reflections Of Sex
Romeo And Julian
Secret Sex 1 & 3
Seeds Of Love
Sex Is In The Air
Slave Auction
Stargazing 5
Summer Fever
These Bases Are Loaded 2
Trade
Voyeur, The

Wharfmen, The

ONY LARSON
Friends are Best
Men Who Dare

CHI CHI LA RUE
Born 1959 in Hibbing,
Minnesota. Real name
Larry Paciotti. Fabulous
and famous drag queen
porn director. Has also
appeared on screen in non-
sexual roles. Her autobiog-
raphy *Making It Big: Sex
Stars, Porn Films, And Me*,
was published in 1997 and
is a must-read for porn
fans.
Bitter She Males
Breaking Out
Davey and the Cruisers
(actor)
Goosed (bi) (actor)
Hardbody 2000 (host)
Headlock (actor)
The Hills Have Bi's
Hung Riders
Mannequin Man (actor)
Night of the Living Bi-Dolls
Revenge of the Bi-dolls
Stairway to Paradise
(actor)
Steel Garters
Switchcraft (non-sexual)
Valley of the Bi-Dolls

THOMAS LASZLO
Blond, 1999 Hungarian
model.
Hungarian Heat
Raging River

SEAN LAURENCE
A youthful-looking, brown-haired model from the 1980s.
Air Male
Better Than Bi
The Big One
Big Surprise
Black Bullet
Cabin Fever
Dirt Busters
Dreaming About Dick
In His Corner
In the Raw
More
My Sister, My Brother
New Recruits
Night Boys
Spokes 2

TOM LAW
Closed Set 2
501
Mr. Wonderful
Wild Oats

JAY LAWFORD
Any Boy Can

AARON LAWRENCE
A New Jersey native. An author, as well as a porn star, he penned the memoir *Suburban Hustler: Stories of a Hi-Tech Callboy* in 1999.
The Dream Team
Pushover

JAISON LAWRENCE
Balls of the Wild

SEAN LAWRENCE
Airmale
Bi-Surprise
The Big One
BulletPac 12: Black Bullet
Cabin Fever
Dirt Busters
Dreaming About Dick
The Graduation
In His Corner
In the Raw
More
New Recruits
The Night Boys
The Rockmore Files
Solo Flight

BILLY LAWTON
Trilogy

TONY LAZZARI
(aka Tonyboy)
Slave Toy
Sting: A Taste For Leather

DREW LEAD
All The Way Inn
Hot Stuff

BRAD LEATHERWOOD
A well endowed model from the 1980s. Died in 1990.
Black Magic, White Heat
Competition
Max Makes it Big
Outpost
Rehearsal

JOEY LABEAU
1990s model.
Staten Island Sex Cult

JONATHAN LEBEAU
Woody's

MARC LEBLANC
One More Time

PAUL LEBLANC
French Erections

PATRICK LEDEUX
All Heated Up

TOM LEDUC
Hard to Come By
The Intruders
Muscle Up
School Daze

BOBBY LEE
In His Corner

BRANDON LEE
Born March 18, 1979 in Mobile, Alabama. Late 1990s Asian model. Dark hair, 5'7". Lives in Los Angeles.
Asian Persuasion 1 & 2
Dial "S" For Sex
Fortune Nookie
Harley's Crew
Stag Party
Throat Spankers

DENNIS LEE
Black Men Do!
Black, Sex & Leather
Taking The Plunge

GABRIEL LEE
Best of Leather: Part 1
    Leather Dream
Leather Obsession 5

Look Of Leather
Mr. Blue
Orgies Pt 4

GORDON LEE
Any Excuse For Sex
Behind His Back
Desert Maneuvers
Dirty Leather
Driven By Lust
Leather Watch
Palm Springs Cruisin'
Sex And The Single Man
Sucker
Tight Leather

JAMIE LEE
VamBires

JEREMY LEE
(see Jason Miller)

JIMMY LEE
Fatique Relief
Paramedic Alert
Rites of Spring

MARK LEE
Back To K-Waikiki

MIKE LEE
The Bigger They Come
You Want Muscles?

RICK LEE
Butt Boys in Space
Cool Hand Dick
Foxhole
Grid Iron
The Grip of Passion:
   Love or Lust
Hot and Bothered
Idol Worship

Just Between Us, You
Promise
L.A. Sex Stories
The Mad Masseur
Off Duty Maneuvers
Painted
Party Hard!
Sexabition
White on White
Wild and Loose

ROB LEE
Asian Persuasion 2

RONNIE LEE
Big Time
Hard Choices

TOM LEE
Leather Report
Minute Men 2

TORI LEE
Anonymous Sex

JASON LEERY
Any Way I Can

ANDREW LENNOX
A late 1990s Australian
model.
Australian For Leather
Fetish Sex Fights 3
Switchcraft

CRUZ LENNOX
Layin' Pipe
Road To Hopeful, The

JOHN LEON
Staten Island Sex Cult

MARK LEONARD
Non-Stop
Under Construction

ROY LEONARD
A 1990s model.
Big Salami, The

MITCH LEVEC
A 1990s model.
Northern Exposures
Sure Shot

ROBERT LEWIS
Bijou

TONY LEXUS
Born September 9, 1969,
Iowa. 5'8," 7" cock.
Versatile bottom. Brown
hair. Late 1990s model.
All About Sex
Balls to the Wall 35
Cockpit, The
Fireside Brats
Freshman Fever
Hard Up
Homo Erectus
Hot Male Mechanics
Man-Time Stories
The Men of Dream
Canyon
Night In Leather
9 Holes
Pinball Wizard
Sex Trigger
Sexual Thoughts
Sinplicity
Splat
Stiff As Nails
Summer Seduction
Taking The Plunge
Tell Me About Sex

The Staff
The Wall
Threesomes
Tight Places
Tutor Me
WeHo Alley
Working Day and Night

ANDY LI
Oriental Encounters

REN LICKETT
(see Ren Adams)

DENNIS LINCOLN
(aka Choice Thomas)
Popular, black '90s model.
Adventures of A. Rocky
    and Bill Winkler, The
A.W.O.L.
Bam 2: Thug
Black American
Black Balled 2
Black Brigade
Black for More
Black Moves
Black Power
Forever Hold Your Piece
Freaks
Guarding the Jewels
Marine Chronicles, The
Mt. Fuckmore

STEVE LIPARITI
Handsome, dark-haired,
mature,'90s model.
Anal Sex Toys
Hey Tony! What's The
    Story?
Hole Patrol
Nuts, Butts And Glory
Sex Between The Lines
Shower Room Slave

SONNY LISTZ
A youthful, blond, 1990s
model from Germany.
The Big Merger
Black and Blue
The Brawnzmen
Coming Together
Deception I: Happy
Birthday to You
Deception II: Hard Justice
Down, Down, Down
    (wrestling)
Fast Company
Foreign Competition
Friends & Lovers
The Ivy League
Jackpot: On the Road to
    Vegas
Male Seduction
Malibu Pool Boys
The Meaning of Sex
My Own Private Mexico
The Naked Prey
Personal Service
Rings
A Scent of Man
Young and Notorious

TYRONE LITTLE
Black Mouthfuls

THOM LITTLEWOLF
Best Friends
Two Handsful

THOMAS LLOYD
Born June 28, 1967,
Topeka, Kansas. 6'3," 7"
cock, top. Resides in West
Hollywood. Very popular,
cute, hairy late '90s model.
Chi Chi La Rue's
    Hardbody 2000.2

Fallen Angel 2
Hard Times
Hard Working Men
Muscle Fantasies Vol. #1
Redwood

RICHARD LOCKE
Born 1941. Died
September 25, 1996 from
AIDS-related illness. One
of the first true porn stars
from the 1970s.
Best of the Superstars
Cruisin' the Castro
Daddy Dearest
The Diamond Stud
Dreamer
El Paso Wrecking Corp.
Forbidden Letters
Gemini
Heartstroke
Hot Shots, Vol. 5: Leather
Hot Shots, Vol. 7: Daddies
Hot Shots, Vol. 12:
    Uniforms
Kansas City Trucking Co.
L.A. Tool & Die
Magnum Griffin, Vol. 9
Magnum Griffin, Vol. 10
Magnum Griffin, Vol. 12
Pool Party
Passing Strangers
Robin's Egg Blue Hanky
    Left
Sins of Johnny X

JACK LOFTON
A masculine, dark-haired
1980s model.
Airmale
All Night Long
Big Boys of Summer
Blow Your Own Horn

Bubble Butt
California Dreamin'
Cruisin'
Dickey-Lickey
Flexx
Great Balls of Fire
Guilty
Highway Patrol
Hitchhiker: Manual
Transmission
Jack it Up
My Brother, My Lover
Piece Work
The Pledge Masters
Ranger Nick
Ride the Swell
Seduction
Seduction 1-5
Sex Waves
Size Talks
Soldiers
Spokes 2: The Graduation

MIKE LOFTON
(aka Tommy)
Ex sailor turned porn star.
Buddies 2-3
The Hitchhiker
The Hunger
Military Gang-Bang
Military Sex Acts 1
One Hot Summer
Real Cowboys
Young Stallions

JOSEF LOG
Collage 2
Coming From Above
In Thrust We Trust
M.A.G.I.C.
Recruit Me
Steal My Stuff

DAVE LOGAN
This blond, British import,
from the mid '90s, resides
in London.
Boot Black 1 & 2
By Invitation Only
CD Ram
Down on It
Driven to It
The Fluffer
The Guy Next Door
GV Guide Gay Erotic Video
    Awards 2
Hot Properties
Hot Stuff
Idol Dreams
Jawbreaker
Look of a Man
Lunch Hour 2
New Pledgemaster
On the Mark
One Man's Poison
Oral Fixation
Posing Strap
Rawhide
Roll in the Hay
Sunsex Boulevard
These Bases Are Loaded 2
True Stories
When the Boss Is Away
Whitefire

PETER LOGAN
Gang of 13
Lick it Up
First Time Tryers #12

BILLY LONDON
Was brutally murdered
in1990.
Black Fantasies
Bulge: Mass Appeal
Grip Of Passion

Hard Choices
Head of the Class
Hot Wired!
Imperfect Strangers
Sex Drive 2020
Sex Waves

BRYCE LONDON
An Oklahoma native and
1990s model.
Tales From the Foxhole

DEAN LONDON
I Do!
Route 69

LONDUN
A cute, dark-haired youth
from the mid 1990s.
Bite, The
Sex Between the Lines

BURT LONG
Cult of Manhood
Heat Goes On

JAMES LONG
Five Hard Pieces
Harley's Angels

JOHN LONG
Pure Fantasies
Spanking Master

JUSTIN LONG
The Games We Play

RICK LONG
(see David Burrill)

ROBERT LONG
Black Workout 2
Forbidden Black Fantasies

TAD LONG
Man Watch

TERRY LONG
Big Favors
Hard
Mansplash
Peterbuilt Boys
Rushes
Seattle Sea Hunks
Slumming
The Spirit is Willing
Texas Size 12
Uncut Club of L.A.
When a Stranger Comes

TIM LONG
A youthful model from the 1980s.
Memories of 18
Touch of Class

MICHAEL LONGSTAFF
Homo Erectus

CHASE LONGWOOD
Black Mouthfuls

CHRIS LOPEZ
(aka Jack Dallas, Torsten Witte)
A 1980s model.
Hustler Way
Spin the Bottle Orgy
Trade Off

LUIS LOPEZ
Boys Behind Bars 1 & 2
Powergrip

MIGUEL LOPEZ
(see Mike Lamas)

DANIEL LORD
Leather Lover
Virgin Territory

KRIS LORD
Dark-haired, hunky, mid-'90s model.
Bad Boys Ball
Bondage Memories
Down Home
Driving Hard
Grapplin'
Live From Key West
My Own Private Kentucky Studs
Shadows in the Night
Straight Pick-up
Take Me Home

TONY LORENZO
(see Tonyboy)

JASON P. LOVE
Cat's Tale
Party In My Pants

STEVEN A. LOVE
Cumpetition
Good Old Days
In Thrust We Trust

WINSTON LOVE
A.W.O.L.
Black Balled
Black Brigade
Black Gang-Bang
Black in the Saddle
Black Leather Gang Bang
Black Patrol
Black Renegades
Ho Ho Ho!!!
Hot Mix
Inter-Racial Interrogation

Marine Chronicles, The
Raw Meat 1
Raw Meat 5
The Soul Patrol
Special Forces
Underboss, The

MARK LOVETT
A blond, hairy-chested, early 1990s model.
Dicks' Service Center
Freeze Frame
Fantasy Suite
Trail Tales

JASON LOWE
Briefs

KEITH LOWE
Southbay Boys

TIM LOWE
Born in 1967. A handsome, dark-haired hunk-next-door. Married, he was one of the biggest gay-for-pay names of the late '80s. Returned briefly to the biz in the 1990s.
Angels By Day, Devils Bi Night
Bare Bottoms
Bi Madness
Big & Thick
Blow Out
Boot Camp 1 & 2
Buttsluts of the Castro
Center Spread 2
Davey and the Cruisers
Down Under
Fratrimony
Full Service
Hardball

Hard-on Hard Bodies
The Hole
Interview, Vol. 2
The Journey
Les Hommes
Lowe Down
The Main Attraction
Midnight Riders
Nude & Rude
Offering
Paradise Found
Power Force
Powerline
The Rites of Fall
The Rites of Summer
The Rites of Winter
Seduction III: Passion
   Obsession
Steel Away
Stud Vision
Superhunks 2
Tease Me!
Texas Size 12
Tim Lowe's Weekend
   Adventure
Top This
Trip to Paradise Beach
Wide Receiver
William Higgins Screen
   Test #2
Wolfboy
Young Gladiators

JIRI LUBOV
A 1990s Czech Republic
model.
Lucky Lukas

CHRISTIAN LUC
Born December 26,
Hungary. 5'10," 8" uncut.
Versatile. A late '90s hairy
daddy.

Good Enough To Eat
Hairsteria
Johnny Come
Leather Buddies
Mr. Fix It
The Playboy
The Pool Party
Uncut Glory

LUCKY LUC
dark-haired, hairy-chested,
mature 1980s model. Died
March 2, 1992 from AIDS-
related causes.
Absolutely Uncut
Everyday is the Fourth of
   July (dir. & actor)
First Experiences
   (dir. & actor)
Foreskin Dreams
   (dir. & actor)
F...... Good! Just Do It
   (dir. & actor)
Giving & Taking it All
Harrassment (dir. & actor)
It's So Good It's F...... Bad!
   (dir. & actor)
Lucky Hustlers (dir. & actor)
Pounding Hard
   (dir. & actor)
Red Hot Redheads
   (dir. & actor)
Screwing Around
   (dir. & actor)
Straight Dudes
   (dir. & actor)
Street Trash (dir. & actor)
Traffic School (dir. & actor)
Uncut Lucky Devil
   (dir. & actor)
Uncut Lucky Luc
   (dir. & actor)
Uncut Fever, Part 1 & 2

(dir. & actor)

MICHEL LUCAS
Born March 10. This hand-
some, horse-hung, dark-
haired, Russian-born actor-
turned-director, started his
own company in 1998.
Back in the Saddle (Dir.)
Basic Plumbing 2
The Chosen
High Tide
Maximum Cruise
Red Alert

MIKE LUCAS
Hotel Montreal
Male Call

LUKE
(aka Phillip Wagner)
Boys From Riverside Drive
Dirt Bikes
Full Service
Hot Shots
Inevitable Love
Just Blonds
Times Square Strip
Upperclassiman

KARL LUNDGREN
(see Karl Bruno)

KIRK LUNA
1970s model.
Adam & Yves
Drive!

DOLPH LUPIN
Men On-Site
New Meat
Northwest Passage

LARRY LUST
Leather Lover
Room 328

LANA LUSTER
(see Vince Harrington)

DAN LYNN
Men and Steel
Move Over Johnny

PHILIPPE LYON
Breakin'Em In

BEAU LYONS
Batter Up!

LEO LYONS
A Vermont native. Cute,
youthful, blond, 1990s
model.
Dirk Yates' Private
Collection 130 & 134
God, Was I Drunk
Tales From The Foxhole

SCOTT LYONS
Born in Duluth,
Minnesota. 5'8," 9 1/2"
cock. Versatile. Young,
blond, '90s model resides
in Los Angeles.
Alley Katt
Beach Buns
Bear Mountain Patrol
Boot Camp Buddies
Deep In The Brig
Dream Team
Getting Straight
HOMOgenized
Jeff Stryker's Underground
Marine Crucible
Meet Ray Harley

Men in Blue
Mountain Patrol
9-1/2"
Pool Play
Runway Studs
Sex Fly
Spectrum
Tall Tail

STEVE LYONS
(see Damien)

M

FREDDY MAC
A handsome, hairy-chested,
Puerto Rican model from
the 1980s.
Hot Hispanic Homebosy
Raunchy Ricans
Spanish Harlem Knights

RYAN MACALLEN
Cat's Tale
Male Call
Party In My Pants

JAYSON MACBRIDE
Anything, Anytime
Broadway Boys
Catching Up
Cherokee Station
Dirty Picture Show
Hand-In-Hand Preview
   Tape #1
Harley's Angels
Hot House
Hunk
Navy Blue Hanky Left
New York Construction Co.
A Night at the Adonis
Pool Party

Red Ball Express
Safe Sex
Sex magic
Video Encounters of the
Sexual Kind
White Hanky Left

DICK MACK
Rough Ideas
Tramps
Wildside

SYDNEY MACKENNA
A British model from the
1980s.
Carnival in Venice
Sex Oasis

SKIP MACKINTOSH
California Boys
Revenge of the Nighthawk

GEORGE MADERA
Full Service
Private Dick
Undercover

BOBBY MADISON
(aka Brian Michaels)
Below The Belt
The Bigger The Better
Brother Load
Catalina Down and Dirty
Catalina Men
Director's Best: William
   Higgins, Vol. 1
F. Stop
Foreign Competition
French Lt.'s Boys
In Heat
Leo and Lance
The Master of Disciple
Pipeline

Sex in the Great Outdoors,
  Part 2
Something Wild
Studio X
Sum Young Mahn

PAUL MADISON
Brother Load
Bigger & Better
Bronco Bunch
Home Movies
Kiko Maestras
Taxi
Wide Load
Young Olympians
Young Warriors

KIKO MAESTRAS
Bigger & Better
Bronco Bunch
Home Movies
Taxi
Wide Load
Young Warriors

JOE MAGNUM
Best Of Leather: Part 2
Leather Obsession
Orgies Pt 2
Outlaw Bikers
Tom Katt

ROD MAJORS
Latin looking mid '90s
model, discovered by
Kristen Bjorn. Reportedly
moved to Germany.
All About Last Night
Beat Off Frenzy
Bi-Conflict of Interest
Built Tough
Come And Get It
Conflict Of Interest

Everybody Does It
Forever Hold Your Piece: 2
Grease
Guest Services
Hot Springs Orgy
Hung Up
Idol Country
Jawbreaker
Laid To Order
Lunch Hour 2
Man Country
Man To Men
Manticipation
Montreal Men
Northern Exposures
Power Trip
Secret Sex 2
Taste Of Leather 2
Woody's

LUCIEN MALLARD
Thick & Creamy
Under the Sign of the
Stallion

MALLEEK
Glory Holes of San
Francisco

MALO
Dune Buddies
A Night at the Adonis

DANIEL MALONE
Buddy System
Ten is Enough

**HOGAN MALONEY
(see Alec Campbell)**

ERIC MANCHESTER
Born in 1965. A dark-
haired, gay-for-pay leg-

endary bottom from the
'80s. Lives in San
Francisco.
Ball Blasters
Best Bi Far #2
The Best of Eric
  Manchester
A Big Business
Bulge: Mass Appeal
Crosswire
Down for the Count
The Exchange
'57 Pickup
Giant Men
Giant Splash Shots 2
Giants
Head of the Class
Hot, Hung And Hard
In Your Wildest Dreams
Mannequin Man
Men Of Size
Plunge, The
Powerline
The Rites Of Summer
Sex Drive 2020
Sex Waves
Spokes 2: The Graduation
Superhunks
They Grow Em Big
Touch Me: It's Hot, I'ts
Tender

MANDINGO
Bronc Rider
Dirt Bikes
A Night at the Adonis
Sex Magic
Weekend Lockup

ERIC MANDRELL
Printer's Devils
Strictly for Ladies Only

NICK MANETTI
(aka Nick Mannetti)
The Abduction 2&3
At Your Service
Basket Fever
Beach Blanket Boner
The Calendar Men
Come Back, The
Day Dreams
Dirty Pool
Erector Set
Favors
Good Vibrations
Hard Ass
A Hole Different Ball Game
Home Wrecker
Hose Men
Hot Ticket
Hustlemania
Impacted
In the Mix
It's a Gang #2
Men on a Budget
Ouch
Picture Perfect 2
Powertool 2: Breaking Out
The Producer
Roughed Up At The Spike
Running Wild
Secrets and Fantasies
Sex Shooters II
Silverlake Inn
Slippery When Wet
Smoke Screen
Stiff
Sucker
Surrogate Stud
Sweat Motel
Tattoo Parlor
Temptation
Ten Plus 2
Through the Looking Glass
Toilet Tramps

Tongue and Cheek
Totally Exposed
Transparent
V-8
Vice Cop
Voltage
X-treme Close-Up

KIRK MANHEIM
Badlands
Bronc Rider
Flashback
More DickFisk

CHRISTOPHER MANN
The Big Lift
Big Time
Danny Does Dallas!
Danny's Back
Dude Ranch
Gimme it All
Hot Shots, Vol. 27:
    Super Studs
Hot Wired
Imperfect Strangers
Let me Be Your Lover Boy
Obsessed
On Fire
Pounder
Reunion
Unloading It
Who's Dat Boy?
You Bet Your Ass

DAVID MANN
A New York model from
the early 1990s.
Broadway Boys
Screen Test
Sleaze
Young Yankees

JOHN MANN
13th Step

LARRY MANN
(aka Larry Young)
976-MANN

LEE MANN
Beyond Hawaii
Delivery Boys
Director's Best: William
Higgins, Vol. 1
Preppy Summer
Razor's Edge

M. VIC MANN
Attack of the Amazing
Colossal Latino

MARC MANN
Hairy, older model, now
runs a video store in
Southern California.
Barely Tamed
Beater's Digest
Cumplete & Uncut
Daddy for Dessert
Distinguished Gentlemen
Digital Fantasy - 2nd Byte
Executive Action
General Mann's Hawaiian
Vacation
Hard Working Daddies
Hoods & Helmets (Cameo)
ISO: Heavy Metal Fantasy
Manly Persuasion
Men: Skin & Steel
Real Men of the New West
Stiff Summer Cocktails
Working Stiffs

MICHAEL MANN
(see Michael Ram)

SCOTT MANN
Anonymous Sex
Object of My Erection, The
Policemen's Balls

VICTOR MANUEL
Militia Men

MIKE MANZONI
My Dick Is Bigger 2

ETHAN MARC
Born June 30th, New
Orleans. 5'8," 7 1/2" cock,
bottom. Cute, clean cut,
boy-next-door, late '90s
model.
Aussie Pool Party
Bootie Nights
Cadet
Cowboy Jacks
Demolition Man
Rosebud
Swank
Tailspin

VITO MARCHELLI
Hotel Montreal
Party In My Pants

JOHN MARCUS
Into Leather Part 2
Leather Lover
Leather Party
Leather Virgin
Summer Obsession
Tempted
13th Step
3-Some

JUSTIN MARINO
Czech Republic model.
Lucky Lukas

TONY MARINO
A cute, youthful, dark-
haired Italian model from
the 1980s.
Angelo Loves It!
Bad Boys Club
Ball Bustin' Boys
The Best of John
Davenport
The Bigger They Come
Cruisin' West Hollywood
Head of the Class
Heatwaves
Hot Wired
Military Men
Mountain Fever
Perfect Summer
Powertool
Sex Drive 2020
Spokes II: The Graduation
Uncontrollable Obsession
Unloading It
The Voyeur
The Young Cadets

VINNIE MARINO
(aka Ray Acosta) Cute,
boyish Cuban model from
the 1980s.
Beat this Beef
Boy Oh Boy
Cruising Park
Hard Men 2
Hot Rods: Young & The
  Hung 2
Interview 1
Spanking Master 2

DAVE MARK
Asian Knights
Oriental Encounters

JOE MARKHAM
Big Deal
Connoisseur Collectros
Classics
First Time Around 1972
Fist Full
Magnum Griffin 1
Male Stampede
Muscle, Sweat & Brawn
Round-Up

SONNY MARKHAM
Born July 27, 1976 in
Chicago, Illinois. 5'8," 8-
1/2" cock. A Chicago resi-
dent. Popular bodybuilder
from the '90s.
Dare Devils
Dark Side of the Moon
In Man's Country
Mavericks
Trying it On for Size
Working It Out

JEFF MARKS
Hard Ball
Lust Boys
Power Force

JOSEPH MARKS
Conflict Of Interest

LOREN MARKS
Every Which Way

MATTHEW MARKS
(aka Clint Parker, Mark
Angeles, Mark Matthews)
dark-haired, macho, bisex-
ual, 1980s model.
Big Favors
Big Shooters
Bi Bi Love

Foreplay
Good Men Get Bad
Hard
Island Heat
Men on the Loose
Naked Lunch
Nightcrawler
Rushes
Sex Hunt
The Spirit is Willing
Tough Iron
You Want Muscles?

STEVE MARKS
(aka Steven Marks or Steve
Marx) Steve was a televi-
sion weatherman in
Chicago before becoming a
porn star.
Another Man's Pleasure
Below The Rim
Bi-Conflict of Interest
Big River
Built Tough
Chi Chi Larue's Hardbody
    Video Mag. 3
Conflict Of Interest
Courting Libido
Deep End
Diamond Stud, The
Fantasy Fights 5 & 6
Fox's Lair
Getting Even With David
Hard Lessons: Sex Ed 2
Hot Cargo
Hung Riders, The
Idol Country
In Your Ear
Making Of A Gay Video
Prisoner Of Love
Ruthless
Secret Sex 3: The Takeover

LEE MARLIN
Best of the Superstars
The Boys of Riverside
Drive
Down to the Farm
Grease Monkeys
Hand-in-Hand Preview
    Tape #1
His Little Brother
Just Blonds
New York Men
Rear Deliveries
Roommates
Tub Tricks

BILL MARLOWE
(aka Damian Harris) a
dark-haired, late '80s, and
early '90s model. Lives in
San Francisco.
Back to Front
The Best of Matt Sterling 2
Big Delivery
Bi Intruder
Black Pack
Brawn's Rod
Brief Encounters
Buttsluts of the Castro
Castro Commando
Cruisin' the Balcony
Disconnected
Dogs in Heat
Easy Riders
Everybody Does It
Exposed
Fast Idle
Fidelity
Gorgeous
Hard Ass
Heat in the Night
Hot Pursuit
In a Jock's Locker
Inside Karl Thomas

Just Between Us,
    You Promise
Leather Lust
Leather Story
Live Bi Me
Long Hard Ride
The Lust Boys
Lust, Sex & The
Covermodel
Male Instinct
Male Seduction
Male Triangle, The
Manstroke
Motor Crotch
Nothin' Nice
Over The Edge
Penetrating Moves
Private Dick
Sex Crimes
Sex Guys And Videotape
Shadows In The Night
Sizzle
Solo Satisfaction
Special Handling
Star Gazing 2
Stiff Cocktail
Stud House
Sunsex Boulevard
Switch Hitters 7
Take It Like A Man
Taken 2 The Max
Tales Of The Backlot
Temptation
Ten Is Enough
Top It Off
Voice Male
What Men Do

LEE MARRON
Razor's Edge

KURT MARSHALL
Died October 10, 1988

from AIDS-related illness.
Night Flight
Other Side Of Aspen 2
Sizing Up
Splash Shots

TODD MARSHALL
Rawhide

DAVE MARTIN
Big Shooters 2
Boys Just Wanna have
  Sex
Caribbean Cruising
Flesh Tones
Freshman Fantasies
Good Men Get Bad
Ivy Blues
Men on the Loose
Outpost
Show and Tell

VAL MARTIN
Born to Raise Hell
Moving
Performance
Sextool

ARMANDO MARTINEZ
After Hours
Board Meeting
I Love Foreskin
Uncut Latins

ROD MARTINEZ
All That Jizz
Bootie Nights

DANNY MARTINO
(see Danny Russo)

ADRIANO MARQUEZ
Born August 25.

Into Leather
Men
Raw Material
We've Got Them All

ERIC MARX
Alley Boys
Erotikus
Hot Cargo
New Pledgemaster
Penetrating Moves
Reveille
Rival, The
Sexual Suspect
Slave Auction
Stud House
Swallow
Vice Cop

BRAD MASON
A mature, 1980s model
known for his tattoos.
Advocate Men Live 2
Blue Angel
Cum-pany Ass-ets
Extreme Urge
Falconhead 2
Giants, Part 1
Hot Off the Press
Hot Shots, Vol. 6: Kinky
Hotel Hell
Jacks Are Wild
Job Site
Lovers and Friends
Mind Games
More Mind Games
One in a Billion
Rising Desire

BRODY MASON
Outdoor Ecstacy
You've Got Male

CHAD MASON
976-Stud

DIRK MASON
Any Boy Can

DOUG MASON
Gunslingers
Kept After School

MARK MASON
Born: April 20, 1964, West
Virginia. 6'2," 8" cock. A
dark-haired leather daddy
top from the late '90s.
Australian For Leather
The Best of Advocate Men
Big Guns II
Billy 2000
Deep In The Brig
Erota-Wrestling
Give & Submit
Maximum Performance
Muscleforce #2 - Mark
The Orgy Experience
Sharp Shooters
Thunder Balls
Uninvited, The

TONY MASON
Black Attack
Black Force
Black Lust, white Passion
Working Hard for the
Money

TODD MASS
Bi-Conflict of Interest
Making Of A Gay Video

AUSTIN MASTERS
Ass Lick Alley
Aussie Pool Party

Australian For Leather

BROCK MASTERS
1990s model.
Chip Daniels' Video
Studbook
Time Cops

BUDDY MASTERS
Cult of Manhood
Max makes it Big

DICK MASTERS
Died of spinal cancer in
March 1990. A handsome,
blond, Dallas, Texas native
and a porn star legend
from the late '80s with an
11" cock.
Best Of All 2
Bi and Beyond
Black and Beyond: The
    Darker Side
Deep in Hot Water
Director's Best: John
Travis, Vol. 1
Foxhole
Heat in the Night
Just Between Us, You
    Promise
L.M.L. Uncut
Manrammer
Nut Busters
Size Talks
Ten is Enough

DOUG MASTERS
1990s model.
Oasis
Wrestling

LEO MASTERS
Born October 13, 1970 in

Santa Barbara, California.
5'8," 8" cock. Late '90s
bottom.
Action on Melrose
At First Glance
Behind His Back
Big Boyz Club 4
Club Butt 2: Private Party
Come As You Are
Danger Alley
Desert Maneuvers
Desert Paradise
Dickin' Around
Dirty Dreaming
The Drifters
Full Release
Gone West
Hard Times
Hurricane Hard-on
It's a Gang #1
Looking For Mr. Goodhead
Max Hardware
My Own Private Mexico
O is for Orgy
On the Move
Penetration on
Pennsylvania Avenue
Poolman Cometh, The
Sexcuses
Skinny Dipping
Special Deliveries
Swimming Pool Orgy
Touch Me There
Uniforms Only
Wet Load
Wet Sex
You've Got Male

PHILLIP MASTERS
(see Cole Youngblood)

ZAIRE MASTERS
Black Balled 2

Black Men Do!
Gettin' Ma Freak on 2

MARC MASTERSON
Gut Reaction
Jumpin' Jacks

AKOS MATAYOS
Sure Thing

ROD MATHESON
Holding Their Own:
    Self-Sucking Soldiers
Lusty Leathermen:
Mechanic on Booty

PAUL MATTA
(see Ted Matthews)

REUBEN MATTA
A Spanish Fantasy

BEAU MATTHEWS
A 1980s model.
Afternoons
Bad Habits
Big Shooters #6
California Boys
Every Which Way
Greenhorn
Hard & Throbbing
Hard Fantasies
How I Got the Story
I Do!
Men of Action II
Men of the Midway
Obsession: The Ultimate
    Experience
Pleasure Beach
Skin Deep
Tony's Initiation
Turned On

BRUCE MATTHEWS
Sure Thing

BULL MATTHEWS
(see Michael Ram)

CHIP MATTHEWS
The Boy Next Door
Convertible Blues
The Cut Club
Daddy Hunt
Deception, Part 1 & 2
The Extra Day
4 Alarm Studs
Hot and Bothered
Hustlemania
In the Men's Room
Keep in Touch
Macho Money
Mack Pack, Vol. 3:
   Splash Tops
Mechanics on Duty
Midnight Hard-On
Mounted Police
Movers and Shakers
No Cruisin' Zone
One and Only Dominator
The Orgy Club
Rear End Window
Santa's Coming
Secret Boys Club
Secret Report
Selling It
Tennis Court Daze
The Whole 9 Yards

CODY MATTHEWS
Born June 10, 1978,
Kentucky. 6'0," 7 1/2" cock,
versatile. Cute, blond, late
'90s model.
Relatively Speaking
Something Very Big

Uncle Jack

DIRK MATTHEWS
Full Load
Head of the Class

RICK MATTHEWS
Born February 26, 1976 in
the Midwest. 5"7," 7"
cock. Beefy, dark-haired
bottom from the late '90s.
Desert Heart
Family Secrets
Focal Length
Get It On Line
Island Guardian
Live Feed
Raw Material
Sit Tight
Stock
Suck Daddy
Sunsex Blvd. 2
Switchcraft
Take One: Guys Like Us
Up For Grabs

SCOTT MATTHEWS
Late 1990s blond model.
Apprentice, The
Home Bodies
Iron Will
Man Trade Solos
964 Dicks St.
Shameless

TED MATTHEWS
(aka Paul Matta) dark-
haired, early '90s model.
Action on Melrose
Alone At Last
Bedtime Stories:
   Tales to Keep You Up
The Best of Chad Knight

Best of Titan: Collector
   Series 2
The Big Date
Boner
The Brawnzmen
Built to Last
A Cut Above
Deep End
Dirty Pillow Talk
Fighting Dirty
Foot Fetish
Frat House: Memories of
   Pledge Week
The Fresh Men
Hard Talk
Hell Weekend
Hologram
Hot Pursuit
Joey
Johnny Hormone
Juice Bomb
Knight Heat
Mandriven
Manplay
Midnight Sun
Muscles and Thickness
Neighborhood Games
A Night With Strangers
Nude Science
Pits, Tits and Feet
Powertool 2: Breaking Out
Pure Attraction
Rump Ranger
Sex Depot
Sex in the great Outdoors,
   Part 3
Sex Shooters 2
Single White Male
Skuff
Speelbound for Action
Sterling Ranch
Stiff Piece
Straight To The Zone

Studz
Too Damn Big!

TOM MATTHEWS
Ass Lick Alley
Bi-Sexual Nation
Gang of 13
Lick It Up
Live Feed
Suck Daddy
Thick as Thieves

NICK MAURO
The Hustlers
Split/Image

CLAY MAVERICK
Born July 15. Hunky, dark-haired model from the late '90s.
An American Man
Beverly Hills Hustlers
The Big Shot
Billy 2000
Dynastud 3
Handsome Drifters
Hard Focus
Naked Highway
Sex Rangers, The
Sting: A Taste For Leather
West Hollywood Hope

STEVE MAVERICK
Chase Is On, The
Chi Chi Larue's Hardbody Video Mag. 3
Coach's Boys, The
Cody Exposed
Easy Prey
Military Issue 2
On The Mark
One More Time
Secret Sex

Summer Daze
Sunsex Boulevard
Trade

BRIAN MAXON
A porn star legend from the '80s.
Best Bi Far #2
Big & Thick
The Big Switch
Briefs: The Best of John Summers
Maximum Maxon
Paul Norman's World of Sexual Oddities
Sizing Up
Splash Shots
Switch Video #2
The Troy Saxon Gallery, Vol. 1
Two Handfuls

**CHAD MAXWELL
(see Mark Tayler)**

DEAN MAXWELL
Born May 29, 1973, Los Angeles. 5'9," 7-1/2" cock. A hairy and versatile model from the late '90s.
All That Jizz
Always Available
Animus
Ass Lick Alley
Aussie Pool Party
Bed and Breakfast
Coal Miner's Son
Cockland
Danger Zone
Dare Me
Desert Sands
The Drifter
Eatin' Crackers In Bed

From Hair to Eternity
Gang of 13
Going West
Greased Lightning
Guarding The Jewels
Hairsteria
Hard To Keep Down
Hot Tub Fever
Lick It Up
Mall Cruisin'
Mount The Big One
My Best Friends Woody
Over The Rainbow
Picture Perfect
Rendezvous At The Golden Gate Rent To Bone
Sandsblasted
Sand Storm
69in' In The Shade
Spiked
Uniforms Only
Wanna Be In Pictures?
West Hollywood Sex Party

JAKE MAXWELL
You've Got Male

**TROY MAXWELL
(see Kevin Kemp)**

BRIAN MAXX
Full Package
His Big Brother
Hot Copy
How To Get A Man In Bed
In Your Ear
Inches Away
It Happened One Day
Man About Town
Men of Forum
Night Walk
Night Watch 2
Prisoner Of Love

Saddle Tramps 2
Single For The Weekend

RANDALL MAXXON
A handsome, 1990s dark-
haired daddy.
Eight Men In
Favors
Hand Jobs 3
Hologram
Hot Ticket
It's A Gang: Video Series 1
Sex Crimes
Silverlake Inn
Summer Fever

JIM MAYER
Blue Summer Breeze

HAWK MCALLISTAR
Born November 7, 1967,
Boise, Idaho. Resides in
Los Angeles. 6'3," 8"
uncut. A popular, blond top
from the '90s.
Clothes Make the Man
Cram Course
Earning His Keep
Flesh and Blood
Heat Wave
Hot Tub Fever
Idol in the Sky
Law of Desire
Leather Obsession
Mall Cruisin' X-L
Marine Obsession
Men Only
More than Friends
Mount The Big One
Nude Getaway
A Real Man
Sand Storms
Saving Ryan's Privates

Something About Larry
Streets of LA
Urgent Matters
Wall, The 1 & 3
West Hollywood Sex Party
Wild Sex in America

GLENN MCALLISTER
Billy's Tale
Full Length
Wet Load

DOUG MCCALL
(see Steve Wright)

BLAKE MCDONALD
Anonymous Sex
The Best of Surge II
Big Boys of Summer
The Best Stallions
BulletPac 12: Black Bullet
Century Mining
Dirty Load
The Golden Boys
Hard Disk Drive
Hollywood Gigolo
Hot Shots, Vol. 36:
    Student Affairs
Hot Shots, Vol. 38:
    Uncut Hunks
Hot Shots, Vol. 41:
    Rim Shots
Lusty Lovers
Men of Action II
More Than a Mouthful
My Brother, My Lover
Nightcrawler
Quickies #7
Rodeo
Slumming
Stud Struck
Studbusters
Texas Size 12

What the Big Boys Eat

CHRIS MCDONALD
You Want Muscles?

TOMMY MCGILL
Measuring Up

SHAWN MCIVAN
(see Brian Hawks)

BROCK MCKAY
Cute, beefy, blond model
from the 1990s.
Orgies Partt 3
The Selection Part 1 (Solo)
The Sex Files
Titan Men
We've Got Them All

KYLE MCKENNA
Born October 27, 1968,
Pennsylvania. Very hand-
some and buffed, boyish-
looking brunet. 5'9," 6 1/2"
cut. Late '90s bottom.
Academy, Tlhe
Ace In You Face
Balls In Play
Best of Leather: Part 1
Butt Bruisers
Captive Men 6
Chip Daniels' Video
    Studbook
Das Butt
Down On Me
Extreme Measures
Homosexual Tendencies
Hot Cops 3: The Final
    Assault!
Hung Jury
Idol In The Sky
In The Deep End

In The Mix
Invaders From Uranus
Johnny Hormone
Leather Men
Leather Obsession 5:
   Mission Possible
Leather Training Center
Link To Link
Morning, Noon & Night
One the Prowl Again
The Player
Ranger In The Wild
Raw Recruit
Reform School
Confidential
Reunion
Sex Files, The
Shoot The Chute
Skuff
Sure Thing
A Tale of Two Brothers
Vacation Spot

CHRIS MCKENZIE
(aka Brad Alman, Todd
Anders & Jeremy Wynn)
A blond, boy next door,
1980s model.
Between the Sheets
Bigger & Better
Birthday Boy
California Dreamin'
Campus Glory Holes
Clothes Make the Man
Cyber Sex
The Diamond Stud
Exiled
Fidelity
Hard Corps
Hard to Take
Honesty
Honorable Discharge
Hot Copy

Jackhammer
Joker's Wild
Junior Crew
Just Do It (Jeremy Wynn)
The Lust Boys
Male Taboo
More of a Man
Mirror, Mirror (Brad Alman)
Object of Desire
Ram Man 3
Ready to Serve
The Rise
Scoring
Sex, Lies and
Videocassettes
Sexmates
Sizzle
Strictly Confidential
Superhunks
Swim Meat 1 & 2
Ten is Enough
Trading Up
Undergear
Wide Load
X-Poseur

DAVID MCNEIL
1980s model.
Big Shooters #6
Chain Reactions
Class Reunion
Gayracula
Hard Money
Knockout
Malibu Days, Big Bear
   Nights

SHAWN MC WILLIAMS
1980s model.
Tony's Iniation
Wilde House

BUCK MEADOWS
Resides in Amsterdam.
Big Thrill ,The
Hotel California
French Connections 1
In Deep: Miles To Go

RAY MEDINA
Gayracula
Rawhide (1981)

MELCHOR
(see Melchor Diaz)

CISCO MELENDEZ
Beeper Boyz of el Barrio
Bodega Boyz
Hispanic Monuments 2
Latin Showboyz

TEO MELENDEZ
Attack of the Amazing
Colossal Latino

ANTHONY MENGETTI
(aka Tony Mengetti)
Bear It All
Dirty White Guys
Face Riders
Fire & Desire
Harley's Crew
Hung Riders 2
Leather Intrusion 1
Leather Obsession
Leather Obsession 6:
   The Search
Meet Ray Harley
Men 4 Men On The Net
On the Net
Men With Tools
Room Mated
Shoot the Shoot
Slave Trade

Smell of a Man 1 & 2
South of the Border
Throat Spankers
Time in the Hole
Tomorrow Will come
Wet Warehouse 2

JOHN MERCADO
(see John Dante)

ERIC MERRILL
Cum-Pany Ass-Ets
Jacks are Wild
SunKissed

JIMMY METZ
Afternooners
Bore 'n Stroke
Hard to Come By
The Intruders

ANDREW MICHAELS
(see Chuck Barron)

BRAD MICHAELS
Born March 19. Mature,
hairy-chested, dark-haired,
late 1990s model.
Deep Desires
Family Secrets
High Stakes Wrestling
  3 & 4
Immersion
Los In Las Vegas
Rescure 69-11

BRIAN MICHAELS
(see Bobby Madison)

CHRIS MICHAELS
(1980s)
Fire Island Fever
A Night At The Adonis

CHRIS MICHAELS
Dark-haired, late 1990s
model and boyfriend of
Matthew Anders.
Cream Team, The
The Man Hunt
Uninvited, The
Weho Confidential

DAMIEN MICHAELS
Good Old Days
In the Black
Screen Test Magazine 1

DEREK MICHAELS
Bootie Nights

DEVON MICHAELS
(see Ren Adams)

ERIK MICHAELS
Acres of Ass 1 & 2
The Big Thrill
Jumpin' Jacks

GAVIN MICHAELS
Late 1990s model.
Nude Science
When A Man Wants A Man

JEFF MICHAELS
Pushover
Quick Relief
Relentless
Stop At Nothing
You've Got The Touch

JOSHUA MICHAELS
Redwood

KEVIN MICHAELS
The Hollywood Kid

LANCE MICHAELS
(See Dirk Adams)

MATT MICHAELS
Skin Deep
Stud Struck
Young Guys

PAUL MICHAELS
Bare Bottoms
Boys on the Block
Just Between us
Make a Wish & Blow
She's a He
Some Men are Bigger
  than Others
Tender Trick

PETER MICHAELS
Flyin' Solo
Smell of a Man 2
Straight Cocksuckers

RAPHAEL MICHAELS
(aka Rafael Michaels)
My Best Friends Woody
Skinny Dipping
Swimming Pool Orgy

SEAN MICHAELS
(aka Shawn Michaels)
All-American Boy
The All-American Girl
  (hetero)
Anal Revolution (hetero)
Big Shooters #2
Black in the Saddle Again
  (hetero)
Blonds Do It Best
Getting It
Heavy Petting (hetero)
Hot Male Mechanics
Hot Men

Ivy Blues
Malibu Days/Big Bear
  Nights
Oriental Temptation
  (hetero)
Robin Hood (hetero)
Shameless (hetero)
Straight Boys Do!
Straight to Bed
Takin' it to the Jury
Victoria's Secret Life
  (hetero)

SHANE MICHAELS
Auto Erotica: The Best of
  Sex in Cars
Ball Bustin' Boys
Below the Belt
Bi Bi Love
Bi Sexual a Go-Go
Bi-Sexual Fantasies
Big & Thick
Boys Just Wanna Have
  Sex
Heat Goes On
Hollywood Gigolo
Hot and Bothered
Internatinal Skin
Ivy Blues
Make it Hard
Mansplash
Naked Lunch
Spanking 11
The Spirit is Willing
Two by Ten
Two Handsful
White on White

STEFAN MICHAELS
Hard 1 & 2
It's Raining Men
Young Guys
Young Shooters

STEVEN MICHAELS
Grizzly

TROY MICHAELS
I Live For Sex

LAURENT MICHEL
Horizons

ARPAD MIKLOS
Thick as Thieves

ZOLY MIKLOS
Raging River

CHRISTIAN MILANO
It Happened One Day
Just One Favor

JORGE MILANO
Beach Buns
Latins
Straight Exposure
Uncut Weekend
You Sexy Thing!

RICK MILANO
Big Deposit
Latin Sex Thing
Spin the Bottle Orgy

COREY MILES
Full Package
Hungry Eyes
Nasty Rumors
No Reservations
Point Of View
Possession
Rear Ended
Ruthless
Sexual Suspect
Tainted Love
Trophies: Class Of '94

KEVIN MILES
Betrayed
Cowboy Jacks
In Deep: Miles To Go
Link
Male Box
The New Coach
Soaked
Stock
The Taking of Jake

DAVID MILKEN
Cummin' Of Age
Mountain Cruisin'
Summer Money

CHRISTOPHER MILLER
A Tale of Five Brothers

DON MILLER
Breaker Blue
Soul & Salsa 2

DUNCAN MILLS
(aka Duncan Miles, Duncan
Miller, Don Dawson)
Cute, young-looking
Latin/Asian-looking model
from the late '90s.
Bootie Nights
Cramming for the Big One
Gang Bang Ranch Hand
Gay for the Weekend
Going West
Greased Lightening
Guarding the Jewels
Hard Times
Hard Working Men
Hawaiian Vacation 2
K-Waikiki
Latin Balls 2: Huevos
Logan's Journey
Mall Crusin' X-L

Measure For Measure
My Secret Lust
Outdoor Ecstacy
Paul Morgan's Raw Meat 3
Red Blooded Americans
Sands Storms
Sexpionage
Spank Me, Man!
Uniforms Only
Virtual Sexuality
While the Cat's Away
www.Orgy
Young Slaves in Training

JASON MILLER
(aka Jeremy Lee)
Born March 18, 1977,
Walla Walla, Washington.
5'11," 7" cock. Blond, boy-
ish model from late '90s.
Blade Studs
Hot Sheets
Lambda, Lambda, Lambda
Pleasure Principle
Reform School
Confidential
Something Very Big

MARK MILLER
A legendary top from the
'80s.
The Best of Street Times
   Video
The Big Switch (bi)
Dick's Service Center
Dynastud
Executive Action
Friend to Friend
Giant Men
Giants
Hot Shots, Vol. 14:
   Tight Buns
Inch by Inch

Lovers, Cheaters and
Maneaters
Nightflight
Party Line
Sizing Up
The Switch is On
Switch Video #2
Taking the Dive
Tender Trick

VINCENT MILO
Boot Camp 2
Fantasy Boys

ADAM MITCHELL
Greenhorn
Hardhat
Rough Cut

BRAD MITCHELL
A dark-haired, 1980s
model.
Cocktales
Cruisin 2
Deep in Hot Water
Heat in the Night
Made for You
Mandriven
Manrammer
Pledge Masters

JEFF MITCHELL
Desert Sands
Freshman Recruits
Hairsteria
Journal, The
My Best Friends Woody
Penetration on
Pennsylvania Avenue
Phi Kappa Sucka'
Poolman Cometh, The
Romping Roommates
Skinny Dipping

Swimming Pool Orgy
Turn of Events
When The Wife's Away

MIKE MITCHELL
Dreamen: Dirty Dialogue
Dreamer
Hollywood Liberty
Twelve at Noon

MILES MITCHELL
Face to Face
Flashbacks

ROD MITCHELL
Come Closer

TODD MITCHELL
All American
Born To Be Wild
Bull Pen
Call Boy
Come Closer
Come With Me
Hot Cargo
It Happened One Day
MVP: Most Valuable Player

TOM MITCHELL
Bigger Than Huge
Powertool
Private collection Screen
Test
Sizing Up
Splash Shots
Spring Training

RANDY MIXER
(aka Cody Feelgoode)
This bottom man was
reportedly discharged from
the Navy for being gay.
Alley Action

Bedroom Lies
The Big Showoff
Bi-ology: The Making of
Mr. Right
The Bodymasters
The Brawszmen
Chain Male
Chi Chi LaRue's Hardbody
Video Mag. 3
Choose Me
Circle of Fire
Cocksure
Deception, Part 1 &2
Down Bi Law
Dude Beach
Exposed
G.I. Jocks: Out of the
Ranks
Handjobs 2
Hard Talk
Head Over Heels
Hollywood and Vine
Hologram
Idol Universe
Intensive
It's A Gang: Video Series 1
Long Distance Lovers
Mentor
Mix It Up
Muscles and Thickness
My Cousin Danny
One and Only Dominator
1230 West Melrose
Palm Springs Paradise
Payne In The Ass
Piece Of Cake
Playing With Power
Posing Strap
Possession
Rear Ended
Ring Of Fire
Sex In Wet Places
Songs In The Key Of Sex

Special Deliveries
Sperminator
Tony's Big Brother
Waterworks
Wet Sex
X-Treme Close-Up

MOCHA
A popular black model
from the '90s.
Adventures of Rocky and
Bill Winkler, The
A.W.O.L.
Bam 2: Thug
Black American
Black Leather Gang Bang
Black Power
Black Rose, The
Black Warriors
Ho Ho Ho!!!
Hooked on Ebonics
Marine Chronicles, The
Mt. Fuckmore
Other Side of Big Bear
Stroke My Digits

CORY MONROE
(aka Eric Reiker)
Anywhere, Anytime
Bad Boys Dormitory
Bait
Ball Blasters
The Best Stallions
Bi Day/Bi Night
Bi-Swingers
Black Lust/White Passion
Boys Camp Memories
Cabin Fever
Cashload
Castro Commands
Climactic Scenes #101
Crusin' for Lust
Danny Does Dallas

Dirt Busters
Dogs in Heat
Double Exposure
Double Standards
Freshman
Giants
Guilty
Guys Who Crave Black
Cock
Hawaiian Heat
Hollywood Gigolo (cameo)
Hot on His Tail
Hot Pages
Hot Shots, Vol. 14: Tight
Buns
In a Jock's Locker
It's the Size that Counts
J.D. Slater's Confessions
Male-O-Gram
Man's Hand #115
The Massage Boys
Men in Motion #1
Men of Action
Men of Size
Men on the Loose
Mikey Likes It
Neverending Studs
New Recruits
Nine-and-a-Half Inches
Oh, Brother!
On Top
Play Safely
Pretty Boy
P.S. Connection #1
Pump
Quickies #5
Scores
She-Male Desires
She-Male Reformatory
Show it Hard
Southern Comfort
The Spirit is Willing
Spring Break

Brad Stone, Size Videos

Lance, Laguna Pacific/Malibu Studios

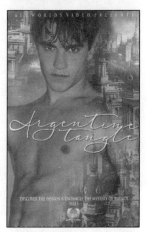

Javier Duran, All Worlds

Vince Rockland, Crystal Crawford/IMD

Kurt Marshall, Falcon Studios

Kurt Stefano, Jocks Studios

Bam, Jett Set Productions

Tom Brock, Huge Video

Chance & Johan Paulik, Bel Ami

Tony Donovan, L.A. Heat Video

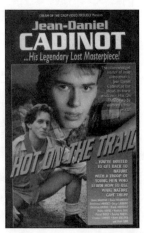

Denis Beauvais & David DiLorenzo, Cadinot

Mark Slade, Studio 2000

Roger, Falcon Studios

Kip Noll, Trademark Studios

Lane Fuller, All Worlds

Jeff Stryker, Huge Videos

Aiden Shaw, Falcon Studios

Scott Nichols, TCS Studios

Andel, Czech Mate/All Worlds

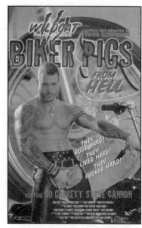

Bo Garrett, Wildcat Productions/IMD

Joey Carr & Vic Hall, Junior Studios

Bobby Blake, Brick House Entertainment

YMAC Video

Rex Chandler, Falcon Studios

Scott Aaron, YMAC Video

Rick Donovan, First Place Video

Adam Hart, All Worlds

Gianfranco, Catalina

Bill Henson, Falcon Studios

Steve Hammond, Falcon Studios

Steve Henson, Huge Video

Mason Jarr, All Worlds

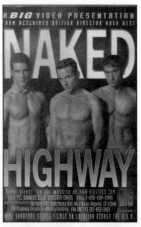

Clay Maverick, Kurt Young, Ty Harman, BIG Video

Burt Edwards, Falcon Studios

Alec Powers, Minotaur

Steve Rambo, Catalina

154

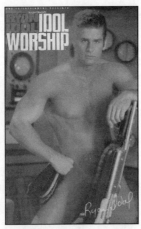

Idol Worship, Planet Group

Huge Video

Kevin Williams, Falcon Studios

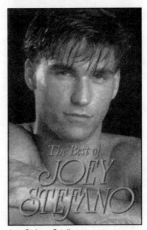

Joey Stefano, Catalina

Jeff Palmer, Falcon Studios

Ken Ryker, Men of Odyssey

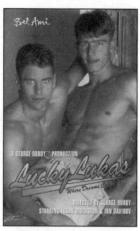

Lukas Ridgeston & Ion Davidov, Bel Ami

Ryan Fox, Steve Fox, Ty Fox, Stuido 2000

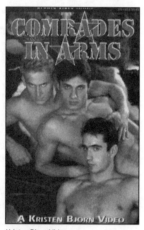

Kristen Bjorn Video

Sebastian, Brad Posey's Club 1821

Tom Steele (front), Filmco

Tommy Cruise, Deluxe Entertainment

Split Decision
Sticky Business
Strokers
Student Bodies Too
Tall Tales
3-Way Cum, Vol. 1
Tough Iron
Trans Europe Express
Trisexual Encounters
  3, 5 & 6
Video Games, Vol. 8
Working Hard for the
  Money

JAKE MONROE
First Timer
Fully Serviced
No Faking It

MICK MONROE
New In Town
Tutor Me

PAUL MONROE
Alleycats
Doing It
Falconhead
Gold Rush Boys
Huge
Nighthawk in Leather
Revenge of the Nighthawk

CARLOS MONTANA
Forum Video Magazine
The Hideaway
One More Time
Romeo & Julian

CHRISTIAN MONTANA
Schlong Blade

FERNANDO MONTANA
Serviced

Sting: A Taste For Leather

JIM MONTANA
A Blond, baby-faced 1980s
model from Nevada.
Be My Baby
California Blonds
California Stud Pups
Commercial Sex
Cool Hand Dick
Desert Fox
Don't Kiss Me, I'm Straight
For Sale by Owners
Hawaiian Desire
Hole in One
Honolulu Hard Bodies
Hot for His Bod
Hot Shots, Vol. 47:
  Newcomers
In the Briefs
Junior Crew
Once in a Blue Moon
Pay to Play
Point of No Return
Rockhard 2
Stiff Competition
Tight Jeans
V-8
Weekend Wildcats
Where The Hunks Are
White Steel

MARK MONTANA
(aka Johnny Ringo)
Hoghounds 2
Mavericks
Riptide!

ROB MONTESSA
(aka Gavin Burke)
Biggest One I Ever Saw
Leo & Lance
Something Wild

Student Bodies Too

CARLOS MONTEZ
Bi and Large
Black Book
Men Behind Bars
Sex Behind Bars

MAX MONTOYA
A 1980s, Latin daddy with
thinning hair and a mus-
tache.
Max Makes It Big!
S.F. Packing Company
Stud Search
Uncut Gems: Diamonds In
  The Raw

DAR MOON
The Exchange
Try Anything Once

ANGELO MOORE
(see Angelo)

BOB MOORE
Flesh & Fantasy
Performance
Turned On

JIM MOORE
(aka Cody Richards)
Died November 28, 1988
from AIDS-related compli-
cations.
Auto Erotica: The Best of
  Sex in Cars
The Best of Jon Vincent 1
The Big One
Cruisin'
Heavenly
In Heat
More

Powerline
Taxi
Top Man
Turned On
Wet Dreams

MICHAEL MOORE
The Best of Jon Vincent 1
The Best of Jonathan
  Strong
The Best of Rick Savage
Billboard
Callguys, U.S.A.
Grid Iron
Hard Knocks
Idle Pleasures
Pumping Up: Flexx II
Ram & Jam
Ranger Nick 2
Running Hard
Sailor in the Wild 2
Scorched!
Screwin Screw-Ups
Sex in the great Outdoors 3
Stiff Competition
The Stroke
Tender Trick
Undergear

NICK MOORE
Ass Lick Alley

OPANO MOORE
Black Sex Party
Steal My Stuff!

STEVEN MOORE
(see Angelo)

THOMAS MOORE
Nefarious

TOMMY MOORE
Boys in the Sand

CARLOS MORALES
Back in the Saddle
Betrayed
Staten Island Sex Cult

JOSE MORALES
Anything, Anytime
The Bigger the Wetter
Cum & Get It
Latin Lovers
Latino Dreaming
Navy Blue Hanky Left
New York Men
Oil Rig 99
Oriental Dick
P.M. Preview Tape #2
Trisexual
Video Encounters of the
  Sexual Kind
The Young Ones
Young Yankees

MICHAEL MORALES
Boys Behind Bars 1 & 2

YAN MOREAU
French Erections

JOEY MORELLI
(see Joey Amore)

ERIC MORENO
Bullring
Friction
Rear Ended
To The Hilt

MORGAN
A porn legend of the '80s
reportedly died in an acci-

dent.
Best Little Whorehouse In
  L.A.

BRUCE MORGAN
Connoisseur Collectors
Classics
Lodestar

CASEY MORGAN
Cop Stories #1:
  The Scandal
The Games We Play
Hard To Keep Down
Hard #2
The Selection Part 4 (Solo)

COLT MORGAN
Best Of Leather: Part 3
  Into Leather
Leather Obsession 4 -
  Forever

JOEY MORGAN
(aka Aaron Gunn)
Behind The Barn Door
Bi-Ology
Cody Exposed
Down Bi Law
Foot Fetish
Foot Loose
Leather Me Down Do Me
  Toys
Model Behavior
Morning Rituals 2
Night Heat
Palm Springs Paradise
Razor Closett
Sex Shooters 1 & 2
Takedown
Tony's Thing
Water Sports
Wet And Wild

Wild Obsession
X-Treme Closeup

KELLY MORGAN
Mountain Fever
Southbay Boys

KURT MORGAN
Everything A Man Wants
Powergrip
Pushing The Limit
Whatever It Takes

PAUL MORGAN
(Has appeared under a
variety of names including:
Jon Davis, Rod Harder,
Paul Smith, Scott Burton,
Chris Hard and Dean
Steed). Popular 1990s
model.
Alley Katt
At First Glance
Backseat BJ
Bad Ass Lieutenant
Balls to the Wall 35
Before & After
Behind His Back
Below the Decks
Big Boys Club
Big Deposit
Birthday Blowout
Bi-Sexual Nation
Black Brigade
Body of Art
Burning Desire
CatalinaVille
Caught In The Military #1
Chasers
Cop Stories #1: The
   Scandal
Cruise Park
Cruisin'

Cruisin' the Men of L.A.
Desert Maneuvers
Desert Paradise
Desert Sands
Dial "S" for Sex
Dickin' Around
The Drifter
Drop 'em
Flyin' Solo
Foot Patrol
Fortune Nookie
Four Men
Freshman Recruits
Going West
Hand of Fate
Handsome Ransom
Hawaiian Illustrated
Historic Affairs
Homo House Party
Hot Guys #2
Indulge Part 2
Invaders from Uranus
Iron Cage
Jeff Stryker's Underground
A Jock's Dream
Kept: A Way of Life
Leather Intrusion Case 1:
   Flaming Dragon
A Love Story
Locker Room Sex Brawl
Logan's Journey
Lusty LeatherMen
Mall Cruisin X-L
Marine Crucible
Marine Obsessions
Men in Blue
Men With Tools Part 2 :
   Nailed
Nude Getaway
Nude Science
Orgies Pt 2
Paul Morgan's Raw Meat
   1-5

Penal Pen Pals
Photo-Op
Prime Cut
Runway Studs
Sex Toy Story 2
Sexual Thoughts
Sharp Shooters
The Shoote
Sleeping Booty
Skateboard Sliders
Snafu
So Fine
South Beach Heat
Spankfest 6
Special Forces
Tank Tops
Things to Cum
The 13th Step
Three Brothers
Throat Spankers
Underboss, The
Undress for Success
Wet Daddy
Wet Warehouse #3:
   The Party
Working It Out

REX MORGAN
Faces
Full Load
Hunk
Therapy

SCOTT MORGAN
Outrage
Rough Idea
Tramps

TYLER MORGAN
Any Way I Can
Don't Hold Back
Pushover
Relentless

Stop At Nothing
You've Got The Touch

ANTONIO MORIAS
(see Anthony Gallo)

MIKE MORRIS
California Fox
El Paso Wrecking Corp.
Pieces of Eight

ALFREDO MOSSINNI
Acres of Ass

MR. ED
For His Own Good
Sleeping Booty and Other
  Tails

HANS MUELLER
A blond, well built Austrian
gay-for-pay 1980s model.
Air Male
Bi And Busty
Bi Inferno
Buddy System, Part 1 & 2
Cherry, The
Cruisers: A Reunion Of
  Friends
Desert Fox
Fag Hags
Fatigue Relief
Foreign Affairs
Island Heat
Knock-Out
L.A. Underground
Long Hard Ride, The
Over The Edge
Pay To Play
Raw Footage
Rolls, The
Single She-Males, Singles
  Bar

The Slut
Untamed
Warhead
Weekend Wildcats

DON MUIR
Blue Summer Breeze

MICHAEL MUNSEY
Cruisin' 57
Dynamite
White Hanky Left

TEX MURDOCK
Muscle Up

CHRISTIAN MURPHY
Conflict Of Interest
Making Of A Gay Video
One Track Mind
Playing Dirty

WAYNE MUSKWOOD
Das Butt 2

N

JOHN NAGEL
Royal Flesh

SCOTT NEELY
Copsucker
Fluid
Leather Lust
Splashdown

GUNNAR NEILSON
Australian For Leather
Skuff

DAVE NELSON
Handsome, mature, blond,
late 1990s model.

Bi-Sexual Nation
Coal Miner's Son
Internal Affairs
God Was I Drunk
Goosed (bi)
Policemen's Balls
Serviced

GARR NELSON
Very cute, blond, boy next
door, 1980s model.
Sex Hunt

GARY NELSON
Cruisin' '57

MARK NELSON
Discharged
Eagle pack 2
Size of the Matter 2

MARC NEMETH
Iron Will

GARARD NEMOUR
Carnival in Venice
Thick 'n Creamy
Tough & Tender
Under the Sign of the
  Stallion

NICK NICASTE
Doctor's Orders 1 & 2

AARON NICHOLS
American Way, The

BRIAN NICHOLS
Fantasize
Games
Gold Rush Boys
I Do!

JOHN NICHOLS
Like Father, Like Son
Mountain Fever
Soap Studs

MIKE NICHOLS
(aka Mick Nichols)
Born April 30.
An American Man
Another Man's Pleasure
Asian Persuasion
Autofellatio Biographies
Big as They Come II
Big River
The Big Score
A Body to Die For
Cat Men Do!
Cop Out
Cruisin' 3
Erotikus
Glory Holes of San
Francisco
Inches Away
INNdulge Palm Springs
Invaders from Uranus
Link
Marine Crucible
Measuring Up
Mountain Patrol
My Sister's Husband
Nightwatch 2
Party of One
Photoplay
Pocket Rockets
Swallow
Throat Spankers
Whatever you Say, Sir!

JOHN NICHOLSON
Big Time
Hard Choices

JASON NIKAS
(aka Patryk Strait)
Born August 17, 1972,
Arcadia, California. 5'10,
"8" cock. Handsome young
'90s bottom.
All About Sex
Always Available
Analized
Back in the Saddle Again
Bathroom Cruisers
Bedroom Buddies
Below the Decks
Billy 2000
Camp Pokahiney
Cramming For The Big
One
Cum: Stories to Tell
Cyber Sex
First Timer
Fountains of Youth
Freshman Fever
Friendly Desire
Give It To Me Straight
Goodfellas/Badfellas
GV Guide All-Star Softball
Game #1
Hard Corps
Hard Labor
Hidden Agenda
Hip Hop Hunks
I am Curious Leather
In The Penthouse
In The Shadows
Jamie Hendrix's
Interviews 1
A Jock's Tale
Magic Bed
Mr. Blue
Nasty Rumors
New In Town
No Faking it
Nymphomania

On To Something Big
One Way or the Other
Open Windows
Palm Springs Cruisin'
Paradise Inn
Pinball Wizard
Playing Dirty
Relentless
San Francisco Sex
Sand Storms
Sex and the Single Man
Sex Toy Story
Something Very Big
Splat
Sudden Urge
Summer Money
Tailspin
Tempted
Threesomes
Total Deception
Virgin Tales #1: The Show
Wanna Be In Pictures?
West Hollywood Hope
Wet Dreamers
Whitefire
Wild Bill
Working Stiff
You've Got The Touch
Zebra Love

DOUG NILES
All Night Long
The Best of Mike Henson
Bi and Beyond III
Director's Best: John
Travis, Vol. 1
Engine #69
A Friendly Obsession
From Maui with Love
Innocence Found
Man in Motion
Miles of Niles
My Best Buddy

Plunge, The
Powerful 2
Private Collection
Screentest
The Rites of Spring
Seduction IV: Sex Storm
Sex in Tight Places
Sexpress
Trip to Paradise Beach, A
Undercover

DREW NOLAN
Big River
Deep End
Forced Entry
Full Package
Hole, The
Hot Summer Of Sex
No Reservations
Possession
Whitefire

CHIP NOLL
Born May 7, 1980, Erie,
Pennsylvania. 5'8," 7 1/2, "
cock. Entering the biz at
18, this cute, blond, bottom
with Swedish/German
good looks, became very
popular in the late '90s.
Dirk Yates Private
Collection #124
First Time Tryers #13
God Was I Drunk
Iron Will
Love Inn Exile (softcore)
Opposites Attract
Private Passions
Sexy Spank 2
Spanked
Sting: A Taste For Leather

CHRIS NOLL
1980s model.
Cuming Of Age
Fantasies
Flashback
Hard-Up
Kip Noll's Casting Couch
Sizzlin' Studs
Summer of Scott Noll

JEFF NOLL
Jeff Noll's Buddies

KIP NOLL
A dark-haired, boy next
door, porn legend of the
late '70s, early '80s.
Al Parker's Flashbacks
Auto Erotica: The Best of
 Sex in Cars
The Best of Kip Noll
The Boys of Venice
Brother Should Do It
BulletPac 1
Class of '84, Part II
Cuming of Age
Erotica Video 30 #6
Flashback
For You, Edition #1
Grease Monkeys
Kip Noll & the Westside
 Boys
Kip Noll's Casting Couch
Kip Noll Superstar
Pacific Coast Highway
Roommates
Super Studs
Try to Take It
William Higgins Preview
 Tape #1

CAREY NORTH
Blue Summer Breeze

BRUCE NORTON
Hard Luck Number
Island of Passion

DEREK NOVAK
Four in Hand
Strictly for Ladies Only
Young Olympians

TIAGO NUNES
Brazilian Bath Boys
Breakin'Em In
Euromen

O

MARSHALL O BOY
1990s model and founder
of the "O Boys" club in Los
Angeles.
Behind His Back
Bi Sex Club
Leather Temptation
Meet Me At The Orgy
Sex Toy Story #2
Sleeping Booty and Other
 Tails
Tell Me About Sex
Working It Out

CASEY O'BRIAN
1990s, brown-haired model.
Anal Attraction
Big Shots
Cowboys Get The Blues
 Filth
Free Your Willy
From Hair to Eternity
Great Lengths
Group Therapy
Hang 8 1/2
Hidden Man
Motor Crotch

Party Favors
The Player
Poolman
Round 1
Sex Gallery
Sexcess
Special Reouest
Steamed
Tattoo Parlor
Where The Night Takes You

CHRIS O'CONNOR
A 1990s model.
A Lesson Learned
Happily Ever After

DEAN O'CONNOR
Entering the biz at 18, this cute, dark-haired, boy-next-door bottom from the Mid- west became very popular in the late '90s.
Live Feed
Nefarious
Red, Hot & Safe
Ryker's Revenge
Something Very Big This Way Comes
Technical Ecstasy
Young Men On The Pleasure Trail

STEVE O'DONNELL
Born May 20, 1969, Michigan. Resides in Las Vegas, Nevada. 6'," 7 1/2" cock. Versatile. Cute, boy next door model from the 1990s.
Alley Boys
Apprentice, The
Bustin' Loose
Cat Men Do

Code of Conduct 1- Stripped
Code of Conduct 2- Deliverance
Das Butt 2
Download
Family Values
Flavor of Men
Flesh and Blood
Four Men
Grease Guns
Heatwave
HOMOgenized
Hot Cops 3
Indulge
INNdulge Palm Springs
LA Boys
Law of Desire
Lucky Strokes
Malibu Beach Hunks
Men Only
Party of One
Raw Material
Sex and Sensuality
Sexual Suspect
Street Smarts: Sex Ed 5
Striptease
Ultimate Reality
Vacation Spot
We've Got Them All
Working it Out

ODYSSEY TWINS: GABRIEL & OSCAR
Hardbody 2000
Ryker's Revenge
Twins

SCOTT O'HARA
Died February 18, 1998 at age 36 in San Francisco. Cause of death reported as Kidney failure resulting from

his HIV infection. One of the big name stars of the '80s, he wrote his acclaim-ed autobiography *Autopornography* in 1997.
Advocate Men Live 1
Advocate Men Live 4
All the White Boys
Below the Belt
California Blue
Cum Shots 102
Double Standards
Head Over Heels
Hot Shots, Vol. 14: Tight Buns
Hot Shots, Vol. 26: Self-Service
Hung and Horny
In Your Wildest Dreams
Jocks
Lovers & Friends
The Massage Boys
Mr. Drummer Finals
New Recruits
Old Reliable #52: The Guy Next Door
Old Reliable #72: J/O Collection #5
The Other Side of Aspen
Oversize Load
Ramcharger
Rough Riders
Sgt. Swann's Private Files
Sex Hunt or You Get What You Pay For
Slaves for Sale
Stick Shift
Switch Hitters 2
Video Games 1 & 4
Winner Takes All

DOUGLAS O'KEEFE
Handtools

Hard Men
Screen Test 1

MIKE O'LEARY
Printer's Devils
Strictly for Ladies Only

RUBEN OMAR
Come With Me
Moving Target

CHRIS ONASIS
(aka Christopher Onasis)
The Beat Goes On
The Bigger They Come
Eagle Pack 8
Every Inch a Winner
Freshman
Hard at Play
Idle Pleasures
Low Blows
Muscle Fever
Rushes
Sex Hunt
Slumming
Solitary Sin
Tough Iron

CHAD O'NEIL
Show & Tell
Big Shooters 1

MARK O'NEILL
Anonymous Sex
Apply Within
Hard To Keep Down
Hustler Way
Spin the Bottle Orgy
Trade Off

CHRIS ORION
Bring Your Own Man
Cousin Buck

Hot Roomers
Long Johns
Rough Idea
Screen test
They All Came
Tramps

DANIEL ORLEANS
French Erections

DANNY ORLIS
Real name Rich Merritt. A
Marine Corps officer, Rich
appeared on the covers of
The New York Times mag-
azine and *The Los Angeles
Times* before being outed
by the *Advocate*, in 1998,
as a former porn star.
Bad Moon Rising
Best Of Leather: Part 3
Breakthrough
Bullseye
Leather Obsession 2
Reflections in the Wild

PATRICK O'ROURKE
Mo' Bigga Butt
Sure Thing

SHAWN O'TOOLE
Early Erections
Lovers
Star Search

SPARKY O'TOOLE
A cute, young, blond porn
star legend from the '80s.
Angelo Loves it
Big Boys of Summer
The Big One
Bubble Butt
BulletPac 11: Battle of the

Bulges
Butt Darts
California Dreamin'
Camp Y.M.C.A.
Climactic Scenes #101
Commercial Sex
Danny Does 'em All
Frat Brats
Full Load: Maximum
  Overdrive
Hard Rock High
Hard to be Good
Hot Shots, Vol. 22:
  Raw Rears
Hot Shots, Vol. 24:
  Hot Hunks
Hot Shots, Vol. 32: Dirty
  Daddies
Hot Shots, Vol. 40: Glory
  Holes
Hot Shots, Vol. 41: Rim
  Shots
In Deep
Inside Expose
Larger Than Life
Las Vegas Orgy
Locker Room Sex
Love Muscle
Men in Motion #3
Mountain Fever
My Brother, My Lover
Orgy at the Funhouse
Paddle Brats
Pretty Boy
A Real Man Wouldn't
  Leave
Ride the Swell
The River
Show it Hard
Sizzle
Sparky's Wild Adventure
  (dir. & actor)
Spring Clean-Up

Stud Fuckers
Surfer Guys
Swim Meat
Tasting Mr. Goodbar
3-Way Cum, Vol. 1
Top Man
The Young Cadets

SEBASTIAN O'VAU
Peterbuilt Boys
Sun Kissed

JERRY OVERTON
Times Square Stud

P

DAMON PAGE
Born in the Northeast. 6'0,"
9" cock, versatile bottom.
Handsome black model
from the late '90s.
Fallen Angel 2
Focal Length

DAVID PAGE
A 1970s model.
Adam & Yves

RANDY PAGE
California Jackoff
Fantasize
Hot Numbers, Vol. 1-2-3
Like a Horse
Master of Disicipline
Pleasure Mountain
Something Wild
Winner Takes All

VINCENT PALADINO
Ciao Bello 2

DEREK PALMER
Objects of Desire

JEFF PALMER
Born March 27, 1975 in
Argentina. Resides in West
Hollywood, California. 5'9,"
9-1/8" uncut. A very popu-
lar young Latin model from
the '90s.
Betrayed
Chosen
Heatwave
Manhandlers
Player
Sting: A Taste For Leather
Stripped: Code of
    Conduct 1

JIM PALMER
Locker Jocks 1982

RICK PANTERA
Eight Men In
Find This Man
Foot Fetish
Group Therapy
Head Bangerst
Morning Rituals I2
Private Dancer
Sex Shooters 2
Smells Like A Man
Sperminator, The
Stripped Down
Wet Sex
White Spy

KEITH PANTHER
(see Dirk Caldwell, Eric
Dahl)

FRANCOIS PAPILLON
Advanced Disrobics

Full Grown, Full Blown
Interview 1
Solo Flight
Weekend Workout
The Young & the Hung

T. J. PARIS
Measure For Measure

TRISTAN PARIS
A cute, brown-haired, blue-
eyed 1990s model.
Big Thrill, The
In Deep: Miles To Go
Mercury Rising
Red Alert 1988
Sit Tight
Skuff
Sting: A Taste For Leather

AL PARKER
Died August 17, 1992 from
AIDS-related complica-
tions. Considered by most
to be the biggest superstar
of the 1980s. A versatile top
or bottom, Parker became
a director and operated his
own video company Surge.
Advocate Men Live 2
    (interview only)
America's Sexiest Home
    Videos 1
Anywhere, Anytime
Best of Buckshot: Chute
Best of Colt, Vols. 3, 4, 10,
    11, 13
Best of Surge, Vol. 1:
    Feed Me
Better Than Ever
    (dir. & actor)
Buckshot
Century Mining (dir.)

Challenger
Cum Shot Bears
Dangerous! (pro.)
Fanta-Size
Fast Idle
A Few Good Men (pro.)
Flashback (dir. & actor)
Games (pro. & actor)
Gay Voices, Gay Legends
   (interview)
Hard Disk Drive (dir.)
Head Trips (dir. & actor)
Heavy Equipment
High Tech (dir.)
Inches
Kinky Stuff (dir. & actor)
Make it Hard
Night Alone with Al Parker,
   A (dir. & actor)
One in a Billion
   (dir. non-sex)
The Other Side of Aspen
Overload
Oversize Load (dir.)
Performance (cameo)
Rangers (dir. & actor)
Rocks and Hard Places
Scout's Honor
So-Low (dir.)
Strange Places, Strange
Things (dir.)
Surge Men are Very
Receptive
   (dir. & actor)
Surge Men at Their Best
   (dir. & actor)
Taxi
Therapy (cameo)
Timberwolves, Part 1-2
Turbo Charge (dir. & actor)
Turned On (pro. & actor)
Wanted
Weekend Lock-Up

CLIFF PARKER
Born March 30. Hairy, mid-
'90s daddy. Has been in
relationships with Cougar
Cash and York Powers.
Abduction 2: The Conflict
All About Steve
Boot Black 2
Command Performance
Desert Drifters
Desert Oasis
Get It On Line
Grand Prize
Hot Pursuit
Keeping Time
Nightwalk
The Other Side of Aspen 3
The Other Side of Aspen 4
Pressure
Reunion
River Patrol
Shoot
Summer Buddies
Sure Thing
That Old Whorehouse
True Stories
The Road to Hopeful
Total Corruption 2
Wild Country

DIXON PARKER
Shameless

FRANK PARKER
Born September 25th,
Tallahassee, Florida. 5'10,"
7" cock. Versatile, hairy,
leather daddy from the late
'90s.
Ass, Balls, Cock
Bachelor Party
Big Guns 2
Biker Pigs From Hell

Boss Man
Doctor's Order's
Fallen Angel 2
F-Train To Castro
Johnny Come Home
Link To Link
Too Many Tops
Youthful Offenders

JEFF PARKER
Rebel

REED PARKER
Born July 5, 1969, Tampa,
Florida. 5'10," 7 1/2" cock.
Bottom. Late '90s model.
Analized
Bootie Nights
Caught By Surprise
The Coach's Punishment
Coal Miner's Son
Gang Bang Revenge
Get It on Part 2
Hard Times
In and Out Express
Journal, The
Leather Confessions
Leather Connection
Leather Temptation
Leather Triangle
Leather Watch
Male Box
Oklahomo
On Leave In LA
The Peeping Tom
Red, White and You
Sex And The Single Man
Spanking Master 4
Street Smart
Tight Leather
Things You Can Do In
   Leather
Weho Confidential

RICKY PARKER
A.W.O.L.
Black Renegades
Black, Ripped & Stripped
Hung Man Meat
Other Side of Big Bear

WESLEY PARKER
(see K.C. Hart)

BOBBY PARKS
God Was I Drunk

DANNY PARKS
All-American Boys
Best Friends II
Catalina Orgies
Frathouse Memories
Hot Male Mechanics
Route 69
Tough Competition
William Higgins Preview
    Tape #2

MICHAEL PARKS
A dark-haired, early 1990s
model.
The Best of Michael Parks
The Best of Rick Savage
The Best of Ryan Yeager
Big Bang
Classified Action
Elements of Passion
Foxholes
Glory Hole of Fame 1 & 2
Male Taboo
More of A Man
Object of Desire
Read My Lips
Revenge: More Than I Can
    Take
The Rise
Superman 87

Trade-Off

RODNEY PARKS
Shooting Stars

GLENN PARMLEY
Do Me Evil

TRAVERS PATEKE
Raging River

HORST PATRE
(aka Zsolt Borbely, Arpad)
Born May 10 in Budapest..
A cute, young, dark-haired,
late 1990s Hungarian
model. 5'10", 8-1/2" uncut.
Fresh
Raging River
Sex Garage

PATRICK
Hotel Montreal
Last Call
Male Call
On The Job
Opportunity Knocks
Party In My Pants

SHANE PATRICK
All That Jizz
Over the Rainbow

RICK PATRIOT
Freshman Fever
Magic Bed

ROCCO PASSOLINI
Bijou

TICO PATTERSON
A popular 1980s bisexual
model.

Bait
Bi-Coastal
Faces
Fanta-Size
The Golden Boys
Head Trips
Jackoff Giants
Manholes #1
Man O'Man
Men in Motion #4
Old Reliable #1
Old Reliable #99: Some
Old Friends, Part 3
On the Bi-Side
Rodeo
Room Service Plus
Shooting Stars #1: Chris
    Thompson
Stud Struck
Therapy
Windows

JOHNNY PAUL
Just Blondes

LOGAN PAUL
(see Rob Stone)

JOHAN PAULIK
Born March 14. A Czech
Republic native. This cute,
6" tall, 7" uncut, barely-legal
model with boy-next-door
good looks was discovered
by Bel Ami's George Duroy.
Along with Lukas
Ridgeston, he has become
one of the biggest names—
and dicks—of the 1990s.
An American In Prague
Blue Danube
Boy Oh Boy
Chain Reaction, The

Frisky Summer
Johan's Big Chance
Lukas' Story 1-2
Moments With Johan
Out at Last
Plowboys, The
Sauna Paradiso
Siberian Heat
Summer The First Time
Sunshine After The Rain
You're Gorgeous

DUFF PAXTON
Kansas City Trucking Co.
Three Day Pass

GEORGE PAYNE
Anything, Anytime
The Back Row
The Best of Superstars
Centurians of Rome
The Erotic History of
Christopher Rage 1
Four Letters
Hand-in-Hand Preview
  Tape #1
Kiss Today Goodbye
Le Voyeur
Light Blue Hanky Left
Men Between Themselves
Men Come First
Navy Blue
Olive Drab Hanky Left
Safe Sex
You Got it All

THOM PAYNE
(see Tom Katt)

CARLOS PAZ
A Spanish Fantasy

KEVIN PEARCE
In Deep: Miles To Go

DANA PEARSON
All the Right Boys
All the Way In
Big Favors
Big Shooters 1 & 2
Chip Off the Old Block
F-Stop
Frat Brats
In Deep
Manholes #1
Men in Motion #6
Never Big Enough
One, Two, Three
Rooms
Show and Tell
Star Shots #6
Summer Heat
Video Games, Vol. 10

JEREMY PENN
Born April 23. The ultimate,
mid '90s blond jock next
door with mainstream
model good looks.
California Kings
Current Affairs
The Freshmen
High Tide
Hot Wheels
Manhandlers

ANTONIO PEREZ
Home Work

JOSH PEREZ
(see Joshua Scott)

JONNIE PERRINO
A dark-haired 1990s youth.
Lambda, Lambda, Lambda 2

DOUG PERRY
Mid '90s porn star daddy.
Another Man's Pleasure
By Invitation Only
Courting Libido
Forced Entry
Hard Lessons
Jawbreaker
Midnight Run
Ruthless
Thriller
Wild Horses

JAMES PERRY
Born December 15th,
New York. Resides in West
Hollyood. 5'10," 7" cock.
Cute, dark, late 1990s
bottom.
Bitanic
Driven By Lust
Genderella
Hawaiian Vacation 1 & 2
Jockstrap
The Uninvited

BRAD PETERS
Died May 31, 1994 from
AIDS-related complications.
Bait
Brothers Should Do It
Main Attraction
Man O'Man
Men Will Play
Midnight Special #1
Rangers
Skin Flix
Squirts 1: After the Shoot
These Bases Are Loaded

DREW PETERS
A Michigan native. A young,
blond, late '90s model.

Manhungry
Mantasy Island
Soaked
Wet Warehouse 3
Young Shooters (Solo)

SHAWN PETERS
Ball Bustin' Boys
Boys Town: Going West
Hollywood
California Wet
Collage
Desert Heat
Dirty Jocks
Drawing Tricks
The Exchange
Fleshtones
Growing Years
Internatinal Skin
Make me hard
Mansplash
Nine-and-a-Half Inches
Pleasure Peak
Spring Semester
Squirts 1: After the Shoot
Sudbusters

WADE PETERS
Before & After
The Big Shot
A Body to Die For 2
Logan's Journey
Rosebud
Stag Party
Throttled
Wet Warehouse #3:
    The Party

ALEX PETERSON
Bend Over Buddies
Hungarian Rhapsody

URI PETROV
Raging River

MARC PEUGEOT
Bat Dude
The Buddy System
Pool Boy
Thumbs Up
Tips
Wet Dreams

CHRIS PHIFER
(see Sean Diamond)

IAN PHILIPS
Boystown
Century Mining Company
Faces
Flesh
Seven Card Stud
Strokers
Studbusters
Windows

STEVE PHILIPS
Mr. Wonderful

ARTHUR PHILLIPS
French Lieutenant's Boys

BRAD PHILLIPS
A handsome, brown-haired,
1980s model.
Bad Boys, Vol. 2
Bi-Mistake
Castro Commando
The Company We Keep
Crosswire
Cum Shots #102
Deep in Hot Water
Dogs in Heat
Flexx
Full Service

He-Devils
Hot, Hung & Hard
Hot Pursuit (non-sex)
Hot Shots, Vol. 28, 29, 42
House Boys
In a Jock's Locker
Intruders
Long Hard Ride
Man in Motion
Manimal
The Men of 550
Motor Sexual
Offering
Ranch Hand
The Rites of Spring
Rooms
Seduction
Spare Room
Straight Boys Do
Stud Vision
Superhunks II
Surge Men are Very
    Receptive
Surge Men at Their Best
Swap Meat
Switch Hitters IV: The
    Grand Slam
That Old Whorehouse
Tim Lowe's Weekend
    Adventure
Touch Me
Undercover
The Young and the Hung

BUCK PHILLIPS
Crossing the Line
Take One: Guys Like Us

COLE PHILLIPS
As Time Goes Bi
Exiled
Men In Love
Sex In Tight Places

Spring Fever
Ten Plus (Vol. 2)
Tough Guys

DINO PHILLIPS
Born December 13, 1969
in Chicago, Illinois.
Resides in Los Angeles. 6,'
8" cock, versatile top. In
1999 this busy dancer, pro-
fessional model, actor and
writer formed his own
video production company.
Alex's Leather Dream
Arrested Voyer
BG Wrestling & Spanking
   1994 to 1998
Biagra
Big Riggs
Bitanic
Boys From Bel Air
By Invitation Only
Chi Chi La Rue's
   Hardbody Video Mag. 2
Come With Me
Desert Paradise
Forever Hold Your Piece
Gay For The Weekend
Gay Weekend Away
The Gigilo1s Fantasy
Guest Services
Hard Lessons/Sex Ed 2
Happily Ever After
Hardball
Hawaiian Vacation 1 & 2
The Heat Of The City
Hell Weekend 2
Hot Cops 2
Hot Springs Orgy
Hot Tub Fever
Initiation 2
In The Mix
Into Leather

Keep The Tip
Lesson Learned, A
Lockerroom Sex Brawl
Mount The Big One
Night We Met, The
A Night With Todd Stevens
Object of My Erection, The
Opposites Attract
Penetration on
Pennsylvania Avenue
Pheromones
Please Don't Tell
Provacative
Quick Study/Sex Ed 1
Red, White, & You
Right Hand Man
Runway Studs
The Rush
A Score Of Sex
Sexy Spank 2
Showboys
Skateboard Sliders
Smooth Strokes
S.N.A.F.U.
Spank Me Man!
Star Contact
Talk Dirty To Me
Taxi Tales
Tempted
Threesome
Together Again
Too Damn Big
Too Many Tops
Travelin' Wild
Trixxx of the Trade
Urge, The
VamBires
Watering Game , The
Wet Warehouse
WeHo Alley
West Hollywood Sex Party
Wild Sex In America

DOUG PHILLIPS
Brian's Boys

GREG PHILLIPS
Brian's Boys

JACKSON PHILLIPS
Born February 27. The
self-described Susan Lucci
of porn retired from the
business at the end of
1998.
Desert Train
Double Crossed
Flashpoint
Guest Services
How to Get a Man into Bed
Immersion
Into Leather
A Lesson Learned
The Men of South Beach
Midnight Run
Military Sex Pass
Other Side of Aspen 3&4
Palm Springs Weekend
Police Daddy Marco
Rear Ended
Reform School Confidential
Rookie Patrol
Street Smarts
Tourist Trade
Uniform Code
Weekend Sex Pass

MIKE PHILLIPS
(see Michael Brandon)

NICK PHILLIPS
Provacative

ROD PHILLIPS
A very popular, boyishly
handsome blond, 1980s

model. Committed suicide
June 7, 1993 by overdose.
Also had AIDS.
Bare Tales
The Best of Joey Stefano
The Biggest One I Ever
  Saw
Boys Town: Going West
  Hollywood
Winner Takes All
Giants, Part 1
Guess Who's Coming
Hard Steal
Hologram
Men & Films
Outlaw Bikers
The Plunge
Spokes
Too Big For His Britches
Windows
Winner Takes All

DEAN PHOENIX
Born in Mexico. Dark-
haired, 5'8-1/2," 9" uncut,
top. Cute, with a sweet,
boyish smile. Former
Marine and 1990s model.
Resides in San Diego.
Complexx
First time Tryer's #9
God Was I Drunk
Jarrhead
A Lesson Learned
Mantasy Island
Pucker Up
Sexfly
Snafu

PETER PHOENIX
Lust Shack

TONY PIAGI
Born July 25. Florida resi-
dent and mid '90s Italian
bottom.
Try Again
Friction
Full Package
Indulge
Major Meat
Mavericks
Men

MARC PIERCE
Leather Men
Leather Night
Vacation Spot

STEVE PIERCE
Born August 28, 1964,
Detroit, Michigan. Light-
brown hair, 6'2," 7" cock,
with a Prince Albert and
both nipples pierced. Late
'90s daddy.
The Big Thrill
Black Gang Bang
Bondage Buddies
Bound and Debauched
Boyfriends
Burnin'
Butt Sluts of The Castro
Cell-Shocked
The Chosen
Code of Conduct 1 & 2
Do Me Dirty
Dr. Good Glove
Electro Anal Kink #2
Eyes of Larry Stars
Fire In The Hole
Flesh and Blood
Foolin" Around
Hell Bent For Leather
Hustler's Blues

Johnny Hormone
Lap It Up
Leather Lust
Leather Tricks
Lovers Lane
Marine Obsessions
Masters Sex Toys
Military Sex Initiation
Naked Underneath
Nude and Rude
Plow Me
Poolman Cometh, The
Principal of Lust
Private Parts
Rent A Fantasy
Roped and Punished
San Francisco Sex
Sex Is in The Air
Skinny Dipping
Special Delivery
Straight Construction Site
Swimming Pool Orgy
Video Store Sex Studs
Washed Out Anal Buddies
Worked Over

DAVID PIERRE
Born January 3 in France.
Late '90s Mature, French
model. 5'9," 8" cock.
Americans In Paris
Billy Herrington's Body
  Shop
Bite 2, The: Bloodline
Chi Chi La Rue's
  Hardbody 2000.2
Desert Hart
Full Up!
Gang of 13
Hard Body 2000
Humidity
Iron Will
Jockstrap

Lick It Up
Live Feed
964 Dicks St.
Stock
Suck Daddy

JEAN PIERRE
Ft. Lauderdale Hustlers
Men of Rio 1
Mykonos 1 (Les Minets)

JIMMY PIKE
Black And Beyond
Island Heat
Karen's Bi-Line
Painted
Poetry & Motion

JOSH POWELL
Road To Hopeful, The

ALEC POWERS
Born July 17. Resides in
Nevada. Blond, very popu-
lar gay-for-pay '90s model.
All The Way Inn
Beat Patrol
Bi Voyeur
Born To Please
Boys From Bel Air
Boys Next Door, The
Center Spread
Dare Devils
Fox's Lair
GV Guide All-Star Softball
    Game 1
Hard Bodyguard
The Hills Have Bis
His Big Brother
Hot Day In La
Hose 'Em Down
House Of Tricks
Hung Up

Idol Inn Exile
Insiders, The
Intensive
Keyhole
Lube Job
Magnified
Man To Men
Manhattan Skyline
New Pledgemaster
Night We Met, The
Nights In Eden
Physical Education
Pitch A Tent
Please Don't Tell
Power Driver
Quick Studies-Sex Ed. 1
Ready For It
Redwood
Reveille
Revenge Of The Bi-Dolls
Shaved Dick Slave
Single For The Weekend
South Beach Heat
Squeeze Play
Tourist Trade
Uncut Weekend
Urgent Matters
Wanted
Whitefire
Wide Receiver

AUSTIN POWERS
Handsome, mature-looking,
dark-haired and horse-hung
1990s bodybuilder and
model. Owns Get Fit, a personal training company.
Jock Trade

JEFF POWERS
Wolfboy

MATT POWERS
Cute, young looking, dark-
haired, 5'11" 1980s porn
star.
The Best of Matt Powers
Lifeguard on Duty
Lunch Hour
The Main Attraction
Muscle Force
Skin Torpedoes (solo)

MIKE POWERS
Locker Jocks 1982

NOLAN POWERS
Pressure

STEPHEN POWERS
Porno Tonight Show, The

TERRY POWERS
The Escort

YORK POWERS
Born June 12. Hunky, dark-
haired, '90s model. New
York resident.
An Officer and His
    Gentleman
Basic Plumbing
Below The Rim
Best of Leather: Part 1
The Bi-Ologist
Boot Black 2
Catch The Big One
Chi Chi Larue's Hardbody
    Video Mag. 2
Club House #5
Come And Get It
Come Closer
Cramming For The Big
    One
Cumback Kid

Desert Paradise
Getaway, The
Getting It Firm
Hard Drive
Hard Times
Hot Blades
Hot Cops 2
Immersion
It's A Gang: Video Series 1
Just Can't Stop
Leather Obsession
Long Play
Lowe Down
Magnified
Malibu Pool Boys
Man Construction
Mix It Up
Moving Target
Personally Yours
Pure Sex
Rags To Riches
River Patrol
Ryker Files, The
Sexcuses
Sex Police
Shadow Dancer
Slam Bam Thank You Man
Smokescreen
Smooth Operator
Stiff
Summer's Tall Tales
Tall Tales
Thick Of It
Think Big 2
Teecha Sucks
Wanted

MARTIN PRAVDA
Andel's Story 2: The
Running of the Bulls

BUDDY PRESTON
Boys From Riverside Drive

Caught in the Act
Gunslingers
Main Attraction
Pacific Coast Highway
These Bases are Loaded
Times Square Strip

MITCH PRESTON
(aka Scott Sampson)
Fifty Seven Pick Up
Group Therapy
Liquid Love
Mix It Up
Ranger Nick
Ride The Swell

LES PRICE
Chain Reactions
Fade Out
Hot Shots 6

RICKY PRICE
Daredevils
Young Guys
Young Shooters (Solo)

JASON PRIDE
Dick Undercover
Earning His Keep
GV Guide All-Star Softball
   Game 1
Hard Corps
Hard On Demand
Leather Playhouse
Leather Watch
Leather Weekend
Male Order Sex
More Than Friends
Pure Sex
Sexologist
Sex Trigger
6969 Melrose
Smooth Strokes

Squeeze Play
Thick Of It

PAGAN PRINCE
Mavericks
Travelin' Wild

TONY PRINCE
Hot Shots 3, 4
These Bases are Loaded
Wrestling Meat 1, 2

ERIC PRINCETON
Mount The Big One
West Hollywood Sex Party

JIM PULVER
A very handsome, buffed
and popular blond 1980s
model.
Bare Tales
The Best of All Matt
Sterling
Bigger Than Huge
Bigger Than Life
Direftor's Best: John Travis,
   Vol. 1
Forced Entry
For You, Edition #5
Full Load: Maximum
Overdrive
In Hot Pursuit
Inch by Inch
Mark Reynolds Videolog
Out of Bounds
Reflections 2
Somebody Is Watching
Stryker Force
Tales of the Backlot
Wide Receiver

JOE PUMP
Happiness is a Big Cock

JOE PURCELLI
A Matter Of Size
Best Of All

Q

JEFF QUINN
A very cute, 1980s boy-
next-door model and for-
mer *Playgirl* centerfold with
blond hair and blue eyes.
AC/DC Hookup
Best Bi Far 1 & 2
The Best of All Matt
   Sterling
The Best of Mike Henson
Big Guns
Bigger Than Life
Catalina Classics
Giant Splash Shots 2
Hot Rods: The Young & the
   Hung 2
Inch by Inch
Innocence Lost
Paul Norman's World of
   Sexual Oddities
The Switch is On
The Troy Saxon Gallery 1

R

MARC RADCLIFF
Resident of Orange
County, California. 5'8".
Angels Bi Day, Devils Bi
   Night
Backyard Boys
The Best of Back Alley
   Video
Bi Mistake
Brotherly Love 1 & 2
California Stud Pups

Dueling Dicks
Hard Rock High
The Harder the Better
Heart Beat
Interview, Vol. 2 & 3
New Love
The Night Boys
Painting Party
Rainstorm
The Rolls
Say Goodbye
Sex Shooters
She-Males Undercover
Show it Off
Spanking New: Drive it
   Home
Spring Clean-Up
Stud Sensors
Swim Meat 2
Tease Me!
Tell Me Something Dirty

ERIC RADFORD
A cute, brown-haired boy-
next-door 1980s porn star.
Bad Boys Club
Big & Thick
Bulge: Mass Appeal
Catalina Down and Dirty
Catalina Men
Cruisin' West Hollywood
Director's Best: John
   Travis, Vol. 1
Hot Rods: The Young and
   the Hung II
Rockhard
They Grow 'em Big
An Uncomfortable
   Obsession
The Voyeur

KARL RADFORD
(aka Karl Redford)

All Men Do It!
Bedroom Lies
Born To Please
Bulletin Board Buddies
Center Spread 2
The Come Back
Cut Above, A
Cruisin' The Balcony
Cyber Sex
Dynastud 2: Powerhouse
Exiled
Fully Serviced
Hard Drive
Hard Labor
The Hideaway
Hot Cops 2
Hot Guys
Keep The Tip
Leather Playhouse
Men of Forum
Men With Tools
Mentor
Nasty Rumors
Night In Leather
Oral Fixation
Personally Yours
Reflections Of Sex
Rival, The
Satisfacion
Scent Of Leather
Score Of Sex
Sex Posse
Sexcess
Solicitor
Spring Fever
Steel Away
Stiff
Surrogate Stud
Trickmaster
Working Day & Night

ANTHONY RAGE
Come Closer

CHRISTOPHER RAGE
(aka Chris Rage)
Died April 24, 1991 from
AIDS-related complications.
Versatile top or bottom
daddy and 1980s actor
and director.
Best Of The Superstars
Drive
Hidden Camera
Le Voyeur
Outrage 1 & 2
Queer: The Movie
Rough Idea
The Shaft
Sleaze
Street Kids
Toilet Tramps
Wildside

DYLAN RAGE
Tenderloin
Pleasure Ridge

JOHNNY RAHM
Born June 11. A dark-
haired, mature-looking,
1980s model.
All About Steve
All the Way In
Alone At Last
Badlands
Be My Baby
Bedtime Stories: Tales to
Keep You Up
The Big Merger
The Big Switch III: Bachelor
Party
Black Alley-South of the
Border
Body Search
Boner
The Boxer 2

The Boy Next Door
Boys Will Be Boys
The Brawnzmen
Breaking & Entering
Brotherly Love 2
Come Clean
Craze!
Daddy Hunt
Dare Devils
Deception 1 & 2
The Devil and Danny
Webster
Exiled
Express Male
The Extra Day
Fast Company
The First Time
Friends & Lovers
G.I. Jocks: Out of the
Ranks
Going Down in Style
Here Comes Peter
Hidden Man
Hollywood and Vine
In Your Face
Interview, Vol. 4
Jackhammer
Kick Boxing: Getting Below
the Belt
King of the Mountain
Kiss-Off
Latino Playmates
Leather Angel
Low Riders
Male Seduction
Male Triangle
Manhandler
Man Play
Master Piece
The Meaning of Sex
Mess Hall Maneuvers
Midnight Hard-On
Midnight Sun

Mounted Police
Movers and Shakers
My Cousin Danny
My Own Private Mexico
A Night With Strangers
On the Lookout
Once in a Blue Moon
Open House
Oral Report
The Orgy Club
Point of Return
The Pornographer
Preferred Stock #1
Return to Badlands
Rock-Hard
Santa's Coming
Sex Bazaar 1 & 2
Smokin' Butts
The Spanking Master 2
Straight To The Zone
Sunsex Boulevard
Toilet Tramps
Trading Up
Tricked
2 Hard Up
X-tasy

RICHARD RAINES
(aka Rich Raines)
Born September 14.
Mature, late 1990s model.
Fast Action
Hard To Keep Down
Hot Spot
Outdoor Ecstacy
Tall Tail

ANSEL RAINIER
(see Darryl Weld)

NICK RAINS
Big Boyz Club 3
Danger Zone

Poolman Cometh, The
Skinny Dipping
Swimming Pool Orgy
Virtual Sexuality

MICHAEL RAM
(aka Michael Mann & Bull
Matthews)
Bi-Bi Love (Michael Mann)
Bi-Coastal
Bi-Heat, Vol. 1-4
Bi for Now
Bisexual Fantasies
Bisexual Swingtime
Boys Town: Going West
Hollywood
California Wet
Cruisin' for Lust
Days Gone Bi
Foreplay
Hard
Hot Shots 17, 19, 34, 38
Ivy Blues (Michael Mann)
L.A. Boiling Pt.
Lusty Lovers
Men of Action II
Men on the Loose
More Than a Mouthful
Never Big Enough
Nightcrawler
   (Michael Mann)
P.S. Connection 1 & 2
Play Safely
The Spirit is Willing
Tyger Tales

STEVE RAMBO
Born November 25, 1957
in Rochester, New York.
Resides in Palm Springs,
California. 5"9," 8-1/2"
cock. Hunky, hairy, mature
1990s model with dark

hair.
Ace in Your Face
Big Guns 2
Cat Men Do
Catalinaville
Chicago Erection Company
Detour
Dudes
Hell Bent For Leather
Hot Properties
Hot Springs Orgy
International Male Leather
   Initiation
Logjammer
Male Box
Mountain Jock
Night of the Living Bi Dolls
Nutt Crackers
Palm Springs Weekend
Priority Male
Ranger in the Wild
Right Hand Man
The Roommate
Street Boyz
Studio Tricks
Tainted Love

DICK RAMBONE
Hung & Horny
Hot Shots 2

CHRIS RAMSEY
(aka Eric Carson)
Billboard
French Kiss
Hot Summer Of Sex
In Man's Country
Renegade, The
Say Goodbye

MATT RAMSEY
(aka Peter North, Peter
Ramsey)

A very popular, dark-haired,
'80s star from Orange
county, California. Left gay
videos to do straight
videos.
Backstrokes
Below the Belt
Big & Thick
The Bigger the Better
Blond Riders (hetero)
Catalina Classics
Cataline Five-O (hetero)
Cheeks IV: Backstreet
   Affair (hetero)
The Company We Keep
Cousins
Director's Best: William
   Higgins, Vol.1
East L.A. Law (hetero)
Euromen
Friends and Lovers
   (hetero)
Getting It
Hand Jobs, Vol. 1
Hot off the Press
Interviews, Vol. 1 (hetero)
The Life of the Party
   (hetero)
Like a Horse
Master of Discipline
A Matter of Size
More Mind Games
Naked Juice
Party Doll a Go-Go, Part 1
   (hetero)
Sex in the Great Outdoors 2
Sizing Up
Speelbound (hetero)
Two Handfuls
Valley of the Bi Doll
The Way We Were (hetero)
Young Gladiators

MIKE RAMSEY
Behind Closed Doors
Best Of All
The Bigger the Better
Briefs (Compilation)
Like A Horse
Route 69

TROY RAMSEY
Bi & Beyond 2
The Big One
Bi-Coastal
Pizza Boy
Powerline
Sweat & Wet
The Young & the Hung

SCOTT RANDSOME
Born July 26, 1972 in
Torrance, California.
Resides in Orange County,
California. 5'8," 8-3/4"
cock. Hunky, blond body-
builder and '90s model.
Catalina Weekend
Cumming Attractions
Fame & Flesh
Fantasy Fight 1,2, 3, 5 & 6
Fun in the Sun
Greased Up
Hollywood Muscle Boy 4-8
Jockstrap Wrestling 16-21
Manhattan Skyline
Mavericks
Personals
Riptide!
Secret Sex 3
Sex in the Great Outdoors 4
Summer of Scott
    Randsome
Sunsex Boulevard
Total Corruption 2:
    One Night in Jail

Wanted

DANIEL RANGER
Sure Shot

PAUL RAPALLO
Handsome, dark-haired,
1980s model.
The Best of Jonathan
Strong
The Best of Rick Savage
Bi & Sell
Bi-Cycling
Hot Shots, Vol. 44: Golden
    Boys
Long Hard Ride
Manhandler
The Men of Tough Guys
Private Workout
Probation
Running Hard
Scorched!
Smokin' Butts
Spare Room
Tough Guys Do Dance

MATTHEW RAVEN
All Men Do It
How To Get A Man In Bed

KYLE REARDON
Born July 23.
Games We Play, The
Hot Firemen
A Love Story
The Selection Part 4 (Solo)
Skuff
Tall Tail
Throttled

MARK REBEL
The Best of All Matt
    Sterling

Fantasize
Hot Numbers, Vol. 1, 3, 4
Like a Horse
The Mark Reynolds
    Collection Videolog
One Size Fits All

COLE REECE
Born October 7, 1971, El
Paso, Texas. 5'8," 8"
cock, versatile (usually
bottom). Hairy '90s daddy.
Balls In Play
Big Rigs
Cockland
Cum: Stories To Tell
Dirty Leather
Doggy Style
First Timer
Four Men
From Hair to Eternity
Hard up
Hustler Way
Jamie Hendrix's
    Interviews 1
Leather Lover
Leather Watch
Locker Room Lust
Marine Fever
MVP: Most Valuable Player
My Dick Is Bigger 2
No Faking It
The Playboys
Real Cocksuckers
Sex and The Single Man
Sex Toy Story
Sexual Thoughts
Smell of a Man 2
Spin the Bottle Orgy
Sucker
Summer Obsession
Summer Of '44
Talk Dirty To Me

The Playboys
The Pounderosa
The Rush
Trade Off
Virgin Tales #1
Voyeur

DYLAN REECE
Aussie Pool Party
Flesh and Fantasy 2
Hotel California
Sting: A Taste For Leather

ERIC REECE
Ft. Lauderdale Hustlers
Royal Flesh

C.J. REED
Spin the Bottle Orgy

GUY REED
Sure Shot

LOGAN REED
Born April 30. Hairy-chested, light-brown hair. Late 1990s model.
Back in the Saddle
Beach Buns
Before & After
Billy 2000
CatalinaVille
Chip Daniels' Video
Studbook
Home Bodies
Hotter Than Hell
Jeff Stryker's Underground
Logan's Journey
Meet Ray Harley
Men Only
Mountain Patrol
Ryker's Revenge
Soaked

Shooting Stars
Straight White Male
SWM
A Tale of Two Brothers

TRENT REED
Abduction 2
The Backroom
Billy's Tale, A Modern Day
   Fable
Dickted
Do Me Dirty
Idol Country
Flashpoint
Manhattan Skyline
Mavericks
Other Side Of Aspen 3 & 4
Rags To Riches
Renegade, The
The Road To Hopeful
Swallowers, The
Toolkit
Wild Horses
X-Treme Close-Up

CARLO REESE
Beach Dreamer
Warlords

ALAN REEVES
Family Secrets
He's Worth It
Hot Guys #3
In Man's Country
Orgies Pt 3
The Pornographer
Ripe For Harvest
The Selection Part 1 (Solo)
While I Was Sleeping

CODY REEVES
Webmaster

JOE REEVES
(aka Joe Reeve)
A legendary top from the '80s.
Boys of Company F
California Summer
Company We Keep
Gold Rush Boys
Good Hot Stuff
Hard Money
Huge 1
Student Bodies Too

MARCELO REEVES
Born May 12th, Brazil.
Resides in New York. 5'8," 9" uncut, top. Popular late '90s Latin model.
Back in the Saddle
Big Guns 2
Country Hustlers
For Your Pleasure
Hard
He's Worth It
Hot Guys #3
Indulge
Island Guardian
Jumpin' Jacks
Latins
Leather Intrusion Case 4
Leather Men 2
Leather Obsession 1 & 3
A Love Story
Matador
Men
Men Only
Morning, Noon & Night
Objects of Desire
Orgies Pt 2 & 3
Red Alert
The Road Home
The Selection 1 (Solo)
Stock

Turn of Events
The Visit
We've Got Them All

TANNER REEVES
Born January 3, 1962 in
Detroit, Michigan. Resides
in Santa Ana, California.
6'4," 9" cock. One of the
most prolific models of the
'90s.
All Man: Hard as Steel
At Your Service
Bedroom Lies
Best of Daryl Brock
Bi Conflict
Big Drill
Blowout
Body of Art
Boot Black
Boot Camp Buddies
Bootie Nights
Boys From Bel Air
Brief Exchanges
Captain Stud and his
   Seamen
CD-Ram
Centerspread 2
Chi Chi LaRue's Hardbody
   Video Mag. 1
Clubhouse
Come Closer
Conflict of Interest
Constant Hunger
Cruise Control
Cybersex
Dildo Pigs
Dirty White Guys
Dream Men, Erotic Men
Drop 'Em
Dynastud 2
Eaten Alive
Friendly Desire

Getting in Tight
Hairy Chested Hunks
Hand to Hand
Handsome Ransom
Hard Bodyguard
Hard Drive
Hidden Instinct
Hole Patrol
Horny & Hung, Vol. 12
Hot Cops 2
Hot Laguna Knights,
Hot Stuff, Video 10
Hustling Roommate
Idol Country
Idol Inn Exile
Illicit Love
In the Mix
In/Out Masseur
Initiation 1 & 2
Insiders
Intensive
Knight Gallery 2
Leather Intrustion 3
Leather Lover
Leather Obsession 6
Leather Virgin
Leatherworld
License to Thrill
Long Play
Lust Shack
Male Order Sex
Man Construction
Man To Man
Measure For Measure
Masculine Men
Military Issue 2 & 3
Mind Blower
More Than Friends
Moving Target
MVP: Most Valuable Player
Navy Seals
A Night With Todd Stevens
Nymphomania

Outcall Lover
Outlaw Bikers
Palm Springs Cruisin'
Peep-O-Rama
Phone Mates
Physical Education
Pitch A Tent
Playing Dirty
Politically Erect
Poolside Passions
Prisoner of Love
Punk
Pure Sex
Raw Stock
Receiving End
Reflections of Sex
Remembering Times
   Gone Bi
Reunion
Roundup
Santa Monica Place
Sex Posse
Sexabition
6969 Melrose
Sleeping Booty
Solicitor
Stockade
Stud Valley
Studs in Uniform
Summer Daze
Summer Of Scott
   Randsome
Surrogate Stud
Tight End
Too Big to Handle
Top Men
Trade, Malibu Sales
Trickmaster
Trixxx of the Trade
Wear It Out, Spectrum
Wharfmen
White Walls

HANS REGER
(see Chaz Holderman)

STEVE REGIS
In 1998, using his real
name Randy Wendelin, he
appeared in the San
Francisco stage musical
Dirty Little Showtunes!
As Time Goes Bi
Body Search
The Brawnzmen
Brief Encounters
Cocksure
Cruising Park
Desert Drifters
Hair Klub For Men Only
Hard Ass
Hey Tony! What's the
    Story?
Honolulu Hard Bodies
Into the Night
License to Thrill
Manplay
Masculine Men
Men in Love
The Muscle Club
Muscleman
Pacific Coast Highway 2
Palm Springs Paradise
Powertool 2: Breaking Out
Sex Crimes
Sex in Tight Places
Snowbumz
Studz
Sunsex Boulevard
Ten Plus 2
Tough Guys
Voice Mail
Waterworks
X-treme Close-Up

JACKSON REID
Born February 11, 1959,
New Jersey. 6'0," 8" uncut,
versatile. A late '90s hairy
daddy with a mustache.
Bad As We Oughtta Be
Best of Titan: Collector
    Series 2
Fallen Angel 1 & 2
Johnny Come Home
Leather Inndulgence 2
Swell
Tight Fit

ERIC REIKER
(see Cory Monroe)

ERIC REIKERT
Oh, Brother!

KURT REIKERT
Oh, Brother!

RAND REMINGTON
Big Shooters 6
Gayracula
Knockout

TONY RENO
South Beach Heat

DEVON REXMAN
Gut Reaction
One More Time
Playing Dirty

CARLOS REY
(see Eddie Valens)

JOHNNY REY
Popular dark-haired, '90s
model.
Beat Off Frenzy

Bed & Breakfast
Boys From Bel Air
Cool Moon
Cut Vs. Uncut
Dish
Fever
Forum Video Magazine
Full Release
G.I. Jocks: Out Of The
    Ranks
Inside Karl Thomas
Insiders, The
Leather Teddy
Male Triangle, The
Masquerade
Men 4 Men On The Net
Midnight Run
More Than Friends
Night Watch
Nude Science
Nymphomania
O is for Orgy
Party Line
Personally Yours
Portholes
Posing Strap
Risky Sex
Romeo And Juliant
Score Of Sex
Sexcuses
Sex Is In The Air
Smooth Strokes
Toilet Tramps
Twin Exposure
Wall 3, The
Wanted
While I Was Sleeping

VALENTINO REY
Desert Sands
My Best Friends Woody

ANTHONY REYES
Getting Personal
Rent To Bone

DANIEL REYES
www.Orgy

RICHARD REYES
Born February 24.
Bare Bodies
Black In Demand
Black, Ripped & Stripped
Black Sex & Leather 1 & 2
Caught In The Military 2
Latin Sex Thing
Leather Intrusion Case
 1- 3
Love In Dakota
Supersize It
Wall 3, The

BOB REYNOLDS
Laguna Adventure
Show it Off
Some Men are Bigger than
 Others

MACK REYNOLDS
1990s model.
Skateboard Sliders

MARK REYNOLDS
Died in 1989 of a heart
attack.
Back Room, The
Beat Patrol
Big Score, The
Big Showoff
Black And Beyond
Breaking & Entering
Buttsluts Of The Castro
Cruisin' The Balcony
Do Me Dirty

Dreams Come True
Easy Prey
Everybody Does It
G-Squad
Hotel Hombre
A Letter To Three Men
Lunch Hour
Man To Men
Men Together
Mind Blower
Picture Perfect 2
Power Trip
Salsa Fever
Say Goodbye
Sliders
Stud Wanted
Waterworks

MAVERICK REYNOLDS
Bound for Leather
Hot Spot
Link 2 Link

R.J. REYNOLDS
Big Man on Campus
A Night at Halstead's
Three Day Pass
Wet Shorts

TRENT REYNOLDS
A 1990s model.
Saugatuck Summer

REX
The Best of Kevin Williams
The Best of Mike Henson
Faces
Full Load
Glory Hole of Fame
Hot Rods
Therapy

JUSTIN RHODES
(aka Geoffrey Spears) A
versatile, dark- haired,
1980s model.
Backstrokes
Bad Boys Dormitory
The Beat Men
Beginnings
Big & Thick
Black & White Hustle
The Boys of Wilde Island
Boxing Delight
Brother Hustlers
Campus Jocks
Cashload
Climactic Scenes #101
Cum Shots 102
Down to His Knee
Drawing Tricks
Foreplay
Hard Line
Hot Shots, Vol. 18, 23, 27,
 37, 42, 50
It's The Size That Counts
Larger Than Life
Lustful Paradise
Manheat
Manimal
Man Size
Men on Call
Mikey Likes It
Overseas Trade
Play Safely
Pretty Boy
Quickies #3-4
Rainstorm
Rooms
Show it Off
Size Counts
The Size of His Toys
Squirts #3: Hot Encounters
Stiff Sentence
Streaks

Sunday Brunch
Sunstroke
Tease Me!
Think Big
Too Big For His Britches
Tyger Tales
The Voyeur
When a Stranger Comes
Where the Hunks Are

RICKY RHODES
(aka Mikey & Ricky
Masters)
Ball Blasters
The Best of Eric
Manchester
Cashload
Down for the Count
Full Grown/Full Blown
Hot on His Tail
It's the Size That Counts
Locker Room Sex
Man Size
Obsession: The Ultimate
Experience
Pure Fantasies
Star Shots #4
Southbay Boys
Sunstroke
Too Big For His Britches

ALFONSO RIBEIRO
Amazon Adventure
Caracas Adventure
Mystery Men
Paradise Plantation

TONY RICCI
Happily Ever After

PHILIP RICE
Meet Me At The Orgy

TOBY RICH
Rope Tricks

MARC RICHARD
Sure Shot

BO RICHARDS
Afternooners
The Cruiser
Four in Hand
Gunslingers
Main Attraction

CODY RICHARDS
(see Jim Moore)

JAY RICHARDS
Addicted
Any Way I Can
The Boys of New Jersey
Can't Say No
Don't Hold Back
Driveshaft
Every Man's Desire
Everything A Man Wants
Friends are Best
Guys Just Can't Stop
Hidden Instincts
Make it Count
Men Grip Tighter
Men Matter Most
Men Who Dare
The Naked Truth
Natural Response
19 Good Men
Nothing Else Matters
One Way or the Other
Point Of Entry
Powerdrive 500
Powergrip
Pushing The Limit
Pushover
Raw Impulse

Relentless
Shameless
Stop At Nothing
Suckulent
Total Impact
Ultimate Desires
Uncensored
Unexpected Persuasion
Untamed Seductions
Whatever It Takes
The Wild Guys
The Young Stimulators
You've Got The Touch

KYLE RICHARDS
First Timer
Gaywatch
Hard Up
Hard Ball
Hot Male Mechanics
Leather Playhouse
Mountain Cruisin'
Naughty Little Brother
No Faking It
Obsessive Desires
One Track Mind
Phone Mates
Pleasure Ridge
Scent Of Leather
Spring Fever
Top Men
Virgin Tales #1
Wear It Out

TROY RICHARDS
1980s model.
Boys of San Francisco
Class of '84
More Mind Games
Pacific Coast Highway

ZACH RICHARDS
Cute, young, dark-haired

model from the late 1990s.
Won the Probe award for
Hottest Rising Star in 1999.
An American in Moscow
The Art of Lust
Goosed
In Touch Auditions,
Volume 3 (solo)
Jockstrap
Late Night Porn
Marine Obsessions
The Mob Connection
Picture Perfect
Spiked
Underboss, The

BRAD RICHARDSON
A very popular and very
handsome 1980s blond
model.
All the Way
Auto Erotica: The Best of
Sex in Cars
The Best of Kurt Bauer
Best Wishes
The Big One
Man's Hand #13-14
Mr. Wonderful
Out of Bounds
Runaways
Top Man

JOHNNY RIDER
Born January 5, 1973 in
Boston. Cute, young, 5'10"
blond bottom. Late 1990s
model.
Batter Up!
Doctor's Orders 1 & 2
In Deep: Miles To Go
Hotwired: Viewers' Choice
Mo' Betta Butt

LUKAS RIDGESTON
Born April 5. A Czech
Republic native. This cute,
5'10" tall, 7" uncut, model
with "all-American" boy-
next-door good looks was
discovered by Bel Ami's
George Duroy. Has
become one of the most
popular porn stars of all
time.
Frisky Summer 2
Lucky Lukas
Lukas' Story 1-3
Out At Last
Tender Strangers

TAMAS RIDGESTONE
Very cute, boyish-looking,
dark-haired Czech model.
East of Berlin

BOB RIKAS
Left Handed
Rugged Man

NICK RILEY
1990s model.
Sting: A Taste For Leather

ROBERT RILEY
Insertion
Naked Underneath
The Selection Part 2 (Solo)

DAVID RINALDO
Brown-hair, brown-eyed,
1990s model.
Beach Buns
Hard Focus
My Brother's Friend
On the Prowl Again

JOHNNY RINGO
(see Mark Montana)

CHASE RITE
Bear to the Bone
Country Hustlers
The Flavor of Leather
The Flavor or Men

SAM RITTER
A 1980s model.
Balls to the Wall 35
Behind His Back
Dirty Leather
Leather After Midnight
Leather Intrusion Case
2 & 4
Militia Men
Sex On The Beach

ANGEL RIVERA
Brothers
Buckets of Love
Hawaiian Heat
Young Warriors

CARLOS RIVERA
Shameless

DANNY RIVERA
Tiger's Brooklyn Tails

JEAN RIVERA
Born May 15. Resides in
Argentina. Native
Argentinians Jean and
Marco Antonio are lovers
who came to the U.S. in
1997 and entered the porn
video business. They
returned to their native
country where they continue to make porn videos for

American studios.
Current Affairs
First Time Tryers 6
Indulge 2
Positively Yours
Winged

MICHAEL RIVERA
(aka Carlos Velasquez)
Gangsters at Large
Hand of Fate
Hot to Trot
South Beach Heat
Swell

STEVEN RIVERA
Working Pleasure

DANIEL RIVERO
Gang of 13
Lick It Up

DUSTY RIVERS
Good Samaritan, The

JORDAN RIVERS
(aka Jordan, or Julian in
his straight videos.) Dark-
haired, horse-hung, ex-
Marine and late '90s
model.
Choke 'Em
Fly Bi Night
Hard to Swallow
Hung Heroes 2
Just You and I

ROCCO RIZZOLI
(see Georgio Canali)

DOUGLAS ROBB
Gay Weekend Away

BILLY ROBERTS
The Bartender
Summer Money

BRIAN ROBERTS
Rosebud
Throttled

MIKE ROBERTS
Born September 20, 1958
in Chicago. 6'1," 8" cock.
Top. Late '90s, hairy
daddy.
Chances
Chapters
Fallen Angel 2
Outcast

RANDY ROBERTS
Dream Doll
Gang Bangers
Movers 'N' Shakers
Pay to Play
Raw Footage
Tongue Dancing
True Confessions

ROB ROBERTS
Suck Daddy

SCOTT ROBERTS
All the Right Boys
California Homegrown
Class Reunion
Cousins
Desert Heat
Growing Years
Nothing but the Best
A Physical Education
Play Safely
P.S. Connection 1
Rebel 1980s

JOHN ROBERTSON
A dark-haired 1990s model.
Bedtime Tails
Gang Bang Alley
Hollywood Kid, The
Jackpot
Lords of Leather
Sex Between the Lines
Sex Games

GABRIEL ROCAS
Bear Hug
Club Butt 2: Private Party
Cockland
Hard on Site
Sex Invaders
Uniforms Only

NATHAN ROCCO
Afternoon Delight
Boys in the Office
Brown Paper Wrapper
Exiled
Heaven Too Soon
Hell Knight
Hotel L.A.
How Big is Danny?
Huge Double Impact
Knight Out with the Boys
Mein Kock
Method & Madness
The Making of "Knight Out
    with the Boys"
Never Enough
976
Off Duty Maneuvers
On Cue
The Orgy!
Primitive Impulses
Private Moments
Right Here, Right Now
The Rolls
Room for Rent

Savage Blue
Steel Pulse
Straight Studs
Stroke 'N' Men
Tempting Tommy
Whistle While You Work
Who's Gonna Get It?
Wild Streak
Willing to Take It

CHRIS ROCK
Born April 21 in Delaware.
Dark-haired, mature-look-
ing, 5'10," 7" cock, versa-
tile. Late '90s model.
Apprentice, The
Before and After
Body Worship 24
Descent
Fantasies in White and
   Black
Forced Service
Hand of Fate
Logan's Journey
Public Submission
Ranch Hands
Sex Invaders
Stock
Wild Sex in America

HAL ROCKLAND
Born February 11. One of
three brothers, all in the
industry.
The Backroom
By Invitation Only
Flashpoint
Other Side of Aspen 3 & 4
The Renegade
Saddle Tramps
Three Brothers

SHANE ROCKLAND
Born December 23, 1972
in Darmnstadt, Germany.
5'10," 9" uncut, top. One of
three brothers, all in the
industry.
A Body to Die For
Military Issue #3
The New Coach
Orgies Pt 1
Scenes in Leather
Sure Thing
Three Brothers

VINCE ROCKLAND
Born December 29, 1973
in Germany. Resides in
Hollywood, California. 5',
9," 8" cock, uncut. One of
the legends of gay porn.
The most popular of three
brothers, all in the industry
in the 1990s.
All Men Do It
Best of Leather 3
Bi Norma Jeanie
Bi Voyeur
Bi Invitation Only
Body Worship 24
Breakaway
A Brother's Desire
By Invitation Only
Chip Daniels' Video
Studbook
The Complexxx
Curious (Bi)
Driven to It
Electrocorrective Bondage
Fame And Flesh
Foul Play
Hands On
Hot Cops
Hotter Than Hell

House Of Tricks
How to Get a Man Into Bed
Into Leather
Jawbreaker
Jeff Stryker's Big Time
Keyhole (Hetero)
Leather Obsession 3 & 4
Male Tales (DVD)
Matinee Idol
Military Issue 2,3
Montage
My Brother's Keeper
Nightheat
9-1/2"
Your Knees
Orgies 1, 4
Perfect Ten's
Porn Fiction
Possession
Private Passions
Quick Change (Trans)
Rock Off (solo)
Rock Solid
Roped and Used
Saddle Tramps 1 & 2
Sex Invaders
The Sex Pit
She-Male Latex (Trans.)
The Stalker
Three Brothers
Thriller

JOHN ROCKLIN
A well built, blond, early
1990s model.
Big Guns
Dreaming of You
Handtools
Military Men
Screen Test #1
Splash Shots II
The Switch is On
William Higgins Screentest 1

DAVID ROCKMORE
A porn star legend from
the '80s.
Airmale
Cowboys & Indians
Davey and the Cruisers
Grid Iron
Hole in One
Jumper
Powertool 2
The Rites of Manhood
The Rockmore Files
Sizzle
Sterling Ranch
Tease Me!

RICK ROGUE
All Men Do It!
Anal Attraction
Balls to the Wall 35
As Time Goes Bi
Barracks Glory Hole 3
California Surfsiders
Dick Diving
Free Your Willy
Friendly Desire
Hard Up
Hole In The Wall
Knight Heat
Leather Triangle
Low Rent
Sex On The Beach
Things You Can Do In
    Leather
Threesomes
Tutor Me!
Wall, The
Working Pleasure
Young Memories

VINNIE ROCKO
Bear it All
Bear to the Bone

Bound for Leather
Chicago Bearfest
Fluid
Porno Tonight Show, The
Viva Latino

GREGG ROCKWELL
Born October 9.
The Big Thrill
Caught In The Military 1
Coal Miner's Son
Hard To Keep Down
Opposites Attract
Throttled
Tomorrow Will Come

JOEY ROCKWELL
(aka Scott Ryan)
Attraction
Cocktales
Heat in the Night
Interview 2
Sex Lies & Video
Cassettes
Show it Off

DEAN RODNEY
Made to Order
Doctor's Orders
Porno Tonight Show, The

JESUS RODRIGUEZ
A Spanish Fantasy

MIGUEL RODRIGUEZ
Ft. Lauderdale Hustlers

ROGER
A dark-haired, porn legend
from the 1970s.
Bondage Voyeur
Bullet Gold, Vol. 1-3
Erotica Video 30—#7

Garden Party
Good Neighbors
Hand in Hand Preview
    Tape #1
Heavy Equipment
Hot House
House Painter & Bigger
Than Life
Hunk
A Night at Adonis
Sex Machine
Sex Magic
Super Studs

BLAKE RODGERS
Skuff

BRYON ROGERS
Men Matter Most
Stop At Nothing
You've Got The Touch

ERIC ROGERS
An early 1990s model.
Black Magic/White Heat
Boys Night Out
Cult of Manhood
Hot Shots, Vol. 19: Black
    and White Buns
Hot Shots, Vol. 22, 23,
    27, 34
Jack City
Men: Skin and Steel
Max Makes it Big
Raw Footage
The Size Counts
Who's Dat Boy

JIM ROGERS
California Boys
Dangerous
Doing It
Games

Greenhorn
Hot Lunch
Palace of Pleasures
Turned On

KENNETH ROGERS
Boys of Beverly Hills
California Wet
4/Hour 4/Skin
The Prostitute
Rodeo
Uncut Club of L.A.

K.J. ROGERS
Late '90s model.
Black Balled 2
Black Men Do!
Black Patrol
Link 2 Link

KIRK ROGERS
Bottoms Up

NICK ROGERS
Died from AIDS-related
complications.
Arcade
The Best of Colt, Vol. 1 & 2
Bullet Gold, Vol. 1 & 3
Grease Monkeys
The Idol
Malibu Days/Big Bear
Nights
Performance
Rangers
Rough Cut
Sex Machine

RICK ROGUE
All Men Do It
Friendly Desire
Intrusion
Leather Confessions

Leather Connection
Leather Desires
Leather Party
Leather Triangle
Man About Town
Nasty Rumors
Sex And The Single Man
Tell Me About Sex
Things You Can Do In
    Leather
Tight Leather
Tutor Me
Working Day & Night

CHRISTOPHER ROJAS
1990s model.
Something About Larry

ADAM ROM
Born April 17, 1970 in
Western Russia. Resides
in Hollywood, California.
5'10," 7" uncut, versatile.
Cute, '90s model, works
mostly behind the scenes,
these days.
After Hours
Alibi For A Gang Bang
Alley Boys
Born To Please
Call Rescue 911
Cram Course: Sex Ed 3
Cumbustible
Hard Ass
Hard Labor
Hot Cops 3: The Final
    Assault!
Hot Male Mechanics
In Man's Country
Oral Alley
Personals
Pleasure Ridge
Point of View

Rescue 69-11
Rocket Rider
Sex Invaders From Uranus
Showboys
Take One: Guys Like Us
Taking The Plunge
Top Men
Ultimate Reality
Uncut Weekend

GIO ROMANO
J.S. Big Time
Night Walk
Nutt Busters
Sexual Suspect

NICK ROMANO
A dark-haired, Italian,
1980s model.
Alley Action
Any Excuse For Sex
The Best of Matt Powers
The Best of Scott Bond
The Brawnzmen
Buddy System 2:
    Camouflage
Built to Last
Carnival Tales
Casting Couch
Climactic Scenes #101
Come and Get It
Come as You Are
Crusin' Park
The Drifters
Fetish
Fighting Dirty
Foreign Competition
For His Own Good
Give It To Me Straight
Guyz n-the Burbs
Hollywood Tails
Hot Shots, Vol. 45:
    Latin Fever

Leather Angel
Leather Watch
Lifeguard on Duty
Lights! Camera! Action!
Midnight Hard-On
Moment of Truth
Object of Desire
O is for Orgy
On the Rocks
Power Play
The River
Secret Meeting
Sex Trigger
Steam Room
Stickpussy
Tell Me About Sex
Tight Jeans
Vice Cop
Where the Hunks Are
White Steel
You Bet Your Ass

JOE ROMERO
Born February 15, 1967,
Burbank, California. 6'0,"
9" cock, top. Late '90s
daddy.
Alex's Leather Dream
Best of Leather: Part 1&2
Big Boyz Club 4
Biker Pigs From Hell
Born To Wild
Call Boy
Chip Daniels' Video
Studbook
Come Closer
Courting Libido
Cyber Sex
Do Me Dirty
Dream Lover
Driven Home
Erotikus
Escort, The

Everybody Does It
Find This Man
Fire In The Hole
Folsom Street sex
Getting Even with David
Hoghounds 2
Homebody Hoodlums
Forum Video Magazine
Hot Cops
Hot Properties
Hot Pursuit
Intrusion
Jock Off
Just One Favor
Leather Obsession 1 & 2
Leather Tricks
Millitary Issue 3:
    Ask & I'll Tell
New York Close-Up
New York Pick Up
Night We Met
Oral Fixation
Orgies 1-4
Overcharged
Peep O'Rama
Photoplay
Politically Erect
San Francisco Sex
Sex in Dangerous Places
Sex is in the Air
Sex Play by Russo
Sexxs Pitt
Shoot 'n' Porn
Slave Camp 2
Swallow
Technical Ecstasy
Tom Katt
Total Deception
Wet Dreamers
Wet Warehouse

MIKE ROSE
1990s model.

Technical Ecstasy

TONI ROSE
1990s model.
Choke 'Em 3

JASON ROSS
Dark-haired, handsome
1980s model.
A New Mexico native.
The Abduction 2&3
Bedroom Eyes
Bedtime Stories: Tales to
    Keep You Up
Behind the Eight Ball
The Best of Michael Parks
The Best of Ryan Yeager
Between the Sheets
The Big Ones
Blond Justice
Callguys, U.S.A.
Club Men
The Cockeyed Eagle
The Devil and Danny
Webster
Fantasy Man
Fetish
Glory Hole of Fame 2
Hard Moves!
Hard Steel
Hawaiian Desire
Head Struck
Hot Shots, Vol. 45:
    Latin Fever
Hot Summer Knights
The Long Hot Summer,
Part 2
The Making of "Knight Out
    with the Boys"
Method & Madness
Object of Desire
One Night Stands
Open House

Piece Work
Pull the Trigger
Raising Hell
Ram Man 3
Rock-Hard
Smokin' Butts
Songs in the Key of Sex
Stranded: Enemies and
    Lovers
Summer Knights
Tattoo Love Boy
Top Brass
Toy Boys (dir.)
Traffic School Was Never
    Like This!
Trail Tales
Underground Homo
Hardcore

JOHN ROSS
Born April 28, 1968 in
New York. 5'10," 7" cock.
Cute, boyish, '90s model.
Resides in Los Angeles.
At First Glance
Back Seat BJ
Cadet
Bustin' Loose
California Deep Woods Inn
Chip Daniels' Video
    Studbook
Chompin' at the Bit
The Corporate Ladder
Deep in the Brig
Expose
Fantasies of White & Black
Hotter Than Hell
Inter-Racial Interrogation
Journal, The
Locker Room Sex Brawl
Male Box
Marine Crucible
Maximum Cruise

Mountain Patrol
Opposites Attract
Red Blooded Americans
Reform School Confidential
Said & Done
Sex Club Initiation
Straight Exposure
Tease, The

KEVIN ROSS
Rebel 1980s

STEVE ROSS
An early 1990s model.
Ace in the Hole (solo)
Bad Boys Club
Bare Tales
The Best of Eric
    Manchester
The Best of Kevin Williams
Bigger & Better
The Boys of Summer
Brother Hustlers
Catalina Classics
Crusin' West Hollywood
Cum Shots 101
Fever Pitch
Head of the Class
Hitchhiker: Manual
Transmission
Manimal
Mannequin Man
My Brother, My Lover
Out of Bounds
Probe Vol. 3: Tom Brock
Switch Hitters III
The Switch is On
They Grow 'em Big
An Uncontrollable
    Obsession

DANIEL ROSSI
Home Bodies

MARCO ROSSI
Born October 16, 1970 in
Queens, NY. Resides in
Laguna Beach, California.
5'10," 7" cock. Rossi is a
hunky, Italian gay-for-pay
bodybuilder from the
1990s.
Ace in the Hole
Back Room
The Bartender
Best of Leather: Part 1
Best of Sam Abdul
Chi Chi LaRue's Hard Body
    VideoMag. 3
Day of Decadence
Double Vision
Dripping Hard 3
Driven to It
Fame & Flesh
The Getaway
Greaseguns
Hands On
Hot Guys
House Rules
How to Get a Man in Bed
Idol Country
International Male Leather
    Uncut
Knight Gallery
Lana Exposed
Latex Meltdown
Leather Obsession 2
License to Thrill
Long Play
Look of a Man
Man's Touch CD
Marco Rossi—A
    Wanted Man
Masquerade
Mess Hall Maneuvers
Military Issue
Mirage

Night Fall
Nightheat
Orgies Pt 2
Romeo & Julian
Stripper Service
Stroking It, Uncut 1
Tom Katt
Total Corruption
The Urge
Virtual Viewer Photodisc
A Wanted Man
We've Got Them All

VINCE ROSSI
Brian's Boys

PETER ROTH
Redwood

LEE ROY
Drawing Tricks
Flesh Tones
Hot Latinos
Show & Tell
Valley Boys

VIC RUBINO
Born October 5, 1975 in
Mt. View, California.
Resides in North
Hollywood, California. 6,'
7-1/2" cock. Young, hairy,
'90s daddy in training.
As Big As It Gets
Good Dick Hunting
Grease Lightning
HOMOgenized
Hustler Way
Sand Blasted
Sand Storms
Spin the Bottle Orgy
Trade Off
West Hollywood Stories

TOM RUCKER
A dark-haired, youthful-
looking, 1980s model from
Canada.
The Best of Back Alley
   Video
It's Good to Be Bad
Naval focus
Obsession: Hot Rocks of
   Steel
Paradise Beach
Perfect Summer
Point of No Return
Sailor in the Wild
Sex in the Great Outdoors,
   Part 3
Stud Sensors
Tough Guys Do Dance
A Trip to Paradise

NICK RUFFIN
A brown-haired, early
1990s model.
After Hours
The Recruiter
Self-Made Men
When Straight Men Stray

LOGAN RUNNER
Dark-haired, boyish-looking
1990s model.
Object of My Erection, The
Something About Larry
You've Got Male

AL RUSSELL
O is for Orgy
Sex Toy Story #2
Sleeping Booty and Other
   Tails

CLAY RUSSELL
Behind Closed Doors

Behind the Greek Door
Breaker Blue
The Boys of Venice
Cop Daddies Playtime
The Cruiser
El Paso Wrecking Corp.
Fast Friends
Hard at It, Vol. 2
Heatstroke
Hot Off the Press
Hot Shots, Vol. 12:
   Uniforms
Police Stories
Six Card Stud
Snowballin'
Star Shots #5
Trick Time
Wintertime

DAVE RUSSELL
Dark-haired, hot and hand-
some Italian-looking model
from the late 1990s.
Take One: Guys Like Us
Urgent Matters

JAKE RUSSELL
Off Duty

JOE RUSSELL
Laguna Beach Lifeguards
Off Duty

LUC RUSSELL
Flashpoint
Nutt Crackers
Raw Material
Rear Ended
Room Service
Said & Done
Tainted Love

SCOTT RUSSELL

Bedroom Lies
Below The Rim
By Invitation Only
Hard Bodyguard
Idol Dreams
Idol Inn Exile
Jawbreaker
Mean Streak
Mentor
Physical Education
Receiving End
Road To Hopeful, The
Secret Sex 3: The Takeover
Shadowdancer
Summer Of Scott Randsome
Voyeur, The
Wanted

TY RUSSELL

Cute, Italian, mid '90s top from Denver.
Abduction 2: The Conflict
Bigger The Better 2, The
Billy's Tale
Cd-Ram
Desert Oasis
A Few Fresh Men
Hart Throb
The Hideaway
Highway Hunks
House Of Tricks
Imagination: Action Gone Wild
Jawbreaker
License To Thrill
Party Line
Physical Education
Protector, The
Roll In The Hay
Somebody Is Watching
Toilet Tramps

Tony's Big Brother
Twin Exposure

DANNY RUSSO

(aka Danny Martino)
Down for the Count
Heatwaves
Powertool
Spring Break

DONNIE RUSSO

Beat Cop, The
Best of Sam Abdul
Born To Be Wild
Bound And Creamed
Captain Stud And His Seamen
CD-Ram
Chase Is On, The
Chi Chi Larue's Hardbody Video Mag. 4
Cody Exposed
Donny's Dirty Sex Garage
Down For The Count
Find This Man
Forum Video Magazine
Grease Guns
Home Alone
Horny Brothers
Idol Dreams
Idol Inn Exile
Insiders, The
In The Jeans
Intruder: Robbery, Torment, Fantasy
J.D. Slater's S.M.U.T.
Long Play
Military Issue
Military Secrets
New York After Hours
Night Watch
Nuts, Butts And Glory
On The Mark

Oral Fixation
Pits, Tits And Feet
Romeo & Julian
Rough Night At The Jockstrap Gym
Roughed Up At The Spike
Roughed Up In Boston
Roughed Up In L.A.
Russo's Sex Pig
Sex Clubs Of San Francisco
Sex-A-Holics
Slave Workshop Boston
Spank Me Paddle Me
Stargazing 5
Summer Of Scott Randsome
Taste Of Leather
These Bases Are Loaded 2
Thief's Punishment
Tickled Butch Guys
Torture Alley
Total Corruption
Total Deception
Tough Guys
Wet Fantasies

JEAN RUSSO

Asian Persuasion 2

ANDREW RYAN

Knockout
Workout
Young Olympians

ASHTON RYAN

American Way, The

ERIC RYAN

A popular, dark-haired, Italian-looking model from the 1980s.
The Best of Surge II

Better in Bed
Bi-Heat, Vol. 3: Bellhops
Bi-Heat, Vol. 4: Dial-a-Doll
Bi-Heat, Vol. 5: Male
  Hustlers
Bi-Heat, Vol. 6: Co-
  Worker's Wife
Bi-Heat, Vol. 8: Sharon's
  Houseboys
Bi-Heat, Vol. 9: Men's
  Room
Body Scorchers
The Boys in the Back
  Room
The Boys of Venice
Centurians of Rome
Century of Mining
Days Gone Bi
Dynamite
Early Erections
Giants, Part 1
Glory Hole of Fame
Hand-in-Hand Preview
  Tape #1
H.E.A.T.
Hot Roomers
Hot Shots, Vol. 7: Daddies
Hot Shots, Vol. 22: Raw
  Rears
Hot Shots, Vol. 27: Super
  Studs
Hot Shots, Vol 32: Dirty
  Daddies
Hot Shots, Vol. 34: More
  Orgies
Hot Shots, Vol. 37: Penal
  Code
Job Site
Juice
Just Blonds
Leo and Lance
Lewd Contact
Lovers and Friends

Magnum Griffin, Vol 7
Magnum Griffin, Vol. 9
Master Hyde
Mustard Hanky Right
Navy Blue Hanky Left
New York Men
Non-Stop
Old Reliable #37: Superior
  Men
Old Reliable #59: Some
Old Friends 2
Old Reliable #115: All
  Grown Up
Screen Play
Sighs
The Size Counts
Stiff Sentence
Stroke: Foreskin Fantasy
Texas Size 12
Tough Guys
Tough Iron
Tough Stuff
X-tra Large
Young Yankees

JACK RYAN
(aka Kent Austin)
Born in 1977. Resides in
West Hollywood. Dark-
haired and handsome '90s
model.
Cream Team, The
Over the Rainbow

KENNY RYAN
Hotel Montreal
Male Call

MICHAEL RYAN
Alone & Private
Casting Couch 3
House Rules
Platoon

MIKE RYAN
(see Eric Stryker)

ZEFF RYAN
(aka Jeff Ryan) dark-
haired, 1980s model. Died
January 1994 from AIDS-
related complications.
Blue Moves
Classified Action
Come and Get It
The Devil and Danny
  Webster
Dial Justice
Executive Action
The Experiment
The Grip of Passion: Love
  or Lust
Hawaiian Desire
Hot Shots, Vol. 45: Latin
  Fever
Las Vegas Love Gods
Movers and Shakers
Moving In
Once in a Blue Moon
Party Hard!
Radioman
Ready to Serve
Rear Window
The Slut
Stud Ranch
To Protect and To Serve
Traffic School Was Never
  Like This

JASON RYDER
1990s model.
Ass Lick Alley
Skuff
Splashdown!

LEE RYDER
Died July 10, 1991 from

AIDS-related complications. A legendary top from the '80s, from Laguna Beach, California.
All American Boys
Biggest One I Ever Saw
Bikers Liberty
A Few Good Men
Giants, Part 1
Hard
Hot Shots, Vol. 7: Daddies
Huge 1 & 2
Men And Films
Screen Play
Spokes
Sticky Business
2X10
The Wilde House
Winner Takes All

STEVE RYDER

A long-haired, 1980s model.
Big Switch 3: Bachelor Party, The
In Your Face
Majestic Knight
Mandriven
Scoring

KEN RYKER

Born August 17, 1972 in Chonju, Korea. Resides in Arizona. 6'4," 11" cock, bisexual top. This 1990s blond, hairy, horse- hung hunk is considered by most to be one of the biggest porn stars of all time.
All About Teri Weigel
The Backroom
Big River

Idol Promises
Mass Appeal (bi)
The Matinee Idol
New Pledgemaster
Other Side of Aspen 3 & 4
Red, Hot & Safe
The Renegade
The Ryker Files
Ryker's Revenge

S

MARK SABER

All About Sex
At Your Service
Backdrop
Back in the Saddle Again
Beach Blanket Boner
Big As They Come
Big Box Office
Born to Be Wild
Brats
Conflict of Interest
Disconnected
Dorm Fever
Down Home
Down & Out
Dude Beach
The Escort
Express Male
Frat House: Memories of Pledge Week
GI Jocks: Out of the Ranks
Group Therapy
Hardball
Hidden Agenda
Hidden Instinct
Hush
Hustlemania
I Dream Of Weenie
Idol Universe
Impacted

It's A Gang, Video Series 1
Leather Weekend
Macho Money
Mack Pack #5: Toolkit
Men In Love
Muscle Bound
MVP: Most Valuable Player
Nasty Rays
On The Lookout
Open Windows
Overcharged
Overload
Playing Dirty
Powertool 2: Breaking Out
The Predators: Vol. 1
Rawshock
Room Service
Sex Trigger
Sex, Guys And Videotape
Slave Auction
Stud House
Superstud Fever
Trick Stop
True
The Whole Nine Yards
Wild Ones, The
Young And Notorious

MARK SAGE

Action on Melrose
Brats
Buddy System
Carnival
Casting Couch
Cruising West Hollywood
Foot Loose
Heat
Leather Me Down, Do Me Toys
New Love
Snowbound
Thumbs Up
The Voyeur

VIRGIL SAINCLAIR
1990s model.
Betrayed
Sit Tight

DREW SAMPSON
Pressure

SCOTT SAMPSON
(see Mitch Preston)

RUSTY SAMUELS
Big Showoff
Diamond Stud, The
Dirty Pillow Talk
Everybody Does It
Hardhats
In Your Ear
Invitation
Playground, The
Point Of View
Principal of Lust
River Patrol
San Francisco Sex
Stop In The Name Of Sex

DAVID SANCHEZ
Hispanic Monuments 5
Mucho Macho Private
Collection 1

FERNANDO SANCHEZ
(aka Raul)
Hairsteria
Young Men On The
Pleasure Trail

MITCH SANDER
Late '90s model.
Bound for Leather
Dial "S" for Sex
Link
Link 2 Link

Stag Party

JEROME SANDERSON
A 1970s model.
Seven in a Barn

MARTIN SANDOR
Dark, handsome and
slightly hairy young 1999
Hungarian model.
Hungarian Heat

DUSTY SANDS
(see Sean Fox)

EMILIO SANDS
Black Power
Club Butt 2: Private Party
Desert Sands
Dickin' Around
Foot Patrol
Freshman Recruits
Gay for the Weekend
Hard on Site
L.A. Daze
Opposites Attract
Paul Morgan's Raw Meat
    2,3 & 5
Red Blooded Americans
Sands Storms
Sodom
Touch Me There
Young Men On The
Pleasure Trail

RICK SANDS
Black Balled
Boot Camp II
Fantasy Boys
Hard to be Good
Make a Wish and Blow
One Hot Day
Paramedic Alert

The Recruiter
Rumble
Sud Squad

MARK SAUNDERS
(see Eric Stryker)

CHAD SAVAGE
Born June 16, 1980.
Resides in San Diego. 5'6,"
7" cock, blond-haired, blue
eyed, boy-next-door with a
thick dick. Reportedly the
younger brother of Luke
Savage.
Another Man's Hand
First Time Tryers

LUKE SAVAGE
1990s blond, jock next door
model. Resides in San
Diego.
Beach Buns
Black Balled 2
Boomerang
Choke 'Em 3
Jarhead

NICK SAVAGE
Cadet

TOM SAWYER
A dark-haired, 1990s model
Coach's Boys, The
Imagination
Latin Magic
Painting Party
1230 West Melrose

BILLY SAX
A 1990s model.
Ass Lick Alley
Aussie Pool Party

Australian For Leather
Flesh and Fantasy 2
Gang of 13
Low Riders

STEVE SAX
Buffed, brown-haired,
1990s model
Men Only

T.J. SAX
Bedtime Tails

BEAU SAXON
A mid '90s model. Resides
in Northern California and
now works mostly behind
the scenes.
Backstage Pass
Bottoms Up
Call to Arms
Forced Entry
Mavericks
One Man's Poison
Pocket Rockets
Rear Ended
Road To Hopeful, The
Trucker's Sex Dog

TOMMY SAXX
A late 1990s model.
Sometimes blond, some-
times brown-haired, this
youthful and husky Missouri
native now lives in
Colorado.
I Know Who You Blew Last
    Summer
Skateboard Sliders

TONY SCALIA
Four Card Stud
Wet Warehouse #3:

The Party

NICK SCHULTZ
Below the Belt
Collage 2
Good Sex!
Hard Disk Drive
Poker Studs
Voyeur

SCORPIO
All Tied Up
Best of the Superstars
Black Hanky Left
Boots and Saddles
Centurians of Rome
Christopher Rage's Orgy
Death of Scorpio
The Erotic History of
    Christopher Rage, Vol. 1
Grey Hanky Left
Hand-in-Hand Preview 1
Hot Shots, Vol. 5: Leather
    In Heat
In Search of the Perfect
    Man
Just Blonds
Light Blue Hanky Left
New York Men
P.M. Preview #2
Private Collection
Red Hanky Left
Rock Creek Gang
Sleaze
Street Kids (cameo)
Style

AARON SCOTT
Long, brown-haired, hand-
some 1980s model.
Busted
Cabanna Boys
California Blonds

Desert Fox
In the Briefs
The Long Hot Summer 2
Male Taboo
Painted
Read My Lips
A Real man Wouldn't
    Leave
The Rod Squad
Stryker's Best Powerful
    Sex
Summer School

ADDISON SCOTT
Born April 11. 6'2," with a 9"
cock. Mature, shaved head-
ed, blue eyed, 1990s
Falcon exclusive. Resides
in Massachusetts.
French Connections 2
Hot Wired: Viewers' Choice
Sting: A Taste For Leather

CHRISTOPHER SCOTTT
A Chicago native. Moved
to West Hollywood in late
1999. A cute, boyish-look-
ing, 1990s model with
brown hair. He tells us that
he's part German and part
Native American Indian. An
intelligent and warm guy,
on and off the set.
The Chosen
French Connections 2
Gang Bang Jocks
High Tide
Hot Wheels
I Know Who You Blew Last
    Summer
In Deep: Miles To Go
Red Alert
Sting: A Taste For Leather

DYLAN SCOTT
Leather After Midnight
Back To K-Waikiki

FRANCIS SCOTT
1990s model.
Northern Exposures
Woody's

HUNTER SCOTT
After Hours
Bedroom Lies
Bi-Conflict of Interest
Big Score, The
Blow Me Down
By Invitation Only
Center Spread 2
Conflict Of Interest
Dreaming In Blue
Fluffer, The
Hot Guys #3
Interview #2
Jawbreaker
Just Men
   (Gino Colbert Dir)
Leather Triangle
A Letter To Three Men
Look Of A Man, The
Major Meat
Male Triangle, The
Manticipation
Midnight Run
Moving Target
Orgies Pt 1
Pitch A Tent
Power Driver
Raw Material
Road To Hopeful, The
Seeds Of Love
Sexologist (Adam Hart Dir)
Slave Auction
Street Smarts: Sex Ed 5
Together Again

Tyler Scott- A Day Of
Decadence
Wanted Man, A
Working Stiff

JACOB SCOTT
Aching for Punishment
Chapters
Fortune Nookie
Gang of 13
Hot to Trot
Lick It Up
Link 2 Link
Mr. Fix-It
Wet Daddy

JAKE SCOTT
Bi Bi Love
Big Shooters #2
Extreme Urge
Fleshtones
Hard Disk Drive
Heat Goes On
The Last Surfer
Men of Action II
My Straight Friend
Show & Tell
Strokers

JASON SCOTT
Batter Up!

JEREMY SCOTT
Died from AIDS related
complications.
Anywhere, Anytime
The Arousers
Bad Boys Dormitory
The Best of Kip Noll
Black Force
The Boys of San Francisco
Class of '84, Part 1 & 2
Foreplay

Giants, Part 1
Glory Hall of Fame
Hardline
Hot, Hung & Hard
Hot Shots, Vol. 3: Cum
   Contest
Hot Shots, Vol. 4: Contest
   Continues
Hot Shots, Vol. 21: Big
   Ones!
Hot Shots, Vol. 29: More
   Raw Rears
Juice
Just Do It
Little Brother's Coming Out
The Lone Star
Kip Noll: Superstar
Making it Huge
Manholes 1 & 2
Men and Steel
Men in Motion #6
Mind Games
More Mind Games
Move Over, Johnny
Never Big Enough
Pacific Coast Highway
Palace of Pleasures
Probe, Vol. 4: Black &
   Blond
P.S. Connection #1
Rock Creek Gang
   (co-dir. & actor)
Sex in the Great Outdoors
Shooting Stars #3: Michael
   Cummings
Shooting Stars #4: Jeremy
   Scott
The Size Counts
Split Decision
2 X 10
William Higgins Preview 1
Working Hard for Their
   Money

JOSHUA SCOTT
(aka Josh Perez)
Born December 27,1961,
Philadelphia. 5'10," 7 1/2"
cock. A '90s bottom.
The Big Showoff
Bi-Sexual Nation
Black Gang-Bang
Boss Man
Chicago Meat Packers
Doctor's Orders 2
Fallen Angel 2
The First Time
Flesh and Fantasy 2
Focal Length
F-Train To Castro
From Hair to Eternity
Hairsteria
Hard for the Money
Leather Story
Link
Midnight Run
9-1/2"
Night Feast
Ranch Hands
Redwood Ranger
Slave Trade
Someone is Watching
What Men Do

NOLAN SCOTT
Coal Miner's Son
When The Wife's Away

RYDER SCOTT
1990s model.
Never Too Big
Rear Ended
To The Hilt

T.J. SCOTT
(aka T.J. Anderson, T.J.)
A blond, 1980s model.

Bare Bottoms
The Best of Street Times
    Video
Bi-Cycling
Blow Your Own Horn
Board Meeting
California Wet
Concrete Lover
Hard Men at Work
Hollywood Hunks
International Guide to
    Fellatio
Interview, Vol. 2
Lee Hunter's Laguna
    Adventure
More Mind Games
The Rolls
Sweet Meat, Lost
Innocence
Switch Hitters V: The Night
    Games
Undergear (as T.J. Scott)
X-tra large

TYLER SCOTT
A mature, blond, 1990s
model.
All About Steve
Bed & Breakfast
Best of Sam Abdul
Chase Is On, The
Chi Chi Larue's Hardbody
    Video Mag. 1
Cody Exposed
The Come Back
Exposed
Forum Video Magazine
Getting It Firm
The Hideaway
In The Jeans
Lowe Down
Man Construction
Military Issue 1 & 2

Obsessively Compulsive
On The Mark
Outlaw Bikers
Romeo And Julian
Solicitor
Tony's Thing
Tyler Scott- A Day Of
    Decadence

TREVOR SCOTT
1980s model.
Eighteen Candles

ZACHARY SCOTT
Born May 7, 1973,
Hollywood, California.
5'11," 9-3/4" cock. Late
'90s model.
Autofellatio Biographies
Chip Daniels' Video
Studbook
Don't Dick With the Devil
Men in Blue
Ryker's Revenge
Skateboard Sliders
Uncle Jack
Whatever Ever You Say,
    Sir
Wild Sex In America

WILL SEAGERS
(aka Matt Harper)
Bi-Surprise
Bullet Gold, Vol. 2 & 3
BulletPac 3: Cowpokes
BulletPac 6: Bruno Will
Cabin Fever
Cruisin' the Castro
Dune Buddies
    (as Matt Harper)
Face to Face
Champs: Will Seagers &
    the Hustler

Fire Island Fever
(as Matt Harper)
Hot Shots, Vol. 11: Men's
Room
J. Brian's Flashback
Jocks
L.A. Tool & Die
The Massage Boys
Peagusus II: Hot to Trot
Star Shoots #5
Wanted

SEBASTIAN
Late '90s Latino model.
Adventures of A. Rocky
and Bill Winkler
All That Jizz
Chance Encounters
Coal Miner's Son
Deep In The Forest
The Drifter
Driven By Lust
Mt. Fuckmore
Underboss, The
Uninvited, The

SEBASTIAN
Real name is Simon Rex.
In the 1990s, this incredibly
handsome, Italian model
went on to become an MTV
host, has done TV commer-
cials and a Fox TV sitcom.
Young, Hard & Solo 2 & 3
Hot Sessions 3

SCOTT SEDGWICK
The Arousers
Hot, High & Horny
Pleasure Beach
Pleasure Mountain

CARL SEER
Leather Connection
Leather Intrusion Case 1
Leather Pit
Sex In Leather
Things You Can Do In
Leather

JAKE SEEVER
Brown-haired, handsome
1980s model.
Hot Property
Texas Size 12
Three the Hard Way
Too Hard to Hold
Warlords

TONY SERRANO
Men Matter Most
Stop At Nothing
Whatever It Takes

JOHN SEXTON
Best Of Leather: Part 3
Hotter Than Life
Into Leather Part 2
Leather Obsession 5
Low Riders

SHANE
Locker Jocks 1982

BOB SHANE
Anything Anytime
Cell Block #9
Heatstroke
Navy Blue Hanky left
Red Ball Express
Tough Guys
The Young Ones

JACK SHANE
Jacks Are Better

JOE SHANE
Any Boy Can

RONNIE SHARK
(see Bill Harrison)

STEVE SHANNON
Bi-Sexual Nation
Cream Team, The

IAN SHARP
Discovered by Chi Chi
LaRue. Only made one
film, as far as we know.
Chi Chi LaRue's Hard
Body Video Mag.

KEVIN SHARPE
Bedtime Stories
Challenge, The
Fetish
Headstruck
Poetry & Motion
Their Wild Ways

AIDEN SHAW
Lives in London. He left the
business but made a
comeback in 1998. He is
also a highly acclaimed
author.
The Art of Touch I & 2
The Backroom
Black Leather, White Studs
Boot Black 2
Breakaway
Chi Chi LaRue's Hardbody
Video Mag. 4
Command Performance
Danger Alley
Descent
Dirty Dreaming
Disconnected

Forced Entry
Grand Prize
Greaseguns
Hand Jobs
Hot Pursuit
Hush
License to Thrill
Lovers, Tricks & One Night
    Stands
Mess Hall Maneuvers
The Midnight Sun
New Pledgemaster
Night Force
On the Mark
Palm Springs Paradise
Reunion
Ripped
Roll in the Hay
Secret Sex
Steam Room
Summer Buddies
Voice Male
Wet N Wild
Workin' Hard

NEAL SHAW
Best of Buckshot
Chip Off the Old Block
Easy Entry
Every Which Way
Triple Treat
What the Big Boys Eat

BRIAN SHAWN
The Big Showoff
Do Me Dirty
What Men Do

SHANE SHEPARD
Caribbean Cruising
Delivery Boys
Poker Studs
Salt & Pepper Boys

Size of the Matter 2
Spank Your Buddy
Squirts 3
Tub Stubs

SKIP SHEPPARD
Kansas City Trucking Co.

JAKE SHOT
Gang of 13
Lick It Up

JUSTIN SIDE
(aka Justin Syde)
Interview #1
9 Holes
Man Watch
My Dick Is Bigger 2
Plugged In
Swallow
Tutor Me!

DAVID SILVA
(see David Dabello)

JACK SIMMONS
Born December 11th,
California. 6'2," 10" cock,
top. Popular black '90s
model.
All You Can Eat
Backseat BJ
Balls in Play
Best of Titan: Collector
    Series 2
The Big Black bed
Black Heat
Black in the Saddle
Black Mischief
Chained Desires
Cruisin' for a Gang Bang
Dr. Jerkoff and Mr. Hard
Expose

Flashers
The Freshmen
Heat of the City
Hot Sex Pick Up
Humidity
Journal, The
Morning, Noon & Night
Naked Escape
Provacative
Pushed to the Limit
Red Blooded Americans
Reform School
Confidential
Rip 'n' Strip Wrestling
The Rush
Sex Club Initiation
Shoot the Chute
Sodom
Street Boyz
Stuffed
The Taking of Jake
Tease, The
Tourist Trade
Turn of Events
Zebra Love

JOE SIMMONS
Died from AIDS-related
complications. Popular 6'2"
1980s black model.
Advocate Men Live 6:
    Big Buddies
Bad Ass
The Best of Joe Simmons
The Best of Satellite
Bi and Large
Black Alley: South of the
    Border
Black Book
Black Delivery
Black Magic
Black Pack
Blackmates

Black Workout 3
Briefs: The Best of John
   Summers
Catalina's Black Gold
Colored Boys
Cousin Buck
Dirty Tricks
Frank Vickers: Worship
Gettin' Down
Homeboys
I Know What Girls Like
Made in the Shade 1 & 2
Male Power
The Men of 550
My Masters
Oreo Boys
Oriental Dick
Pizza Delivery
Raunch II
Return of Indiana Joan
Safe Sex
Screen test
Sizzling Joe Simmons
Slaves
Soul & Salsa
Soul Dad
Spittin' Image
They All Came
White HankyLeft

PHIL SIMMONS
Do Me Evil

BRETT SIMMS
(aka David Morris)
Ball Blasters
Beach Ballers
Big Favors
Bi-Heat, Vol. 7, 8, 9
Boys Camp Memories
Days Gone Bi
Deep Inside
Desert Heat

Dirty Jocks
Freshman
Good Men Go Bad
Growing Years
Hot on His Tail
Hot Shots, Vol. 10: Sweat
Hot Shots, Vol. 15: Bottoms
Male-O-Gram
Manheat
Muscle Fever
Oasis
Perfect Ten
Summer Heat
Video Games #6
When a Stranger Comes

JOHN SIMMS
Leather Obsession 5
Millitary Issue 3: Ask &
   I'll Tell
O is for Orgy

PHILIPPE SIMONEAU
A hunky, blond, 1990s
French-Canadian model.
Call of the Wild
A Few Fresh Men
On the Rise

DAVID SIMONS
Three Day Pass

B. J. SIMPSON
The Best of Joe Simmons
Bi and Large
Black Book
Black Magic
Black Pack
Black Stallions
Catalina's Black Gold
Duo Series, Vol. 1
Homeboys
Men Behind Bars

TONY SINATRA
(aka Tony Erickson)
Castro Motel
Hard as Steal
Headstruck
Hole in One
Iron Man
Lifeguard on Duty
Pay To Play
Secret Boys Club

DOMINIC SINCLAIR
(aka Dom Sinclair)
Born July 7, 1971, New
York. 6'2," 9 1/2" cock. A
dark-haired, Italian model
from the late '90s.
Back in the Saddle Again
Body Shop
Born To Please
Buttsluts in Leather
Cruising Grounds
Cybersex
Face Down
Fire in the Hole
Force of Nature
Forest Rump
Gaywatch
Getting Ahead
Getting Greeked
Getting it Good!
GV Guide All-Star Softball
   Game #1
Handsome Ransom
Hard Labor
Hidden Agenda
Hot Dreams
Hot Male Mechanics
Hot Properties
I Saw What You Did
Leather Playhouse
Leather Triangle
Love In Dakota

A Night in Leather
Nude Getaway
Obsessive Desires
Outcall Lover
Overcharged
Phonemates
Pleasure Ridge
Scent of Leather
Sex After hours
Sex is in the Air
Sex On The Beach
6969 Melrose
Skinnydippers
Smooth Strokes
Star Maker
Studs in Uniform
Summer Money
The Soul Patrol
Things You Can Do in
   Leather
Top This
Trophies: Class of '94
The Wall
Working Day and Night

STEVE SINCLAIR
Cute, long, dark-haired
model from the early '90s.
Lives in So. California.
Pay For Play 1
Pay For Play 2

VIRGIL SINCLAIR
Dark-haired, jock-next-door
1990s model.
Sting: A Taste For Leather

ROBIN SINNER
California Blonds
Four by Four
Hot Property
Men in Motion #7
Men-TV

The Rites of Spring
Texas Tales
Three the Hard Way
Too Hard to Hold

TONY SKINNER
A 1970s model.
Adam & Yves

JESSE SKYLER
(see Jesse Tyler)

MARK SLADE
(Hetero porn name Frank
Towers) Born September
25, 1968, California.
Resides in Los Angeles.
Beefy, gay-for-pay late
'90s model. 6'4," 9" top.
Billy 2000
Cadet
West Hollywood Hope

B.J. SLATER
A mature, balding 1980s
model and actor with a
beard. A native of Southern
California. Now lives in
Northern California.
Alley Action
Big as They Come
Big City Men
Big as They Come
The Bi Valley
Break In
Brief Exchange
Caged Heat
The Cockeyed Eagle
Command Peformance
Danger Alley
Deception, Part 1 & 2
Delirium
Dirty Laundry

Dirty Pictures
The Drifters
Express Male
Few Freshmen, A
Free Your Willy
Home Wrecker
Horse Meat
Hot Cops 2
Hung in the Balance
Ivy League
Keeping Time
Kiss-Off
L.A. Boot Bottom
Low Rent
Male Seduction
Man Driven
Midnight Hard-On
Night Force
O is for Orgy
Palm Springs 92264
Ram Man 3
Ripped
A Scent of Man
Sex Fix
Sex Shooters
Sexpress
Sleepless in L.A.
Smokin'Butts
Someone in Mind
Star Gazing #1
Steamy Bondage Hard-Ons
Studz
"10" Plus
The Thick of It
Trade-Off
True
Wet Load
Wild Streak

BILLY SLATER
(see Rex Baldwin)

CRAIG SLATER

A hunky, blond 1980s model.

The Abduction
Bedroom Eyes
Between the Sheets
Best of All 2
The Best of Chad Knight
Callguys, U.S.A.
The Challenge
The Cut Club
Glory Hole of Fame 2
Hot Shots 48: International Males
Man of the Year
Mein Kock
Open House
Overload
Pacific Coast Highway 2
the Producer
Rear Window
Callguys, U.S.A.
The Return of Grant Fagan
Score 10
Scoring
Someone in Mind
Spellbound for Action
Tattoo Love Boy
Their Wild Ways
Trading Up
Up and Over

J.D. SLATER

A resident of San Francisco, the former actor is now a music composer. In 1998 he released a CD titled "Themes for Erotic Trance Fractals"—now that's a mouthful!

Anonymous Sex
Bad Boys, Vol. 1
Bait
Bears and Cubs
Breaker Blue
Bring Your Own Man
Caribbean Cruising
Chip off the Old Block
Crazed
Delirium
Dynastud
Encounters of a Different Kind
The Erotic History of Christopher Rage, Vol. 2
Guilty (dir.)
Hand-in-Hand Preview Tape #1
Handsome
Hard
Hard at It, Vol. 2
The Heat Goes On
Hot Men
Hot Roomers
Hot Shots, Vol. 7: Daddies
Hot Shots, Vol. 19: Black and White Buns
Hot Shots, Vol. 34: More Orgies
Hunk
I Need it Bad
In Heat
International Skin
J.D. Slater, Top to Bottom
J.D. Slater's Confessions (dir. & actor)
J.D. Slater's S.M.U.T.
Manholes #1
Meat (dir.)
Motor Sexual (dir. & actor)
Mud! Apocalypse Again!
My Masters
New York Men
A Night Alone with Al Parker
Nightcrawler
One, Two, Three
Outrage
Ranch Hand
Rough Idea
Seduction II: The Heat Goes On
Seduction III: Passion Obsession
Shooting Stars #5: J.D. Slater
Social Studies
Soul & Salsa 2
Studbusters
Tramps
Turbo Charge
2 X 10
Video Games, Vol. 10
Voyeur
What the Big Boys Eat

MIKE SLATER

Throttled

J.T. SLOAN

(aka Justin Sloan)
Born September 25. Handsome, dark-haired Canadian model from the 1990s.

After Hours
The Backroom
Bedroom Lies
Best Of Leather 2 & 3
Boys Next Door
Bullseye
Centerspread
Chi Chi LaRue's Hardbody Video Mag. 3
Chip Daniels' Video Studbook
Come With Me
Country Hustlers
Deep End

Diamond Stud
Dino Dreams On
Fast Action
Fetish Sex Fights 3
For Your Pleasure
Freshman Recruits
Gamemasters
GV Guide All-Star Softball
   Game 1
HOMOgenized
Hot Cargo
Hot Firemen
Hot Guys #2
Hot Stuff
The Hotel
How to Get a Man Into Bed
Idol Country
Idol in the Sky
Jawbreaker
J.S. Bigtime
Killer Looks
Leather Bound
Leather Obsession 1-4
Leather Playhouse
Les Hommes Au Natural
A Letter To Three Men
Link to Link
Live Feed
Locker Room Lust
Man Country
Man to Men
Man Trade Solos
Manticipation
Mavericks
Men
Naked Highway
Never Too Big
New Pledgemaster
Night Walk
Night We Met
No Reservations
Nude Science
Orgies Pt 1

Physical Education
Pitch a Tent
The Pornographer
Quick Study
Rawhide
The Rival
The Ryker Files
Scenes in Leather
Single For The Weekend
Skateboard Sliders
Snafu
South Beach Heat
Suck Daddy
Travelin' Wild
Turn of Events
The Visit
Wanna Be In Pictures?
While I Was Sleeping

SANDY SLOAN
Born May 22, 1966 in
Glendale, California. 5'10,"
7 1/2" cock, bottom. Blond,
boy-next-door late '90s
model.
Beach Buns
Chip Daniels' Video
Studbook
Freshman Getaway
Weekend
Getting Straight
Hand of Fate
HOMOgenized
Lambda Lambda Lambda
   #2 —Lessons In Greek
Pucker Up
Return To Camp YMAC
Sand Storms
Sex Fly Sex Invaders
Sex Lie
Stag Party
Technical Ecstasy
Throttled

Time Cops
Weekend at My Brothers
White Tails Black Tails
Young Men On The
Pleasure Trail

BRANDON SMALL
A Lesson Learned
SWM

JUSTIN SMALL
Male Call
Party In My Pants

BILL SMITH
Arkansas Luggage
Spank Your Buddy
Wrestling 8, 10, 22

CAMERON SMYTH
Mantasy Island

WALTER SOARES
Breakin 'Em In 1 & 2
The Men From Ipanema
O is for Orgy

DAVIDE SOLARI
Journey To Italy
Summoner, The

DAVE SOMMERS
Cashload
Freshman Fantasies
Nine and a Half Inches
Sailor in the Wild
X-tra Large

TOM SOUTHERN
Chi Chi La Rue's
   Hardbody 2000.2

BILLY SPARKS
Eighteen Candles

STEVE SPARKS
Hot Cops
Top Men

JOE SPEARS
Beat Patrol
Bi-Conflict of Interest
Conflict Of Interest
Flashpoint
Making Of A Gay Video
Man Country
Manticipation
Shadowdancer
Together Again
Too Dam Big!
Wide Receiver

GEOFFREY SPEARS
(see Justin Rhodes)

RANDY SPEARS
A 1980s straight porn star
who appeared in a few
gay-for-pay vids.
Hotel California
Men On Site
Straight To Bed
Stud Squad

ZAK SPEARS
A very popular hairy model
from the '90s. This
Minnesota-native left the
business in the mid-'90s at
the height of his popularity
and now reportedly works
as a personal trainer in Los
Angeles.
The Abduction 2 & 3
All About Steve

Backstage Pass
Boot Black
CD-Ram: Sex Star
Interactive
Chi Chi Larue's Hardbody
Video Mag. 2
Coach's Boys, The
Dish
Fluffer, The
Getaway, The
GV Guide Gay Erotic Video
Awards 2
Hand Jobs 3
Hologram
House Rules
License To Thrill
Look Of A Man, The
Model Behavior
Network Q #28
Night Watch
On The Mark
Oral Fixation
Posing Strap
Rags To Riches
Secret Sex 1 & 2
Sex Crimes
Solicitor
Summer Fever
Sunsex Boulevardt
Supermodels Of Advocate
Men
These Bases Are Loaded 2
Too Big To Handle
Too Dam Big!
Total Corruptiont
Wild Ones, The

DEAN SPENCER
1990s model.
Biker Pigs From Hell
Fetish Sex Fights 3
Man Trade Solos
964 Dicks St.

West Hollywood Hope
Underboss, The

MATT SPENCER
Blond Australia model
discovered in late 1990s.
Absolute Aqua
Absolute Arid
Taken Down Under

SPIKE
A dark-haired Ohio native
discovered by Chi Chi La
Rue.
Acres of Ass 1 & 2
Billy Herrington's Body
Shop
The Bite 2
Chi Chi La Rue's
Hardbody 2000.2
Hotel California
Final Link, The
Full Up!
Lick It Up
Read Bi All
Sex Play by Russo 2
Spiked
Stock
Wet Fantasies

ROB SPITFIRE
Splashdown!

MICKEY SQUIRES
Anywhere, Anytime
The Best of Colt,
Vol. 2, 3, 10, 12
The Best Stallions
The Brig
Face to Face
Fade Out
Fade In
J. Brian's Flashbacks

Joys Of Self Abuse
The Muscle Clue
Red Ball Express

PETER ST. JAMES
Balls of the Wild
Cat's Tale

MITCHELL STACK
1990s model.
Black Balled
Link to Link
Wet Warehouse #3: The
Party

BO STALLION
Black For More
Driven Home
GV Guide All-Star Softball
Game 1
Mr. Blue
Officer And His Gentleman

BULL STANTON
Blue Blake's former lover.
Nothin' Nice
The Wild Ones

DEREK STANTON
Born October 27, 1955 in
Baltimore, MD. Resides in
Huntington Beach,
California. 6,' 8-1/2" cock.
A porn star legend from the
'80s still making videos in
the late '90s.
Bad Bad Boys,Hand-in-
Hand
Best Of Kip Noll
The Best of Stud
The Best of the Biggest
Boys of Venice
Brothers Should Do It

Catalina Orgies, Vol. 1
Class of '84, Part 1 & 2
Class Reunion
Deep Fantasies
Face to Face
Family Values
Glory Hole of Fame
Grease Monkeys
Hard Core
Hardhat
The Idol
Jocks
Kip Noll: Superstar
L.A. Tool and Die
Members Only
Men Under The Hardhat
Performance
Printer's Devils
Rear Deliveries
Route 69
Sex in the Great Outdoors
Strange Places and
   Strange Things
These Bases Are Loaded
Tricking, Nova Fortuna
Wet Shorts
William Higgins Preview
   Tape #1
X-tra Large

CHRIS STARR
(see Chris Ladd)

ETHAN STARR
Born May 29th,
Connecticut. 5'6," 7" cock,
bottom. Late '90s model.
Analized
Bootie Nights
Complexxx
Dick Will Hunting
Driven by Lust
First Time Tryer's #8

Gang of 13
Goosed (bi)
Inside Men 1
Jamie Hendrix's
   Interviews 1
The Man Hunt
The Pounderosa
69—Made in the Shade
Tail End of Summer

RICKY STARR
Latin model from the '90s.
All The Way Inn
Big As They Come 2
Boot Black 2
Cruisin' for a Gang Bang
Daredevils
The Insiders
A Jock's Tale
Switchcraft
West Hollywood Hope

CHAD STEELE
Bedtime Tails
Best of Sam Abdul
Live Feed
Military Issue
Weho Confidential

CHRIS STEELE
Born March 7 on Carswell
Airforce Base in Fort
Worth, Texas. 6,' 7 1/2"
cock, top. A Studio 2000
exclusive. When he's not
on screen, this dark-haired
daddy runs a bar in Dallas.
Night Riders
Cadet
Relatively Speaking
Uncle Jack

CURT STEELE
Physical Education

DAMION STEELE
Everything A Man Wants
Powergrip

JACK STEELE
Anywhere, Anytime
Desert paradise
Hot, High & Horny
Jacks Are Better
Surfer Blue

JASON STEELE
Died February 25, 1995
from AIDS-related compli-
cations.
Beef
The Best of Both Worlds
The Best of Surge
    Vol. 1 & 2
Bi-Ceps
Big Bear Men
Chip Off the Old Block
Hard Disk Drive
Hung and Horny
Manholes #1
Nine Skins
Paradise Park
Ranch Hand
Strokers
Studbusters

JIM STEELE
Cute, blond and boyish
1980s model.
Advocate Men Live!
Below The Belt

KURT STEELE
Physical Education
Slip It In

Squeeze Play

LANCE STEELE
Bootie Nights

MARK STEELE
Bedtime Tails
Bi-Anonymous
Big City Men
Blond Obsession
Brats
Cocksure
Crusing Park
Dickted
Dirty Leather
Dirty Works
Disconnected
Dorm Fever
Dreams Come True
Favors
Fever
Frat House: Memories of
    Pledge Week
Horney Rent Collector
Interview #2
It's a Gang
Juice Bomb
Leather Teddy
Mack Pack 1, 2, 3
Man's Hand #121
Men of Steel
Mess Hall Maneuvers
My Cousin Danny
Nasty Rays
Olympic Proportions
Party Animals
Private Games
Rebel 1980s
Slick Willies
Spring Fever
State of Mind
Straight to the Zone
Stud Ranch

The Swallowers
Transparent
The Visitor

ROB STEELE
Bi-Sexual Nation
Internal Affairs

TOM STEELE
Handsome and hung,
dark-haired 1980s legend.
Owned a popular bar in
Galveston, Texas known as
the Steel Door.
All the Way In
Behind Closed Doors
The Best of All Matt
Sterling 1 & 2
Come Clean
Four Card Stud
Hard as Steele
Heat in the Night
Highway Patrol
Hotel L.A.
Interview, Vol. 3
Offering
One Night Stands
The Other Side of Aspen 3
The Pledge Masters
Powerline
Powertool 2
Sailor in the Wild 2
Say Goodbye
Seduction 3: Passion
    Obsession
Two Handfuls 2
Undercover

TROY STEELE
Born October 22.
Born To Be Wild
Flyin' Solo
Goodfellas/Badfellas

Jump On It
Leather Obsession 5
Leather Watch
Leather Weekend
Look Of Leather
Militia Men 1 & 3
Orgies Pt 4
Scent Of Leather
To The Hilt
Wear It Out
Wet Warehouse

GLENN STEERS
Died September 17, 1994
from AIDS-related illness.
A masculine porn star legend from the early '80s
who made a brief comeback in the early '90s.
Big Bang
The Company We Keep
Good Hot Stuff
One In A Billion
Stiff Competition

JOEY STEFANO
(Real name Nicholas
Anthony Iacona) Born
January 1, 1968 in
Chester, Pennsylvania.
Died November 21, 1994
of a drug overdose in
Hollywood, California at
age 26. One of the most
popular gay porn stars of
all time.
All About Last Night
The Best of Adam Grant
Best of All 2
The Best of Joey Stefano
The Best of John Vincent 1
The Best of Street Times
   Video

Bi Golly
Big Bang
Billboard
Buddy System 2:
Camouflage
Chi Chi Larue's Hardbody
   Video Mag. 1
Dildo Kings
Fidelity
Down & Out
Fond Focus
French Kiss
G-Squad
GV Guide Gay Erotic Video
   Awards 1
Hard Knocks
Hard Moves!Hard Steal
Hole in One
Horsemeat
Idol Eyes
Innocence Found
Inside Vladimir Correa
Joey
Karen's Bi-Line
The Legend of Joey
   Stefano
Les Hommes
Man in Motion
Man of the Year
Men of Forum
More of a Man
My Cousin Danny
Obsessivley Compulsive
On the Rocks
One Man's Poison
Plunge
Prince Charming
Privilege
Pumping Up: Flexx II
Ranger Nick II
Raw Footage
Revenge: More than I Can
   Take

The River
Rock-Hard
Say Goodbye
A Scent of Man
Scoring
Screwing Screw-Ups
Secret Dreams
Sex in Wet Places
Sex, Lies and
   Videocassettes
Smokin' Butts
Song in the Key of Sex
Soul Dad
State of Mind
Strip Search
The Stroke
Stryker's Best Powerful
   Sex
Sweet in the Bootie
Temptation
Tommy Boy
To the Bone
Total Impact
Uncut Club
Undergear
Videolog 2: Director's Cut
The Visitor
What Men Do

KURT STEFANO
Born in January 11,
Oregon. 5'10," 7-3/4" cock,
bottom. Handsome, dark-
haired '90s model.
Caught in the Act 2
Caught In The Military 2
Cop Out
Cowboy Jacks
Dark Side of the Moon
Good Samaritan, The
Grease Guns 2
Hot Guys 4
Hot to Trot

Hotter Than Life
Hustler Blue
Initiation 2
Johnny Hormone
Latin Obsession
Leather Intrusion Case 2
A Love Story
Malibu Beach Hunks
Men With Tools Part 2 :
    Nailed
Night of the Living Bi-Dolls
9-1/2"
Sleeping Booty and Other
    Tails
Star Maker
Summer of '44
Supersize It
Sure Thing
Toolbox

LES STEIN
(aka Les Stine)
A usually hairy-chested,
1980s model.
All Night Long
Boot Camp 1 & 2
Boys on Fire
Butt Darts
Climactic Scenes #101
Corporate Head
Cream of the Crop
Dueling Dicks
Fantasy Boys
Fetish
Flexx
From Maui With Love
Fucking Around
Gays, Bis, She-Males and
    Hermaphrodites
Guys Who Crave Black
    Cock
Hard Labor
Hard to be Good

Head of the Class, Part 2
Headin' West
In His Corner
In the End Zone
Inside Vladimir Correa
Make a Wish and Blow
Manhandler
Mechanics on Duty
Men at Worl
Mix N' Match
Neptune
Night Maneuvers
Nuts and Butts
Pool Boy
Pretty Boy
Prince Charming
The Rites of Fall
The Rites of Winter
Rumble
Seduction 1 & 2
Sex, Guys and Videotape
Size Talks
Smokin' Butts
Stud Fuckers
Tasting Mr. Goodbar
Texas Size 12
Unchained Men
V-8

LEE STERN
All the Right Boys
All the Way In
Bondage Voyeur
Brother Load
Chain Reaction
Class Reunion
A Few Good Men
The Other Side of Aspen 2
Southern Comforts
The Wilde House

FRANK STERLING
(aka Dixon Hardy)

Back in the Saddle Again
Big Box Office
Caribbean Cruising
Come And Get It
Dangerous
Elements Of Passion
Head of the Class
Holding Their Own: Self-
    Sucking Soldiers
Hose Man
It's A Gang: Video Series 1
Las Vegas Orgy
Leather Me Down Do Me
    Toys
Looking Good
More Than Just Strangers
Olympic Proportions
One And Only Dominator
Powerful 2
Sand Blasters
Sex Toy Story
6969 Melrose Lane
Skinny Dippers
Slut, The
Smells Like A Man
Sticky Gloves
Tennis Court Daze
Turbo Charge

JOSHUA STERLING
Born August 13.
Best Of Leather 1 & 2
Call Boy
How To Get A Man In Bed
Idol Universe
Leather Bound
Leather Obsession
Lost In Las Vegas
Nights In Eden
Orgies Pt 3
Sexologist
South Beach Vibrations
Top To Bottom

BILL STETSON
Choke 'Em 3

ANDREW STEVENS
Caught In The Military 1

BRENT STEVENS
Hold Me Again

BRYCE STEVENS
Pinball Wizard
Plugged In
Taking The Plunge

CARL STEVENS
Party In My Pants

COREY STEVENS
American Way, The

CORT STEVENS
Born October 4. A Denver
native. A blond, boy-next-
door looking '90s model.
At Your Service
Bound to Rise
By Invitation Only
Chi Chi LaRue's Hardbody
   Video Mag. 4
College Jocks' Foot Fetish
Cruisin' the Balcony
Cumback Kid
Daredevils
Erotic Confessions
Getting In Tight
Hand to Hand
Hard Bodyguard
Hot Cargo
Hot Day In L.A.
How To Get a Man Into
   Bed
Hustler's Blues
It Happened One Day

Jet Streams
Masculine Men
Meanstreak
Mirage
Nasty Rumors
Nightheat
The Other Side of Aspen
   3 & 4
Receiving End
Revenge of the Bi Dolls
Rescue 69-11
Roped and Delivered
Risky Sex
Smooth Operator
Stud Valley
Summer's Tall Tales
Tony's Thing
Too Damn Big!
Underwraps
The Urge
Wet Dreams
Wet Warehouse
Whitefire

CRAIG STEVENS
A.W.O.L.
Bam 2: Thug
Black Leather Gang Bang
Black Renegades
Black, Ripped & Stripped
Hung Man Meat
Marine Chronicles, The
Redwood
Straight Cocksuckers

DREW STEVENS
Wet Warehouse #3:
   The Party

JEREMY STEVENS
Apply Within
Ft. Lauderdale Hustlers
Royal Flesh

JOEY STEVENS
A late 1990s model.
Alley Katt
Apprentice, The
Deep Desires
A Jock's Dream
New In Town

KORY STEVENS
A 1980s model.
Locker Jocks

MICHAEL STEVENS
Ass Lick Alley
Both Ways (bi)

MITCHELL STEVENS
Born October 22nd,
England. 6'2," 8" uncut,
bottom. Blond, hairy, late
'90s model.
Ass Lick Alley
Aussie Pool Party
Bar None
Big Guns 2
Buttmunch
Cowboy Jack's
Immersion
Mercury Rising
Read Bi All
Spiked
Stock
Swell
Up For Grabs

ROB STEVENS
Flesh & Fantasy
Kip Noll & the Westside
Gang
Rear Admiral
Rear Deliveries
Wanted

SEAN STEVENS
(aka Sean Stevins)
Back in the Saddle

TODD STEVENS
Born June 26. Dark-haired,
hung-huge '90s model.
Resides in New Jersey.
Clothes Make The Man
Download
Homogenized
Hot Copy
I Am Curious Leather
In Man's Country
Men Matter Most
Mr. Blue
Pushing The Limit
Put It Where It Counts
Renegade, The
Sex Session
Titan Men
Urgent Matters

WAYNE STEVENS
Grizzly

NICK STEVENSON
Grizzly
Sleeping Booty and Other
   Tails

MARC STEWART
The Big Thrill
California Kings
Full Up!
Hotel California
Red Alert

RAY STOCKWELL
A very handsome, dark-
haired, early '90s model
who only did three videos.
Advocate Men Live! 5

Full Load: Maximum
Overdrive
Sailor in the Wild 2

ARMSTRONG STOKER
Acres of Ass 1 & 2

ALEX STONE
Born July 30. Early '90s,
dark-haired daddy.
Another Man's Pleasure
Aussie Pool Party
Before & After
The Big Black Bed
Boys on Fire
Dirty White Guys
Fallen Angel 2
Fetish Sex Fights 3
Flexx
Fond Focus
Great Balls of Fire
He Devils
Hot Shots, Vol. 42:
   Face Shots
Jawbreaker
Link 2 Link
Lip Lock
Lunch Hour
Manstroke
My Brothers Best Friend
Pay to Play 2
Phi Kappa Sucka
The Pledge Masters
Powerfull II
Pay to Play II
Ram Man 2
Rites of Manhood
The Rites of Winter
Rocket Ryder
Rock Solid
Room-Mated
Seduction III: Passion
   Obsession

Shoot the Chute
Stag Party
Stone's Alone
Stryker's Best Powerful
   Sex
Superhunks II
Weho Confidential

ANTHONY STONE
Bi-Sexual Nation
Male Box
Switchcraft

BRAD STONE
Dark-haired, mid '90s
model. Lives in Southern
California. Still makes
occassional appearances
at clubs across the
country.
The Abduction 3
Bi and Beyond 2
Built Tough
Foul Play
Men of Size
Pump
Ready for It
Show it Hard
Summer Fever
Wild Horses
Workin' Stiff

CHARLIE STONE
(aka Charlie Warner) A
1980s gay-for-pay actor.
Best Of All 2
Butt Darts
Engine 69
Entertainment Bi-Night
'57 Pickup
Hard to Be Good
Heat in the Night
I Like to Watch

Lovers Coming Home
Mix 'n Match
Naked Juice
Offering
Powerful II
Seduction
Superhunks II
Tasting Mr. Goodbar

CHRIS STONE
Born in Costa Rica. Resides on the East Coast. Dark-haired, mid '90s model.
Back to Front
Basket Fever
Beach Blanket Boner
Bedtime Tails
Behind the Eight Ball
Best Of All 2
The Best of Joey Stefano
The Best of Street Times Video
Bi-Anonymous
Big Bang
Billboard
Bonus Pay
The Boxer 2
Buttsluts of the Castro
Callguys, U.S.A.
The Carnival
Cellblock Sinner
Club Men
Club Pleasure
Crucial Encounters
Dickted
Dream Doll
Erector Set
Foreign Affairs
Hang 8-1/2
A Hole Different Ballgame
Honolulu Hard Bodies
Hawaiian Desire
Hot for His Bod

Hot Shots, Vol. 41: Rim Shots
Hot Shots, Vol. 45: Latin Fever
Hot Shots, Vol. 48: International Males
Hotel Hombre
Hustlemania
Idol Eyes
Idle Pleasures
I Dream of Weenie
I Love Foreskin
Impacted
Heads or Tails
Jarheads for Sale
Las Vegas Love Gods
Latin Bandit
Latin Encounters
Latin Escorts
Latin Hustle
Liquid Love
Los Hombres
Love of Lust
Lovers Coming Home
Low Blows
Mack Pack #1: The Swallowers
Mack Pack #2: Dicked
Male Taboo
Mating Game
Men of the Moment
Nude & Rude
Open House
Paradise Beach
Pin Me
Preferred Stock #1
Private Workout
The Rumpster
Sailor in the Wild 2
Scorcher
Score 10
Sex in the Great Outdoors, Part 3

Smokey
The Sperminator
Steamed
Steel Pulse
Stiff Competition
Sugar Britches
Superstud Fever
Surrogate Stud
The Swallowers
Their Wild Ways
Ten Plus 2
Through the Looking Glass
Trading Up
Trick Time
A Trip to Paradise Beach
True Confessions
Up and Over
White Spy
Who's Gonna Get It?

ERIC STONE
Born in 1960, died December 24, 1996, reportedly of natural causes at age 37. A hairy-chested daddy from the mid '90s.
Driven: No Turning Back
First Timers
Hidden Man
Male Instinct
Manhandlers
The Other Side Of Aspen 4, The Rescue
Powergrip
Ranger In The Wild
Ripe For Harvest

JARROD STONE
Freshman Fever
To The Hilt

JEFF STONE
Anything, Anytime

Cherokee Station
Hard Disk Drive
In the Name of Leather
Juice
More Mind Games
Red Ball Express
Subway
Tough Guys
Trisexual

MAX STONE
Born October 2. Mature,
shaved-headed, late
1990s model.
Best of Leather 1 & 3
Blow Me Down
Born To Be Wild
Fast Action
Faultline Sextime
Flesh and Fantasy 2
Idol Universe
I.M.L. Uncut
Leather Bound
Leather Obsession 1-6
Night Walk
Nutt Crackers
Oral Fixation
Orgies Pt 3 & 4
That Old Whorehouse
Things You Can Do In
    Leather
Wet Warehouse
Wild Ones, Thet

RIP STONE
Blond, buffed '90s model.
Resides in Los Angeles.
All About Sex
Best Of Leather: Part 3
Boot Black 2
Cop Sins
Deep Desires
Diamond Stud

Down in the Dirt
For Your Pleasure
Forced Entry
Fox's Lair
Full Package
The Guy Next Door
Handball Marathon 3
High Stakes Wrestling
    3 & 4
How to Get a Man Into Bed
I.M.L. Uncut
Into Leather
Is Your Big Brother Home?
Keyhole
Muscle Bound
Muscleforce #6 - Rip
Night Walk
An Officer and His
    Gentleman
Prisoners of Lust
Rear Ended
The Selection Part 1 (Solo)
Score of Sex
Sex House
Street Smarts: Sex Ed 5
Tainted Love
We've Got Them All

ROB STONE
(aka Logan Paul)
Download
Hot Summer Of Sex
Sex Wrestling

STORM
1990s, dark-haired Italian
model. Resides in New
York.
Alley Action
Big Bang
Bed Tales
The Best of Jonathan
    Strong

Boys on Call
Boys Will Be Boys
Brotherly Love 1 & 2
Busted
Don't Hold Back
Extra Day
Extra Sex
Find This Man
Firstmate
French Kiss
Hidden Instincts
Kick Boxing: Getting Below
    the Belt
Knockout
Latin Tongues
Les Hommes
Lust
Make it Count
Man in Motion
Manplay
Men Matter Most
Morning Ritual
Natural Response
New York Close-up
19 Good Men
Northern Exposures
One Way or the Other
Orgy Club
Pacific Fever
Painted
Puppy Dog Tales
Powergrip
Pushing the Limits
Pushover
Ram Man 3
Raw Stock
Ready to Serve
Sex Bazaar 1 & 2
Slave Trainer
Smokin' Butts
Snowbound
Stiff Competition
Switch Hitters VI:

Back in the Bullpen
Taken by Storm
Tight Jeans
Videolog 2: Director's Cuts
You've Got The Touch

MARTY STORM
A 1970s model.
Seven in a Barn

RANDY STORM
Alley Action
Arms of Forgiveness
Basket Fever
Big Box Office
The Big Merger
Black Leather, White Studs
Blond Obsession
Boys in the Office
Brief Exchanges
Burgle Booty
Buttsluts of the Castro
Captive Men 5
Come and Get It
Cool Moon
Cops, Jocks & Military Feet
Crazed
Daddy, Daddy
Dare Devils
Deception, Part 1 & 2
Destination: West
   Hollywood
Elements of Passion
Express Male
The Extra Day
Favors
Frat House Memories of
   Pledge Week
Gang Bang Alley
Get It On
Grapplin'
Hell Knight
Hell Weekend

A Hole Different Ballgame
Hustlemania
In The Men's Room
In The Penthouse
Interior Motives
The Ivy League
Key West Bellhop
L.A. Underground
Leather Angel
The Legend of Mine 69
Lost Loves
Love Muscle
Major Owens
Man Construction
The Meaning of Sex
Midnight Hard-On
Movin'
Muscles and Thickness
My Cousin Danny
Nasty Rays
Need You Tonight
A Night With Strangers
Nude & Rude
One and Only Dominator
The Orgy Club
Palm Springs 92264
Pitts, Tits and Feet
Playing Dirty
Private Moments
Puppy Dog Tales
Rassle
Raw Stock
Rear End Window
Return to Badlands
Right Here, Right Now
The Rolls
Roughed Up In L.A.
San Francisco Bed &
   Breakfast
Santa's Coming
Secrets and Fantasies
Selling It
Sex Gallery

Sex Shooters 2
Shooters
6969 Melrose
Slave Trainer
The Slut
Special Request
Steamy Bondage Hard-On
Stockade Studs
Straight Studs
Strong Man Scent
Summer Daze
Surrogate Stud
Take It Like A Man
Thick Of It, The
Through The Looking Glass
Top To Bottom
Tricked
Two Fistful
2 Hard Up
Underground
Wear It Out
Whistle While You Work
Who's Gonna Get It?
Wild Obsessions
Wild Streak
X-Tasy
You Bet Your Ass

STEPHEN STRAIGHT
Balls of the Wild
Male Call
Party In My Pants

PATRYK STRAIT
(see Jason Nikas)

JONATHAN STRANTON
Cashload
Freshmen Fantasies
Full House
Heat Goes On
It's the Size that Counts
Let Me Be Your Loverboy

Male-O-Gram
Sticky Business

KEITH STRATTON
Big As They Come
Possession

RICK STRATTON
Badlands
Boys in the Office
Callguys, U.S.A.
Classified Action
Daddy Hunt
Delusion
Elements of Passion
Flesh Den
For My Eyes Only
Guyz 'N-the Burbs
Hawaiian Desire
Hot Shots, Vol. 49:
   Torrid Trips
In the Men's Room
Movin'
On Cue
One and Only Dominator
Packin' a Piece
Prison
Return to Badlands
Steam Room
Tennis Court Daze
Their Wild Ways

ALEXANDER STRAUSS
1990s Czech Republic
model.
English Student, The
Lucky Lukas

FRANK STRONG
Batdude & Throbbin'
A Friendly Obsession
From Maui with Love
Illusions

Long Hard Ride
Sizzle
Spare Room
Stud Search
Tongue Dancing
Wolf Boy

JAY STRONG
A 1990s Studio 2000 exclu-
sive.
It's Raining Men
Rosebud

ERIC STRYKER
(aka Noel Kemp, Mike
Kelly, Mike Ryan and Mike
Saunders) Died from AIDS-
related illness.
Alleycats
Alone & Private
   (as Mike Ryan)
Arcade
Asian Knights
Best Bi Far
The Best of Buckshot
Big Guns
Bore 'N' Stroke
Easy Entry
Firsts
Good Hot Stuff
Grizzly
Hot Shots, Vol. 1: All Star
   Review
Hot Shots, Vol. 3: Cum
   Contest
Hot Shots, Vol. 4: Contest
   Continues
In Hot Pursuit
Innocence Lost
It Starts With A Knockout
   (non-sex)
Magnum Griffin, Vol. 9,
   10 & 12

A Matter of Size
My Best Buddy
Not Just Friends
Platoon
Powerline
Rawhide
Sighs
Student Bodies
Switch Video #1
Thinking Big
Video Games, Vol. 12
Wresting Meat 2
The Young Cadets

JAKE STRYKER
The Diary
Family Affair

JEFF STRYKER
Born August 21. The horse-
hung, gay-for-pay superstar
top of the '80s and '90s.
The Best of All Matt
   Sterling
The Best of Jeff Stryker
The Best of John
   Davenport
The Best of Mike Henson
Bigger Than Life
Busted
Catalina Classics
Catalina Down and Dirty
Cummin' Together
Director's Best: John
   Travis, Vol. 1
Dreaming of You
Every Which Way
Heiress
How to Enlarge Your Penis
In Hot Pursuit
Jamie Loves Jeff 1 & 2
Jeff Stryker: A Romance
   Video for Women

Jeff Stryker's Favorite
Sexual Positions
(hetero how-to)
Jeff Strykers' Underground
J.S. Big Time
Just You & Me (dir. & actor)
Les Hommes
The Look
On the Rocks
Powerfull 1 & 2
Strike Back (dir. & actor)
(non-sex)
Stryker Force
Stryker's Best Powerful
Sex
Strykin' it Deep
(dir. & actor)
Superman
The Switch is On
The Tease
10 Plus 1 & 2 (dir. & actor)

RICK STRYKER
A young, blond 1980s
model. Claimed to be Jeff
Stryker's brother.
Every Which Way
Powerfull 2
Ten Plus
Undercover

T.J. STRYKER
A dark-haired, 1980s
model from Canada.
All Hands on Dick
Boy Oh Boy
Cross Over
Head of the Class
Hung Guns
The Look
Never Say Good-Bi
Nine Inches Plus
Ranger Nick

Streaks
They Grow 'Em Big

PATRIC STUDDS
Born April 2.
Behind His Back
Sucker
Tempted
Touch Me There
Virgin Territory

DANO SULIK
Czech Republic native.
5'8," uncut, youthful blond.
A 1990s George Duroy, Bel
Ami discovery.
Accidental Lovers
English Student, The
Frisky Summer
Gangbangers
Lucky Lukas
Lukas' Story 2
Lukas' Story 3
Sauna Paradiso

MATT SULLIVAN
Beyond Hawaii
Delivery Boys
Heroes

ALEX SUMMERS
Club 18-23
The Games We Play

BO SUMMERS
A Denver resident and
popular blond bottom from
the early '90s.
Abduction 2: The Conflict
All American
All the Way Inn
At Your Service
Behind the Barn Door

Below the Rim
Bi-Ology
Bodymasters
Bullseye
Cat Man Do!
CD RAM: Sex Star
Interactive
Chip Daniels' Video
Studbook
Deep End
Down Bi Law
Family Values
Fly Bi Night
Hand to Hand
Hart Throb
The Hole
Hollywood Knights
Hot Cargo
Hot Laguna Knights
Hot Stuff
Hot Ticket
Idol in the Sky
Idol Universe
The Insiders
Jawbreaker
Long Distance Lovers
Lowe Down
Lucky Stiff
Manhattan Skyline
Marine Crucible
Meanstreak
Mountain Patrol
1230 West Melrose
Palm Springs Paradise
Rawhide
Remembering Times
Gone Bi
Revenge of the Bi Dolls
Risky Sex
Sex in Wet Places
Shadow Dancer
Single White Male
Solicitor

Somebody Is Watching
Stud Valley
Summer's Tall Tales
Take Down
Ty's Back
Video Head
Wet Load

ALEX SUMMERS
The Games We Play
Winged

BRIAN SUMMERS
Attraction
Heartbeat

DANNY SUMMERS
(aka Danny Sommers)
Born March 11. A
Pittsburgh native. A very
busy blond 1990s model.
The Abduction 2&3
Aaron Austin : A Day in
the Life
Apollo Does Danny
Beach Blanket Boner
Best of All 2
The Best of Danny
Sommers
The Big Splash
Blue Collar, White Heat
Brief Encounters
Choose me
Club Sex-A-Holics
Cocksure
Cops, Jocks and Military
Feet
Crossroads
Danny's Dirty Sex Garage
Danny Sommer's Day Off
Danny's Back
A Day in the Life
Down Home

Down In The Dirt
Face Down
Fan Male
Find This Man
First Times
For My Eyes Only
Frat House: Memories of
Pledge Week
A Gay Man's Guide To
Safe Sex
Guys in Jocks and Jockeys
Hard at Work
Heads or Tails
Honolulu Hard Bodies
How Big Is Danny?
Hot Blades
Immoral Thoughts
Inner Circle
The Ivy League
A Jocks Tale
Jumper
Key West Bellhop
Key West Voyeur
Kiss Off
L.A. Sex Stories
Lava Flow
The Legend of Joey
Stefano
Live From Key West
Loaded
Long Distance Lovers
Lust Letters
Majestic Knights
Male Instinct
Man Alone
Mandriven
Manhattan Skyline
Manplay
Memories of Summer
More You Get, More You
Need
Naughty Little Brother
Night Force

Off Duty Maneuvers
On the Lookout
The Other Side of
Aspen 3 & 4
Personally Yours
Piece of Cake
Pits, Tits & Feet
Poolside Passion
Powertool II
The Predators, Vol. 1
Privilege
The Producer
Rearended
Release Yourself
Rings
Ripped
Roommate
Roughed Up at the Spike
Rump Ranger
Saddle Tramps 2
Sailing to Paradise
(Secret) Shore Leave
Sex Bi Lex
Sex in Tight Places
Sex Shooters
Shake That Thing
Score 10
Slave Workshop Boston
Smells Like a Man
Someone in Mind
Songs in the Key of Sex
Spank Me, Paddle Me
Summer's Tall Tales
Superstud Fever
Take Down
Tickled Butch Guys
To Thine Own Self Be True
Tough Guy
Trade Off
True
Truth, Dare or Damien
Visitor
Videolog 2: Director's Cut

Wharfmen
White on White
Who's Gonna Get It?

VIC SUMMERS
The Best of Joey Stefano
The Best of Matt Powers
Billboard
The Main Attraction
Private Dick
Sailor in the Wild 2
Sex in the Great Outdoors,
   Part 3

GLENN SWANN
Discharged
Sgt. Swann's Fantasies
Sgt. Swann's Private Files
The Size of His Toys
Video Games, Vol. 1 & 4

T.J. SWANN
A popular 1980s and '90s
model.
Basic Black, Vol 2 & 5
Big Black Brother
Black and Proud
Black Lust/White Passion
Black Sex Party
Black Sweat
Black Workout 2
Old Reliable #138: Black
   on Black
Hunk
Salt & Pepper Boys
Switch Hitters #1
That Boy Next Door
What The Big Boys Eat

FRANK SYLVANO
1990s bottom from the
Czech Republic.
Best of Titan: Collector

Series 2
Call to Arms
Gut Reaction
Jumpin' Jacks

GABOR SZABO
HUNGarians

T

JOSH TAGER
Doctor's Orders 2
Porno Tonight Show, The

SCOTT TANDY
Fire In The Hole
Leather Lust
Men Together
Unexpected Persuasion
What Men Do

BUCK TANNER
Callguys, U.S.A.
Dreamen: Dirty Dialogue
Grid Iron
Hard-on Hard Bodies
Hot Shots, Vol. 46:
   Street Man
Idol Eyes
Man in Motion
The Plunge
The Rockmore Files
The Rolls
Slam Dunk
Swap Meat
"10" Plus
Their Wild Ways
Toy Boys

DANE TARSEN
Faultline Sextime
Leather Obsession Part 3

Night Walk
Playing With Fire
Prisoners Of Lust
Sex & Sensuality
Sex Wrestling
Swallow
Tools Of The Trade

ROBSON TAVARES
Alex and His Buddies

BRANDON TAYLOR
Fully Serviced
Hard Labor
Jump On It
No Faking It
Pleasure Ridge
Top Men

BUTCH TAYLOR
A mature, blond, 1980s
model.
Beach Dreamer
Bi Mistake
Big Memories
Biggest Piece I've Ever
   Had
Boys Will Be Boys
Busted
Catalina Blonds
Catalina Men
The Cockeyed Eagle
Crosswire
Cum Shots 102
Director's Best: John
Travis, Vol. 1
Dirty Tricks
Excess
Fratrimony
A Friendly Obsession
Full Service
G.I. Mac
Hard-on Hard Bodies

He-Devils
Hot, Hung & Hard
Hot Shots, Vol. 21:
    Big Ones
Hot Shots, Vol. 29: More
    Raw Rears
Lovers
Made for You
The Main Attraction
Manimal
More of a Man
Muscleforce
The Next Valentino
Offering
Paradise Found
Ranch Hand
Seduction
Sex Junkies
Size Talks
Straight Boys Do
Surge Men are Very
Receptive
Switch Hitters IV: The
    Grand Slam
Texas Size 12
Think Big
Touch Me
A Trip to Paradise Beach
Undercover
Wet

CAMERON TAYLOR
Any Way I Can
French Erections
Home Bodies
Northern Exposures
Shooting Stars

CHRISTIAN TAYLOR
Born in 1980 in South
Dakota. Resides in St.
Paul, Minnesota. Cute,
blond-haired, youthful-

looking model. 5'8" with a
7" cock. Late 1990s model.
American Way, The
Double Cross
Heartland, The
Visit, The

COLBY TAYLOR
Big Thrill, The
Desert Hart
Four Card Stud
Summer Reunion
Up For Grabs

COLE TAYLOR
A porn star legend from
the '80s.
All Hands on Dick (bi)
The Best of Surge, Vol. 2
The Biggest One I Ever
    Saw
Boys Just Wanna Have
    Sex
Climactic Scenes #101
The Company We Keep
Fanta-Size
'57 Pickup
Full Grown/Full Blown
Guys Who Eat Cum
Hard Fucking Buddies
The Harder the Better
Head Trips
Heroes
Hollywood Gigolo
Hot Shots, Vol. 7: Daddies
In Too Deep
Lifeguard
Lovers & Friends
Magnum Griffin, Vol. 6
Making It Huge
Motel California
Muscle Studs
Nightcrawler

Oasis
One Size Fits All
Perfect Ten
Pound Your Pud: Eagle 7
Room for Rent
Sighs
Strokers
Sunstroke
Thinking Big
Tight Friendship

CORY TAYLOR
Hard Ball
Leather Weekend
Nutt Busters
One Track Mind
Scent of Leather
Sex Trigger
Squeeze Play
Steel Away
Thick of It
Wear It Out

DALLAS TAYLOR
(aka Bill Tuck)
All About Sex
All Heated Up
Any Excuse For Sex
At First Glance
Backstage Pass
Basket Fever
Bedtime Tales
Best of Leather: Part 1
The Big Drill
Black Fantasies
Blow Me Down
Blue Moves
Boot Black
Born To Please
Butt Boys in Space
The Challenge
Come and Get It
Convertible Blues

Courting Libido
Cruise Control
Dallas Does Hawaii
Delirium
Dial Justice
Earning His Keep
Exiled
Fan Male
First Timer
Fully Serviced
Goodfellas/Badfellas
Group Therapy
Hang 8 1/2
Hard Ball
Heat
The Hideaway
Hoghounds 2
Hot House Lodge
Hot Shots, Vol. 48: International Males
Hot Shots, Vol. 50: Men At Work
Hung Up
Idol Inn Exile
Indecent Proposition
In The Men's Room
The Insiders
Jock City
Keep The Tip
Knight Heat
Knight Out With The Boys
Latex Meltdown
Leather Obsession
Leather Playhouse
Leather Story
Leather Temptation
Liquid Love
Long Play
Lowe Down
Lunch Hour 2: Sweating Grease
The Mad Masseur
Madness & Method

Majestic Knight
Male Order Sex
Mein Kock
Men On Call
Men Together
Method Madness
The Making Of "Knight Out With The Boys"
Mr. Blue
Night Watch
976-Hot!
Nymphomania
Obsessive Desires
Obsessively Compulsive
O Is For Orgy
The Orgy!
Party Animals
Party Hard
Peep-O-Rama!
Phone Mates
Physical Exam
Playing Dirty
Power Driver
Powertool 2
Privilege
Pure Sex
Reflections Of Sex
Revenge Of The Bi-Dolls
Rhythm: Men In Motion
The Rod Squad
Romeo And Julian
Roughed Up At The Spike
San Francisco Sex
Sex Toy Story
Sexologist
Shoot 'N' Porn
Slave Auction
Sparkle
Stiff
Stripper Service
Stud House
Summer Daze
Summer Obsession

Summer Of Scott
Randsome
Sunday Brunch
Surrogate Stud
These Bases Are Loaded 2
Thursday Morning Workout
To Protect And To Serve
Top Men
Top To Bottom
Toy Boys
Trade
Transparent
Trickmaster
2 Hard Up
Valley Of The Bi Dolls
Visit, The
Wear It Out
Wet Fantasies
Working Day & Night

FRANK TAYLOR
Cute, youthful bottom.
Uncut. Dark-haired, 1999
discovery.
How the West Was Hung
Lambda Lambda Lambda 3
Stalled

JAKE TAYLOR
Born October 20. Mature,
hairy-chested, dark-haired
1990s model.
Das Butt 2
Dirty Leather
Family Secrets
Hardhats
Interview #3
Lip Lock
Man Watch
On The Prowl
Plugged In

JOSH TAYLOR
A young, blond, early '90s model.
Advocate Men Live 7
The Big Ones
Crusin' Park
Dare Devils
Honorable Discharge
Hot Guys 2
In The Jeans
In Your Face
Junior Crew
Knight Heat
Knights of Thunder
License to Thrill
Lunch Hour
Mission Accomplished
Muscle Talk
Need You Tonight
Poetry & Motion
Pumping Up: Flexx II
Pure Attractions
Ranger Nick II
The Rolls
Skin Tight
Snowbumz
Strictly Forbidden
Stripper Service
Stroke 'N Men
Totally Exposed
Where the Hunks Are
Young and Notorious

KEN TAYLOR
Bam 2: Thug
Black Power

MITCH TAYLOR
Backdrop
Best of Sam Abdul
Brats
Down Home
Idol Thoughts

Imagination: Action Gone Wild
Into The Night
Kiss Off
Made To Get Laid
Mindscape 1 & 2
Naked Prey
Night Force
Predators, The
Private Dancer
Skin Tight
Stripper Service
The Whole Nine Yards

RICK TAYLOR
Falconhead 2
Hard Money
Therapy
Windows
X-tra Large

ROBBIE TAYLOR
Even Steven
Any Way I Can
Driveshaft
Everything A Man Wants
Happiness is a Big Cock
Natural Response
Unexpected Persuasion
You've Got The

ROD TAYLOR
A 1970s model.
Seven in a Barn

SCOTT TAYLOR
Died December 22, 1994 of AIDS-related causes.
Best of the Superstars
Boys of Venice
Flashback
My Masters
Rough Cut

Strange Places, Strange Things
Turned On

STEVE TAYLOR
Dangerous
Flashback
Inches
Therapy
Turned On
Wanted
Weekend Lockup

ZAK TAYLOR
A Montana native and late '90s model.
Flesh and Fantasy 2
Object of My Erection, The
Return to Camp YMAC
Up For Grabs

KARL TENNER
(aka Alexi Romanoff)
Czech Republic model.
Cute, boyish, late '90s model.
An American In Prague
English Student, The
Hotel California
In Deep: Miles To Go
Johan's Big Chance
Lucky Lukas
Serviced
Stock

TREY TEMPEST
Bi Madness
Big Merger, The
Bound Boys In Slave Hollow
Boys Of Wilde Island
Busted
Cool Hand Dick

Devil And Danny Webster
Driven By Lust
Kickboxing
Memories Of Bamboo Island
Memories Of A Lost Summer
Mindscape 1 & 2
Movers & Shakers
Newcomers
Oral Report
Preferred Stock #1
Safe Sex: A Gay Man's Guide
Summer School
Takin' Care Of Mike

DEAN TEMPLE
Sit Tight

ALEX THOMAS
All the Way In
Behind the Eight Ball
The Best of Ryan Yeager
The Big Ones
Break In
Breaking & Entering
Dirty Pictures
Double Exposure
Exiled
Hot Shots, Vol. 46: Street Meat
How Big is Big?
Immoral Thoughts
Inner Circle
The Ivy League
Joker's Wild
Jumper
Knight Moves
Knight Out With the Boys
Las Vegas Love Gods
Majestic Knight
Male Seduction

Model Behavior
The Orgy!
Overnight Service
Personal Service
Power Play
Pure Attraction
Rassle
Read My Lips
Ready to Serve
The Roommate
Sex in Wet Places
Stranded: Enemies and Lovers
Summertime Blues
Their Wild Ways
Tony's Big Brother
Toy Boys
Trick Time

BERNARD THOMAS
Splashdown!

CHOICE THOMAS
(see Dennis Lincoln)

DEREK THOMAS
Buffed, blond 1990s model.
Dive!
Hot Summer Of Sex
On The Prowl
Smooth Operator
Take It Deep

GREG THOMAS
A young, blond, early 1990s model.
Brother Trouble 1 & 2
First Experiences

KARL THOMAS
(aka Carl Thomas)
A blond, boy-next-door, 1980s model.

Basket Fever
Best Of All 2
Big City Men
The Big Ones
The Bigger They Come
Biggest Piece I've Ever Had
Brother Trouble 1 & 2
California Dream Inn
Can't Say No
Dildo Kings
Cellblock Sinner
Don't Hold Back
Don't Kiss me, I'm Straight
Driveshaft
For Your Pleasure
Hard Talk
Holding Their Own: Self-Sucking Soldiers
Hot Guys 3
Hot House Lodge
How To Get A Man In Bed
Huge Torpedoes
Idol Thoughts
Imagination: Action Gone Wild
Impacted
Inside Karl Thomas
Jockathon
The Naked Truth
Man of the Year
Man Driven
Mission Accomplished
Muscle Talk
Nothing Else Matters
One More Time
Other Side of Hollywood
19 Good Men
Powerdrive 500
The Predators, Vol. 1
Pushover
Put It Where It Counts
Right Before Your Eyes

Robert Prion Uncensored
Scorcher
Sexposure 2
Stripper Service
Texas Tales
Thrust Fault
Toilet Tramps
Tool Kit
Toolbox
Total Impact
Unexpected
Up Close And Sexual
Whatever It Takes
Working Day & Night
Young And Notorius

LANCE THOMAS
Hard #2
Insertion
Men With Tools Part 2 :
    Nailed Orgies1
The Selection Part 2 (Solo)
Wet Warehouse #3: The
    Party

MATTHEW THOMAS
All Heated Up
Best of Leather: Part 1
Both Ways (bi)
Burning Desire
Cramming For The Big
    One
Crossing Over
Desert Paradise II:
    Revenge!
Hawaiian Vacation 2
Hard Times
Hotel Montreal
In The Shadows
Just Blondes
Leather Obsession 2
Male Call
Meet Me At The Orgy

O is for Orgy
Orgies Pt 2
Outdoor Ecstacy
Party In My Pants
Postcards From Montreal
    Part 1 & 2
Something About Larry
Touch Me There

NEIL THOMAS
(Terry Gardner) A brown-
haired, well-hung, early
'90s model and L.A. native.
All Night Long
Attraction
Beach Dreamer
Cousins Should Do It
Engine #69
Excess
Flexx
Foxhole
Hard to be Good
Head of the Class, Part 2
Headin' West
Hot Shots, Vol. 41: Rim
    Shots
Innocent Bi-Standers
Locker Room Sex
The Lust Boys
Major Meat
Mix N' Match
Neptune
Powerful II
Private Workout
Revenge: More Than I Can
    Take
The Rites of Winter
Seduction 1, 2, 3
Soldiers
Stiff Competition
Tim Lowe's Weekend
    Adventure
Tips

Warlords
X-Poseur

RICK THOMAS
Beat Patrol
Diamond Stud, The
Driveshaft
Hidden Instincts
Men Matter Most
Natural Response
Point Of Entry
Powergrip
Power Trip
Pushing The Limit
Put It Where It Counts
Up Close And Sexual

SHADOE THOMAS
(see Jason Broderick)

SHANE THOMAS
Club 18-23
Love In Dakota
The Selection Part 3 (Solo)

VINCENT THOMAS
The Best of Surge II
Big Favors
Flesh
Hard
Hot Shots, Vol. 8: Orgies
Hot Shots, Vol. 15: Bottoms
Hunk
Thinking Big
What the Big Boys Eat

BLADE THOMPSON
A Beefy, blond, 1990s
actor-turned-director in
1998.
Behind the Barn Door
The Best of All Matt
    Sterling 2

Best of Sam Abdul
Driven Home
Drop 'Em (Dir.)
4 Alarm Studs
Friction
Full Body Contact
Hand Jobs 2
Hole Patrol
Hose 'Em Down
Idol Worship
Imagination: Action Gone
  Wild
It's a Gang, Video Series 2
Johnny Hormone
Just Men (G. Colbert Dir)
L.A. Sex Stories
Lap It Up
Leather After Midnight
Leather Confessions
Leather Night
Leather Virgin
Men 4 Men On The Net
Muscle Bound
The Other Side of
  Hollywood
Protector, The
Red, White & Blue
Rex: Take One
Score 10
Sex Change
Sexual Thoughts
Splash Tops
Squeeze Play
Total Corruption 2
View To A Thrill 2: Man With
  The Golden Rod
White On White
Winged

BRIAN THOMPSON
Below The Belt
Big Shooters 3
Class Reunion

A Few Good Men
Fleshtones
French Lt's Boys
Frat House Memories
Lusty Lovers
Men in Motions #3
Men of Action
Military Men
Never Big Enough
Sailor in the Wild
Santa Monica Blvd.
Sex in the Great Outdoors
  1 & 2
Studbusters
William Higgins Preview
  Tape #2

CHRIS THOMPSON
(aka Chris Thomson, Chris
Cairns, Chris Deconnett) A
dark-haired, 1980s model.
Bad Boys, Vol. 7
The Best of Surge, Vol. 2
Bi-Ceps
Body Scorcher
Boys Just Wanna Have
  Sex
California Summer
Campus Jocks
Century Mining
Cruisin' for Lust
Double Exposure
Faces
Firsts
Flesh
Full Grown/Full Blown
Getting It
The Golden Boys
Gotta Have It
Growing Years
Hot Men
Hot Shots, Vol. 10: Sweat
Ladies Choice

Manheat
Manholes #1
Men and Steel
Men in Motion 4 & 7
Never Big Enough
New Wave Hustlers
Nightcrawler
Nine-and-a-Half Inches
Pipeline
P.S. Connection #1
Seven Card Stud
Shooting Stars #1: Chris
  Thompson
Solo Studs
Spring Break
Studio X
Windows

DAVID THOMPSON
Born February 4, 1965,
Meadowbrook,
Pennsylvania. Resides in
Hollywood. 6'1," 8 1/2"
cock, versatile. Handsome
and hunky, dark-haired
dancer, model and director
from the 1990s.
Best of Leather: Part 1
Exposed
For Your Pleasure
Full Package
Gang of 13
Guest Services
Guy Next Door, The
Heat of the City
Humidity
Indulge
In Your Ear
In Your Eye
Just Men
Leather Dream
Leather Obsession 5
Leather Triangle

Lick It Up
Marine Crucible
Mavericks
Men At Work
Nightwalk
Orgies Pt 4
Personal's
Ryker Files
Sex & Sensuality
Showboys
The Staff
Tainted Love
Unexpected Persuasion
Wet Fantasies
When A Man Wants A Man
Wild Sex in America

SCOTT 'GADOR' THOMPSON
Boys of West Hollywood
Giants
Hot Shots 1
Hotel Hell
Jobsite
Jock Empire
Longhorn Cowboys

SKY THOMPSON
Born April 13. 1990s model.
Four Card Stud
Glory Holes of San
   Francisco
Happily Ever After
Leather Desires
Manhungry
Our Trespasses
Red, Hot & Safe
Wet Warehouse #3:
   The Party

THOR
Absolutely Uncut
Beater's Digest

Men: Skin and Steel
Skinner Jacks
Trash, Vol. 8: Uncut Cocks
Uncut Gems: Diamonds in
   the Raw

GRIFF THORSEN
Born in Boston,
Massachusetts. 6'2,"
7-1/2" cock, versatile.
Blond, late '90s model.
Beach Buns
The Hotel
Mr. Fix-It
Rosebud
Stag Party
Twins
Uncle Jack

JOHNNY THRUST
1990s model.
The Drifter
Jockstrap
Skateboard Sliders
Spiked
Suck Daddy
Switch Hitter 10
WeHo Alley

CHRIS THUNDER
Like Father, Like Son
Playing With Fire

SERGE TIMAR
Slightly hairy 1999
Hungarian model.
Fresh
Hungarian Heat
Raging River

T.J.
(see T.J. Scott)

LOUIE TONG
One Night Alone
Oriental Dick
P.M. Preview Tape #2
Screen Test Spittin' Image

EMERICK TONCKA
Cute, young Cadinot dis-
covery.
Insatiable

TONY BOY
(see Tony Lazzari)

ANTHONY TORRES
Always Available
Latin Sex Thing

ANTONIO TORRES
Off Da Hook 2

ENRIQUE TORRES
A Spanish Fantasy

VINNIE TORRINO
Beach Dreamer
Pin Me

JACK TOWER
Backstage Pass
Can't Say No
Make it Count
One Way or the Other

VINNIE TRAVINO
Beach Dreamer
Brother Trouble 1 & 2
Fatique Relief
Foxhole
From Maui with Love
Hot Shots, Vol. 34: More
   Orgies
Pin Me

Texas Size 12

ARIK TRAVIS
The Best of Danny
Sommers
Break In
Dicked
Dirty Pictures
Fan Male
Malibu Pool Boys
Man Alone
Max Hardware
Reunion
Someone in Mind
Star Gazing #1
True

DANE TREMMELL
Kansas City Trucking Co.

**CLIFF TRENT
(see Trent Black)**

T-SPOON
Popular black model from
the '90s.
A.W.O.L.
Black & Blue
Black In Demand
Black Leather
Black Leather Gang Bang
Black Renegades
Black, Sex & Leather 1 & 2
Black Warriors
Cruisin' for a Gang Bang
Ho Ho Ho!!!
Inter-Racial Interrogation
Marine Chronicles, The
A Tale of Five Brothers
Tiger's Temptation

STEVEN TUCK
Anonymous Sex

You've Got Male

COLE TUCKER
Born October 23, 1953,
New York. Resides in
Boston. 6'0," 8 1/2" cock,
versatile. Famous for his
tattoos, cigars and fisting,
this porn daddy from the
'90s is one of the most
popular porn stars of
the decade.
Acres of Ass 1 & 2
Big Guns 2
Bound For Leather
Catalinaville
Chip Daniels' Video
Studbook
Down on Me
Fallen Angel
Family Values
Flesh and Fantasy 2
Grease Guns 2
House of Games
Leather Obsession #6
Link to Link
Logan's Journey
Private Passions
Ramrod
Slick

JEFF TURK
Bulging Jockstraps
Help Wanted
The Other Side of Aspen
1 & 2
Oversize Load
Stroke 2

JOHN TURNMILL
Caller, The

JEFF TURNER
Solo Flights
Too Big for His Britches
Weekend Workout

RICKY TURNER
Auto Erotica: The Best of
Sex in Cars
Ball Bustin' Boys
The Best of Jeff Stryker
The Best Stallion
Bi-Coastal
Bi-Sexual Fantasies
Big Shooters
The Body Scorchers
Catalina Down and Dirty
Chip Off the Old Block
Firsts
Getting Off Campus
Hot Shots, Vol. 10: Sweat
Hot Shots, Vol. 11: Men's
Room
Hot Shots, Vol. 37: Penal
Code
Ivy Blues
L.A. Boiling Point
The Look
Make it Hard
More Than a Mouthful
Nasty Rays
New Wave Hustlers
Oasis
On the Bi Side
Rodeo
Seven Card Stud
Social Studies
Spring Training
Stroke #19
Swing Set
Totally Awesome
Underground Homo
Hardcore

TYKE
The Best of Alexander
 Marshall
The Best of Jonathan
 Strong
Caged heat
G.I.
Hardline
It Happened One Day
Leather Sex Club
The Lust Boys
Power Force
Sizzle
Stiff Craving
Tough
Underground Homo
Hardcore
Who's Dat Boy
X Marks the Spot

CODY TYLER
Billy Herrington's Body
 Shop
Internal Affairs

DUKE TYLER
(see Mark Tyler)

JESSE TYLER
(aka Jesse Skyler)
Blond model from the mid
1990s.
Abduction 2: The Conflict
Best Of Leather: Part 3
Come As You Are
Dirty Pool
Dirty Works
Dreams Come True
Earning His Keep
For His Own Good
Hardball
Hard On Demand
Hot Guys #4

House Rules
How To Get A Man Into
 Bed
Leather Obsession 2
Lost Loves
More Than Friends
Morning Rituals 2
Nutcrackers
O Is For Orgy
Pinned
Pocket Rockets
The Pornographer
Private Dancer
Pure Sex
Selling It
Sex Is In The Air
Sex Trigger
Spare The Rod
Thursday Morning Workout
Trophies 2
Vacation Spot
While I Was Sleeping
Working Day And Night

JOSE TYLER
Over the Rainbow

JUSTIN TYLER
Eighteen Candles

KIP TYLER
Alley Action
Bedtales
Big Box Office
The Big Splash
Boys Will Be Boys
Breaking and Entering
Brown Paper Wrapper
Coming Home
Destination: West
Hollywood
Flesh Den
Frat Pack

Friends & Lovers
Heat
Immoral Thoughts
Mating Game
Mindscape 1
Personal Service
Preferred Stock #1
Rings
A Scent of Man
Sex Bazaar 1 & 2
Tennis Court Daze
Willing to Take It

MARK TYLER
(aka Duke Tyler, Chad
 Maxwell, Sam West)
A Body to Die For 2
Military Bound
My Master's Training
That Old Whorehouse
Wanted: Bondage Trainee

TIGER TYSON
Popular black '90s model.
Off Da Hook 1 & 2
Screentest USA: NY 2
Sweatin' Black
Tiger's Brooklyn Tails
Tiger Untamed
Vivid Man Raw 5: Sweatin'
 Black

U

GASPAR URGE
Young, blond 1999
Hungarian model.
Hungarian Heat
JOHNNY UTAH
A mature, blond, bisexual
model from the 1990s.
Bl-Ology

Billy's Tale: A Modern Day
Fable
Club Utah
Down Bi Law
Valley Of The Bi Dolls

V

EDDIE VALENS
(aka Carlos Rey)
An early 1990s model.
Backyard Boys
The Best of Back Alley
Video
The Best of Jonathan
Strong
Black Alley: South of the
Border
Black Salsa
Blacks & Latinos Working
Hard
The Boxer 2
The Boys of Wilde Island
Butt Boys in Space
For Sale By Owner
Great Balls of Fire
Hawaiian Desire
Hispanic Panic
Hole in One (Carlos Rey)
Hombres
Hot for His Bod
Hot Shots, Vol. 45:
Latin Fever
Inside Expose
It's Good to be Bad
Latin Jackoff
Latino Nights: Noches
Latinas
Latinos Working Hard
Motorcycle Madness
My Fantasy
New Love

Rainstorm
Rock-Hard
Shacking Up
Straight Boys Do!
Surfer Guys
Taken by Storm
Weekend Wildcats

DUNCAN VALENTINE
Big Boyz Club 4
Dickin' Around
Internal Affairs
Latin Balls 2: Huevos
Over the Rainbow

RAPHAEL VALENTINO
Nude Science
Opposites Attract

TONY VALENZUELA
Positively Yours
Red, Hot & Safe

KIRK VALIANT
French Erections

PATRICK VALIANT
French Erections
Sure Shot

MARTIN VALKO
A Czech Republic native
and a George Duroy
discovery.
Accidental Lovers
Lukas' Story
Lukas' Story 2
Lukas' Story 3
The Plowboys
Tender Strangers

RICK VAN
(See Geoffrey Karen Dior)

DAREN VAN LAAN
Czech Republic model.
Lucky Lukas

EDDIE VAN NESS
(see Chris Dano)

ANTHONY VEGA
Can't Say No
Hot Tub Fever
Mount The Big One
Phi Kappa Sucka'
West Hollywood Sex Party

MARC VEGA
Casting Cocks (solo)

ROBERT VEGA
Daddy Dearest
Giants, Part 2
Hot Off the Press
International Skin
Juice
Job Site
Lifeguard
Mansplash
Men of Action
Quickies #1
Screenplay
Tough Studs

ANTONIO VEGAS
Can't Say No
Driveshaft
Every Man's Desire
Natural Response
Nothing Else Matters
Point Of Entry
Unexpected Persuasion
Whatever It Takes

PETER VEGH
Cute and young 1999

Hungarian model.
Hungarian Heat

**CARLOS VELASQUEZ
(see Michael Rivera)**

PIERCE VENDETTA
Late 1990s model.
Nude Science

NICOLAS VERNANT
An American In Prague
Johan's Big Chance

RALF VERNIER
(aka Rodolphe Vernier)
Czech Republic model.
Cute, young '90s model.
Insatiable
Lucky Lukas

MIKE VESPA
Fast Action
From Hair to Eternity
Grizzly
Lap It Up
Male Box

**JEFF VICKERS
(see Jon Vincent)**

FRANK VICKERS
Died February 24, 1991
from AIDS-related causes.
The Best of Buckshot
Easy Entry
Frank Vickers I: Solo
Frank Vickers II: Worship
Frank Vickers III: Man
   After Man
Good Hot Stuff
Hayfever
Magic of Power

Pumping Oil
Triple Treat
Worship
Worship 2

SHAWN VICTORS
1970s and '80s porn star.
Big Men on Campus
Class of '84: Part 1
Dirty Picture Show
Flesh
L.A. Tool & Die
Palace of Pleasures
Performance
Rear Deliveries
Strokers
Three Day Pass
Wet Shorts

ALEX VILLABOAS
Alex & His Buddies
Breakin' 'Em In 1 & 2
Master Strokes
Pumping Fever

JON VINCENT
(aka Jeff Vickers)
Born December 17, 1962 in
New Orleans. This mature,
dark-haired model was one
of the top performers of the
1980s.
Aaron Austin: A Day in the
   Life
All to Yourself
The Best of Kevin Williams
The Best of Kurt Bauer
The Best of Jon Vincent 1
The Bi-Analyst
Bi-Intruder
The Big Merger
The Bite
Blue Collar White Heat

Boner
A Day in the Life
Deep Inside Jon Vincent
First Timers: Amateur
   Trilogy #1
Gays, Bis, She-Males &
   Hermaphrodites
GV Guide Gay Erotic
Video Awards 2
Handjobs 3
Hard Ball
Hard Knocks
Heavenly
Idol Thoughts
Inside Vladimir Correa
The Look
Lords of Leather
Man Talk
Masculine Men
The Moon Also Rises
Muscleman
Paradise Beach
Porn Fiction
Power Play
Rassle
Revenge: Much More
Than I Can Take
Ride the Swell
The Roommate
Screwing Screw-Ups
Seduction II: The Heat
Goes On
Seduction IV: Sex Storm
Seduction V: Taking Full
Charge
Surfer Guys
Tommy Boy
A Trip to Paradise Beach

MICHAEL VINCENT
Best Bi Far 1 & 2
Best Friends 2
Bi and Beyond

A Big Business
Big Packages
The Big Switch
Hot Shots, Vol. 14: Tight
  Buns
Hot Shots, Vol. 15:
  Bottoms
Hot Shots, Vol. 26: Self
  Service
Hot Shots, Vol. 36:
  Student Affairs
Hot Shots, Vol. 39: Uncut
  Hunks 2
Incessant
Magnum Griffin, Vol. 8
Magnum Griffin, Vol. 10
Magnum Griffin, Vol. 13
Mustang Ranch
On Top
Star Shots
Stick Shift
Sunstroke
Switch Video
Tease Me!

ROSS VINCENT
Stock

TONY VINCENT
Daytime Voyeur

MICHAEL VISTA
Born January 2, 1965, Los
Angeles. Resides in West
Hollywood. 5'10," 7" cock,
bottom. A dark-haired
daddy from the '90s.
All You Can Eat
Ass Lick Alley
Aussie Pool Party
Bi Witched
Caught in the Military
  1 & 2

Cop Stories #2: The
  Cover Up
Cream Team, The
Crossing Over
Cruise Park
Cruisin'
Desert Paradise
Doggy Style
Dude Watch
Getting Ahead
Hot Spot
I Saw What You Did
In The Bushes
Kept: A Way of Life
Killer Looks
Lap It Up
Leather Lover
Meet Me At The Orgy
O Is For Orgy
Oral
Policemen's Balls
Rope Tricks
Saving Ryan's Privates
Sex Camp
Sex Toy Story 2
Sexcuses
Sexpionage
Size Does Matter
Stag Party
Starmaker
Sucker
Supersize It
Talk Dirty To Me
Tempted
Cock Lock
Weho Confidential
www.Orgy

ROBERTO VISTA
Born August 10. Resides in
New York City. 7" cock, versatile. Cute, youthful-looking 1990s Latin model.

Back in the Saddle
Home Bodies
Shooting Stars

ELEC VOUGHN
Anal Attraction
Cowboys Get The Blues
Free Your Willy
The Hollywood Kid
Homo Erectus
Leather Desires
Oh, So Tender
Party Favors
Sex On The Beach
Skin Tight
Stud Wanted
Weho Confidential
  (Non-Sexual)
West Hollywood Stories
Where The Night Takes You

W

DANNY WADE
Youthful, blond, early 1990s
boy-next-door model.
Runaways
Screen Test 2
Undercover

TRAVIS WADE
Born September 17. Dark-
haired, youthful and hung
thick and long. Late 1990s
model.
Hardline
The Chosen
The Freshman
Mercury Rising
Stock

BILL WADKINS
A mature, dark-haired, 1990s model.
Big Lift, The
Blond Obsession
Gang Bang Alley
Newcomers
Thunder Blue
Voice Male
Wet 'n Wild

MARK WADSWORTH
1990s gay for pay daddy.
Chapters

ANTHONY WAGNER
Bullring
Friction

BOSCH WAGNER
Anything, Anytime
Blue Angel
Broadway Boys
Christopher Rage's Orgy
Goodjac 5: Yardogs
High Tech
In Your Wildest Dreams
Manholes
Raunch 2
Wildside

HONUS WAGNER
Choke 'Em 3

PHILLIP WAGNER
(see Luke)

RYAN WAGNER
Originally from Indianapolis. Now lives in San Diego with boyfriend Bryan Kidd. Will always be known as one of the porn stars

who was befriended by Andrew Cunanan in 1997.
Audition to Be a Bottom
Birthday Blowout
Bound and Gagged 3
Butt Bruisers
Clothes Make the Man
Cram Course: Sex Ed 3
Greased Up
Happily Ever After
Hawaiian Lei
Hardbodies: Vol. 5
Hardhats
Hot Copy
I Live For Sex
Like Father, Like Son
Lip Lock
Matador
Nick and Phil's Boner
   Adventure
Ripe For Harvest
Rim City
Spankfest 2
Sex Ed Cram Course 2
Taken and Shaved
Thick of It
Ultimate Reality
Erotic Combat
Magic Hands 9

CHRIS WALKER
My Dick Is Bigger 2

LUKE WALKER
Winged
MASON WALKER
Born June 14. Brown-haired, youthful, late 1990s model.
Urgent Matters

ROB WALKER
Any Way I Can

One Way or the Other
Shameless

NATHAN WALTERS
Always Available
Hard Working Men
Working It Out

PERRY WARD
Absolutely Uncut
Beater's Digest
Men: Skin and Steel
Uncut Lucky Luc
Uncut Fever, Part 1

TOM WARD
Manly Persuasion

TONY WARD
Full Release

CHARLIE WARNER
Deep Inside Jon Vincent
Lunch Hour
Pay To Play 1 & 2
Stroke, The

JERRY WEBB
Any Boy Can

DARRYL WELD
(aka director Ansel Rainier)
Born September 18, 1965. Died July 24, 1991 from AIDS-related causes. A 1980s actor-turned-director. His real name was Darren Eugene Harris. A New Mexico native.
Attraction
Batdude and Throbbin'
   (dir.)

Brotherly Love
Concrete Lover
(actor & dir.)
Cruisers: A Reunion of
Friends (actor & dir.)
Dueling Chicks
Fatigue Relief (actor & dir.)
'57 Pickup
Gang Bangers
(as Ansel Rainier)
Great Balls of Fire
Guys with Tight Asses
Heart Beat
Hot Shots, Vol. 47:
Newcomers
Hot Shots, Vol. 49: Torrid
Trios
Kevin Goes Wild (dir.)
Mix N' Match
Naval Focus (dir.)
Ranger Nick
Seduction IV: Sex Storm
Seduction V: Taking Full
Charge
Sunday Brunch
Taxi
Teammates (dir.)
Tempting Tommy
The Thirteenth: It was On
a Friday (actor & dir.)
Wet Dreams
X-Poseur
Young Warriors

BRANDON WELLS
A 1990s goteed daddy.
Best Of Leather: Part 3
Big Packages
Boy, Oh Boy!
Centerspread 3
Excess
Hard Balls
Hard Rock High

Hot Cocks
How To Get A Man Into
Bed
Into Leather
Las Vegas Orgy
Leather Obsession 3 -
Illusion
Manticipation
Militia Men
Pocket Rockets
Ram Man
The Rites of Summer
Show it Off
Smooth Moves
Sunsex Blvd.
Taste of Leather 2

**ADAM WEST
(see Aaron Brandt)**

CUTTER WEST
Born September 8.
Beat Off Frenzy
Boys From Bel Air
Center Spread
Crossing The Line
Driven Home
Getting In Tight
Hard Bodyguard
His Big Brother
Hot Cargo
Hot Guys #2
Hot Stuff
House Of Tricks
Insiders, The
Leather Virgin
Limited Entry
Lost In Las Vegas
Manhattan Skyline
Men of Forum
Men With Tools Part 2 :
Nailed
Military Issue 2

Nude Men Can Jump
Officer And His Gentleman
Physical Education
Playing With Fire
Ready For It
Receiving End
Reunion
Revenge Of The Bi-Dolls
The Sex Files
Sexpionage
Single For The Weekend
Slip It In
Squeeze Play
A Tale Of Two Brothers
Too Dam Big!
Vacation Spot
Whitefire

JAY WEST
Coming True
Keep The Tip
Total Deception

JIM WEST
Four Card Stud
Sure Thing

JORDAN WEST
Call to Arms
Four Card Stud
Four Men
A Love Story
Road Home, The
The Selection Part 3 (Solo)

MARK WEST
In his fourties, Mark was
one of the older porn stars
in the business when he
became popular in the
early '90s.
All About Steve
Blow Me Down

Boot Black
Boys From Bel Air
CD-Ram
Chase Is On, The
Cody Exposed
Fluffer, The
The Games We Play
Getaway, The
Hot Guys #4
Indulge Part 2
Inter-Racial Interrogation
Jawbreaker
Like Father Like Son
Lunch Hour 2: Sweating
  Grease
Man Country
Midnight Run
Oral Fixation
Party Line
Posing Strap
Roll In The Hay
Saddle Tramps 1 & 2
Secret Sex
The Selection Part 4 (Solo)
Sunsex Boulevard
Taste Of Leather
These Bases Are Loaded,
  Part 2
Too Dam Big!

MATT WEST
1990s model.
Ass Lick Alley
Cadet
Daredevils
Hot Mix
Object of My Erection,
  The
1-800-Hunk
WeHo Alley

SAM WEST
(see Mark Tyler)

TED WEST
Brian's Boys

TOM WEST
Cut Vs. Uncut
Express Male
Leather Teddy
Voyeur, The

TONY WEST
The Big Shot
Burning Desire
Crammin' For the Big One
Desert Paradise 2
Driven By Lust
Freshman Years
Hawaiian Vacation
Locker Room Lust
My Brother's Best Friend
Red, Hot & Safe
Sexy Spank 2
Sharp Shooters
Sleeping Booty and Other
  Tails
The 13th Step

TRENT WEST
Behind His Back
Desert Paradise II:
  Revenge!
Sex Toy Story #2
Sleeping Booty and Other
  Tails
13th Step
VamBires

WADE WEST
Cute, young, blond,
smooth-bodied 1990s
model.
Center Spread 3
Freshman Fever
Magic Bed, The

Splat

DEX WESTEN
On the Mark

DOUG WESTON
All-American Boy
Big & Thick
The Bigger the Better
French Lt's Boys
Gayracula
A Matter of Size
Tough Competition
Triple Treat

HAUS WESTON
A Vermont native.
Tales From The Foxhole

CODY WHILER
Born May 29, 1970 in
Monroe, Louisiana. 5'10,"
8" cock, bottom. A '90s
model.
Big Bear Lake
Burning
Hell Bent For Leather
Hot To Trot
Hung Riders 2
Leather Desires
Leather Obsession #6
Link
Meet Ray Harley
Naked Escape
Ranger in the Wild
Red, White and Blue
Take One: Guys Like Us

JEFF WHITE
Young-looking, blond Jeff
was in an auto accident in
1997. He made a come-
back in 1999.

Skateboard Sliders
Tail Spin
West Hollywood Hope

MICHAEL WHITE
Blond, handsome 1980s
model.
The Best of Street Times
   Video
California Blonds
Daytime Voyeur
Foreign Affairs
In the Briefs
In the Stretch
Idol Eyes
John Summers Screentest
   Mag. #1
Knockout
Lovers Come Home
Man In Motion
Private Workout
Shooters
Sugar Britches
Tender Trick
View to a Thrill: Man with
   the Golden Rod
Wet Fantasies
Where the Hunks Are

RANDY WHITE
Alone At Last
Best of Sam Abdul
Blue Collar, White Heat
Brief Encounters
California Dream Inn
Cocksure
Cruising Park
Damien, One Night of Sin
Disconnected
Down, Down, Down
   (non-sex)
Dream Team
Easy Riders

Forum Video Magazine
Four Alarm Studs
   (dir. & actor)
Getting It Firm
GI Jocks: Out of the Ranks
Good Vibrations
GV Guide Gay Erotic
   Video Awards 2
Handjobs
Heads or Tales
The Hideaway
Idol Worship
Indecent Proposition
It's a Gang, Video Series 1
Jockaholics
Juice Bomb
The Legend of Joey
   Stefano
Low Rent
Night Force
Open House
Open Windows
Piece of Cake
Reflections of Sex
Release Yourself
Rex: Take One
Romeo & Julian
Roommate, The
Sailing to Paradise
Sex Crimes
Slick Willies
Solicitor
The Sperminator
   (Actor & Co-Dir.)
Strip Search
Stripper Service
Sunsex Boulevard
Taste Of Leather
The Thick Of It
Twin Exposure
Tyler Scott- A Day Of
   Decadence
Wanted Man, A

Wet And Wild
Wet Load
Wharfmen, The
White On White

SEAN WHITE
I Live For Sex

TOM WHITE
Danger Zone

BRAD WHITEWOOD
Caught In The Military #1
Cop Stories #1: The
   Scandal

ALEX WILCOX
A late 1990s model.
At First Glance
Bootie Nights
Man Trade Solos
My Secret Lust
964 Dicks St. (Nine Sixty
Four Dicks St.)
Opposites Attract
Young Men On The
Pleasure Trail

ADAM WILDE
Born July 7. Actor turned
agent, lives in Columbus,
Ohio. While living in San
Diego he was one of the
porn stars who was
befriended by Andrew
Cunanan, the serial killer
who murdered Gianni
Versace in 1997.
Hot Guys #4
Inches Away
Indulge Part 2
Lip Lock
The Selection Part 3 (Solo)

My Sister's Husband
Reunion
Studio Tricks
Total Corruption 2
Wet Warehouse Part 2:
    Drenched

ALEX WILDE
Boot Black
Fluffer, The
One More Time
Pitch A Tent
Rawshock
Saddle Tramps
Sexabition
Sexcess

BRANDON WILDE
Dark-haired 1980s model.
Born 1957. Murdered in
1996 in Pensacola,
Florida.
Battle of the Bulges
Big Shooters #5
Blonds Do it Best
Blue Moves
Body Scorcher
Buck's Excellent Adventure
Cat Burgler
Cruisin' West Hollywood
Dreaming About Dick
Dueling Dicks
Excess
Fantasy Bytes
Getting It
Getting Off Campus
Hard To Hold
Health Club Gigolo
Heroes
Hot Splash
In His Corner
Ivy League
Let Me Be Your Lover Boy

My Sister, My Brother
976-CUMM
The Rodz
Seven Card Stud
Studvision
Teammates
Totally Awesome
Windows

HUNTER WILDER
Laguna Beach Lifeguards

MATT WILDER
A Jock's Dream
Cop Stories #1: The
    Scandal

PETER WILDER
Born April 28. Young,
blond, 1990s model.
Analized
Billy Herrington's Body
    Shop
Bootie Nights
Boys on Fire
California Stud Pups
Commercial Sex
Full Up!
Hard Balls
Hot Mix
Humidity
A Love Story
Manhungry
MVP: Most Valuable Player
Naked Underneath
Nefarious
964 Dicks St.
Nude Science
Orgies Pt 4
Over the Rainbow
Pay to Play 2
Point of No Return
Runway Studs

Straight Talk
Tight Jeans
Turn of Events
Wanna Be In Pictures?
Weekend Wildcats

KEVIN WILES
Behind Closed Doors
The Best of Back Alley
    Video
The Best of Jeff Stryker
Big Guns
Boys, Boys, Boys
Cat Burglar
Catalina Down and Dirty
Concrete Lover
Cruisin' for Lust
Foreplay
Gang Bangers
Heavy Cruisin'
Hot Cocks
Hot Shots, Vol. 8: Orgies
Hot Shots, Vol. 20: More
    Tight Buns
It's Good to be Bad
Kevin Goes Wild
The Look
Major Meat
Midnight Riders
Motel California
P.S. Connection #1
Romanti-Spank
Spring Break
Stiff Sentence
Stud Sensors
Teammates
Ten is Enough
Tim Lowe's Weekend
    Adventure
Undergear

ED WILEY
A hairy-chested, dark-

haired model from the late 1970s. Made a comeback in the 1990s.
The Best of Colt, Vol. 2
The Best of Colt, Vol. 12: Prowlers
BulletPac 7: Pier Pals
California Boys
Centurians of Rome
Fanta-Size
Fuck Truck
Full Service
Head Trips
Jocks
Someone is Watching
Stud Struck

ART WILLIAMS
Black Brothers
Black Forbidden Fantasies
Black Orient Express
Black Sex Therapy
Cum-pany Ass-ets
J. Brian's Flashbacks
Jacks are Wild
The Pizza Boy—He Delivers
Style

BRETT WILLIAMS
Action on Melrose
Below the Decks
The Best of Back Alley Video
Brother Hustlers
Built to Last
Clippers
Cousins Should Do It
Cum Shots 101
Daddy Hunt
Danger Alley
Delusion
Desert Sands

The Drifters
Drop 'Em
Extra Sex
Fond Focus
Guys N' The Burb
GV Guide All-Star Softball Game 1
Hair Klub For Men Only
Heads Or Tales
Hole In One
Hot Shots, Vol. 42: Face Shots
Immoral Thoughts
Iron Man
Jock City
Keep In Touch
Lovers Coming Home
Lovers Lane
Majestic Knight
Mechanics On Duty
Mix It Up: Black
Passions/White Dreams
Phi Kappa Sucka'
Photo-Op
Pumping Up: Flexx 2
Quick Relief
The Rise
Romeo & Julian
The Roommate
Smell Of A Man 2
Snowbumz
Steam Room
Stud Vision
Tell Me Something Dirty
True Confessions
Untamed
You Bet Your Ass

BRUCE WILLIAMS
Bijou

BRYAN WILLIAMS
Brothers Behaving Badly

CASEY WILLIAMS
Blond, mid '90s model.
Blowout
Centerspread 2
Come With Me
Feels So Good
Fire in the Hole
Friction
Hard Lessons
Illicit Love
Knight Gallery 2
Man to Men
Night Watch 2
Spring Fever
Stock
Summer Blazes
This End Up
Wear It Out

CHRIS WILLIAMS
Died September 11, 1991 from AIDS-related illness.
Bare Tales
The Best of Kurt Bauer
Catalina Blonds
Making it Big
Military Men
My Best Buddy
New Zealand Undercover
Out of Bounds
Perfect Summer
Spokes 2: The Graduation
Steal My Stuff
The Young Cadets

GRANT WILLIAMS
(see Grant King)

GUNTHER WILLIAMS
Royal Flesh

JEROD WILLIAMS
House of Tricks

KEVIN WILLIAMS

One of the biggest names in gay porn in the late 1980s. This hunky, blond, jock-next-door bottom won the Hall of Fame award at the 1997 Gay Erotic Video Awards. Made his comeback in 1998 in Falcon's *Betrayed*, looking better than ever. Lives in San Diego

Bad Boys Club
Bare Tales
The Best of All Matt
  Sterling 2
The Best of Kevin Williams
Betrayed
Big Bad Boys
Big Guns
The Boys of Summer
Catalina Blonds
Hot Rods: Young and the
  Hung 2
Hotwired: Viewers' Choice
In Your Wildest Dreams
The Look
On the Bi Side
Out of Bounds
Stryker Force
The Switch is On
William Higgins Screen
  Test #1

KURT WILLIAMS

Big Men on Campus
Gold Rush Boys
Hot Numbers, Vol. 1, 2, 3
Kansas City Trucking Co.
Revenge of the Nighthawk
Snow Balling
Straight
Twelve at Noon

Wintertime
The Young Olympians

LANCE WILLIAMS

Brothers Behaving Badly
Sting: A Taste For Leather

SEAN WILLIAMS

The Beat Goes On
California Summer
Cashload
Growing Years
Hard Choices 1 & 2
Hot Wired
Imperfect Strangers
Looking Good
Obsessed
A Physical Education
Pound Your Pud
Pounder
Sticky Business
Unloading It

SWEET WILLIAMS

(aka Sweet William)
The correct spelling of his name is Williams, according to the actor himself. Born November 1, 1965, Southern California. Resides in West Hollywood. 5'8," 8" cock, bottom. A '90s model.

Academy, The
Adventures of A. Rocky
  and Bill Winkler, The
Biker Pigs From Hell
Black Cargo
Body Shop
Burning Desire
Camp Pokahiney
Cruise Park
Cruisin'

Das Butt
Desert Maneuvers
Desert Paradise 2
Dirty Leather
Flashpoint
Flexing Solo
Flyin' Solo
Forced Service
Full Body Contact
Handsome Ransom
Hot Cops 3: The Final
  Assault!
Hung Jury
Internal Affairs
Latin Stories
Leather After Midnight
Leather Connection
Leather Desires
Leather Dream
Leather Intrusion
Leather Lover
Leather World
Locker Room Lust
Lovers Lane
Lube Job
Lust Shack
Marine fever
Meet Me At The Orgy
Men 4 Men
Men of Magnum
Men Under Siege
Missionary Position
Mt. Fuckmore
O Is For Orgy
Oklahomo
On The Net
Penetration on
Pennsylvania Avenue
Phi Kappa Sucka'
The Playboys
Red Blooded Americans
Romping Roommates
Roughing It

Runway Studs
Secret Admirer
Sex Toy Story 1 & 2
Sleeping Booty and Other
  Fairy Tails
Straight Talk
Studs In Uniform
Trixxx of the Trade
Olympians, The
Other Man, The
Spider's Kiss, The
Straight Talk
13th Step
Timeless Encounters
Virgin Territory
Wall 3, The
White Nuts/Black Bolts
White Tails/Black Tails
Wolf's
Working Pleasure

TONY WILLIAMS
Men In The Sand 2

TOBY WILLIS
Youthful 1970s model.
A Ghost of a Chance

EARL WILSON
A 1970s model.
Adam & Yves

GLENN WILSON
A 1970s model.
Adam & Yves

MATTHEW WINDSOR
(aka Matt Windsor)
A blond, 1980s model
from England.
Airmale
Attraction
Beach Dreamer

Below the Rim
Best of Leather: Part 1
The Best of Street Times
  Video
Bi-Medicine
Bisexual Experience
Boner
Boot Camp 1 & 2
Brawn's Rod
Cabana Boys
Carnival Tails
Castro Motel
Coming True
Cop Stories #1: The
  Scandal
Cruising Park
Cyber Sex
Dick Undercover
Dirty Leather
Excess
Exiled
Fantasy Bytes
Fatique Relief
Favors
Gidget Goes Bi
Hardass
Hardball
Hawaiian Desire
Highway Patrol
Hollywood Hunks
Honolulu Hard Bodies
Hotter Than Life
Illusions
Intrusion
Keep The Tip
Kink
Leather Bound
Leather Confessions
Leather Me Down, Do
  Me Toys
Leather Men 2
Leather Obsession
Leather Playhouse

Leather Party
Leather Pit
License To Thrill
Long Hard Ride
Lords Of Leather
Made To Get Laid
Male Seduction
Manplay
Man About Town
Men At Work
Men In Love
The Moon Also Rises
Moment Of Truth
Motor Crotch
Mustang Ranch
Neptune
A Night With Strangers
Nymphomania
Orgies Pt 3
Overseas Trade
Pool Boy
The Rites Of Manhood
A Scent Of Man
Seduction 3: Passion
Obsession
Sex Depot
Silverlake Inn
Skin Tight
Smoky
Solid Flesh
Straight Boys Do!
Strip Search
Stryker's Best Powerful Sex
Studmania
Summer Daze
Supersize It
Surfer Guys
Sweet In The Bootie
Taken To The Max
Things You Can Do In
  Leather
Tips
Top To Bottom

Total Deception
Vice Cop
Warloads
Wolf Boy
You Bet Your Ass

JUSTIN WINGER
A long-haired, blond youth
from the early 1990s.
Big Splash
Hard Action
Keep In Touch
Off Duty Maneuvers
Pay To Play 3

JAMIE WINGO
Anything, Anytime
The Best of Jon King
Brothers Should Do It
Find This Man
Hot Male Mechanics
Inevitable Love
J. Brian's Flashbacks
Leo Ford: The Making of a
   Superstar
Malibu Days/Big Bear
   Nights
Mark Reynolds Videolog
Summer Fantasy
Wild Oats

TERRY WINTER
Cruisin' '57

BRETT WINTERS
Born June 7. Handsome,
dark-haired '90s model.
Resides in Long Beach,
California.
Advocate Men Live 7
Beach Head
The Best of Back Alley
   Video

The Best of Jonathan
   Strong
The Best of Rick Savage
The Best of Street Times
   Video
Big Dare
Blond Justice
Bodywaves
Butt Boys in Space
Butt Sluts of the Castro
Casting Couch
Crucial Encounters
Deep Inside Jon Vincent
Desert Fox
Easy Prey
Feels So Good
Fidelity
Free to Be Wild
French Kiss
The Guy Next Door
Hard to Take
Heaven Too Soon
Hoghounds
Hot for His Bod
Hot Shots, Vol. 45: Latin
   Fever
Hot Shots, Vol. 47:
   Newcomers
Hot Shots, Vol. 49: Torrid
   Trios
Interview
In the Briefs
Iron Man
J.S. Big Time
Junior Crew
Kink
Leather Story
Liplock
Long, Hot Summer
Mandriven
Manhandler
Mein Kock
Men Together

Mountain Patrol
Naked Truth
New Love
Object of Desire
On The Prowl
Original Sin
Poetry In Motion
The Pornographer
Raw Recruits
Rock Hard 2
The Rolls
Say Goodbye
Sex Fly
Shoot 'N' Porn
Slammers
Spanking New
Steel Pulse
Stiff Competition
Stroke 'N Men
Sugar Britches
Sunday Brunch
Tailspin
Taken by Storm
Tempting Tommy
Three on Their Knees
Tight Jeans
To the Bone
Underground Homo
Hardcore
Uniform Ball
Where the Hunks Are
White Steel
Willing to Take It
Young Hearts, Broken
   Dreams

TORSTEN WITTE
(See Chris Lopez)

DAMON WOLF
Born February 20, 1964 in
Las Vegas. 5'7," 7" cock,
versatile. A '90s model.

Backstage Pass
Catalinaville
The Chosen
Detour
Friction

KEVIN WOLF
Cute, young, blond 1990s model.
Made to Order
Renegade, The

SEAN WOLF
Apply Within
The Games We Play

WILL WOLFE
Choke 'Em 3

WOLFF
German porn star who came to the U.S. to make movies in the mid '90s and then returned to Europe where he became one of the biggest names in porn. Autobiography published in Germany in 1998.
Big Score, The
Boot Black
Call To Arms
Captain Stud And His Seamen
Hard Bodyguard
Idol Country
Lost Loves
Lovers, Tricks & One Night Stands
Mess Hall Maneuvers
Military Issue 2
Nutt Busters
Outlaw Bikers
Party Line

Physical Exam
Rigid Video, Volume 1
Seeds Of Love
Summer's Tall Tales
Vice Cop
Wild Ones, Thet
Working Stiff

KRIS WOLFF
Ass Lick Alley
Slave Toy

MARK WOLFF
Born September 5, 1967 in Vancouver, British Columia, Canada. Resides in New York City and Vancouver, Canada. 5", 10-1/2," 8" cock. Bodybuilder and mainstream model whose handsome face has graced the cover of numerous magazines.
Blake Onassis: Exposed!
California Muscleboy Pro Wrestling 2
Canadian Built Muscle Club 3
Canadian Built Wrestling Club 1,2,3,
Exposed
Feel the Power
Flex Appeal
Four-Star Fantasy
Mark Wolf: Bashed, Beaten, Battered Mark Wolff—Totally Dominated
Mark Wolff Rockhard
Mark Wolff's Four Star Fantasy
Maxon vs. Wolff
Muscle Fantasies 1, 2
Muscles in Paradise

The Ring
Titans
Totally Dominated

KURT WOLFFE
House of Tricks

AUSTIN WOOD
Redwood

GRANT WOOD
Born February 14, 1971, Glenview, Illinois. Resides in Los Angeles. 5'11," 7" cock, bottom. A popular '90s model and director.
An Interview with Dax Kelly
Bad Ass Lieutenant
Blade's Real World, Men of Raleigh Durham
Curious?
Desert Paradise
Dirty White Guys
The Hotel
Hot Laguna Knights
How to Pleasure a Man
Humidity
In the Mix 96
Interview With A Goddess
Killer Looks
Late Night Porn
Latins
Lust Shack
Lusty Leathermen:
Mechanic on Booty
Men of Dream Canyon
Palm Springs Cruisin'
The Pounderosa
Red, Hot & Safe
Rescue 69-11
Sex 4 Hire 2
Sex in America

Star Contacts
Sexcuses
3-Some
Voyeur
Wild Sex In America
You Sexy Thing

B.J. WOODS
Bear Hugs

ROBERT WOODS
Do Me Evil

TOM WOODS
Boys Will Be Boys
Cockeyed Eagle, The
Lords Of Leather
Lovers
Manplay

CALVIN WORTH
Beach Ballers
Down To His Knee
Boots And Saddles
Boys From Riverside Drive
Broadway Boys
Dynamite
Erotica Video-30 #5
Eyes of a Stranger
Full House
Gemini
Giuseppe
Heavy Equipment
High Riders
Hot House
Hottest Hunks In Town
Hunk
Jacks
Jocks
Junior Cadets
Kansas City Trucking Co.
Killing Me Softly
A Married Man Who Had

Them All
Navy Blue
New York Construction Co.
A Night At The Adonis
Palace Of Pleasure
Sea Cadets
Sex Machine
Sex Magic
Too Big For His Britches

JACK WRANGLER
Gay-for-pay superstar of
the '80s who appeared in
gay and straight videos.
An author, he wrote an
autobiography titled *What's
a Nice Boy Like You
Doing?* He also wrote the
book for the Broadway
musical "Dream." After
leaving the porn business
he married singer
Margaret Whiting. He now
lives in New York.
Anything, Anytime
Boots and Saddles
Broadway Boys
The Boys of Riverside
   Drive
Cum Shots Bears
Dynamite
8" or More
Eyes of a Stranger
Gemini
Guess Who's Coming?
Hand-in-Hand Preview
   Tape 1
Heavy Equipment
High Riders
Hot House
Hot Shots, Vol. 4: Contest
   Continues
The Hottest Hunks in Town

Hunk
Jack Wrangler (non-sex)
Jocks
Junior Cadets
Kansas City Trucking Co.
Killing Me Gently
Light Blue Hanky
 B.J. Movie
Magnum Griffin, Vol. 9
Magnum Griffin, Vol. 12
A Married Man
Mustard Hanky Right
Navy Blue
A Night at the Adonis
New York Construction Co.
Palace of Pleasures
P.M. Preview Tape #2
Sex Machine
Sex Magic
Superstuds
Wanted
White Hanky Left

DAVID WRIGHT
A 1990s model.
Saugatuck Summer

ERIC WRIGHT
Manhungry

ETHAN WRIGHT
Anonymous Sex
Gang Bang Ranch Hand
Gay Weekend Away
Outdoor Ecstacy

JARED WRIGHT
With light brown hair, this
mature 1990s model
became famous for fisting.
A San Francisco resident.
French Connections 1-2
Link 2 Link

Mr. Fix-It
Power Fist
Rear End Alignment

STEVE WRIGHT
(aka Doug McCall)
Balls of the Wild
Big & Thick
Bigger They Come, The
Hard & Throbbing
Inch by Inch
In Hot Pursuit
In Your Wildest Dreams
Two Handfuls
Tyger Tales

JEREMY WYNN
(see Chris McKenzie)

Y

JOSEPH YALE
Three Day Pass

STEFAN YANOS
(see Sergei Jordonov)

BRIAN YATES
Bedroom Eyes
The Boy Next Door
Dirty Pictures
The Ivy League
Man Alone
Prince Charming
Rings
Truth, Dare or Damian
V-8

BUCK YEAGER
The Night We Met

CHRIS YEAGER
Any Excuse For Sex
At Your Service
Body of Art
Dick Undercover
For His Own Good
GV Guide All-Star Softball
  Game 1
Hard On Demand
Home Wrecker
Leather Confessions
Leather Connection
Leather Night
Leather Pit
Leather Playhouse
Leather Triangle
Leather Weekend
Men At Work
O is for Orgy
Plugged In
Pure Sex
Sex In Leather
Sex Trigger
Stud House
Taking The Plunge

NICK YEAGER
Billy Herrington's Body
  Shop
The Complexxx
Fit For a Man
Straight White Male
SWM

RYAN YEAGER
Handsome, dark-haired
1980s model. Voted Best
Newcomer of the Year by
Adult Video News maga-
zine in 1989.
Airmale
The Best of Michael Parks
The Best of Ryan Yeager

The Best of Scott Bond
Buddy System 1 & 2
Davey and the Cruisers
Fond Focus
Head Struck
In Your Face
Jumper
King of the Mountain
Powertool 2
Pumping Up: Flexx II
The Rise
The Rockmore Files
Screwing Screw Ups
Stranded: Enemies &
  Lovers
Three's on Their Knees
Uncut Club

GREGOR YELSON
Young, blond Russian and
a 1990s Falcon exclusive.
Hotwired: Viewers' Choice
In Deep: Miles To Go
Serviced
Stock

DAVID YORK
Slip It In
Urgent Matters

ERIC YORK
A blond, buffed Norwegian
model from the '90s.
All About Sex
Beat Patrol
Boys Next Door
Bull Pen
Centerspread 2 & 3
Conflict of Interest
Cop Daddies Playtime
Courting Libido
Driven Home
Fire in the Hole

Hidden Instinct
Hose 'Em Down
Hot Cops 3: The Final
  Assault!
Hot Guys #4
Hot Stuff
Hung Riders
Laguna Beach Lifeguards
Leather Men 2
Leather Virgin
Magic Bed
Maneuvers
The Men of South Beach
My Best Friends Woody
My Dick Is Bigger 2
Night We Met
Orgies Pt 3
Peep-O-Rama
Power Trip
Prisoner of Love
Rival, The
The Selection Part 1 (Solo)
The Sex Files
Squeeze Play
Sunshine Supermen
While I Was Sleeping

STEVE YORK
A porn star legend from the
'80s with one of the biggest
dick's in the history of the
business.
The Big Surprise
The Boys of San Francisco
Buster Goes to Laguna
Cumming of Age
Dirt Bikes
For You, Edition #1
F Truck: Use Me
Hand-in-Hand Preview
  Tape #1
Hard to Swallow
Hot Shots, Vol. 30, Hot

Jocks
Johnny Harden and
Friends
Magnum Griffin, Vol. 7
Performance
Private Collection
Strokers
William Higgins Preview
  Tape #1
Wrestling Meat 1 & 2

BILLY YOUNG
A 1970s model.
Adam & Yves

BRANDON YOUNG
Any Way I Can

CHRIS YOUNG
1990s model.
Raw Meat 5
Skateboard Sliders

DILLON YOUNG
One Way or the Other
Shameless

JARED YOUNG
Bad
The Best of Alexander
  Marshall
The Best of Black Knights
The Best of Jonathan
  Strong
Blond Justice
Dark Men
Extra Sex
G.I.
The Men of Tough Guys
Nasty Nights
Pleasure Theatre
Sex, Lies and
  Videocasettes

Slippery When Wet
Stiff Craving
Tough Guys Do Dance
Undergear

JAMIE YOUNG
Desert Paradise
Pleasure Peak

JORDAN YOUNG
Born May 25. When he's
not acting, cute '90s model
Jordan writes screenplays
for mainstream movies as
well as porn videos.
Inches Away
Lip Lock
Lost In Las Vegas
Naked Truth
Night Watch 2
Our Trespasses
Pick Up
Point Of View
Rescue 69-11
Ryker Files, The
Total Corruption 2

KEVIN YOUNG
(aka Robert Flores) A cute,
dark-haired, boy next door
from the early 1990s.
Acapulco Dreaming
Batdude & Throbbin'
Bare Bottoms
Black Orient Express
The Boys of Wilde Island
Cowboys & Indians
Cum Shots 102
Dream Doll
For Sale by Owners
Gang Bangers
Hung & Horny
I Love Foreskin

Midnight Riders
My Fantasy
Orgy at the Funhouse
Overseas Trade
Screwing Screw Ups
Seduction V: Taking Full
  Charge
Sex Waves
Stud Vision
Taxi
Warlords
Wet Dreams
Young Hustlers

KURT YOUNG
Born August 20 in
Maryland. 5'11," 9" cock,
top. The handsome '90s
model lives in Hollywood,
California.
Beverly Hills Hustlers
Dream Team
Family Values
Flesh and Blood
Handsome Drifters
Heat of Passion
Hot Summer of Sex
Men Only
Naked Highway
A Night With Todd Stevens
On the Prowl
On Your Knees
Rosebud (non-sex)
Showboys
Sodom
Tradewinds

LARRY YOUNG
(see Larry Mann)

Shawn Young
(see Corky Adams)

TONY YOUNG
Sparky O'Toole's Excellent
Adventure
Summer School
Tempting Tommy

COLE YOUNGBLOOD
(aka Phillip Masters)
Born December 5, 1972,
Harrisburg, Pennsylvania.
5'11," 10" cock. This boy-
ish-looking top with the
huge dick is a popular
1990s model.
Auto Fellatio 2
Big Guns 2
Cat Men Do
Cockfight
Cram Course: Sex Ed 3
Download
Family Secrets
Indulge
Inndulge Palm Springs
On The Prowl
Studio tricks
Take It Deep
The Road home
Ultimate Reality
We've Got Them All
Why Marines Don't Kiss

Z

CHRISTOPHER ZALE
(see Cody Fields)

TYLER ZANE
Spiked

ANDY ZEE
Billy Herrington's Body
Shop

TONY ZEREGA
Born February 27, 1966 in
New York City. 6'1," 7"
cock, versatile. A hairy,
'90s porn daddy.
Best of Titan: Collector
  Series 2
Catalinaville
Cowboy Jacks
Fallen Angel
Fit For a Man
Fluid
Immersion
A Love Story
My Brother's Best Friend
Orgies Pt 2
Pressure
Skuff
Stud Fee
Swell

PATRIK ZSOLT
Dark, handsome young
1999 Hungarian model.
Hungarian Heat

PAVOL ZUREK
Very cute, boyish, Czech
Republic model.
Lucky Lukas

Video Title Index
(Title, Studio & Date)

Backseat BJ (All Worlds)	1997
Backstage Pass (Hot House/Bullship)	1994
Backstrokes (John Summers) [solo]	1988
Backwoods (Jocks Video 42)	1996
Backyard Boys (Avalon Video)	
Bad (Back Alley Prod.)	1990
Bad as I Wanna Be (Brush Creek Media)	
Bad As We Oughtta Be (Brush Creek)	
Bad Ass (Rage)	
Bad Ass Lieutenant	
(Iron Clad Pro./ U.S. Male)	1997
Bad Bad Boys (Hand-in-Hand)	
Bad Boys (Action Video/Knight Men)	
Bad Boys Ball (Greenwood/Cooper)	1995
Bad Boys Club (Catalina)	1988
Bad Boys Dormitory (LeSalon)	
Bad Boys 1- 32 (Western Visuals Video)	
Bad Habits (Celsius Prod.)	1983
Bad Moon Rising (All Worlds)	
Badboys (Stallion Video)	
Badlands (Planet)	1992
Bad Russian Boys (Moscow Nights)	1998
Bait (HIS Video)	1986
Ball Blasters (Hard Hunks Collection)	1992
Ball Bustin' Boys (Stroke Video)	
Balls In Play (All Worlds Video)	
Balls of the Wild (Video 10/ Celestial Ent)	1999
Balls Out (Planet)	1993
Balls To The Wall 1-36 (Totally Tight)	1990-98
Bam 1 (Bacchus)	1997
Bam 2: Thug (Brick House)	1998
Bangcock Boys Town (East/West Prod.)	1992
Bar None (All Worlds)	
Bar Wench, Apply Within (Bent Prod)	1998
Bare Bodies (Metro)	1998
Bare Bottoms (Avalon)	
Bare Tales (Sierra Pacific)	1988
Bareback (Dick Wadd Prod.)	
Barely Tamed ((Altomar)	1996
Barn Storm (Sierra Pacific/Fox)	1996
Barracks Glory Hole 3-6 (All Worlds)	1996-98
Bartender, The (Forum Studios)	1995
Basic Black #7	
Basic Plumbing (Falcon Video Pac)	1993
Basic Plumbing 2 (Falcon Video Pac)	1998
Basket Fever (Vizuns Video)	
Basketballs (Stallion)	1995
Bat Dude (In Hand Video)	1989
Bathroom Buddies & Plumbers Helpers	
(Vivid Video)	
Bathroom Cruisers	
Batter Up! (Hot House/Plain Wrapped)	1997

Battle of the Bulges (LeSalon)	1988
Battling Briefs (BG Wrestling)	
Be My Baby	1984
Beach Ballers (Wall to Wall Video)	1986
Beach Blanket Bedtime Stories	
Beach Blanket Boner (BIG Ent.)	1992
Beach Buns (All Worlds)	1998
Beach Dreamer (By Attractions)	1989
Beach Head (All Worlds)	1998
Beach Heat	
Beached (All Worlds)	1982
Bear Hug	
Bear it All (All Worlds)	
Bear Mountain Patrol	
Bear Sex Party (Brush Creek)	1996
Bear to the Bone (All Worlds)	1997
Bearly Tamed (Altomar)	
Bears and Cubs (Adam & Co.)	1989
Beat Cop, The (Bijou)	1992
Beat Goes On, The (Image Video)	
Beat Men, The	
Beat Off Frenzy (Catalina)	1994
Beat Off Frenzy 2 (Catalina)	1995
Beat Patrol (Minotaur)	1995
Beat Street Boys	
Beat this Beef	
Beater's Digest (Altomar)	1988
Beaverly Hills Cop (Essex)	
Bed & Breakfast (Odyssey)	1994
Bed Tales (HIS)	1991
Bedroom Buddies	
Bedroom Eyes (Vivid)	1991
Bedroom Lies (Vivid Video)	1995
Bedtime Stories: Tales to Keep You Up	
(Catalina)	1991
Bedtime Tails (Erotic Men)	1998
Beef (Wall to Wall)	1988
Beef Jerky (Catalina)	
Beeper Boys of El Barrio	
(Mucho Macho/All Worlds)	1998
Before & After (Forum Studios)	1998
Beginnings (Another Video Co.)	
Behind Closed Doors (Falcon VidPac 61)	1988
Behind His Back (Sex Video/Video 10)	1997
Behind the Barn Door (Catalina)	1993
Behind the Eight Ball (Vivid)	1991
Behind the Greek Door (4 Play Video)	
Below the Belt (Bijou)	1985
Below the Decks (Blade/Video 10)	1997
Below the Rim (Palomino)	1994
Bend Over Buddies (YMAC)	1999
Berlin Army Nights (Cazzo Films/Vid. 10)	1997

Black & Hung, Part 2 (filmco)
Black & Latino Working Hard (Pleasure)
Black & Lethal (Bacchus) 1997
Black & Proud 2 (Filmco Video) 1996
Black & White Hustle (Quickies)
Black Aces, The Caballero
Black All American 1 & 2 (Planet) 1990
Black Alley: South of the Border (Catalina) 1990
Black American (Erotic Men) 1998
Black and Beefy (Sierra Pacific) 1997
Black and Beyond: The Darker Side 1989
Black and Blue (New Age/Video 10) 1996
Black and Bound, Vol. 1 & 2
Black and Huge 2 (Rebel Video) 1989
Black and Lethal (Bacchus Releasing)
Black and Proud
Black Assets: The Movie (Dark Shades)
Black Attack (Catalina) 1996
Black Attack 2 (Catalina) 1997
Black Balled (Rawhide) 1998
Black Balled (Straight Video)
Black Balled 2 (All Worlds)
Black Balls (Stylus Men) 1999
Black Betrayal (Associated Video) 1991
Black Bi Demand (All Worlds Video) 1998
Black Bolts, White Nuts (All Worlds)
Black Bomber (Barbar Video) 1991
Black Bone Parties (Rawhide Video)
Black Bone-A-Thon Vol. 1-4 (Bacchus)
Black Book (Satellite Video) 1989
Black Boot Diaries (All Worlds)
Black Brigade (U.S. Male) 1998
Black Brother/White Brother
Black Brothers (Video Tape Exchange) 1985
Black Bullet (LeSalon Video)
Black Bun Busters (VCA)
Black Cargo (Thor Productions)
Black Champions [solo] 1990
Black Deja (Nubian Video) 1997
Black Delivery (Satellite Video) 1986
Black Dynasty (Caballero)
Black Entry (All Worlds) 1998
Black Fantasies (HIS Video) 1991
Black for More (Catalina Video) 1994
Black Forbidden Fantasies (Video Ex.) 1985
Black Force (Catalina) 1988
Black Gang Bang 1-8 (Bacchus)
Black Gold (All Worlds) 1993
Black Hammer (Associated Video) 1991
Black Handfulls IV (Nubian)
Black Hanky Left
Black Heat 1970

Black Heat (All Worlds)
Black Hombres (Satellite Video) 1986
Black Horses (Bacchus)
Black Hot Rods (All Worlds)
Black In Demand (Thrust Studios) 1997
Black in the Saddle (Catalina) 1996
Black in the Saddle Again [hetero]
Black Jack Fever
Black Jacks (Stallion Video)
Black Justice (Odyssey)
Black, Large and in Charge (All Worlds) 1993
Black Leather (Thrust Studios) 1995
Black Leather Gang Bang (Big Video) 1999
Black Leather, White Studs (Planet) 1992
Black Load 1985
Black Lovers (Bacchus Releasing)
Black Lust/White Passion (Filmco) 1988
Black Magic (Catalina) 1988
Black Magic, White Heat (Altomar) 1988
Black Male
Black Man on Top (Brickhouse) 1995
Black Market (Brick House) 1997
Black Mates (Satellite Video)
Black Men Cruising Crenshaw (Nubian) 1999
Black Men Do! (Catalina) 1999
Black Men in Black (All Worlds) 1997
Black Men on Top (Brick House Ent.) 1995
Black Mischief (Jet Set Productions) 1999
Black Mouthfulls 1 & 2 (Nubian/Video 10) 1999
Black Moves (Millennium) 1994
Black Muscle Machine 2
  (Pacific Sun Video) 1999
Black Nubian Fantasies (Nubian Video) 1997
Black On Black (HIS) 1984
Black Orient Express (Checker Board) 1985
Black Pack (Satellite Video) 1988
Black Passions (Marina Pacific)
Black Patriot
Black Patrol (All Worlds) 1998
Black Power (Paradox) 1999
Black Raven Gang Bang (XTC Studios)
Black Renegades (Bacchus) 1999
Black, Ripped and Stripped (Brick House) 1998
Black Rose (Bacchus) 1998
Black Salsa (Filmco Video) 1991
Black Secret (All Worlds)
Black Sex & Leather 2 (Leather Ent) 1996
Black Sex Party (Filmco Video) 1986
Black Sex Therapy (Videotape Exchange) 1985
Black Shafts (Satellite Video) 1986
Black Shakers
Black Sheep of the Family (Coast to Coast)

Boys and Their Toys 2, (Rage Collection)
Boys Behind Bars (Latino Fan Club)   1988
Boys Behind bars 1&2 (Latino Fan Club) 1989
Boys Boys Boys
Boys Camp Memories (LeSalon)
Boys Can't Help It
Boys From Bel Air (Catalina Video)   1996
Boys From Riverside Drive (Bijou)
Boys in the Office (Adam & Co.)   1992
Boys in the Sand (MKS Video)   1971
Boys In The Sand 2 (L.A. Video)   1984
Boys Just Want Have Sex (L.A. Video)
Boys Next Door (Bacchus)   1995
Boys Night Out (VCA Video)   1988
Boys of Baja
Boys of Beverly Hills (Midnight Special)
Boys of Company F, The (HIS Video)   1984
Boys of New Jersey, The
Boys of Riverside Drive, The
Boys of San Francisco, The (W. Higgins) 1981
Boys of Summer, The
Boys of the Hollywood Spa
Boys of Venice (William Higgins Video)   1979
Boys of West Hollywood
Boys of Wilde Island, The
Boys on Call (Rosebud Male)   1992
Boys on Film
Boys on Fire (HIS Video)   1990
Boys on the Block
Boys Town: Going W. Hollywood (Nova) 1984
Boys Will Be Boys 1 (Junior Studios)   1994
Boyz From Da Hood (Blackwolf Ent.)   1999
Boyz in the Band (Bacchus Releasing)
Brandon's Big Weekend (AVI Group)   1999
Brats (Planet)   1992
Brawn's Rod (Rosebud Video)   1993
Brawnzmen, The (Planet)   1992
Brazilian Bath Boys
    (Marcostudio/Video 10)   1994
Brazilian Bath Boys 2 (Marco/Vid 10)   1995
Brazilian Hunks 2 (Bacchus Releasing)   1998
Brazil Nuts (Iron Horse)   1997
Break Down (Brentwood/Bijou)
Break In (Mustang Video Pac 10)   1992
Breakaway (Jocks Video Pac 60)
Breaker Blue (Adam & Co.)   1988
Breakers, Black Star Cockland-Hair
    Trigger #2 (West Hollywood Video)
Breakin' 'Em In 1 (Marcostudio/Video 10) 1997
Breakin' 'Em In 2 (Marcostudio/Video 10) 1997
Breaking and Entering (Planet)   1992
Breaking and Entering (Graphik Arts)   1999

Breaking Out
Breaking Point
Breakthrough (Minotaur)   1995
Breathless (Catalina)   1996
Brian's Boys (/Nova/L.A. Video)   1980s
Brick Bat 1-3 (Brick House Ent.)
Brick Wall, The (T&T)   1998
Brief Encounters (Catalina Video)   1992
Brief Exchanges (HIS Video)   1994
Brief Tales, Blue Men/Sunshine
Briefs (Compilation - John Summers)   1988
Brig, The (HIS Video)
Bring Your Own Man (Spike Video)
British are Coming, The (HIS)   1986
Broadway Boys (PM Prod)
Broadway Studs (Planet)   1992
Bronc Rider (Falcon Video Pac 36)
Bronco Bunch, The
Brothas Gettin' Down, Part 1 (Nubian)   1998
Brother Hustlers (HIS Video)   1989
Brother Load (Catalina)   1983
Brother Should Do It (Catalina)
Brother to Brother (All Worlds)   1996
Brother Trouble (Catalina)   1989
Brotherly Love (Stallion Video)   1990
Brotherly Love 2 (Stallion Video)   1991
Brothers
Brothers Behaving Badly (All Worlds)   1998
Brother's Desire, A (HIS Video)
Brothers Should Do It (Laguna Pacific)
Brown Paper Wrapper (Video Resource)
Bubble Butt (Scorpion Studios)   1989
Buckets of Love
Buck's Excellent Adventure
Buckshot (Buckshot Prod.)
Buddies 2-3   1998
Buddy System 1 & 2, The (Vivid Video) 1989
Buffalo Meat (Vivid Video)
Bugle: Mass Appeal (Catalina)
Built Like A Brick House (Planet)   1991
Built to Last (Planet) 1992
Built Tough (Jocks) 1995
Bulge: Mass Appeal (Catalina Video)   1988
Bulging Jockstraps (Bijou)
Bull Pen (Mustang)
Bullet Gold 1-3: (LeSalon)   1988
Bulletin Board Buddies (Video 10)   1995
Bullpen (Falcon Video Pac)   1995
Bullring (In Deep)   1995
Bullseye (All Worlds)   1995
Bunk Bed Buddies (Bacchus Releasing) 1998
Buns of Steel (Vivid Video)

Colossal Combo, Volume 43 (Leisure Time)
Come and Get It! (Catalina) 1994
Come as You Are (Planet) 1992
Come Back, The (Millennium) 1994
Come Blow Your Own Horn
Come Clean (Filmco) 1992
Come Closer (Thrust Studios) 1994
Come With Me (Forum Studios) 1994
Coming From Above (Bijou Video)
Coming Home (Catalina) 1991
Coming Out: Coming Hard (Planet) 1991
Coming Soon
Coming Together (Mustang Vid Pac 22) 1993
Coming True (Explosive Studios) 1995
Command Performance (Falcon Vid Pac 81)1992
Commercial Sex (InHand Video)
Company We Keep, The (Buckshot)
Complete & Uncut (Altomar) 1997
Complexxx, The (All Worlds) 1998
Compulsion-He's Gotta Have It
  (Falcon Video Pac 72) 1991
Comrades in Arms (Kristen Bjorn) 1996
Concrete Lover (InHand Video)
Confessions (Izzat Prod.) 1989
Conflict of Interest (Forum Studios) 1995
Connoisseur Collector Classics
Constant Hunger (Close-Up Prod.)
Convertible Blues (Cinderfella) 1992
Cool Hand Dick (Planet) 1994
Cool Moon (Winners Media) 1993
Cop Bound
Cop Corruption (BIC) 1998
Cop Out
Cop Sins (Jet Set Productions) 1997
Cop Stories 1: The Scandal (Thrust) 1998
Cop Stories 2: The Cover Up (Thrust) 1998
Cop Training 1-2
Cops (Bijou) 1992
Cops at Play (BIC) 1995
Cops, Jocks & Military Feet (Planet) 1992
Copsucker
Corky's Vacation (L.A. Heat) 1996
Corporate Head (Planet) 1992
Corporate Ladder, The (Steamworx) 1998
Country Hustlers (Oh Man!) 1997
Court Martial (Odyssey Men) 1997
Courting Libido (HIS) 1995
Cousin Buck (PM Productions)
Cousins (Catalina)
Cousins Should Do It (HIS) 1989
Cover Models
Coverboy (HIS)

Cowboy Jocks (Jocks) 1997
Cowboys And Indians (Vivid Man) 1989
Cowboys Get the Blues (Planet) 1994
Cram Course 1 & 2 (Minotaur) 1995
Cram Course: Sex Ed 3 (Minotaur) 1996
Cramming for the Big One (Sex Video) 1998
Craze! (Planet) 1993
Crazed (Adam & Co.) 1988
Crazy Horny Nutz
Cream of the Crop (Catalina) 1994
Cross Over (Stallion Video) 1998
Crossing the Line (All Worlds) 1996
Crossroads (Vivid) 1995
Crosswire (LeSalon) 1988
Crotch Rockets (Fox) 1990
Crotch Watcher (Falcon Video Pac 5) 1975
Crucial Encounters (Planet) 1992
Cruise Control (Catalina) 1993
Cruise Park (Sex Video/ Video 10) 1997
Cruiser, The (LA Video)
Cruisers: A Reunion of Friends (In Hand) 1989
Cruisin' 1, 2 & 3 (Falcon Video Pac 88) 1988
Cruisin' (Iron Horse) 1998
Cruisin' '57 (Toby Ross/Bijou) 1979
Cruisin' For A Gang Bang (Video 10) 1999
Cruisin' for Lust
Cruisin' Park (HIS) 1992
Cruisin' the Balcony (Metro) 1994
Cruisin' the Castro (Bijou Video)
Cruisin' the Men of L.A. (Inferno) 1997
Cruisin' West Hollywood (LeSalon Video)
Cruising Game, The
Cruising Grounds (Bacchus)
Cult of Manhood (Altomar Video)
Cum & Get It
Cum Bustible
Cum Shot Bears
Cum Shots 101 & 102
Cum: Stories To Tell (Bacchus)
Cumback Kid
Cumbustible (All Worlds)
Cummin' Of Age (Surfside /Video 10) 1994
Cummin' Together (Jeff Stryker) 1991
Cumming Attractions (Fox) 1993
Cum-pany Ass-ets (LeSalon Video) 1985
Cumpetition
Cumplete & Uncut (Altomar) 1996
Curious (Vivid Raw) [Bi]
Current Affairs (Falcon) 1998
Customer Service (LeSalon/Brush Creek)
Cut Above, A (Metro) 1994
Cut Club, The (Vivid Man) 1991

Dick Day Afternoon	
Dick Diving (Planet)	1994
Dick Smoke (Vivid Video)	
Dick Undercover (All Worlds)	1996
Dicked (Planet)	1992
Dickey-Lickey	
Dickin' Around (Iron Horse Studios)	1999
Dicks and Robbers (Planet)	1993
Dick's Service Center (Planet)	1990
Dickted (Mack)	1992
Digital Fantasy - 2nd Byte (Jike Monsoon)	1997
Dildo Kings (Stallion)	1994
Dildo Pigs (Stallion)	
Dildo Sex Slaves	
Dino Dreams On	
Director's Best: John Travis, Vol. 1	
Director's Best: William Higgins, Vol.1	
Dirk Yates Private Amateur #100 (All Worlds)	
Dirk Yates Private Collection #124 (All Worlds)	
Dirk's Dirty Sex Garage	
Dirt Bikes (Falcon)	
Dirt Busters (LeSalon)	1988
Dirty Dancin' Auditions (Control T)	1999
Dirty Dreaming (Mustang Video Pac 16)	1992
Dirty Harry #20 (Gentelmen's Video)	
Dirty Jocks (Hard Hunks Collection)	
Dirty Laundry (Planet)	1992
Dirty Leather (Leather Ent.)	1996
Dirty Load (Hard Hunks Collection)	
Dirty Picture Show	
Dirty Pictures (Vivid)	1992
Dirty Pillow Talk (Studio 2000)	1995
Dirty Pool (HIS Video)	1993
Dirty Stories (Mustang Video)	
Dirty Tricks (Video 10)	1990
Dirty White Guys (All Worlds)	1996
Dirty Works (Planet)	1992
Discharged (InHand Video)	
Disconnected (Pride)	1992
Dish	
Dive! (All Worlds)	1996
Do Me Dirty (Video 10/ Tenderloin)	1995
Do Me Evil (Toby Ross/Bijou)	1975
Dock 9 (InHand Video)	
Doctor's Orders 1: Manipulation (Hot House)	1998
Doctor's Orders 2: Dialation (Hot House)	1998
Doctor's Sex Dungeon (Bob Jones)	1993
Doggie Style (All Worlds Video)	
Dogs in Heat (Rosebud Male)	1992
Doin' Hard Time (Pleasure Prod.)	1993
Doing It (Associated Video)	
Domestic Servitude	
Dominator	
Dominique's Bi Adventure (Leisure Time)	1995
Donny's Dirty Sex Garage (Bob Jones)	1993
Don't Ask, Don't Tell (Bijou)	1994
Don't Dick with the Devil (Studio 2000)	1998
Don't Hold Back (Galaxy)	1997
Don't Kiss Me, I'm Straight (Planet)	1991
Don't Lie To Me/Locker Room Billy (Control T)	1994
Dorm Fever (Planet)	1993
Double Crossed (Jocks)	1994
Double Exposure (Vivid)	1994
Double Solitaire	
Double Standards	1987
Double Vision (Mustang)	
Down and Dangerous (Planet Prods)	
Down and Dirty (Planet)	1992
Down and Out (Image)	1992
Down Bi Law (Catalina)	1992
Down Deep (Planet)	1994
Down for the Count (Catalina)	1988
Down Home (Falcon Video Pac 78)	1992
Down In the Dirt (HIS Video)	
Down in the Dunes (Catalina)	1995
Down on It (Catalina)	1994
Down on Me (Mustang)	1997
Down on the Farm (Nova/LA Video)	
Down to His Knee (LA Video)	
Down Under (Catalina)	
Down, Down, Down [wrestling]	
Download (Falcon)	1996
Dr. Discipline	1996
Dr. Good Glove (Hot House/Plain Wrapped)	1995
Dr. Jerkoff & Mr. Hyde (BIG)	1997
Dracula	1971
Dracula Sucks	
Drafted (Planet)	1991
Drawing Tricks	
Dream Doll (By Attractions)	1989
Dream Lover (Catalina)	1995
Dream Maker (Bijou Video)	
Dream Men (Erotic Men/Midnight)	1996
Dream Seeker (Another Video Co.)	
Dream Team (Planet)	1992
Dream Team, The (Studio 2000)	1999
Dream World (Catalina)	1999
Dreamen: Dirty Dialogue (Video 10)	1989
Dreamer (HIS Video)	
Dreamin': A Black And Latin Fantasy (Bacchus Releasing)	
Dreaming About Dick (Cinderella Video)	1989

Forbidden Portraits (PM Productions)
Force of Nature — 1995
Forced Entry (Studio 2000) — 1995
Forced Fuck Fantasies
Forced Pleasures
Forced Service (Centaur Films) — 1998
Foreign Affairs (By Attraction) — 1990
Foreign Competition (Planet) — 1992
Foreplay (LA Video) — 1986
Foreskin Dreams (Intl. Studio) — 1991
Foreskin Fantasy
Foreskin Madness Four for More (Vivid)
Foreskin Quarterly (Brush Creek Media)
Forest Rump (Hollywood Sales) — 1997
Forever Hold Your Piece 1 (Catalina) — 1994
Forever Hold Your Piece 2 (Catalina) — 1995
Fortune Nookie (Catalina) — 1998
Forum Video Magazine (Forum Studios) — 1994
Foul Play (Falcon) — 1994
Fountains of Youth (Bijou Video)
Four Alarm Studs (Planet) — 1991
Four by Four (Size Video)
Four Card Studs (Jocks) — 1998
Four in Hand (Nova/LA Video)
Four Letters
Four Men (All Worlds) — 1997
Four Rooms (J.T. Video) — 1997
Four-hour Four-skin
Four-Star Fantasy (Wolff Prods.)
Fourty Five Minutes of Bondage
   (Pyewackett) — 1994
Fox Tale (All Worlds) — 1997
Foxholes (Catalina) — 1989
Fox's Lair (Studio 2000) — 1995
Frank Vickers I: Solo
Frank Vickers II: Worship (Live)
Frank Vickers III: Man After Man
Frat Brats (Marathon) — 1988
Frat House Memories (Catalina)
Frat House One (Catalina)
Frat Pack (Planet) — 1992
Fratrimony (All Worlds) — 1989
Freaks (Paradox) — 1999
Free Delivery (Iron Horse) — 1998
Free to Be Wild
Free Your Willy (Planet) — 1994
Freeze Frame (Planet) — 1991
French Connections Part One:
   Temptation (Falcon120) — 1998
French Connections Part Two:
   Conquest (Falcon 121) — 1998
French Erections (Hot House/Vision A)

French Kiss (In Hand) — 1990
French Lieutenant's Boys (Catalina)
Fresh (Huge Video/Falcon Intl.) — 1999
Fresh Men, The (Falcon)
Freshman Fantasies (Vivid)
Freshman Fever (Mansplash Studios) — 1995
Freshman Recruits (Pleasure Prod.) — 1999
Freshmen, The (Falcon) — 1997
Freshmen Getaway Weekend (S.I. Inc.) — 1997
Freshman Years
Friction (Hot House/Bullship) — 1995
Friend Of William Spencer
Friend to Friend (Planet) — 1992
Friendly Desire (Forum/Millennium) — 1994
Friendly Obsession, A (Vivid) — 1989
Friends and Lovers
Friends are Best
Frisky Memories (Bel Ami) — 1999
Frisky Summer (Bel Ami) — 1995
From Feet to Meat
From Maui with Love (Vivid) — 1989
Ft. Lauderdale Hustlers (Iron Horse) — 1999
F-Train to Castro (West Hollywood Video)
Fuck Truck (Falcon Video Pac 23) — 1978
Fucked Up (Live Video) — 1986
Fucking Around (Video Exclusives) — 1989
Fucking Good! (Intl. Studio) — 1991
Full Body Contact (Video 10/Blade Prod.) — 1997
Full Grown/Full Blown (Catalina) — 1988
Full House (Vidco)
Full Length (Falcon Video Pac 85) — 1993
Full Load: Maximum Overdrive (Catalina) — 1988
Full Package (Jocks)
Full Release (Pleasure Prod.) — 1999
Full Service (Catalina) — 1989
Full Service (Falcon Video Pac 20) — 1978
Full Up! (Jocks) — 1999
Fully Serviced (Scorpion/Video 10) — 1995
Fulton Street (Bijou) — 1994
Fun and Games — 1973
Fun in the Sun (Catalina)
Fun Size
Funboy Three (Vivid Video)

G

G.I. Mac (Zen Film Prod.)
Galaxy Boys (Renegade) — 1998
Gamemaster (Centaur) — 1997
Games (Surge)
Games of Paris (AVI) — 1992
Games We Play, The (Forum) — 1997

Grease Monkeys (William Higgins Video)
Greased Lightning (Renegade /XTC) 1998
Greased Up (Jocks) 1995
Greaseguns (Studio 2000) 1993
Great Balls of Fire (Cinderfella Video) 1990
Great Lengths
Greenhorn (LeSalon Video)
Grey Hanky Left
Gridiron (Vivid Video) 1989
Grip of Passion, The: Love or Lust
   (InHand) 1990
Grizzly (Catalina) 1999
Group Therapy (Mack Studios) 1993
Growing Years (Vidco)
Grunts (BIC) 1994
G-Squad (Soho Video) 1990
Guarding the Jewels (Renegade/ XTC) 1998
Guess What? (Fantastic Pics.) 1994
Guess Who's Coming? (LeSalon Video)
Guest Services (Catalina) 1995
Guest, The (Planet Group Video) 1992
Guilty
Gunslingers
Gut Reaction (Hot House/Plain Wrapped) 1996
Guy Next Door, The (Catalina) 1995
Guys in Jocks and Jockeys (Bob Jones) 1994
Guys Just Can't Stop (Bijou Video)
Guys Like Us
Guys N' The Burb
Guys Who Crave Black Cock
Guys Who Crave Hard Dicks (Wildside)
Guys Who Eat Cum (Rawhide) 1990
Guys Who Take It
Guys With A Rise (SEMG Film Prods) 1998
Guys With Giant Dicks (Leisure Time)
Guys With Tight Asses (Rawhide)
Guyz n the Burbs
GV Guide All Star Softball Game #1
   (Greenwood Cooper) 1995
GV Guide Gay Erotic Video Awards #1
   (Out & About) 1992
Gv Guide Gay Erotic Video Awards #2
   (Out & About) 1993
Gym Tales (Video 10) 1996
Gypsy for Dicks (Bijou Video)

H

Hair (West Hollywood Sales)
Hair Fetish and Gay Men (Leisure Time)
Hair Klub For Men Only (Planet Group) 1994
Hair Plug (Brute Films/Planet) 1994

Hair Trigger (W. Hollywood Sales)
Hairsteria (West Hollywood Sales) 1999
Hairway To Heaven (Brute Films) 1995
Hairy Chested Hunks (Close-Up Prods.)
Hairy Hunks (Stallion Video)
Hand in Hand Preview tape 1
Hand in the Fire
Hand Jobs 1-3 (Catalina) 1992-93
Hand of Fate (Catalina) 1997
Hand to Hand (Vivid) 1994
Hand to Mouth (Catalina Videos)
Handball Marathon 3 (Pig Play) 1995
Hands On (Mustang Studios) 1994
Handsome (PM Prods.)
Handsome Drifters (Studio 2000) 1998
Handsome Ransome (Inferno Films) 1998
Hand-To-Hand
Handtools 1 & 2 (Catalina) 1990
Handyman, The (Associated)
Hang 10 (HIS Video)
Hang 8-1/2 (Vizuns)
Happily Ever After (All Worlds) 1996
Happy House (Planet Group) 1992
Hard 1 & 2 (Forum Studios) 1998
Hard Act (A-Line Video)
Hard Action (Junior Studio) 1995
Hard and Kinky 14 (Rock and Roll Video)
Hard and Throbbing
Hard as Marble (All Worlds) 1994
Hard as Steele
Hard as Stone (HIS)
Hard as They Come
Hard Ass (Leisure Time) 1996
Hard at It 2
Hard at Play
Hard at Work (Image/Rosebud) 1992
Hard Ball (In Hand) 1989
Hard Ball (Video 10) 1996
Hard Bargains
Hard Body 2000 (Odyssey Men) 1998
Hard Bodyguard (HIS) 1994
Hard Choices 1 & 2 (InHand Video)
Hard Cock Jock (All Worlds)
Hard Core (All Worlds Video)
Hard Corps (Totally Tight) 1996
Hard Disk Drive (Surge)
Hard Drive (HIS Video) 1995
Hard Fantasies (Stroke Video)
Hard Focus (BIG Video)
Hard For the Money (BIG)
Hard Fucking Buddies (Rawhide)
Hard Hats (Mustang) 1996

Hard Knocks (InHand Video)
Hard Labor (HIS Video) 1990
Hard Labor (Spectrum Video) 1995
Hard Lessons: Sex Ed 2 (Studio 2000) 1995
Hard Line
Hard Luck Number (Bijou Video)
Hard Men 1 & 2
Hard Men at Work (LeSalon Video) 1983
Hard Money (HIS Video) 1984
Hard Moves (Image Video) 1990
Hard On Demand (Sex Video/Video 10) 1995
Hard On Hard Bodies (In Hand Video)
Hard on Site (XTC) 1998
Hard Part 1 (Forum)
Hard Pressed (Studio Assn.) 1991
Hard Punishment (Projex Video) 1999
Hard Rock High (Scorpion Studios) 1988
Hard Steel (Catalina) 1990
Hard Talk (Planet Group) 1992
Hard Times (All Worlds) 1998
Hard To Be Good (Catalina) 1989
Hard to Believe (HIS Video)
Hard to Come By (Fox Studios)
Hard To Focus (Planet Group) 1991
Hard To Hold (Vivid)
Hard To Keep Down (Catalina)
Hard to Resist (Back Alley Video)
Hard to Swallow (All Worlds Video) 1997
Hard to Take (Associated)
Hard Up (Midnight Men) 1996
Hard Use (Close-Up) 1998
Hard Working Men (Video 10/Sex Video) 1998
Hard Workout (Filmco) 1997
Hardass
Hardball (Spectrum) 1995
Hardcore (All Worlds)
Harder the Better, The
Hardhat (Jaguar Films)
Hardhats (Mustang)
Hardline (Jocks Video) 1997
Hardworkers (Stallion) 1995
Harley's Angels (PM Prods.)
Harley's Crew (Catalina) 1998
Harrassment
Hart Attack (Hart Productions) 1995
Hart Throb (Studio 2000) 1993
Haulin' & Ballin' (Le Salon) 1987
Hawaiian Desire (HIS) 1991
Hawaiian Dreams (All Worlds)
Hawaiian Eyes
Hawaiian Heat
Hawaiian Illustrated (All Worlds) 1997

Hawaiian Lei (All Worlds) 1997
Hawaiian Vacation 1 & 2 (Video 10) 1998
Hayfever
Hayride (Falcon Video Pac 13)
He Devils (Vidco) 1990
Head Bangers (YMAC Video) 1991
Head of the Class (Catalina) 1988
Head of the Class 2 (Catalina) 1989
Head Over Heels (Seabag) 1988
Head Struck (Catalina) 1991
Head Trip Hunk (Tmx)
Head Trips (Al Parker's/LeSalon Video)
Head Waiter (Bijou Video) 1980
Headin' West (Gino Colbert) 1989
Headlock
Heads Or Tails (Mustang Video Pac 19) 1994
Heads Up (Barbar Video) [solo] 1991
Headstruck
Health Club Gigolo (In Tropics) 1989
Heart Throbs
Heartbeat (10/9 Prod.) 1988
Heartstroke (HIS Video) 1982
Heat (Vivid Video) 1991
Heat Goes On, The
Heat in the Night (Huge) 1989
Heat of Passion (Video Resource)
Heat Of the City (Vivid Man)
Heatwave (Falcon)
Heaven Too Soon (Sierra Pacific) 1993
Heavenly (In Hand) 1988
Heavenly Acts (BFP Video)
Heavy Cruisin'
Heavy Equipment (Cream of the Crop)
Heavy Petting (heterosexual)
Heiress
Hell Bent For Leather (Catalina)
Hell Knight (All Worlds) 1994
Hell Razer 1-3 (Zeus) 1996-99
Hell Weekend (Close-Up) 1993
Help Wanted (Falcon Video Pac 19) 1977
Here Comes Peter (Planet Group) 1993
Heroes ((Nova Studios) 1984
He's Gotta Have It (Image)
He's Worth It (Forum) 1996
Hey Dude! (Planet Group) 1994
Hey Tony! What's The Story? (Bijou) 1993
Hidden Agenda (Bacchus) 1995
Hidden Camera (Christopher Rage)
Hidden Instinct (Catalina) 1994
Hidden Instincts (Bijou) 1992
Hidden Man (Pleasure Prod.) 1994
Hideaway Bed

Hot Roomers	1985
Hot Sex Pick Up	
Hot Sheets (All Worlds)	
Hot Shots, Vols. 1 - 50	1982-90
Hot Splash (Big Ram Prod.)	
Hot Spot (All Worlds)	1998
Hot Springs Orgy (Catalina)	1995
Hot Stuff (In Deep Prod)	1994
Hot Summer Knights (Vivid Man)	1990
Hot Summer of Sex (BIG)	1996
Hot Tamales (Vivid Video)	
Hot Ticket (Falcon)	1993
Hot Times in Little Havana (K. Bjorn)	1998
Hot to Trot (Hot House)	1997
Hot Trash (HIS Video)	
Hot Truckin' (Bijou Video)	
Hot Tub Fever (Locker Room Prods.)	1999
Hot Wheels (Jocks)	1997
Hot Wired (Vidco)	1988
Hot Wired: Viewers' Choice	
(Falcon FVP 125)	1999
Hotel, The (Vivid)	1998
Hotel California (Jocks)	1999
Hotel Hell (HIS Video)	
Hotel Hombre (Planet Group)	1993
Hotel L.A. (Hendrix Prod.)	1992
Hotel Montreal (Celestial Ent.)	1998
Hotter Than Hell (Centaur)	1997
Hotter Than Life (All Worlds)	1997
Hottest Hunks In Town (LeSalon Video)	
Hotwheels (Jocks)	1997
House Boy Training (Redboard Video)	1999
House Boys (Video 10)	
House For Sale Sex (Brick House)	1998
House of Bondage (Grapik Arts)	1995
House of Games (Catalina)	
House of Tricks (Hot House/Primo)	1994
House Painter & Bigger than Life	
(Falcon Video Pac 6)	1976
House Rules (Falcon Video Pac 90)	1993
Houseboys (Scorpion Studios)	1989
How Big is Big? (Planet Group)	1991
How Big Is Danny? (Planet)	1991
How I Got the Story (Nova/LA Video)	
How to Enlarge Your Penis [how-to j/o]	
How To Get A Man In Bed (Forum)	1995
How to Pleasure a Man (Smeg Video)	
Huddle Up (Sierra Pacific)	1998
Huge 1 & 2 (Falcon Video Pac 31)	1979
Huge Black and Delicious (All Worlds)	
Huge Double Impact (Horse Video)	1991
Huge Loads 1 & 2 (J.T.)	1997

Huge Man Meat (Jet Set Prod.)	1999
Huge Torpedoes (Video Resource)	
Humidity (Pulse Productions)	1999
Hummer (All Worlds)	
Hung and Dangerous (Gino Colbert)	1990
Hung and Horny (Balls To The Wall)	1986
Hung and Restless (Balls To The Wall)	
Hung Guns [bi]	1987
Hung Heroes 1-6 (Jet Set Prod.)	1997-1999
Hung in the Balance	
Hung Jury (Hollywood Sales)	
Hung Riders 1 & 2 (Catalina)	1995
Hung Up (Minotaur)	1996
Hung, Paddled And Plugged	
Hungarian Heat (Falcon Intl. FIC-11)	1999
Hungarian Rhapsody (Ikarus/YMAC)	1997
HUNGarians (Sarava)	1998
Hungary for Men (Kristen Bjorn)	1996
Hunger, The	
Hungry Eyes (Catalina)	1995
Hungry for Hole (T&T)	
Hungry Hole (Brentwood Classics)	
Hunk (Nova/Tmx)	1985
Hunk Hunt #1 (Leisure Time)	1995
Hunk Hustlers (Polk Street Prod.)	
Hurricane Hard-on (Planet Group)	1992
Hurts So Good (Falcon)	
Hush (Bad Brad)	1994
Hustlemania	
Hustler Blue (West Hollywood Video)	
Hustler Way (Locker Room)	1998
Hustler's Blues (Graphik Arts)	1999
Hustler's Alley-Men In Demand (Axis)	
Hustlers, The 1-4 (Malexpress)	
Hustling Roommate (Planet Group)	
I	
I Am Curious Leather (Sex Video)	1996
I Do! (MT Prods.)	
I Dream of Weenie (Filmco)	1992
I Lick It 'Cuz I Like It (Tiger Media)	1992
I Like to Watch (Stroke #45)	
I Live For Sex (Video 10)	1998
I Love Foreskin (Tiger Media)	1990
I Need it Bad (Live Video)	
I Saw What You Did (Thrust Studios)	1997
I Wanna Be In Porn! (Bacchus)	1996
I Want More (Falcon)	
I Was a She-Male for the FBI	
I.M.L. UNCUT	
Idle Pleasures (Catalina)	

Intruder: Robbery, Torment, Fantasy
(Close-Up) 1994
Intruders, The (Fox Studios)
Intrusion (Thrust) 1995
Invaders from URanus (Thor) 1997
Invitation (LeSalon) 1995
Iron Cage (Jet Set Productions) 1998
Iron Man (Vivid Man) 1990
Iron Men of Porn, Volume 3 (Vivid Video)
Iron Stallions (Vivd Man)
Iron Will (Mustang) 1999
Is Your Big Brother Home? (Titan) 1995
Island Fever 1989
Island Guardian (Titan) 1996
Island Heat (Vivid) 1989
Island of Passion
ISO: Heavy Metal Fantasy (Altomar) 1995
It Happened One Day (Forum Studios) 1995
It Starts With A Knockout (non-sex) docu.
It's a Gang, Video Series 1&2 (Planet) 1992
It's Good to be Bad (Associated Video)
Its Raining Men (Studio 2000) 1997
It's So Good It's F...... Bad (Intl. Studios)
It's the Size that Counts (Bacchus) 1997
Ivy Blues (Catalina)
Ivy League, The (Jim Steel) 1992

J

J. Brian's Flashback (Bijou Video) 1981
J.D. Slater, Top to Bottom (LA Video) 1988
J.D. Slater's Confessions (LA Video) 1989
J.D. Slater's S.M.U.T. (Live Video) 1994
J.S. Big Time (J.S.Grand) 1995
Jac Attack (Michael Goodwin) 1992
Jack City (HIS) 1992
Jack it Up (InHand Video) 1989
Jack Off Giants 1985
Jackaroos (Kristen Bjorn) 1991
Jackhammer (Vivid Video) 1994
Jackpot: On the Road to Vegas (HIS) 1995
Jacks
Jacks are Better (YMAC) 1979
Jacks Are Wild (LeSalon Video) 1986
Jail Mates (HIS Video)
Jail Punk (Graphic Art Prod.) 1999
Jamie Hendrix's Interviews 1
(Inferno Films) 1999
Jamie Loves Jeff 1&2 (Jeff Stryker) 1987
Jammed Packed (Bentley Films)
Jarhead (All Worlds) 1998
Jarheads for Sale

Jawbreaker (Catalina) 1995
Jeff Stryker: A Romance Video for Women
Jeff Stryker's Big Time (Stryker Prod.)
Jeff Stryker's Favorite Sexual Positions
Jeff Stryker's Underground (HIS) 1997
Jensen Sensation, The
Jet Set Sex (Planet Group) 1992
Jet Stream (Academy Video)
Jiggy This (Totally Tight) 1999
Job Site (HIS Video) 1984
Jock City (Vizuns Video) 1993
Jock Empire (LeSalon Video) 1984
Jock Off [solo] 1995
Jockaholics (Sierra Pacific) 1993
Jockathon
Jocks (Catalina)
Jock's Dream, A (Thrust Studios) 1997
Jocks Tale, A (Image) 1995
Jockstrap (Vivid) 1998
Jockstrap Wrestling 16-21 (BG) 1991-94
Jockstrapped (Jocks) 1996
Joe Briefs (Compilation - John Summers) 1988
Joe's Big Adventure (Jaguar) 1999
Joey (Planet Group) 1992
Johan's Big Chance (Bel Ami) 1998
John Summers Screentest Magazine #1
Johnny Come Home (Brush Creek)
Johnny Harden and The Champs
(Falcon Video Pac 2) 1974
Johnny Hormone (HIS) 1998
Joker's Wild (Vivid Video)
Journal, The (Bacchus Releasing) 1999
Journey (Vivid) 1996
Journey to Italy (Men of Odyssey) 1998
Joys Of Self Abuse
Juice (Mark V Marketing)
Juice Bomb (Catalina) 1993
Juice in the Hood (Nubian/Video 10)
Jump On It (Wanted Video) 1995
Jumper (HIS) 1991
Jumping Jacks (Hot House/Plain Wrapped)
Jungle Heat (Kristen Bjorn) 1993
Junior Cadets (Magnum)
Junior Crew (Planet) 1991
Junior Varsity 2
Junk Yard Dog (Marina Pacific)
Just Between Us, You Promise (Associated)
Just Blondes (Natural Wonders) 1999
Just Can't Stop (Falcon) 1993
Just Do It (Jeremy Wynn)
Just Guys (New Age) 1997
Just In (Oh Man!) 1997

Just in Time (Rosebud) 1993
Just Men (Gino Colbert Pro./New Age) 1996
Just One Favor (Forum Studios) 1995
Just Say Yes (Avalon) 1992
Just You and I (All Worlds) 1998
Just You & Me 1&2 (Rebel/Stallion) 1992

K

Kansas City Trucking Corp. (HIS) 1970s
Karen's Bi-Line (Soho) 1989
Keep in Touch (Planet Group) 1991
Keep The Tip (Thrust) 1995
Keeping Time (Mustang Video Pac 14) 1993
Kept After School (Nova/LA Video)
Kept: A Way of Life (Thrust Studios) 1997
Kevin Goes Wild (InHand Video)
Key West Bellhop (Close-Up) 1992
Key West Voyeur (Bob Jones Video)
Keyhole (Rockland Prod.) 1999
Kickboxer, The (All Worlds)
Kickboxing (Paul Norman) 1991
Kid Brother
Killer Looks (U. S. Male) 1998
Killing Me Softly (PM Prods.)
King of the Mountain (Catalina) 1992
King Size: The Best of J.W. King (HIS)
Kink (Leisure Time)
Kink (Stallion Video)
Kinky Leather Lads (Stallion)
Kinky Stuff (Surge Studio) 1992
Kip Noll & the Westside Boys (Catalina) 1980
Kip Noll: Superstar (William Higgins Video) 1984
Kip Noll's Casting Couch 1983
Kiss Off (All Worlds) 1992
Kiss Today Goodbye (PM Productions)
Knight Gallery 1 & 2 (Vivid Man)
Knight Heat (HIS) 1994
Knight Men #3: Thick & Throbbing (Leisure Time)
Knight Moves (Vivid) 1991
Knight Out With the Boys (Abandon) 1992
Knights in Eden
Knights of Thunder (Barbar Video)
Knockout (Vivid) 1990
K-Waikiki (Video 10/ Sex Video) 1998

L

L.A. Boiling Point (LeSalon Video) 1985
L.A. Boot Bottom
L.A. Boys (Catalina)
L.A. Daze (XTC Studios) 1998

L.A. Plays Itself (HIS) 1972
L.A. Sex Stories (Associates) 1991
L.A. Tool & Die (HIS Video) 1981
L.A. Underground (Planet Group) 1992
L.A.P.D. (Real Video)
Laguna Adventure (Avalon Video)
Laguna Beach Lifeguards (Brick House) 1997
Laguna Summer (Panther Prod.)
Laid For Work (Brush Creek) 1997
Laid Off (Adam & Co.)
Laid To Order (HIS) 1994
Lambda Lambda Lambda 1& 2
    (Hollywood Sales) 1998
Lana Exposed (V-Team Video)
Lap It Up (Blade Prod) 1999
Larger Than Life (HIS)
Las Vegas Love Gods (Conquest) 1991
Las Vegas Orgy (LeSalon Video)
Last Surfer, The (Bijou Video)
Last Taboo, The (Studio 2000) 1996
Late Night Porn (Stable Ent./IMD) 1999
Latex Meltdown (Can-Am/Masta) 1995
Latin Balls 2: Huevos (Stylus Man Video) 1999
Latin Bandit (Planet Group) 1993
Latin Cops (Iron Horse) 1999
Latin Encounters (Planet Group) 1993
Latin Escorts (Video Resource Group)
Latin Gallery (Planet) 1993
Latin Hustle (Planet Group) 1993
Latin Instinct (Planet Group) 1992
Latin Jack-Off (Filmco)
Latin Knockout
Latin Leather 1-3 (Planet Group) 1999-94
Latin Lovers (Wyngate & Bevins)
Latin Lust 2 (Pleasure Prod.) 1998
Latin Magic (Planet Group) 1993
Latin Men (Bijou Video)
Latin Obsession (New Age) 1997
Latin Power (Filmco)
Latin Screen Test Part 2 (L.A. Brown) 1999
Latin Sex Thing (Sex Video) 1998
Latin Showboyz (Latino Fan Club) 1998
Latin Squad (Bacchus Releasing) 1998
Latin Stories (Bacchus) 1997
Latin Submission (Planet) 1993
Latin Tongues (Campus) 1993
Latin X (Planet) 1993
Latino Dreaming
Latino Nights: Noches Latinas (Barbar)
Latino Playmates (Bacchus) 1996
Latino Posse (Bacchus) 1997
Latino Power (Filmco)

Long Play (Triple X Prod.)	1995	(U.S. Male)	1998
Long Shots (Planet Group)	1993	Lusty Lovers (Barbar Video)	
Long, Hot Summer, The (Vivid)	1990		
Longhorn Cowboys (LeSalon Video)		M	
Look of a Man (Mustang)	1994		
Look Of Leather (Leather Ent.)	1996	M.A.G.I.C. (Black Forest)	1987
Look, The (Catalina)	1989	Macho Money (Vizuns Video)	1993
Looking For It (Planet Group)	1994	Mack Pack 1-5	
Looking for Mr. Big (Image)	1993	Mad Masseur, The (Planet Group)	1992
Looking For Mr. Goodhead		Made for You (Falcon Video Pac 63)	1988
(Planet Group)	1992	Made in the Shade 1&2 (Ebony Vid. Intl.)	1999
Looking Good (LeSalon Video)		Made To Get Laid (Forum Studios)	1993
Lords of Leather (Stallion)	1993	Made To Order (Nova/LA Video)	
Los Hombres (Catalina)	1991	Made to Order (Brush Creek)	1999
Lost in Las Vegas (All Worlds Video)	1996	Madness & Method (Abandon)	1992
Lost Loves (Close-Up Productions)	1996	Magic Bed (Man's Best Video)	1995
Love Money (Catalina Video)		Magic Hands 9 (BG Prod.)	1996
Love Muscle (Rosebud)	1992	Magic of Power	
Love of Lust (Adam and Co.)	1992	Magnified (All Worlds)	1994
Love Story, A (Forum Studios)	1997	Magnum Griffin 1-13	
Love Thy Neighbor (Black Forest)		Main Attraction, The (Catalina)	1989
Lovers & Friends		Main Event, The	
Lovers (Live)	1992	Majestic Knight (P.Norman)	1991
Lovers Coming Home (Planet)	1990	Major Meat (Leisure Time)	1997
Lovers Lane (XTC Studios)	1997	Major Owens (Bijou)	1994
Lovers, Cheaters and Maneaters (Barbar)		Make A Wish And Blow (Scorpion)	1989
Lovers, Tricks & One Night Stands		Make it Count (Galaxy)	1998
(Catalina)	1994	Make It Hard (Hard Hunks Collection)	1992
Loving Butch		Make It Hard (PM Prod.)	1985
Low Blows (HIS Video)		Make Mine Black (Barbar Video)	1991
Low Rent		Making it Big (Bijou Video)	1987
Low Riders (Catalina)	1999	Making it Huge (Falcon)	1986
Lowe Down (All Worlds)	1994	Making it Huge (Marathon Films)	1985
Lube Job (All Worlds)	1996	Making of "Knight Out with the Boys", The	1992
Luck of the Draw (Planet Group)	1992	Making Of A Gay Video, The (Forum)	1994
Lucky Lukas (Bel Ami)	1999	Making the Team	
Lucky Stiff (Vivid Man)	1997	Male Box (Catalina)	1999
Lucky Strokes (Fox Studios)		Male Call (Celestial Ent.)	1998
Lukas' Story 1-3 (Bel Ami)	1994-96	Male Instinct (Mustang Video Pac 15)	1993
Lunch Hour 1 (Catalina)	1990	Male Marathon (U.S Male/In-X-Cess)	1997
Lunch Hour 2 (Catalina)	1994	Male Order Sex (Metro Home Video)	
Lure, The		Male Power	
Lust (Planet)	1990	Male Seduction (Stallion)	1992
Lust Boys, The (Sierra Pacific)	1990	Male Stampede (Bijou Video)	
Lust Horizons		Male Taboo (HIS)	1991
Lust in the Hay		Male Tales, DVD (HIS Interactive)	
Lust Letters (Close Up Prod.)		Male Triangle, The (HIS)	1995
Lust Shack (Blade Pro.)	1997	Male-O-Gram (LeSalon Video)	
Lust, Sex & The Covermodel (Bijou)	1993	Malibu Beach Hunks (BIG Video)	1997
Lustful Paradise (Avalon)	1992	Malibu Days, Big Bear Nights	
Lusty Leatherman (U.S. Male)	1998	Malibu Pool Boys (Catalina)	1992
Lusty Leathermen: Mechanic on Booty		Mall Cruisin X-L (Rodeo)	1998

Memories of Eighteen (Avalon)
Memories Of Summer (Vivid) 1992
Men & Film
Men 4 Men On The Net (Forum Studios) 1997
Men and Steel (Spike Video)
Men at Magnum
Men at Work (Cinderfella) 1990
Men Behind Bars (Satellite Video)
Men Between Themselves (PM Prod.)
Men Come First (PM Productions)
Men For All Seasons (All Worlds) 1992
Men From Ipanema, The (Marcostudio) 1998
Men Grip Tighter (PM Productions)
Men in Blue (New Age) 1998
Men in Love (Planet Group) 1992
Men in Motion 1-7
Men In Uniform (Rebel Video)
Men Matter Most (Galaxy Pictures) 1995
Men of 550, The
Men of Action 1 & 2 (LeSalon) 1989
Men of Dream Canyon, The (All Worlds)
Men of Forum 1& 2 (Forum) 1993
Men of Lake Michigan (Catalina Video) 1995
Men of Magnum (U.S. Male) 1998
Men of Rio (Bacchus Releasing) 1998
Men of Size (Size Video) 1991
Men of South Beach, The (Bijou) 1995
Men of Steel
Men of the Midway (LeSalon Video)
Men of the Moment (Planet Group) 1993
Men of Tough Guys, The
Men on A Budget (Planet Group) 1993
Men on Call (Another Video Co.)
Men on Site (Adam & Co.) 1994
Men on the Loose (LA Video)
Men Only (Jocks) 1999
Men Together (Video 10/ Tenderloin) 1995
Men Under Siege (Jet Set Pro.)
Men Under The Hardhat (W. Higgins Video)
Men Who Dare (Bijou Video)
Men Who Work it Alone
Men Will Play (Video Resource Group)
Men With Big Toys (Planet Group) 1992
Men With Tools 1-4 (Forum) 1994
Men: Skin & Steel (Altomar) 1990
Men's Room (Vivid Video)
Mentor (Vivid) 1994
Men-TV (Vivid) 1989
Mercury Rising (Falcon) 1997
Mesmerized (Rage Collection)
Mess Hall Maneuvers (Tyger Films) 1995
Method & Madness

Michael's Leather Dream
Midnight Hard-On (Planet Group) 1993
Midnight Riders (Scorpion Studios) 1989
Midnight Run (Falcon) 1994
Midnight Special 1-6
Midnight Sun (Mustang Video Pac 12) 1992
Mikey Likes It (Vidco Video)
Miles of Niles
Military Bound (Hot House) 1997
Military Gang-Bang 1998
Military Issue 1-3 (Forum) 1994
Military Men (Catalina)
Military Muscle (Academy Studios)
Military Secrets (Close-Up) 1994
Military Sex Acts 1-3 (Body Shoppe) 1998
Military Sex Initiation (Bob Jones)
Military Sex Pass
Militia Men (Wanted Video) 1995
Military Issue 3: Ask & I'll Tell (Forum) 1996
Millennium Man (L'Experience Inedite)
   (YMAC) 1999
Mind Blower (Planet Group) 1993
Mind Games (LeSalon Video)
Mindscape (Vivid) 1992
Mindscape 2 (Vivid Video)
Mindscape 2: The Final Chapter (Vivid) 1992
Mine's Bigger Than Yours (All Worlds) 1992
Minute Man 1-4
Mi Pinga Loca (LA Brown Prod.) 1999
Mirage (Jocks) 1993
Mirage (Totally Tight Video) 1997
Mirage—From the XXX Files (Totally Tight)
Mirror, Mirror
Mission Accomplished
   (Falcon Video Pac 70) 1990
Missionary Position (Hollywood Sales)
Mix It Up: Black Passions/White Dreams
   (HIS) 1994
Mix N' Match (Las Vegas Video) 1989
Mo' Betta' Butt (HH/Plain Wrapped) 1997
Mo' Better Dudes (Planet Group) 1991
Mo' Bigga Butt (HHPlain Wrapped) 1997
Mob Connection, The
Mocha Madness (Adam & Co.) 1988
Model Behavior (Catalina) 1993
Modern Men, Modern Toys (Marksman)
Moment of Truth (Planet Group) 1993
Moments With Johan (Pride Video) 1997
Monsters and Size Queens
   (Pacific Sun Ent.) 1999
Montage (All Worlds Video)
Montreal Men (Kristen Bjorn) 1993

Raw Discipline
   (Projex Video/Close-up Prod.)   1997
Raw Footage (Adam & Co.)   1989
Raw Impulse (Bijou)   1992
Raw Material (Hot House)   1996
Raw Meat 1-5 (Macho Man/Reelwood)   1998-99
Raw Recruits (Centaur Films)   1997
Raw Rimmers (Compilation) (HIS Video)
Raw Shots (Treasure Island Media)   1998
Raw Stock (HIS)   1994
Raw Street Meat, Midnight Man Video
Rawhide (Bijou)   1981
Rawhide (Studio 2000)   1994
Rawhide Roundup! (Buckshot)
Rawshock (Bad Brad)   1995
Razor Close (Planet)   1992
Razor's Edge (All Worlds Video)
Read Bi All (All Worlds)   1998
Read My Lips (InHand)   1992
Ready for It (Studio 2000)   1994
Ready to Serve (Grapik Arts)   1998
Real Cocksuckers (Brick House)
Real Cowboys
Real Men of the New West (Altomar)   1991
Rear Admiral (Marathon)
Rear Deliveries (William Higgins Video)
Rear Delivery (BIC)   1997
Rear End Alignment (Club Inferno)   1997
Rear End Window (HIS)   1992
Rear Ended (Close Up)   1993
Rear Ended (Hot House/Bullwhip)   1995
Rear View (Planet)   1993
Rearin' to Go (Vivid 4-Hour Video)
Rebel (LeSalon/Canyon)   1980s
Rebel Biker (Wildcat Pro.)
Receiving End (Mustang)   1995
Reckless (Planet)   1992
Recruit Me (Bijou Video)
Recruiter, The (All Worlds Video)
Red Alert (Falcon)   1998
Red Ball Express (PM Prods.)
Red Blooded Americans
   (USMale/In-Xcess)   1999
Red Hanky Left (PM Prods.)
Red, Hot & Safe (No Egos Prod.)   1999
Red Hot Redheads (Intl. Studio)   1991
Red, White & Blue (New Age)   1997
Red, White and Red
Red, White and You (Bijou)
Redwood: Escape from Fern Falls (Titan) 1999
Redwood Ranger (Jocks Video Pac 56)   1993
Reflections 1 & 2 (All Worlds)   1994

Reflections in Black (All Worlds)
Reflections in the Wild (All Worlds)
Reflections of Sex (Metro Home Video)   1994
Reflections of Youth (Bijou Video)
Reform School Confidential (All Worlds) 1997
Refried Dreams (Planet)   1996
Relatively Speaking (Studio 2000)
Release Yourself (Planet)   1992
Relentless (Galaxy Pictures)   1998
Remembering Times Gone Bi (All Worlds)
Rendezvous At The Golden Gate Bed
   and Breakfast (10 Percent)
Renegade, The (Falcon)   1995
Ren's Den 1-6 (BG Video)
Rent A Fantasy (All Worlds)
Rent To Bone (Video 10)   1998
Rescue 69-11 (Vivid)   1996
Return of Grant Fagin, The (Vivid)   1991
Return to Badlands (Planet)   1993
Return to Camp YMAC (YMAC/Avalon)   1999
Return to Sunsex Blvd. (Catalina)   1999
Reunion (SteamWorx)   1997
Reveille (Jet Set)   1995
Revenge Of The Bi-Dolls (Catalina)   1994
Revenge of the Nighthawk (HIS Video)
Revenge: More Than I Can Take (Falcon)   1990
Rex Take One (Catalina Video)   1991
Rhythm: Men in Motion (Another Vid Co.)
Ride the Swell (InHand)   1988
Right Before Your Eyes (Planet)   1991
Right Hand Man (Catalina)   1995
Right Here, Right Now (Planet)   1992
Rigid Video, Vol.1 (Rigid)   1991
Rim City (T&T)   1998
Rimming Slaves (Bob Jones)   1994
Rimshot (Jocks Video Pac 45)   1991
Ring of Fire
Ring, The (Wolff Prods.)   1997
Rings (Vivid Video)   1990
Rip and Strip (BG Video)
Rip Colt's Sex-Rated Home Movies
Rip 'n' Strip Wrestling (Close-Up Prod.)
Ripe for Harvest (Falcon)   1995
Ripped (Pleasure Prod.)   1992
Riptide! (Studio 2000)   1996
Rise And Shine (Planet)   1994
Rise, The (Catalina)   1990
Rising Desire
Risky Sex (Odyssey Men)   1994
Rites of Fall, The (Vivid)   1989
Rites of Manhood (Catalina)   1990
Rites of Spring, The (Vivid)   1989

Sizing Up
Sizzle (Scorpion Studios) 1989
Sizzlin' Studs
Sizzling Joe Simmons
Skateboard Sliders (Tribal Pulse) 1999
Ski Tight (Mustang Video Pac 23) 1995
Skin Deep (Catalina)
Skin Flix (HIS Video)
Skin Tight (Falcon) 1993
Skin Tight (Mustang) 1993
Skin Torpedos (Fox Studios)
Skinner Jacks
Skinny Dippers (Winner's Media) 1996
Skinny Dipping (Locker Room) 1999
Skuff (Hot House) 1999
Slam Bam Thank You Man (Squire) 1994
Slam Dunk (Vivid) 1990
Slammers (Planet) 1991
Slave Auction (Palomino) 1994
Slave Brothel (All Worlds)
Slave Camp 1 & 2
Slave Toy (Projex Video) 1999
Slave Trade
Slave Trainer (Bob Jones) 1992
Slave Workshop Boston (Close Up) 1993
Slave Worship L.A. (Luke Bender)
Slaves
Slaves for Sale (Wings Video) 1984
Sleaze (HIS Video) 1982
Sleazy Gang Bang (Oh Man!) 1998
Sleazy Motel Gang Bang (Gangbang)
Sleeping Booty and Other Tails
    (Sex Video/Video 10) 1997
Sleepless In L.A. (Winner's Media) 1994
Sleepless in San Francisco
Slick (Catalina)
Slick Willies (Planet) 1992
Sliders (Tribal Pulse) 1999
Slip It In (Primo Video) 1995
Slippery When Wet (Campus Video) 1993
Slumming (Kosmos) 1989
Slurp
Slut, The (Planet) 1992
Slutty '60s (Locker Room Prod.) 1999
Smell of A Man (Jet Set) 1997
Smells Like A Man (Planet) 1992
Smoke Screen (Mustang Video Pac 24) 1995
Smokin' Butts
Smoking in the Boys Room (Vivid Video)
Smoky (HIS) 1993
Smooth Moves 1 & 2 (First Class Male)
Smooth Operator (Metro) 1996

Smooth Strokes (Video Res. Group)
Snafu (Vivid Man) 1998
Snowballin'
Snowbound (Vivid) 1990
Snowbound In Manhattan
Snowbumz
So Fine (West Hollywood Sales) 1997
Soaked (Jocks) 1998
Soap Studs (LeSalon Video)
Social Studies (HIS Video)
Sodom (Vivid Man) 1999
Soldiers (InHand Video)
Solicitor (Vivid) 1994
Solid Flesh (Vivid) 1993
Solitaire [solo] 1988
Solitary Sin (Eagle) 1989
Solo Flights [solo] 1988
Solo Guys [solo] 1985
Solo Satisfaction (LeSalon) 1994
Solo Studs [solo] 1989
So-Low
Some Body Is Watching (Studio 2000) 1993
Some Men Are Bigger Than Others
    (Tiger Media)
Someone in Mind (Vivid) 1992
Someone to Watch (Vizuns Video)
Something About Larry (Hollywood Sales) 1999
Something Very Big This Way Comes
    (Odyssey) 1998
Something Wild (Nova/LA Video)
Something's Up
Songs in the Key of Sex (HIS) 1992
Sons of Satan (Maverick)
Soul and Salsa 1 & 2 (Adam and Co.) 1988
Soul Dad
Soul Patrol, The (Totally Tight)
South African Son (Cream of the Crop) 1999
South Bay Boys
South Beach Buns
South Beach Heat (Tribal Pulse) 1998
South Beach Summer (Renegade) 1998
South Beach Vibrations (Jet Set Prod.) 1997
South of Market Leather (Video 10) 1996
South of the Border (All Worlds) 1998
Southern Comforts (Vidco) 1986
Souvenirs (Bel Ami) 1997
Spanish Fantasy (Ikarus Ent.) 1999
Spanish Lessons (Latino Fan Club) 1997
Spank Me Paddle Me (Close-Up) 1993
Spank Me, Man! (Close-Up) 1998
Spank Your Buddy
Spanked (BG Wrestling)

Straight Construction Site (Bob Jones)
Straight Dudes (Intl. Studio) 1991
Straight Exposure (Oh! Man Studios) 1998
Straight Men: Caught on Tape
(Brick House) 1997
Straight Pick-up 1-3 (Bob Jones) 1992
Straight Shooters
Straight Studs (Associates) 1991
Straight Studs 2 (Planet) 1992
Straight Talk (Jett Blakk Prod) 1998
Straight to Bed (Catalina) 1990
Straight to the Zone (Zone Films) 1992
Straight Up (Suzy's Secrets) 1992
Straight White Male (All Worlds) 1998
Strait Jacket (Grapik Arts) 1997
Stranded: Enemies and Lovers (Catalina)
Strange Places and Strange Things (Surge)
Streaks (InHand) 1989
Street Boyz (Catalina)
Street Fair Meat (Brush Creek Media)
Street Kids (Rage) 1983
Street Smart (Cadinot/Studio 2000) 1988
Street Smarts: Sex Ed 5 (Studio 2000) 1996
Street Trash (International Studios) 1990
Streets of LA
Strictly Confidential [solo] 1990
Strictly for Ladies Only (W. Higgins) 1983
Strictly Forbidden (Bijou Video) 1984
Strike Back 1990
Strike Line (Planet) 1992
Strip Search (Video Resource Group)
Strip Tease (Vizuns Video) 1993
Stripped Down (Planet) 1994
Stripped, Whipped and Washed
(Bob Jones) 1993
Stripped: Code of Conduct 1 (Falcon)
Stripper Service (HIS) 1994
Stroke It (Planet) 1993
Stroke My Digits (Paradox) 1999
Stroke 'N Men
Stroke, The (Soho) 1990
Stroke: Foreskin Fantasy
Strokers (Vivid) 1987
Strokes (EX Rider Video)
Stroking It, Uncut 1 (Junior) 1994
Strong Man Scent (Planet) 1993
Stryker Force (Matt Sterling) 1987
Stryker's Underground (Stryker Prod.) 1998
Stryker's Best Powerful Sex 1992
Strykin' it Deep
Stud Busters (LA Video) 1985
Stud Fee (Catalina) 1997

Stud Force (Vivid Video) 1987
Stud Fuckers (Comp Tape) (Rawhide) 1990
Stud House (Squire) 1994
Stud Hunters 1 & 2 (VCA Video) 1984
Stud Ranch (HIS Video) 1993
Stud Search (Adam and Co.) 1990
Stud Sensors (Avalon Video)
Stud Show (Stroke Video)
Stud Squad (Filmco) 1991
Stud Struck (LeSalon Video) 1986
Stud Valley (Odyssey) 1994
Stud Vision (LeSalon Video) 1989
Stud Wanted (Planet) 1994
Student Bodies (Magnum Griffin Video) 1984
Student Bodies Too (LeSalon) 1988
Studio Tricks (Catalina)
Studio X (LeSalon Video) 1986
Studmania (Midnight Men Video) 1993
Studs in Uniform (Erotic Men) 1997
Studz (Planet) 1993
Stuffed (Saytr) 1999
Styker Force
Style (Falcon Video Pac 24) 1978
Subway Named Desire (PM Productions) 1994
Suck (Lee Baldwin Ent.)
Suck Daddy (All Worlds Video) 1998
Sucker (Sex Video) 1996
Suckulent (Bijou Video)
Sud Busters
Sud Squad
Sudden Urge (Jet Set Productions)
Sugar Britches (Planet) 1990
Sum Young Mahn
Summer Blazes (Studio 2000) 1995
Summer Buddies (Falcon Video Pac 83) 1993
Summer Daze (HIS Video) 1994
Summer Fantasy (MT Productions) 1982
Summer Fever (Falcon) 1993
Summer Heat (InHand Video) 1986
Summer Knights
Summer Licks (T&T) 1995
Summer Love (Blue Men)
Summer Money (Surfside Studios) 1995
Summer Obsession (Sex Video) 1996
Summer of '44 (Catalina) 1997
Summer of Derek Thomas (BIG)
Summer of Scott Noll, The (Studio TCS) 1981
Summer of Scott Randsome (Catalina) 1994
Summer Reunion (Jocks) 1998
Summer Reunion
(10%/Greenwood Cooper) 1999
Summer School (InHand) 1990

Summer Seduction (YMAC)
Summer, The First Time (Pride) — 1995
Summer's Tall Tales (Marina Pacific) — 1994
Summertime Blues (Vivid) — 1991
Summoner, The (Lucas Kazan Prod.) — 1999
Sun Devils (Always New Video)
Sun Kissed (All Worlds Video) — 1986
Sunday Brunch (HIS) — 1991
Sunsex Boulevard-Gino Colbert's (HIS) — 1994
Sunshine After The Rain (Pride) — 1996
Sunshine Natural Response
(Galaxy Pictures) — 1996
Sunshine Supermen (Bijou) — 1995
Sunstroke (HIS Video) — 1986
Super Hunks (Vivid) — 1988
Super Hunks 2 (Vivid) — 1989
Super Jocks (Falcon)
Super Sex Hour/Raunch-O-Rama (Leisure Time)
Super shots 6P Take Me Home (Mustang)
Super Size It 1 & 2 (Hollywood Sales) — 1998
Super Stud Fever — 1993
Superman 87 — 1987
Supermodels of Advocate Men
(Lib. Publ.) — 1994
Superstars — 1982
Superstud Fever (Conquest)
Sure Shot (Hot House/Vision A) — 1994
Sure Thing (Hot House) — 1997
Surf, Sand and Sex
Surfer Blue
Surfer Guys (InHand Video) — 1989
Surf's Up (Oceans Prods.) — 1987
Surge Men are Very Receptive (Surge) — 1989
Surge Men at Their Best (Surge) — 1990
Surrogate Stud (Vizuns/Planet Group) — 1994
Swallow (Catalina) — 1996
Swallowers, The (Mack) — 1992
Swank (Studio 2000)
Swap Meat (LeSalon Video) — 1989
Sweat & Wet (Private Edition)
Sweat Motel (Planet) — 1993
Sweatin' Black (Vivid) — 1997
Sweet Bi & Bi (Bi Chance Video) — 1999
Sweet in the Bootie (Street Times Video) — 1990
Sweet Meat (LeSalon Video) — 1990
Swell (Titan) — 1998
Swim Meat 1 & 2 (1st Class Male Video)
Swimming Pool Orgy (Locker Room) — 1999
Swing Set
Swing Shift (Pleasure Prod.) — 1989
Switchcraft (Catalina) — 1999
Switch Hitters 1-10 (Intropics/Metro) — 1987-91

Switch is On, The (Catalina) — 1988
Switch Video 1 & 2 [bi] — 1988
Switchcraft (Catalina) — 1999
SWM (All Worlds Video) — 1998

T

Tail End of Summer (All Worlds)
Tailgate Party 2 (Vivid Video)
Tailspin (Studio 2000) — 1997
Tainted Love (Catalina) — 1995
Take A Peek (All Worlds)
Take Down (Studio 2000) — 1992
Take It Deep (BIG) — 1995
Take It Like a Man (HIS) — 1994
Take Me Home (Mustang Video Pac 9) — 1992
Take One-Guys Like Us (Hot House) — 1996
Taken 2 the Max (Campus Studios)
Taken and Shaved (Grapik Art Prod.) — 1995
Taken by Storm (Associated Video)
Taken Down Under
(Jocks Studios JVP 95) — 1999
Taken to the Max (Campus) — 1993
Takin' Care of Mike (YMAC)
Takin' it to the Jury
Taking of Jake, The (Falcon)
Taking the Dive (Planet) — 1991
Taking The Plunge (Man Splash Video) — 1995
Tale of Five Brothers, A (Ebony Vid. Intl.) — 1999
Tale of Two Brothers, A (All Worlds) — 1996
Tales From the Backlot (All Worlds) — 1994
Tales From the Backlot 2 (All Worlds) — 1997
Tales From the Foxhole (All Worlds) — 1999
Tales to Keep You Up
Talk Dirty To Me (All Worlds)
Tall Tale (Mustang) — 1998
Tall Timber (LeSalon Video)
Tank Tops (Hollywood Sales) — 1997
Taste of Leather 2 (Catalina) — 1994
Taste of Leather, A (Catalina) — 1994
Tasting Mr. Goodbar (Stallion Video)
Tattoo Love Boy, The
Tattoo Parlor (Planet) — 1994
Taurus 48 (Taurus) — 1998
Taxi (InHand Video) — 1988
Taxi Tales (All Worlds Video) — 1995
Teacher Sucks (All Worlds)
Team Mates (InHand) — 1989
Tease, The (Stryker Prod.) — 1994
Tease, The (Blue Men/Sunshine) — 1997
Tease Me (Planet) — 1992
Tease (Blue Men)

Tomorrow Will Come (Forum)	1997	Track Meat (Bijou Video)	1976
Tongue Dancing (LeSalon Video)		Trade (Malibu Sales)	1995
Tongue in Cheek (Planet)	1993	Trade Off (All Worlds)	1991
Tony's Big Brother		Trade Off (Locker Room Prods.)	1999
(Mustang Video Pac 25)	1995	Trade Winds (Matt Sterling/Huge Video)	1996
Tony's Initiation (LeSalon Video)		Trading Up (Vivid Video)	
Tony's Thing (Video 10)	1993	Traffic School (Intl. Studio)	1991
Too Big For His Britches (Tyger)	1988	Trail Blazers (YMAC)	
Too Big to Handle (Hot House/Primo)		Trail Tales (Associated Video)	
Too Damn Big! (Catalina)	1994	Training Sessions (Planet)	1992
Too Hard To Handle (Ramrod Video)		Tramps	
Too Hard To Hold (Vivid)	1989	Trans Europe Express	
Too Many Tops (Hollywood Sales)	1998	Transitory States	
Tool Box (BIG)	1997	Transparent (Vizuns Video)	
Tool Kit (Mack)	1992	Trash, Vol. 4: Huge Meat	
Tools Of The Trade (Totally Tight Video)	1995	Trash, Vol. 8: Uncut Cocks	
Top Brass		Travelin' Wild (Mintoaur 2000)	1995
Top it Off (Video 10)	1997	Travels with Macdaddy 1 (Bacchus)	1997
Top Man (Catalina)		Treasure Load (Island Caprice)	1994
Top Man Security (Planet)	1993	Tree Swallow (Vivid Video)	
Top Men (Scorpion Ent./Video 10)	1995	Trick Stop (Vizuns Video)	
Top This (Tenderloin)	1996	Trick Time (HIS Video)	
Top To Bottom (Explosive Studios)	1994	Tricked (Planet)	1993
Tormentor's Conquest (Close-Up)	1998	Tricking (Nova Fortuna)	
Torture Alley (Bob Jones)	1994	Trickmaster (Video/Planet Group)	1994
Total Corruption (HIS)	1993	Trilogy (Scorpion Studios)	1989
Total Corruption 2: One Night in Jail (HIS)	1996	Trip to Paradise Beach, A (Vivid)	1990
Total Deception (Thrust)	1995	Triple Play (Vivid Video)	
Total Impact (Bijou)	1992	Triple Treat (Buckshot)	
Totally Awesome (LA Video)		Trisexual (PM Prod.)	1983
Totally Dominated (Wolff Prods.)		Trisexual Encounters 1-6	
Totally Exposed (Planet)	1993	Trixxx of the Trade (Bacchus Releasing)	1998
Totally Uncut		Trophies 1-3 (Marina Pacific)	1994
Touch Me There (Video 10)	1998	Tropical Heatwave (Marksman)	1988
Touch Me, It's Hot, It's Tender		Trouble Shooters	
(Falcon VidPac 60)	1988	Trouser Trout (Sierra Pacific)	1992
Touch of Class		Troy Likes It (Bentley Films)	
Tough & Tender (Palladin Video)		Troy Saxon Gallery, Vol.1, The	
Tough Choices (Planet)	1991	Trucker Daddies	1998
Tough Competition (Hot Video)	1984	Trucker's Pig Stop (Bob Jones)	1994
Tough Guys (PM Productions)	1994	Trucker's Sex Dog (Bob Jones)	1993
Tough Guys Do Dance (Bijou Video)		True (Vivid)	1992
Tough Iron (Spike Video)		True Confessions (Vivid)	1989
Tough Studs (LeSalon Video)		True Confessions Uncut Club #1,2,5, (Rage)	
Tough Stuff		True Stories (Hot House/Bullship)	1994
Tough Terrain (Jocks Video Pac 54)	1993	Truth or Fantasy (Altomar)	
Tour de Trans		Truth, Dare or Damien (Vivid)	1991
Tourist Trade (Titan)	1997	Truths and Dares (LeSalon)	1995
Toweling Off (Avalon)	1988	Try Again (All Worlds)	1996
Toy Boys (Bijou Video)		Try Anything Once (InHand Video)	1987
Toys Bi Us		Try to Take It (FalconPak 51)	1986
Toys for Big Boys		Trying it On for Size (Studio 2000)	

Tub Studs (Marlowe Dist.)	1985	Underboss, The (U.S. Male)	1998
Tub Tricks (Nova/LA Video)	1982	Undercover (Catalina)	1989
Tube Steak (Planet)	1992	Undergear (Sierra Pacific)	1990
Tuesday Morning Workout (Bijou Video)	1975	Underground (HIS Video)	
Turbo Charge (Al Parker Prod.)	1987	Underground Homo Hardcore	
Turn of Events (Mandatory Pics.)	1999	(Real to Reel)	1990
Turned On (LeSalon Video)	1982	Underground Sex Club (Bacchus)	1998
Turning Tricks (Boiling Point Prod.)		Under Where? (Surfside Studios)	1999
Tutor Me (Surfside Studios)	1995	Undress for Success	1998
Twelve at Noon (Marathon)	1976	Unexpected Persuasion	
Twelve Thirty West Melrose (Catalina)	1992	(Galaxy Pictures)	1996
Twic Pecs (All Worlds Video)	1991	Uniform Ball 1 & 2 (Vivid)	1998
Twice the Fun		Uniform Code-Sex Ed #4 (Studio 2000)	
Twin Exposure (Pleasure Prod.)	1994	Uniforms Only (Blade Productions)	1998
Twin Pecs (Planet)	1991	Uninvited Images (Vivid)	
Twincest		Uninvited, The (Vivid Man)	1999
Twins (Odyssey)	1998	Unique Gay Positions (Leisure Time)	
Two by Ten (Steve Scott)	1985	Unlawful (Fox)	1996
Two Handfuls (Associates)	1986	Unleashed Action (Close Up)	
Two Handfuls 2 (Jocks)	1989	Unloading It (Hard Hunks Collection)	
Two Hard Up (Planet)	1993	Untamed (Leisure Time)	1990
Ty Me Up (Catalina)	1994	Untamed Seductions (Bijou Video)	
Tyger Tales (Tyger Films)	1986	Uomo Italiano (Inferno)	1997
Tyler Scott-A Day of Decadence (Vivid)	1994	Up and Over (Vivid Video)	
Ty's Back (SX)	1997	Up Close And Sexual (Bijou)	1994
		Up For Grabs (Mustang Video Pac 57)	1999
U		Up Front (Big Bone Pro.)	1994
		Uploading It	
Ultimate Reality (Studio 2000)	1996	Upperclasman (Falcon)	
Uncensored (Bijou Video)	1991	Upwardly Mobile (Barbar Video)	1991
Unchained Men (Stallion)	1989	Urge, The (Vivid Man)	1995
Uncle Jack (Studio 2000)	1998	Urgent Matters (XTC Studios)	1998
Uncle Mike Meets Howard			
Uncontrollable Obsession (Stallion)	1988	**V**	
Uncut (Catalina)	1995		
Uncut Club 1-6 (Rage Collection)	1993	V-8 (Vivid)	1991
Uncut Club of L.A. (4 Play Video)		Vacation Spot (Forum Studios)	1996
Uncut Dicks (Rebel Video)		Valley Boys (LeSalon Video)	1983
Uncut Dreams (LeSalon Video)		Valley Heat	
Uncut Fantasies (Intl. Stuidos)	1991	Valley of the Bi Dolls (Catalina)	1993
Uncut Fever 1 & 2 (Intl. Studios)		VamBires (Bi Now Prod.)	1999
Uncut Fuck Buddy		Vampire of Budapest (Bjorn)	1995
Uncut Gems: Diamonds in the Raw		Verdict, The	1999
(Altomar)	1991	Very Receptive (Surge)	
Uncut Glory (Brush Creek Media)		Vice Cop (Totally Tight)	1995
Uncut Latins (Tiger Video)	1989	Victoria's Secret Life [heterosexual]	
Uncut Lucky Devil (Intl. Studios)	1990	Video Dreams (Planet Group)	1991
Uncut Lucky Luc		Video Encounters of the Sexual Kind	
Uncut Weekend (Oh Man!)	1998	(PM Prod.)	1983
Under Construction (Nova/La Video)	1985	Video Games 1-10	1986
Under the Sign of the Stallion (Cadinot)	1986	Video Head (All Worlds Video)	1986
Under Wraps (Metro)	1994	Video Store Sex Studs (Bob Jones)	

Wide Receiver (All Worlds) 1994
Wild and Loose (Planet) 1992
Wild Bill (Midnight Men Video) 1994
Wild Country (Falcon Video Pac 84) 1993
Wild Guys, The (Bijou Video) 1987
Wild Horses (Huge) 1994
Wild Oats (ADI Video) 1984
Wild Obsession (Planet) 1992
Wild Ones, The (Renegade) 1994
Wild Sex in America (Vivid Man) 1999
Wild Side (HIS Video) 1981
Wild Streak (Planet) 1992
Wild Trail (Renegade) 1997
Wilde House, The (LeSalon Video) 1983
William Higgins Preview tape 1 & 2
   (Catalina) 1982
William Higgins Screen Test 1 & 2 1987
Willing to Take It (Catalina) 1992
Windows (Horizon Video) 1985
Windy City Sex Stories (Bijou) 1992
Winged (All Worlds) 1997
Winner Takes All (Falcon VideoPac 34)
Winner's Circle (Brentwood Classics)
Winner's Way (Falcon VideoPac 45)
Wintertime (Stud Search Video) 1991
Wolf Boy (By Attractions) 1989
Woody And His Peckers (Bacchus) 1998
Woody's (Hot House/Vision A) 1994
Worked Over (Close Up) 1998
Workin' Hard (All Worlds) 1995
Workin' it Out (Studio 2000) 1997
Workin' Stiff (Falcon) 1994
Working Day and Night (Thrust Studios) 1995
Working Fantasies (Polk Street Prod.)
Working Hard (HIS)
Working Hard for the Money (R. Stilskin) 1989
Working It Out (Studio 2000) 1998
Working it up with Bobby Joe (Black Forest) 1990
Working Late (Falcon Video Pac 49) 1985
Working Pleasure (Channel 69 Video) 1998
Working Stiff (LBO Ent.) 1997
Working Stiffs (Altomar) 1989
Workman's Compensation (Manhunter) 1997
Workout (HIS Video) 1982
World of Men, A 1996
Worship 1 & 2 (Live Video)
Wrestle shack 1 ((BG East) 1998
Wrestling 1-22 (Old Reliable)
Wrestling Meat 2 (HIS Video) 1981
Wrist, The (YMAC) 1999
www.Orgy (Locker Room) 1999

X

X Marks the Spot (Associated Video) 1993
X-Poseur (10/9 Prod.) 1988
X-Press Male 1997
X-tasy (Planet) 1992
X-tra Large (LeSalon Video) 1984
X-treme Close-up (Catalina) 1993
XXX (Blue Man/Sunshine Films)
XXX (Rawhide)
XXX Volume 10 (Rawhide Video)
XXX, Blue Men You Sexy Thing (Thrust)
XXX.Man.com (All Worlds Video)

Y

You Bet Your Ass (Planet) 1992
You Sexy Thing (Thrust Video) 1997
Young & the Hung, The (Catalina) 1985
Young and Notorious (Planet) 1992
Young Cadets, The (Catalina) 1988
Young Gladiators (10 Plus Video) [solo] 1988
Young Guys (Forum) 1998
Young Hot Studs
Young Hustlers (Scorpion Studios) 1990
Young Jocks (Original Recipe 2)
Young Lovers
Young Man From Nantucket, A
Young Memories (Planet) 1994
Young Men On The Pleasure Trail
   (Boiling Point Prod.) 1999
Young 'N Eager (Rising Stars Video)
Young Olympians, The (Catalina) 1982
Young Ones, The (PM Productions) 1983
Young Shooters (Solo) (Deluxe Ent.) 1998
Young Slaves in Training (Close-Up) 1998
Young Squirts (Avalon) 1988
Young Stallions (Body Shoppe) 1994
Young Stimulators, The (Bijou Video) 1988
Young Warriors (YMAC Video)
Young Yankees (PM Productions) 1984
Youthful Offenders 18-25 (Atkol) 1998
You've Got It All (Falcon Video Pac 15) 1977
You've Got Male (Hollywood Sales) 1999
You've Got the Touch (Galaxy) 1998

Z

Zebra Love (All Worlds)

Video Studios & Buyers' Guide

Not all companies sell direct to customers. In those cases, order through your local adult video store.

ALL WORLDS VIDEO
P.O. Box 33324
San Diego, CA 92163-9988
800-537-8024 or 619-298-8801
FAX: (619) 298-8567
Website:
www.allworldsvideo.com;
http://www.allworldsvideo.com/sales.html
AWVwebmeister@hotmail.com
or sales@allworldsvideo.com

ALLAN ALAN PICTURES
P.O. Box 2069
San Francisco, CA 94126
(415) 243-9609
(415) 243-9611
Website:
http://www.NewMeat.com
E-mail:
purchase1@NewMeat.com

Alpha/Omega see Zeus

Altomar Video see Video 10

AMORY PRODUCTIONS
P.O. Box 1701, London
SW9 0XD
Website: www.dtk.co.uk
E-mail: info@dtk.co.uk

ATOMIC VIDEO
21115 Devonshire St. #221
Chatsworth, CA 91311
(800) 801-1280
(818) 788-3862

Website:
www.atomicvideo.com
E-mail: sam@atomicvideo.com

BACCHUS RELEASING
9718 Glenoaks Blvd. Unit B
Sun Valley, CA 91352
(800) 923-7355
(818) 768-9101
FAX: (818) 768-9660
Website: www.xtv.com
E-mail:
bacchusm@ix.netcom.com

BALLS PRODUCTIONS
KSE P.O. Box 1501
Pomona, CA 91769

BEL AMI VIDEO
484-B Washington St. #342
Monterey, CA 93940-3030
(831) 373-5546
Fax (831) 647-7161
Website:
www.BelAmiOnline.com
E-mail:
store@BelAmiOnline.com

Bello Productions see Odyssey Men Video

BG ENTERPRISES
3940 Laurel Canyon Blvd.,
Ste. 248
Studio City, CA 91604
(818) 501-7585
FAX: (818) 501-1868
Website:
www.SBPaddleCO.com
E-mail:
orders@SBPaddleCO.com

BIG VIDEO ENTERTAINMENT
Post Office Box 550
Hollywood, CA 90078-0550
(800) 359-0320 or
(800) 824-0949
Website: www.bigvideo.com
E-mail: Bigv@bigvideo.com

Birlynn Productions see Bachhus Releasing

Blade Productions see Video 10

Blue Men see Sunshine Films

BOILING POINT PRODUCTIONS International Media Distributors
P.O. Box 112
Santa Monica, CA 90406
(310) 581-0886
FAX: (323) 512-5182
Website:
www.BoilingPointXXX.com
E-mail: BoilinPtPr@aol.com

Brad Posey see Club 1821

Brigade Studios see Video 10

BRUSH CREEK MEDIA
2215-R Market St., #148
San Francisco, CA 94114
(415) 552-1506 or
(800) 234-3877 or
FAX: (415) 552-3244
E-mail:
bcmsales@brushcreek.com

Buckshot Productions see Colt Studio

CAN-AM PRODUCTIONS
P.O. Box 931627
Los Angeles, CA 90064
(800) 603-5109
FAX (310) 474-9645
E-mail: orders@can-am.com

CAMPFIRE HOME VIDEO
(818) 891-5660
Website: www.hunkvideo.com
E-mail:
campfire@hunkvideo.com)

CATALINA VIDEO
P.O. Box 7016
Los Angeles, CA 91357-7016
(800) 562-1891
(800) 562-1897 or
FAX: (818) 708-3160
Website:
www.CatalinaVideo.com
CatMenDo@CatalinaVideo.
com

**CELESTIAL
ENTERTAINMENT GROUP**
9101 West Sahara Ave., Suite
105, Las Vegas, NV 89117

CENTAUR FILMS
P.O. Box 900
North Hollywood, CA 91603-
0900 (800) 446-8843
FAX (818) 508-4541
Website:
www.centaurfilms.com
E-mail:
Sales@CentaurFilms.com

CHANNEL 1 RELEASING
8721 Santa Monica Blvd., #525
Los Angeles, CA 90069
(800) 997-9071
FAX: (800) 997-9073
info@Channel1Releasing.com

CLOSE-UP CONCEPTS
7080 Hollywood Blvd.
Suite 1004
Hollywood, CA 90028
(800) 697-9009
(323) 957-7011
FAX (323) 957-7017
Website:
www.closeupmen.com or
www.closeup-inc.com

CLUB 1821
Box 5282
Santa Monica
CA 90409
(310) 450-9806
FAX (310) 450-9017

Club Inferno Productions see Hot House Entertainment

COLT STUDIOS
P.O. Box 1608, Studio City
CA 91614
(888) 333-2658
(800) 445-2658
(818) 985-5786
FAX (818) 985-2145
Website: www.coltstudio.com
E-mail: coltinfo@coltstudio.com

Czech Mate see All Worlds

Dirk Yates Collection see All Worlds

Ebony Vid International Prod. see International Media Distributors

Enrique Cruz Productions see International Media Distributors

Euroman Productions see Hollywood Sales

FALCON STUDIOS
P.O. Box 880906
San Francisco, CA 94188-0906
(800) 227-3717 or
(415) 431-7722
FAX (415) 431-0127
Website:
www.FalconStudios.com
E-mail: customerservice
@hawk.FalconStudios.com

Far East Features see Catalina Video

45º Productions see Titan Media

Forum Studios see Video 10

FOX STUDIOS
PO Box 641
Venice, CA 90294
(800) 828-4336
FAX: (310) 399-4770
Website: www.foxstud.com
E-mail: foxstud@best.com

Galaxy Pictures see Video 10

GREENWOOD/COOPER
6165 Santa Monica Blvd
Los Angeles, Calif. 90038
(323) 460-4661

HIS VIDEO GOLD
9650 De Soto Ave.
Chatsworth, CA 91311-5012
(800) 421-2386
(800) 458-4336
(818) 718-0202
FAX: (818) 718-8536
Website:
http://www.hisweb.com

HOLLYWOOD SALES
13340 Saticoy St., H
North Hollywood, CA. 91605
(800) 562-5428
(818) 255-0030
FAX: (818) 255-0036
http://www.hollywoodsales.com/
videos
videos@hollywoodsales.com,

**HOT HOUSE
ENTERTAINMENT**
P.O. Box 410990 #523
San Francisco
CA 914141-0990
(800) 884-4687
FAX: (415) 864-8916
Website: www.hothouse.com
E-mail: hothouse@eyecon.com

**Huge Video, Matt Sterling
Productions see Falcon
Studios**

**Icon Men see Tribal Pulse
Prod.**

IN TOUCH, INC.
13122 Saticoy St.
North Hollywood, CA 91605
(818) 764-2288
(800) 637-0101
FAX: (818) 764-2307
Website:
www.intouchformen.com

IN-X-CESS PRODUCTIONS
9400 Lurline Ave., Unit F
Chatsworth, CA 91311
(818) 341-0997
(818) 349-2278
Website: www.inxcess.com

**INTERNATIONAL MEDIA
DISTRIBUTORS**
23192 Alcalde Drive #D
Laguna Hills, CA 92653

(800) 733-3393
(949) 597-8861
(949) 597-8862
E-Mail: imdworld@aol.com

**Jaguar Studios see
Paladin Video**
3333 Glendale Blvd. #3
Los Angeles, CA 90039
(213) 663-8754
FAX (213) 663-3460

**Jean-Daniel Cadinot see
Centaur Films**
P.O. Box 91257
Los Angeles, CA 90009
(800) 222-9622
(310) 574-2329

JET SET PRODUCTIONS
P.O. Box 15517
North Hollywood
CA 91615-5517
(800) 522-5557
(818) 503-7741
FAX: (818) 764-9821
Website: www.jetset2000.com
E-mail: jetorder@earthlink.net

**Jocks Studios see Falcon
Studios**

JUNIOR STUDIOS
3802 Rosecrans, Suite 500
San Diego, CA 92110-3114
(800) 451-7863
FAX: (619) 230-0365
www.RADvideo.com/mannet.
html
E-mail: Sales@RADvideo.com

**KAREN DIOR
PRODUCTIONS**
PO Box 461481
Los Angeles, CA, 90046
Website:
www.gaywired.com/oboy

E-mail: KDior@aol.com

**KRISTEN BJORN
PRODUCTIONS**
P.O. Box 2520
SW 22nd St. #2-213
Miami, FL 33145
(800) 918-9130
FAX: (800) 918-9130
Website:
http://www.kristenbjorn.com
E-mail: KrisBjorn@aol.com

**LaMancha Video see
Video 10**
(800) 861-7501
Website:
www.lamancha-video.com
E-mail:
info@lamancha-video.com

LBO ENTERTAINMENT
7959 Deering St.
Canoga Park, CA 91304
(818) 598-6700
FAX (818) 598-6721
Website: www.lbodirect.com

LEGEND VIDEO
8955 Fullbright Ave.
Chatsworth, CA 91311
(818) 734-4200
(818) 734-4140
E-mail: got_legend@aol.com

**LEISURE TIME
ENTERTAINMENT**
7050 Valjean Ave.
Van Nuys, CA. 91406
(818) 781-2345
FAX: (818) 781-3345

**Lucas Entertainment see
International Media
Distributors**
332 Bleeker Street, Suite K26,
New York, New York 10014

(888) 562-9125
(212) 924-5892
FAX: (212) 924-6514
Website:
http://www.MicheLucas.com.
E-mail: info@MicheLucas.com

**Lucas Kazan Productions
see International Media
Distributors**
7095 Hollywood Blvd. #693
Hollywood, California 90078
(323) 962-9482
FAX: (323) 962-9482
E-mail:
Lucas10@ix.netcom.com

**Mandatory Pictures see
Channel 1 Releasing**

MAN2MAN EROTICA
8033 Sunset Blvd., Suite 237
Los Angeles, CA 90046
(800) 454-5620
(323) 654-1046
FAX: (323) 654-1024
Website:
www.man2manerotica.com
E-mail:
info@Man2ManErotica.com

MANHUNTER VIDEO PROD.
P.O. Box 7664
Baltimore, MD 21207
(410) 788-3193
FAX: (410) 788-1190
Website:
www.manhuntervideo.com
E-mail: Manhunter@home.com

MARCOSTUDIO
8205 Santa Monica Blvd. 1256
West Hollywood, CA 90046
(800) 555-6301 or
(800) 548-4310
FAX (323) 933-5059
marcoman@mtecnetsp.com.br

**Marina Pacific Entertainment
see Jet Set Productions**

**Masta Entertainment see
Brush Creek Media**

METRO HOME VIDEO
16557 Arminta St.
Van Nuys, CA 91406
(818) 988-1067
(818) 988-3928

MSR VIDEOS
1140 N. Fairfax Ave.
Los Angeles, CA 90046
(323) 822-3843
FAX (323) 656-7589
Website: mrsvideos.com

**MUSCLE GODS
PROD./IDIOM, LTD**
7095 Hollywood Boulevard
Suite 855 Hollywood CA 90028
(800) 916-6300
Website:
http://www.MuscleGods.com
E-mail: rob@MuscleGods.com

**Mustang Studios see Falcon
Studios**

NEW AGE PICTURES
P.O. Box 1234
Hollywood CA 90078
(800) 410-4221 or
(800) 771-7179
FAX: (800) 771-7179
Website:
www.ginocolbert.com
E-mail:
NewAgeVideo@hotmail.com

NO EGO PRODUCTIONS
1985 Santa Monica Bl., # 562
West Hollywood, CA 90046
(323) 692-966

Nubian Video see Video 10

O BOYS STUDIO
P.O. Box 29879
W, Los Angeles, CA 90029
(310) 289-8517
Website:
www.gaywired.com/oboy/
E-mail: oboys123@aol.com

**O Men Video see Odyssey
Men Video**

ODYSSEY MEN VIDEO
P.O. Box 77597
Los Angeles, CA 90007-0597
(800) 369-6214 or
(800) 728-0720
(310) 202-9969
Website: www.OGmen.com
E-mail:
customerservice@ogv.com

OH MAN! STUDIOS
8424 A Santa Monica Bl. # 743
West Hollywood, CA 90069
(888) 442-9843
Website:
www.ohmanstudios.com
E-mail:webmaster@
ohmanstudios.com

OUTBOUND VIDEOS
P.O. Box 2048
New York, NY 10116
(212) 736-6869
FAX: (212) 736-0255
E-mail: boyofbobbg@aol.com

**PACIFIC MEDIA
ENTERTAINMENT**
PO Box 9744
Canoga Park, CA 91303
(818) 341-3156
(800) 262-7367
FAX (818) 341-3562
Website:

www.pacificmediaent.com
E-mail: pacificmediaent@
earthlink.net

**Paradox Pictures see
Video 10**
1164 Ventura Blvd. #622
Studio City, CA 91604
(818) 344-2898

PLEASURE PRODUCTIONS
P.O. Box 946
59 Lake Drive
Highstown, NJ 08520
(908) 308-1777
(800) 999-2483
www.pleasureproductions.com

**Pride Xplicit Video see
Odyssey**
456 Sylvan Ave.
Englewood Cliffs, NJ 07632
(201) 569-1385
(201) 569-2998

**Projex Video see Close-Up
Productions**

REDBOARD VIDEO
P.O. Box 2069
San Francisco, CA 94126
(415) 243-9606
FAX (415) 243-9611
Website: www.redboard.com
E-mail:
webmaster@redboard.com

**REED STILSKIN
PRODUCTIONS**
1077 Market St.
San Francisco, CA 94103
website:
www.ebonyvid.com
E-mail:
alex@ebonyvid.com

RENEGADE VIDEO
451 N. La Cienga #1
Los Angeles, CA 90048
(888) 843-3617
Fax: (310) 659-4767
Website:
www.renegademen.com

**Sarava Productions see
Kristen Bjorn Productions**

**Satyr Productions see
Titan Media**

**SCOTT SLOAN
PRODUCTIONS**
7510 Sunset Blvd.
Suite 1402
Los Angeles, CA 90046
Website:
www.scottsloan.com

**Sex Video see Karen Dior
Productions**

S.I., INC.
6922 Hollywood Blvd., #1000
Los Angeles, CA 90028
(323) 871-1225
Website: www.advocate.com

**SIDMORE SHEPHERD
ENT. INC.**
8424-A Santa Monica Bl. #855
West Hollywood, CA 90069
(888)848-7744 or
(323) 848-7744
Website: www.sidmoore.com

**SIERRA PACIFIC
PRODUCTIONS**
Post Office Box 12109
Marina Del Rey, CA 90295
(800) 828-4336
FAX (310) 399-4770

**STABLE ENTERTAINMENT,
INC.**
964 Hancock Ave.,W.
Hollywood, CA
(310) 854-5626
FAX: (310) 854-5696
E-mail: stable2@AOL.com

STUDIO 2000
7510 Sunset Blvd., Suite 1437
Hollywood, CA. 90046
(800) 435-2445
http://www.studio20004men.
com
E-mail:
studio2000jt@earthlink.net

SUNSHINE FILMS
7722 Densmore Ave.
Van Nuys, CA 91406
(888) 442-9843
Website:
www.sunshinefilm.com
E-mail:
adultx@sunshinefilm.com

**10 Percent Productions see
Greenwood/Cooper
Homevideo**

THOR PRODUCTIONS
1425 N. Detroit St.
Suite 401
Los Angeles, CA 90046-4466
(800) 733-3393
Website: www.thorsss.com
thor@thorsss.com

**TIMO/PUERIS
PRODUCTIONS**
1527 Euterpe #3
New Orleans, LA 70130
Website:
www.TimoVideo.com
E-Mail:
VidkidTimo@aol.com

TITAN MEDIA
P.O. Box 420099
San Francisco, CA 94142-0099
(800) 360-7204
(415) 864-6611
Website: www.titanmedia.com
E-mail:orders@titanmedia.com

TOTALLY TASTELESS VIDEO
12420 Montague St, #D
Arleta, CA 91331
(818) 834-7310
(800) 923-7355
FAX (818) 768-9660
www.totallytastelessvideo.com

TRIBAL PULSE PRODUCTIONS
8581 Santa Monica Blvd., Suite 425, West Hollywood, 90069
(877) ICON-MEN or
(310) 289-0884
FAX: (310) 289-0846

U.S. Male see In-X-Cess

VIDEO 10 DISTRIBUTORS
7063 Lexington Ave.
West Hollywood, CA 90038
(323) 962-8504
(800) 548-4310
FAX: (323) 962-6489.
Website: www.GayVid.com

E-mail: GayVid@GayVid.com

Videospoon see Video 10
Web:
http://www.TobyRoss.com
E-mail: TobyRossX@aol.com

Village East Prod. see Video 10

VIVID MAN
15127 Califa St.
Van Nuys, CA 91411
(818) 908-0481
(800) 423-4227
Website: www.vividman.com

WATERSHED PRODUCTIONS
2522 Hyperion Ave.
Los Angeles, CA 90027
(800) 999-1768
FAX: (213) 662-3095
www.watershedproductions.com

WILDCAT PRODUCTIONS
7985 Santa Monica Blvd., #47
West Hollywood, CA 90046
(323) 464-4226
(323) 654-1867
FAX: (323) 464-7712
Website: www.WldcatProd.com
E-mail: wldcatprod@aol.com

WOLFF PRODUCTIONS
P.O. Box 34069, Dept. 238
Seattle, WA 98124
(604) 649-7686
Website: www.MarkWolff.com
E-mail: markwolff@hotmail.com

XTC STUDIOS
451 N. LaCienega Blvd. #1
Los Angeles, CA 90048

YMAC
P.O. Box 91257
Los Angeles, CA 90009
(800) 222-YMAC
(310) 574-2329

Zen Productions see Tribal Pulse

THE ZEUS COLLECTION
P.O. Box 64250
Los Angeles CA 90064
(800) 259-7386
FAX (310) 474-9645
Website: www.ZEUSstudios.com
E-mail: zeustudio@earthlink.net

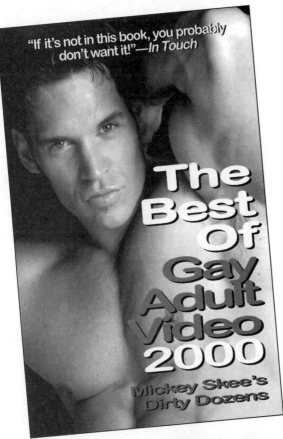

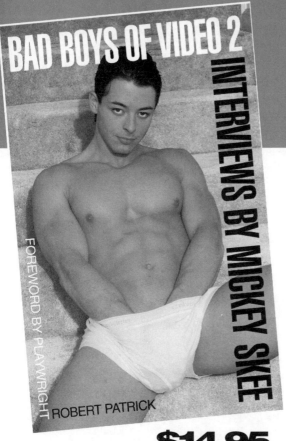

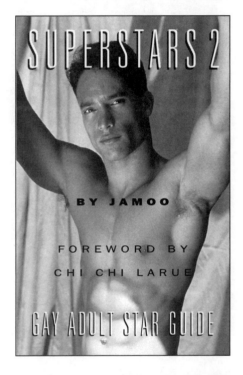

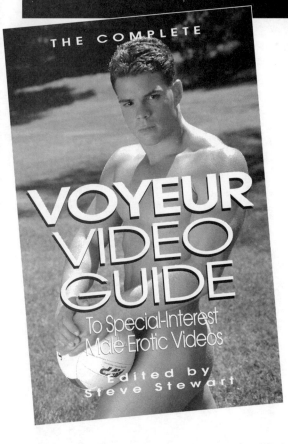

companion press movie & video companion books

BAD BOYS Of Video #1
Porn Star Interviews
By Mickey Skee
224 pages, 5-1/2 x 8-1/2
ISBN# 1-889138-12-6
$12.95 Softcover (Photos)

BAD BOYS Of Video #2
Porn Star Interviews
By Mickey Skee
224 pages, 5-1/2 x 8-1/2
ISBN# 1-889138-19-3
$14.95 Softcover (Photos)

The "BEST OF"
Gay Adult Video 1998
By Mickey Skee
208 pages, 5-1/2 x 8-1/2
ISBN# 1-889138-10-X
$12.95 Softcover (Photos)

The "BEST OF"
Gay Adult Video 1999
By Mickey Skee
208 pages, 5-1/2 x 8-1/2
ISBN# 1-889138-14-2
$12.95 Softcover (Photos)

The "BEST OF"
Gay Adult Video 2000
By Mickey Skee
224 pages, 5-1/2 x 8-1/2
ISBN# 1-889138-21-5
$14.95 Softcover (Photos)

CAMPY, VAMPY, TRAMPY
Movie Quotes
By Steve Stewart
212 pages, 4-1/4 x 6-3/4
ISBN# 0-9625277-6-9
$9.95 Softcover

CASTING COUCH CONFESSIONS
17 Gay Erotic Tales (fiction)
Edited by David MacMillan
192 pages, 5-1/2 x 8-1/2
ISBN# 1-889138-17-7
$14.95 Softcover

COMING OF AGE
Movie & Video Guide
By Don Lort
216 pages, 8-1/2 x 11
ISBN# 1-889138-02-9
$18.95 Softcover

The Films of KEN RYKER
By Mickey Skee
152 pages, 8-1/2 x 11
ISBN# 1-889138-08-8
$18.95 Softcover (Photos)

The Films of KRISTEN BJORN
By Jamoo
152 pages, 8-1/2 x 11
ISBN# 1-889138-00-2
$18.95 Softcover (Photos)

THE FRESHMAN CLUB
18 Erotic Virgin Tales
Edited by David MacMillan
192 pages, 5-1/2 x 8-1/2
ISBN# 1-889138-27-4
$14.95 Softcover (fiction)
AVAILABLE SPRING 2000

FULL FRONTAL, 2nd Edition
Male Nudity Video Guide
Edited by Steve Stewart
144 pages, 5-1/2 x 8-1/2
ISBN# 1-889138-11-8
$12.95 Softcover

GAY HOLLYWOOD, 2nd Edition
Film & Video Guide (non-hardcore)
Edited by Steve Stewart
352 pages, 7 x 8-1/2
ISBN# 0-9625277-5-0
$15.95 Softcover (Photos)

HOLLYWOOD HARDCORE DIARIES
14 Erotic Tales (fiction)
By Mickey Skee
192 pages, 5-1/2 x 8-1/2
ISBN# 1-889138-15-0
$12.95 Softcover

LITTLE JOE SUPERSTAR
The Films of Joe Dallesandro
By Michael Ferguson
216 pages, 8-1/2 x 11
ISBN# 1-889138-09-6
$18.95 Softcover (Photos)

PENIS PUNS Movie Quotes
By Steve Stewart
118 pages, 6 x 4-1/4
ISBN# 1-889138-07-X
$5.95 Softcover

RENT BOYS
18 Erotic Hustler & Escort Tales
Edited by David MacMillan
192 pages, 5-1/2 x 8-1/2
ISBN# 1-889138-25-8
$14.95 Softcover (fiction)
AVAILABLE SPRING 2000

SKIN FLICKS #1
15 Gay Erotic Tales (fiction)
Edited by Bruce Wayne
192 pages, 5-1/2 x 8-1/2
ISBN# 1-889138-16-9
$12.95 Softcover

SKIN FLICKS #2
18 Gay Erotic Tales (fiction)
Edited by David MacMillan
192 pages, 5-1/2 x 8-1/2
ISBN# 1-889138-26-6
$14.95 Softcover

STAR DIRECTORY
Over 2,000 Porn Star Videographies
Edited by Bruce Wayne
384 pages, 5-1/2 x 8-1/2
ISBN# 0-9625277-22-3
$18.95 Softcover (Photos)

SUPERSTARS #1
Porn Star Profiles
By Jamoo
204 pages, 5-1/2 x 8-1/8
ISBN# 0-9625277-9-3
$12.95 Softcover (Photos)

SUPERSTARS #2
Porn Star Profiles
By Jamoo
224 pages, 5-1/2 x 8-1/2
ISBN# 1-889138-20-7
$14.95 Softcover (Photos)

THE VOYEUR VIDEO GUIDE
To Gay Softcore Videos
Edited by Steve Stewart
144 pages, 5-1/2 x 8-1/8
ISBN# 1-889138-05-3
$12.95 Softcover (Photos)

X-RATED Gay Video Guide
Edited by Sabin
448 pages, 5-1/2 x 8-1/8
ISBN# 1-889138-03-7
$12.95 Softcover

companion press order form

PO Box 2575, Laguna Hills, CA 92654 USA

Phone: (949) 362-9726 Fax: (949) 362-4489

Please include your phone number or <u>E-MAIL ADDRESS</u> (for questions about your order):

PRINT Name _____

Address _____

City _____ State _____ Zip _____

PLEASE PRINT CLEARLY. USE EXTRA SHEET OF PAPER IF NECESSARY

Qty	Order or ISBN # last 3 digits only	Title	Price (each)	Price

SHIPPING & HANDLING CHARGES—BOOKS ONLY
U.S. Shipping & Handling Charges (U.S. ONLY)
First book $4.00. $1.00 for each additional book.
Canada Shipping & Handling Charges (Canada)
First book $5.00. $1.00 for each additional book.
Outside U.S. Shipping & Handling Charges (Outside U.S.)
First book $20.00. $1.00 for each additional book.
RUSH FedEx Delivery Charges (U.S. ONLY)
Check one and ADD to above charges ❑ Overnight, **Add** $35.00
❑ 2nd Day, **Add** $25.00 ❑ Saturday Delivery, **Add** $45.00.
CREDIT CARD or MONEY ORDERS ONLY for rush delivery.

Subtotal	$
Discount or Credit (if any)	-
California Residents add 7.75% Sales Tax	$
Shipping & Handling See left for rates	$
ADD RUSH FedEx Delivery Charge	$
TOTAL	$

Check Payment Method
❑ Visa ❑ MasterCard ❑ American Express ❑ Money Order
❑ Check (U.S. only) **(Allow 6-8 weeks.)** Make check payable to COMPANION PRESS.

VISA   MasterCard   AMERICAN EXPRESS

Credit card # _____ Exp. date _____

X Signature required for all orders

I certify by my signature that I am over 21 years old and desire to receive sexually-oriented material. My signature here also authorizes my credit card charge if I am paying for my order by Visa, MasterCard or American Express. We cannot ship your order without your signature.

❑ **Here is my $5. Please send me your complete book flyers. I do not wish to order at this time. (I understand that my $5 will be refunded with my first purchase).**

01/2000